CAMBRIDGE STUDIES

IN

MEDIEVAL LIFE AND THOUGHT

Edited by G. G. COULTON, M.A.
Fellow of St John's College, Cambridge
and University Lecturer in English

PREACHING IN MEDIEVAL
ENGLAND

THE PREACHING SCENE IN A CHURCHYARD.

(*From MS. Fitzwilliam Mus., Cambridge, 22, p. 55.*)

PREACHING IN MEDIEVAL ENGLAND

AN INTRODUCTION TO SERMON MANUSCRIPTS OF THE PERIOD

c. 1350–1450

by

G. R. OWST

M.A. Cantab., Ph.D. Lond.,

Assistant Editorial Secretary to the
Medieval-Latin Dictionary Committee

"ἐκεῖνοι δὲ ἐξελθόντες ἐκήρυξαν πανταχοῦ."

CAMBRIDGE

AT THE UNIVERSITY PRESS

1926

CAMBRIDGE
UNIVERSITY PRESS
LONDON : Fetter Lane

NEW YORK
The Macmillan Co.
BOMBAY, CALCUTTA and
MADRAS
Macmillan and Co., Ltd.
TORONTO
The Macmillan Co. of
Canada, Ltd.
TOKYO
Maruzen-Kabushiki-Kaisha

PRINTED IN GREAT BRITAIN

DEDICATED BY PERMISSION
TO
HIS IMPERIAL HIGHNESS
PRINCE CHICHIBU
OF JAPAN
AS A MEMENTO OF HIS ENGLISH
STUDIES WITH THE AUTHOR:
1925–1926

GENERAL PREFACE

THERE is only too much truth in the frequent complaint that history, as compared with the physical sciences, is neglected by the modern public. But historians have the remedy in their own hands; choosing problems of equal importance to those of the scientist, and treating them with equal accuracy, they will command equal attention. Those who insist that the proportion of accurately ascertainable facts is smaller in history, and therefore the room for speculation wider, do not thereby establish any essential distinction between truth-seeking in history and truth-seeking in chemistry. The historian, whatever be his subject, is as definitely bound as the chemist "to proclaim certainties as certain, falsehoods as false, and uncertainties as dubious." Those are the words, not of a modern scientist, but of the seventeenth century monk, Jean Mabillon; they sum up his literary profession of faith. Men will follow us in history as implicitly as they follow the chemist, if only we will form the chemist's habit of marking clearly where our facts end and our inferences begin. Then the public, so far from discouraging our speculations, will most heartily encourage them; for the most positive man of science is always grateful to anyone who, by putting forward a working theory, stimulates further discussion.

The present series, therefore, appeals directly to that craving for clearer facts which has been bred in these times of storm and stress. No care can save us altogether from error; but for our own sake and the public's we have elected to adopt a safeguard dictated by ordinary business common-sense. Whatever errors of fact are pointed out by reviewers or correspondents shall be publicly corrected with the least possible delay. After a year of publication, all copies shall be provided with such an erratum-slip without waiting for the chance of a second edition; and each fresh volume in this series shall contain a full list of the errata noted in its immediate predecessor. After the lapse of a year from the first publication of any volume, and at any time during the ensuing twelve months, any possessor of that volume who will send a stamped and addressed envelope to the Cambridge University Press, Fetter Lane, Fleet Street, London, E.C. 4, shall receive, in due course, a free copy of the *errata* in that volume. Thus, with the help of our critics, we may reasonably hope to put forward these monographs as roughly representing the most accurate information obtainable under present conditions. Our facts being thus secured, the reader will judge our inferences on their own merits; and something will have been done to dissipate that cloud of suspicion which hangs over too many important chapters in the social and religious history of the Middle Ages.

G. G. C.

Oct. 1922

AUTHOR'S PREFACE

"THERE is perhaps no greater hardship at present inflicted on mankind in civilised and free countries than the necessity of listening to sermons." The Victorian Age of Trollope is more out of date and out of favour with many people than even the Middle Ages themselves; but the sermon, it is to be feared, is in no better odour to-day than when the Victorian novelist wrote his remark. The very "necessity" of hearing it has now disappeared. What is actually the first book to be written on the subject of English Medieval Preaching would seem to call, therefore, for a special word of explanation. To the average Englishman modern sermons may be dull. But the medieval variety, if it has ever occurred to his mind, is probably associated with "empty, ridiculous harangues, legendary tales, miracles, horrors, low jests, table-talk, fire-side scandal," result in the main of a long Protestant tradition, which even reckons Paul's Cross and the Sermons on the Card among its triumphant inventions. If still left with a taste for devotional literature, therefore, he can hardly be expected to waste time upon "monkish superstitions," when the works of Latimer and Jeremy Taylor, Donne and South already stand upon his bookshelves. Not John Wycliffe himself, "morning star of the Reformation," if he rose from the dead, could induce Professor Hearnshaw to listen to his homilies.

English historians and archivists have certainly done little enough to make known what M. Lecoy de la Marche calls "the innumerable written monuments of the pulpit." Emancipated from religion and an old-fashioned culture (yet always the willing slaves of public opinion), they are naturally busy to-day with the weightier material concerns of modern politics and industry. Hence, the whole round of medieval existence is likewise compassed for them in the busy tale of buyings and sellings, the systems of the Courts, the endless reckoning of manor rolls and taxes. Such is the latest fashion in "History," which has now replaced one of treaties, campaigns, and royal escapades. Medieval scholars on the continent, however, especially in

France, while hardly neglectful of other branches of the great medieval tree of knowledge, have long done justice to their sermon manuscripts. The names of Hauréau, Delisle, Langlois, Lecoy de la Marche, Bourgain, to quote but a few, represent but one group which worked industriously half a century ago on the vast collections in the libraries of Paris. Thomas Wright was apparently the first lonely antiquary in England to recognize the value of these quaint homiletic sources. But, apart from a few random editions of Early English Texts since his day, they remained wholly neglected until Dr Gasquet (as he then was) uttered a rousing plea for their study in two essays originally published in the *Dublin Review*. There, again, the matter has been allowed to rest up to the present time. For the survey so enthusiastically planned and recommended by the eminent Cardinal has never been undertaken. Miss Toulmin Smith's hints at the History of Preaching in England which will one day have to be written, in an article in the *English Historical Review* called forth by the publication of Bozon's "Contes Moralisés" in 1889, still constitute a pious dream for the future. One work by an Englishman, Mr J. A. Herbert of the British Museum, is alone worthy to stand by the monumental productions of French scholarship in this sphere. But that, after all, is a learned Catalogue, concerned exclusively with sermon *exempla*.

What, then, are the chief contributions to our knowledge which a study of this much-despised sermon literature is likely to produce? First, a contribution to our knowledge of social life and thought. Pater's "belief that nothing which has ever interested living men and women can wholly lose its vitality,— no language they have spoken, no oracle beside which they have hushed their voices, no dream which has once been entertained by actual human minds, nothing about which they have been passionate, or expended time and zeal" should in itself be a sufficient inducement to study. For the English medieval pulpit assuredly gripped men in its day, had its own peculiar language, its oracles, its dreams, created passions, called forth zeal, as readers will see. But, apart from the mere dilettante— "Homo sum, humani nihil a me alienum puto," our modern social historians declare that they will "now welcome every sidelight, however dim." To glance casually, then, through M. Hauréau's six volumes of manuscript extracts is to convince oneself beyond all doubt of the wealth of illustrative social detail which is to be got from the medieval sermon. Nor shall we wonder at it, if we remember what the medieval preachers were. Political and social champions of the oppressed, reformers of abuses, distributors of news and popular knowledge, writers in prose and verse, jesters and story-tellers, we may well expect them to know and to disclose to us the little secrets of their age. Listen to the preacher as he discourses on the exactions of lords and retainers, the vices of the clergy, the wiles of merchants and lawyers, the fashions of ladies, the sports, labours, sufferings of the common herd! He will tell you all, if you are patient. With Mr Bernard Shaw he would cry—"My conscience is the genuine pulpit article: it annoys me to see people comfortable when they ought to be uncomfortable; and I insist on making them think in order to bring them to a conviction of sin. If you don't like my preaching, you must lump it. I really cannot help it!" Consequently, like Mr Shaw, he will prove a most illuminating critic and satirist.

But, secondly, there is the contribution which our sermons will make to English ecclesiastical history, particularly to the much-debated problems of the state of the medieval church and the causes of the Reformation. For such debates, indeed, the appearance of this little book might almost claim to be timely. For, in it, passages from English synodal sermons are printed for the first time. They will at least serve to remind us that here we have a literature far more intimate and telling in its disclosures than even the Episcopal Registers themselves; yet one which—so far as England is concerned—has been as little explored by the learned Editor of this series as by his critics. Entering medieval chapter-house and church as in a magic cloak, by means of it we are enabled to listen unseen, "behind closed doors," to the clergy as they harangue their own clergy with a frankness and fearlessness only equalled by the confessions of memoir and diary in later centuries. Some of their remarks make peculiarly unpleasant reading. But, until the "ut estimo" of Master Rypon and his kind is thus given heed to again, we shall be compelled to go on listening to the "idle

imaginacions" of professors, propagandists, and journalistic
historians on these points, a hardly less evil fate. Through
ignorance of that insight which sermons alone can give into
the popular as well as the ecclesiastical mind of the times, the
people's arguments, excuses, religious and anti-clerical ideas,
as well as the self-condemnation of the clergy, even so learned
and restrained a work as Dr Gairdner's *Lollardy and the
Reformation* is vitiated. To Gairdner, indeed, Dr Gascoigne's
complaints were almost as exceptional as were those of Wycliffe
himself to Professor Lechler and others. Yet, as a matter of
fact, a hundred pulpits of orthodoxy in England must have been
complaining then in exactly the same strain, if only our historians
could have known it. What shall we say, too, for example, with
the record of medieval preaching now before us, of S. R.
Maitland's pet objections to what he calls "Puritan style," the
unbridled language, and vulgar personal attacks of the Reformers
which he delighted to hold up to our scorn? Did not the
warning voices of the most faithful mariners, clinging to their
post of duty in the storm-tossed, ill-steered Ship of the Church,
ring hoarse and relentless enough, long before the Reformers'
day?

If a study of the sermons is needed to dissipate the errors of
historians, it is needed also to throw fresh light upon the contemporary English literature. Professor Whitney's remark in his
article on "Religious movements in the fourteenth century" in
our Cambridge *History* still holds good over a wide area,—that
much remains to be done in the arrangement of manuscripts.
What sermons may do to illumine the dark places of such a
poem as *Piers Plowman's Vision*, I have already suggested elsewhere. The same fact applies, no doubt, to satire, and to the
drama; and even further to the dark places of symbolism in art.

The present study, however, does not deal directly with
evidence for any of the arguments here indicated: neither is it
concerned with any theological controversies as such. Within
the strict limits of a volume of this kind there is more than
enough to do in first introducing the subject of the Preaching. In
days when the Bar was dumb, and political eloquence unborn,
M. Victor le Clerc has reminded us—"tout discours est pres-
qu'un sermon; parler, c'est prêcher. L'art de la prédication est

tout l'art de la parole." The pulpit is itself a social activity, a centre of picturesque intercourse as well as of "lovelych talkyng" and thinking. Its literature needs much sorting and examination. For, no illustrative material for the historian has any right to be supplied until first the manner and purport of its original delivery has been weighed. The preacher, a man of like passions, prejudices, weaknesses with ourselves, is not discoursing with an eye on his reporters of the twentieth century. He speaks with exaggeration, sometimes with violence, as the mood or the audience prompts him. The very language which he uses may not be his own. Sermon evidence, therefore, can never be too carefully handled, even in its most naïve and voluminous state. Finally, a word concerning the period here chosen. With the medieval pulpit even more, perhaps, than with medieval life and culture in general, we move in a world the motto of which from the first might well be "tout est donné." Hence, in view of the superabundance of our material, it will be convenient to dispense with a chronological survey for the present, and concentrate upon the chief types and characters of a single century which will be broadly characteristic of them all. That century, then, is to be one which saw the full fruit of Mendicant preaching in this country, the revival of our English tongue, an age of mysticism, of simmering revolt, and impending reformation.

This book itself is the fruit of four years' continuous study of the sources. It began from an essay presented two years ago to the Faculty of Theology in the University of London, for which the degree of Doctor of Philosophy was granted. Dr G. G. Coulton first suggested to the author a research upon the "Summa Predicantium" of Bromyard, the "Festiall" of John Myrc, Bishop Brunton's Sermon manuscript, and certain others in the Cambridge University Library indicated in a monograph by M. Petit-Dutaillis. To the Rev. Professor Claude Jenkins, Librarian of Lambeth Palace, he owes the idea of a study of the Preaching itself, and that early stimulus and advice which has led him afield to work upon many manuscripts in many libraries. The unfailing kindness, sympathy and help of these two scholars is to-day the writer's chief joy and solace as he looks back,—*magistri mei perhonorandi et dilectissimi!* For all other sources used, for the method of their treatment, for the many mistakes which recent pressure of duties has made it impossible to eliminate, he takes sole responsibility. Miss Eileen Power, D.Lit., has most kindly undertaken the task of proof-reading. Further, thanks are due to Mr S. C. Roberts for the block from his *Picture Book of British History* (Volume II) which illustrates page 267, and to the University Printer for his advice. Finally, apart from unstinted help given from time to time by officials of the Manuscript Department in the British Museum, acknowledgement is due to the following gentlemen for per-mission to examine MSS., or for references generously supplied, and in many cases for much personal kindness:

In *London*—the Master of the Library of Gray's Inn; and the Rev. Dr H. B. Workman, of Westminster.

In *Oxford*—Mr Falconer Madan, and Dr Craster, of the Bodleian.

In *Cambridge*—Sir Geoffrey Butler, Librarian of Corpus Christi College; Mr Sydney Cockerell, Director of the Fitzwilliam Museum; the Librarians of Gonville and Caius College, and Trinity College (now the University Librarian).

In *Edinburgh*—Dr W. K. Dickson, Keeper of the Advocates Library (now the National Library of Scotland); the University Librarian; the Librarian of the Royal College of Physicians.

Amongst Cathedral Chapter Libraries—at *York*, the Rev. H. T. S. Gedge; at *Lincoln*, the Ven. Archdeacon of Stow, the Rev. Canon W. H. Kynaston, also the Sub-Librarian, and especially the Rev. Canon R. M. Woolley, D.D., for valuable loan of his transcripts; at *Salisbury*, the Rev. Canon Christopher Wordsworth; at *Worcester*, the Rev. Canon J. M. Wilson, D.D.; at *Durham*, Mr Meade Falkner, Hon. Librarian; at *St Alban's*, the late Rev. Canon G. H. P. Glossop.

Last, but not least, to the Librarian and Trustees of Dr Williams' Library, London, for the loan of many books; and to my own college in Cambridge, for hospitality during several visits,—she who stands upon the very site where the great John de Bromyard must often have preached.

G. R. OWST.

Feast of S. Matthias, 1926.
ST ALBAN'S.

CONTENTS

N.B. In all quotations given, the O.E. '*þ*' has been
rendered by '*th*,' as a concession to the general
reader.

ILLUSTRATIONS

PLATES

ILLUSTRATIONS IN THE TEXT

ILLUSTRATIONS

PART ONE

THE PREACHERS

CHAPTER I

"BISHOPS AND CURATES"

"WHO can lawfully preach?" is a typical question put by the *Regimen Animarum*, one of the little hand-books of Canon Law and instruction so plentifully furnished for mediaeval clergy in the fourteenth and fifteenth centuries. The answer is not quite so simple as might be expected, though the main principle underlying it is sufficiently clear and accredited. "Priests, deacons and subdeacons, *if they have preferment and the care of souls (si habeant prelationem et curam animarum)*, because those so entitled preach by reason of their preferment, not by reason of their order."[1]

"Ratione prelationis," this then determines the Church's prime choice of the men called to be her regular spokesmen in the pulpit, the bishop and the "curate" or beneficed parson, who have the authoritative charge of souls. The rest of that vast preaching host of the later middle ages, monks and Mendicants, University graduates in theology, vicars, chaplains, pardoners and recluses, even the Templar and Hospitaller[2], and the rest, are but auxiliaries, to be admitted to the ranks of sacred heraldry[3] only by special privilege, and further license by their own *prelati*, and those of the places where they might preach[4].

[1] MS. Harl. 2272, fol. 9 (De Predicatoribus); compiled 1343 (?).
[2] Specifically mentioned in ibid. fol. 9, also the *Summa Summarum*, bk. v, cap. lix (De Predicatoribus et eorum Predicationibus), and cf. MS. Ryl. 10. D. x, fol. 279 b.
[3] A typical contemporary figure for preachers; cf. *Gesta Rom.*: "Precones, qui illud convivium clamabant"; Rypon (MS. Harl. 4894, fol. 59): "Nuncii vel precursores, procurrentes adventum Domini"; MS. Caius Coll. Camb. 233, fol. 108 b; Bromyard, *S.P.—Predic.*; etc.
[4] Cf. *Cil. Oc. Sac.* (MS. Harl. 4968, fol. 40): "Item predicatores ex privilegiis papalibus constituuntur, scil. religiosi mendicantes...hii qui per prelatos eorum constituuntur ad hoc....Hiis tamen predicatoribus non licet predicare in ecclesiis parochianis sine licentia rectoris,... " etc.; and fol. 42: "...nec presbyter, nec heremita, nec quicunque alius, nisi fuerit prelatus, populo predicare debet, nisi licentiam habuerit, ut predictum est."

O

Yet, as the world knows, it was the auxiliary, in this as in other developments in the history of the Church, who was destined to play by far the most conspicuous part. From the point of view of preaching, the mediaeval *prelatus*, whether as dignitary or merely a humble parish priest, might well be expected to plead before long that that sacred duty must of necessity be shared with others less burdened than himself. If faithfully performed, the elaborate oversight of a mediaeval diocese, the intricate processes of the Church courts, the serving of a country parish, scattered, divided by hill and forest and brook, abominable roads, and even worse class distinctions and jealousies—

> Wyd was his parisshe, and houses fer asonder,
> But he ne lafte nat, for reyn ne thonder
> .   .   .   .   .   to visyte
> The ferrest in his parisshe, muche and lyte[1],—

would seem to leave little time for the requisite study and preparation. On the other hand, when we recall the actual temptations of a secular kind that beset such persons, it is easy to see how "the care of this world, and the deceitfulness of riches" would often "choke the word," rendering many of them unfruitful. The full story of how the spiritual descendants of Francis and Dominic and of the desert hermits eclipsed, in England as elsewhere, the efforts of the "curates" in the production of sermons both written and spoken, will have to be re-told in the pages that follow. But in an opening chapter it may not be out of place to emphasize the fact that, however great the characteristic mediaeval discrepancy between theory and practice here as in other places, the secular clergy at least professed an equally lofty view of the preacher's equipment, whenever they troubled to write about it. When a simple vernacular homilist sets out his exposition of the "fishers of men" in the Gospel, he says, "Be thise fischers ben undirstonde doctoures, the wiche ȝeden doune, thorough mekenes and grace, to the water of wisdom and of mercy, to wasche therin ther nettes, tht is to clense hure beleve and to lere the Lawe of God ...wt the wiche thei shulden drawe in the flodes of this worlde grete men and smale men to the londe of liff, that is, to the blisse of heven." Again, later, "So...alle doctoures shuld lat

---

[1] Chaucer, *Cant. Tales, Prol.* ll. 491–4.

owte in to the worlde holy techynge of Godes lore, for to cache sowles fro synne in to the wey of salvacion."[1] This special association of the preacher with the learned man of the University, which occurs further, for example, in the *Gesta Romanorum* ("sacrae paginae doctores, scil. predicatores, qui habent nos instruere"), and frequently elsewhere[2], was to be seen in the person of the friar as in no other of his contemporaries. The average *curatus* was apparently its living negation. Such a view, too, we might be inclined to associate with the intellectualism of a Bishop Pecock and his marked antipathy to popular preaching. Yet as accepted by all parties it is characteristic of a growing dependence upon the voice of authority in the orthodox religion of the later middle ages. From the panels of the pulpit itself, when pulpits became fixtures in churches, the figures of the four great doctors of the Church stared solemnly down upon the speaker's audience. His own address was enriched most plentifully with sayings at least attributable to those same great doctors. Little wonder, then, if along with the first idea of the preacher as prelate or "curate," there was maintained this other idea of him as essentially a "doctor," no longer indeed expositor of the rank and authority of a Gregory or an Ambrose, but at least one who speaks out of the fullness of his knowledge—"secundum sacram scripturam, et omnes sacros doctores."[3] This type confronts us in particular when we meet with the select preacher for special festivals and events of the year, for convocations and general chapters, the chancellors of cathedral and University, the learned graduates whose visits from Oxford are eagerly awaited. It becomes grotesque, though vivid and amusing, in the persons of ambitious preachers of the day, eager for pulpit fame, with their pedantic Latin phrases, their pompous hoods and furs, their greetings as "Masters" in the market-place.

While churchmen of almost every rank and variety, "lewd and lered," secular and religious, might thus be formally admitted

---

[1] MS. Roy. 18. B. xxiii, fol. 150.

[2] The "fishers of men" as doctors appear in a sermon of Fitzralph, MS. Lansd. 393, fol. 26 b; in Brunton, MS. Harl. 3760; in MS. Add. 21253, fol. 97; etc. The whole is probably derived from a passage in St Gregory. Cf. also *Cil. Oc. Sac.* etc.

[3] Rypon (MS. Harl. 4894).

to the task of the pulpit under one or other of these conditions, others were rigidly excluded. Do you ask if laymen can preach, then the reply is "Certainly not," for them it is a mortal sin[1]. The best advice offered them by the quaint author of an English tract on the Decalogue of the fifteenth century is as follows: "Yf thou be a prest, and havest kunnynge and auctoryte, preche and teche Godes worde to his peple; and yf thou be no prest nother clerk, but on of the peple, thenne bysy the in the halyday to here prechynge of Godes worde, and be aboute with thy goede spekynge and styrynge to brynge thy neyȝebores to betere lyvynge."[2] The contrast in duties is emphasized still more clearly in the opening sentences of John Watton's popular *Speculum Christiani*, which run thus, in an English translation of the period:

A grete differens es be twene prechynge and techynge. Prechynge es in a place where es clepynge to gedyr, or foluynge of pepyl in holy dayes, in chyrches or othe certeyn places and tymes ordeyned ther to. And it longeth to hem th[t] been ordeyned ther to, the whyche have iurediccion and auctorite, and to noon othyr. Techynge es th[t] eche body may enforme and teche hys brothyr in every place and in conable tyme, es he seeth th[t] it be spedful: ffor this es a godly almes dede to whych every man es bounde th[t] hath cunnynge[3].

Women as a class most people would consider quite naturally excluded from the privilege of preaching in the middle ages. Yet, as a matter of fact, there was then one woman who did exercise her regular *prelatio* over a flock, namely the abbess of the nunnery. Moreover, evidence is by no means lacking, from the continent, that in earlier centuries it was not without a considerable struggle that this right of preaching in formal

[1] Cf. *Summa Angelica*, under "Predicare." Lyndwood, *Prov.* adds: "nec publice, nec private"; the *Reg. Anim.*: "quacunque sciencia vel sanctitate polleant" (MS. Harl. 2272, fol. 9); *Cil. Oc. Sac.* (MS. Harl. 4968, fol. 42).
[2] MS. Harl. 2398, fol. 91 b.
[3] MS. Harl. 6580, fol. 2 (written by one Roger Byrde). Here is Watton's original Latin (cf. MS. Harl. 206, fol. 17; MSS. Add. 21202, 22121, etc.): "Magna est differentia inter predicationem et doctrinam. Predicatio est ubi est convocatio sive populi invitatio in diebus festivis, in ecclesiis, seu in aliis certis locis et temporibus ad hoc deputatis, et pertinet ad eos qui ordinati sunt ad hoc, et jurisdictionem et auctoritatem habent, et non ad alios. Informare autem et docere potest unusquisque fratrem suum in omni loco et tempore oportuno, si videatur sibi expedire; quia hoc est eleemosina ad quam quilibet tenetur." Cf. also *Cil. Oc. Sac.* MS. Harl. 4968, fol. 42 b: "Item omnes fideles mutuo tenentur errantes corripere et egentes informare."

fashion in church was completely wrested from her[1]. By the
time that our England of the fourteenth century is reached,
however, nothing so picturesque as M. Lecoy de la Marche's
episodes appears to remain. Bromyard in his *Opus Trivium*,
Lyndwood in his *Provinciale*, the anonymous author of the
Cilium Oculi Sacerdotis[2], for example, all remind you, that
"although learned and holy and 'prelatical,'" she must not
preach where men are present. The Dominican Humbertus
de Romanis' remarks on this subject[3] are worth repeating, if
only because they depict, beyond their immediate application
to the practice under discussion, the general attitude of contemporary preachers toward the opposite sex. Women must be
excluded from the pulpits, he says, first because they lack
sufficient intelligence, secondly because an inferior rôle in
life has been given them by God, thirdly because in such a
position they would provoke immorality; fourthly, owing to the
folly of the first woman, Eve, who as St Bernard pointed out,
by opening her mouth on a certain occasion, brought ruin to
the whole world. One is tempted, nevertheless, to notice that
in spite of these ungenerous remarks alike of the great reforming
Cistercian and the thirteenth-century friar, all following the
example of St Paul, mediaeval woman comes nigh again to
"having a last word" in the matter, even where the English
pulpit is concerned. In its final stages of neglect and decay at
the eve of the Reformation, was it not a distinguished lady, of
holy memory, the Lady Margaret Tudor, patron of no less than
three colleges at Cambridge, who founded preacherships at the
two Universities, still bearing her name, expressly to revive the
dying art?[4] Well may the future generations of men honour
her memory in the prayers and thanksgivings of Benefactors'
Day! Beyond this, indeed, an English preacher of the late
fourteenth century has a remarkable statement in one of his
own sermons to the effect that simple lay-women as well as
laymen were "teaching and spreading the word of God" in

[1] Cf. Lecoy de la Marche, *La Chaire française*, pp. 32–3.
[2] MS. Harl. 4968, fol. 42: "Mulieribus, licet doctae et sanctae et prelatae,
viris predicare non licet." The reference in Lyndwood, *Prov.* Lib. 3, tit. 4,
is to dist. 23. The passage from the *Cil. Oc. Sac.* is actually taken from the
Council of Carthage.
[3] See *Max. Bibl. Patr.* vol. xxv, p. 435.　　　[4] 1502–3.

his day, apparently under the influence of the Lollard movement, to the shame of careless and incompetent priests[1]. As
one thinks of Lauron's satirical print of a Quaker meeting in the
seventeenth century[2], and all that has followed in Christendom
since that woman first stood upon her stool to expound the
Scriptures, there is a tragic irony in learned Doctor Lyndwood's
opening phrase: "Note that not everyone who desires to preach
ought to be admitted to that office."[3]

With a class of preachers firmly established in the heart
of society, a natural curiosity soon arises to discover something
of the personalities and methods of the various leading types
of which it is composed. Here, alas, in the direction of auto-
biographical detail, the contemporary mediaeval sermon proves
as disappointing as its modern counterpart. Even the very
anecdotes, numerous as they are, are borrowed as a rule from
earlier writers, and but very rarely from personal reminiscence.
Sermon diaries or note-books being rarer still, we are thrown
back on the meagre evidence of Episcopal Registers, of Chapter
Acts, upon stray portraits in the secular literature of the times,
or abnormal cases of heretical preaching which caught the
chronicler's attention. These, together with the light which
some brief introductory prologue or series of headings to a set
of homilies may throw on the habits and experiences of their
author, are the principal sources at our disposal. Fortunate
indeed might we have been, if other compilers had followed the
example of brother Robert of Ware, a thirteenth century
Franciscan, who sets forth in the preface to his *Rosarium* of
sermons[4] a sketch of his own early life and conversion to the
Order, for the purpose of illustrating from personal knowledge
the miraculous power of the Holy Virgin he is about to extol.
While autobiography is rare, however, general "figures" and
analogues from nature depicting the kind of man a preacher
was expected to be are common enough. Such curiosities indeed
are always to be found amongst the favourite stock-in-trade of
this particular profession. In Alexander Neckham[5], he had

---

[1] MS. Camb. Univ. Libr. Ii. iii. 8, fol. 149. See below, p. 135.
[2] Collection of Prints at the Brit. Mus.   [3] *Prov.* Lib. 3, tit. 4.
[4] MS. Gray's Inn Libr. No. 7, fol. 62–138. See my article in the *Dublin
Review*, for April, 1925.
[5] (1157–1217.) *De Naturis Rerum*—under "Gallus." Cf. Bromyard,
S.P.—Predic.

appeared as the cock, with his comb and wattles, his morning crowing, his authority in the fowl-house, all carefully delineated in the picture to represent the right homiletical qualities. In Rypon, he is compared to the human stomach in its work of digesting and distributing nourishment for the system—"accipiens cibum, coquit eum in seipsum, et per totum corpus [i.e. the Church] dispergit"[1]; a little later in the same "thema,"[2] to the teeth, with a similar duty, as "with whiteness of purity, bony strength, and immoveable constancy they grind up and disperse the sacred Word." If, however, you consider these a little offensive to modern taste, Dr Bromyard, amid a perfect riot of imagery, will present for your enlightenment the physician to the royal household who must administer herbs and other necessaries, with all skill and firmness, to preserve in health no less distinguished a patient than the king's own son; or again, the royal herald diligently crying his master's proclamations to all men, without fear or favour. Elsewhere, the preachers are likened to the lights of heaven by which men find their way in the darkness of the night[3], no inappropriate simile for the work of the pulpit in the "Dark Ages," as we shall see. Finally, the best-known type of all appears, that of the "Domini canes," of the noble pedigree of Francis Thompson's "Hound," here with their relentless bark protecting the sacred sheepfolds from wolves[4], the poultry-yard from foxes[5], or else full in the chase with Christ, that great huntsman—"the wiche over al other lovithe huntyng of soulis."[6]

Everywhere stress is laid in the current treatises on the fact that before all else deeds and example of life speak as loud if not louder than words. "ʒiff suche men now adayes preche and repreve synne as holy lyvers, men wold be aferde to repreve hem be cause of here holynes...he thᵗ is holy of liff may boldely speke aʒeyns thoo thᵗ be synners."[7] While William de Pagula will have even his village priest "eruditus et doctus, irreprehensibilis et maturus,"[8] if he can, the Dominican, Thomas Walleys, specifies further for one modest alike in dress and

[1] MS. Harl. 4894, fol. 200.   [2] fol. 201.   [3] Ibid. fol. 59.
[4] Bromyard, S.P. etc.   [5] MS. Harl. 4894, fol. 95.
[6] Gesta Rom. Engl. vers. (E.E.T.S.), pp. 110, etc.
[7] MS. Roy. 18. B. xxiii, fol. 75 b.
[8] Oc. Sacer. (MS. Roy. 6 E. l. fol. 27 b) etc. Cf. Cil. Oc. Sac. (MS. Harl. 4968, fol. 42): "eruditum, et prudentem, et providum...," etc.

manner, of frequent prayer and solitary reflection, with all the gifts and graces of a master of elocution[1]. Such a man might well claim, with a clear conscience, his prize among the special crowns of heaven—"called aureals"—awaiting, we are told, all faithful "prechoures, marteres, and maydenes."[2] He toiled in a world full of pitfalls and temptations for those who dared the enterprise.

"Bishops indeed," quotes Dr Lyndwood, "can preach everywhere, unless expressly prohibited by diocesans, following that saying in Matthew, 'Go ye out into all the world and preach!' made to the apostles, in whose place the bishops are their successors[3]. None the less they cannot bestow the authority to preach upon others save within their own dioceses." If the direct instruction of the people lay perforce in the hands of the parish clergy, all *prelati* in the wider mediaeval sense of the word, at the other end of the scale was the prelate in the more restricted modern sense of bishop, archbishop, archdeacon, and the like, pledged to find time amid his many duties to maintain and supervise this particular activity throughout the area of his administration. In fourteenth-century England this might be done in a variety of ways. In support of the programme laid down by the epoch-making Constitutions of Archbishop Peckham, he might encourage the publication and general distribution of vernacular translations and treatises for his clergy like Archbishop Thoresby of York. With Wykeham[4] or Stafford[5] he might check the non-residence and ignorance of individual offenders among the rectors by sending them back to their studies, with the added stimulus of a fine. The audiences he might lure by the attraction of suitable Indulgences. Finally, remembering like Chaucer's priest that practice should ever go

---

[1] See MS. Harl. 635, fol. 6, et seq. in Chap. VIII below.

[2] MS. Roy. 8. C. 1, fol. 137 b, and Adv. Libr., Edin. 18. 6. 15, fol. 2; etc. John the Baptist appears to have qualified as all three! For sources of this tradition see Coulton, *From St Francis to Dante*, 2nd ed. pp. 169, 382.

[3] Cf. also the Letter of Archbp. John Peckham to the Bishop of Tusculum (*Reg. J. Peckh.* (Rolls S.), p. 77): "the Episcopal Order is called by the Holy Fathers the Order of Preachers."

[4] Reg. Wykeham (Hants Rec. Soc.), vol. ii, p. 371, etc.

[5] Reg. Bp. Stafford, of Bath and Wells (Somerset Rec. Soc.), p. 180, and frequently in Reg. Bp. Stapledon of Exeter, etc. See also Wilkins, *Conc.* vol. iii, p. 605: "Item sacerdotes predicti, et alii presbyteri, curati, suis vacent libris."

before precept, even in this duty, he might be as instant as Grossetête or Brunton in exhorting both clergy and laity in person. In the present chapter it is this last-named activity that concerns us more particularly, when the bishop himself appears in the pulpit, with all the added solemnity of some special occasion, or special audience.

AN ENGLISH ARCHBISHOP IN HIS PULPIT, 1399
(*MS. Harl.* 1319, *fol.* 12)

Two sets of episcopal sermons by Englishmen, more or less within the limits of the chosen period, will provide some idea of the labours of the zealous prelate as preacher[1]. They serve

[1] At least a *third* series of English episcopal sermons exists for our period, that of Philip Repingdon, Cardinal, and Bishop of Lincoln (1405 to 1419). As, however, he was once a prominent Oxford Lollard, prior to abjuration of heresy in 1382, and the MSS. were not conveniently to hand for con-

to remind us that even in days when those in office had become a scandal to the whole of Christendom, there was yet here and there a true son of the great Grossetête on English soil. He it was who had put popular preaching first among the priestly duties; who in the year 1238, had actually drawn up a scheme of his own, whereby he might preach sermons to all his clergy in turn grouped in deaneries, to show them how they should henceforth instruct their own people, "since we are debtors in the preaching of the Word of God to all men of our diocese, and we are not able to fulfil this duty with our own mouth, for the multitude of parish churches."[1] Even so doubtful a character as Bishop Thomas de Lisle of Ely, in the centuries before us, has been described as "predicator egregius," rapidly visiting the various districts of his diocese, a faithful and prudent dispenser of the measure of wheat to the Lord's people, scattering the Word of God amongst those committed to his charge with fervent spirit[2].

The first of the collections just mentioned, first both in order of time and biographical detail, contains the sermons of the celebrated Archbishop Richard Fitzralph, of Armagh[3]. The series opens just prior to his appointment to the deanery of Lichfield in 1337. It continues until the year before his death in 1360, when as archbishop and notorious opponent of the friars, he was apparently still preaching at Avignon, "in the chapel of the Lord Pope" (Innocent VI), in spite of the many troubles he had incurred in a famous controversy. He was born

tinuous study, I have neglected these for the present. A writer in the *Church Quarterly Review* (vol. xix, pp. 59–82), declares that the sermons in question are entirely free from "Wycliffist leaven" (p. 72), as might be expected in so ambitious a convert to orthodoxy. MSS. are Caius Coll. 246, and Pembroke Coll. 49, Cambridge: (and also apparently in Lincoln Coll. Oxford). The first of these is the MS. mentioned in Dr J. Venn's *Early Collegiate Life* (Heffer), p. 21. Bp. Sheppey's Sermon MS. (Merton Coll. Oxford, 248) I have not been able to examine yet (d. 1360).

[1] Rypon has an interesting reference to this in one of his sermons (MS. Harl. 4894, fol. 208).

[2] See Wharton, *Anglia Sacr.* vol. i, p. 655. De Lisle was a Dominican.

[3] The copy used here is MS. Lansd. 393 (Dr R. L. Poole, who has not mentioned this in his interesting article on Fitzralph in the *D.N.B.*, refers only to MS. Bodl. 144, which is another copy of the collection): entitled (fol. 11): "Sermones domini Ricardi Dei gratia Archiepiscopi Ardmachani et Hibernie primati, habiti Avinione (?) et aliis locis quampluribus, de diversis sanctis et temporibus."

at Dundalk in Ireland, became a fellow of Balliol College, Oxford, Doctor of Divinity in that University, possibly Chancellor about the year 1333, a dean in England, and an archbishop in his native land ten years later. As in the case of another though less exalted preacher in England, his contemporary, whom we shall have occasion to mention, his death became the signal for an unofficial canonization by the people amongst whom he had toiled. "Seynt Richard Armachan"[1] is indeed almost the one historical figure we can claim to know among the many writers of sermons to be dealt with, all too obscurely, in this study. A single exception need be made in the case of one actually destined to carry on his assault against the Mendicants with fresh emphasis after his death—John Wycliffe. As for our other representative bishop, Thomas Brinton, or Brunton, of Rochester, though once, without doubt, equally eminent and equally renowned, he is now but a dim ghost in the mists of the past. This much, however, may be said of both of them, considered as preachers. Their stern and unsparing attacks on what they conceived to be the abuses of their day prove them to have been prophets indeed, fearing not the face of any man, were he prince or ecclesiastic, who stood before them. The fragmentary record of their journeyings and exhortations would seem amply to fulfil that command, so applicable to the faithful bishop of souls—"Lo thou shalt not nappe, neither slepe, that kepist the puple of Israel."[2]

In the case of Fitzralph of Armagh, we have eighty-eight sermons in Latin, most with place and occasion of delivery noted, together with two other outlines. The earliest examples, dating from 1335 to 1344, belong to an Avignon period, and show visits to the convents of the Minorites and the Preachers (one of them, at a General Chapter), to the Pope's private chapel[3], to the vice-chancellor's chapel, to the "House of the

---

[1] This title actually occurs in one of our fifteenth-century vernacular treatises (on the Decalogue), once ascribed to Wycliffe (MS. Roy. 17. A. xxvi, fol. 12): "As expouneth Seynt Rich. Armachan...."
[2] Thus quoted in an early fifteenth century sermon (MS. Harl. 2276, fol. 67).
[3] MS. Lansd. 393, fol. 153 b (*Sermo...habitus in die cinerum in capella domini Benedicti pape xii*). Sermons preached abroad by Englishmen, during the period, at the Council of Constance, in the year 1416–17 should be noticed in MS. Roy. Appdx. 7 (fol. 6): "per fratrem Galfridum

Apostolic Audience," and one "habitus in audientia causarum."
The remaining Avignon sermons of later date—including one
preached to the Carmelites, as well as the two famous anti-
Mendicant "Propositiones" of 1350, and 1357, in Papal Con-
sistory—can be dismissed in a sentence. It is the English and
Irish series which have the more immediate interest for the
present study. Twenty-four of these, so far as can be made out,
belong to the last two years of the Lichfield period, and illustrate
Fitzralph's homiletic activities as a dean. All seem to have been
delivered originally in English to the people, nine or more in
the cathedral church ("in choro"), two "in the cemetery of the
Hospital of St John," that is to say, from an open-air pulpit
or cross, two at other "chapels" in the city. The place-names
"Brewodde"[1] and Burford, as well as Cannok and Burton,
occurring in connection with others of the group, would appear
to denote Visitation addresses at neighbouring churches of the
diocese. Three others, identified with special processions for
public intercession—"pro rege," etc.—represent a further
typical class of sermons of more than passing interest from their
political character. Two of them delivered in London, that
centre of episcopal fulmination as Brunton reminds us, on the
eve of the preacher's consecration as Archbishop[2], here suggest
perhaps an orator's sudden leap to fame and popularity.

With his new dignity, the variety in Fitzralph's sermon
entries becomes not unnaturally somewhat extended. Without
attempting any exhaustive summary, we may now watch him at
Drogheda in 1349, addressing the Carmelites, strangely enough
in the very year when the Mendicant controversy was to break
out afresh. In the year following he preaches before the clergy
"in latino," assembled at his Provincial Council in that same
city, as also in the year 1354. Several more sermons are given
"ad populum" in 1351 and succeeding years, one of them
another discourse in the open churchyard, this time of the

Schale provincie Anglie, doctorem immeritum universitatis Cantabrigie,
ordinis heremitarum sancti Augustini"; fol. 19: "per magistrum Ricardum
Flemmyng, doctorem in sacra theologia alme universitatis Oxoniensis"
(afterwards Bp. of Lincoln, 1420–31).
[1] Brewood, in Staffordshire.
[2] Cf. fols. 26 b (Sermo in processione facta pro rege et principibus), and
48 (Sermo Ricardi electi Ardmachani in processione Londoni facta pro
rege...). See here in Chap. v.

church of St Mary. Among the scenes of his Irish activity we find such names as Dundalk, "God's Acre," Trim, Louth, "Cowlrath," "Drumeskin," Athboy, Kells, "Tarmfeghym" and "Maundevilleston."[1] It was in London, at Paul's Cross[2], in the year 1356, however, that Fitzralph beat "the drum ecclesiastic" with such challenging violence that the battle over "evangelical poverty" and the privileges of the friars was to rage more fiercely than ever in city pulpit and University schools for years to come. In his defence before the Pope, at Avignon, whither the complaint of his enemies had succeeded in bringing him, the fearless preacher explains the circumstances of that outburst[3]. According to Trevisa's English version[4] of his speech, published eventually as the famous *Defensio Curatorum*, he protests:

Lo, holy fader, I cam yn a tyme to London for certyn nedes of my chirche of Armachan, and fond there wise doctoures stryve upon the beggery and beggynge of the Lord oure Sauyour. And ofte iche was ipreied to preche to the peple in here owne tunge with the protestacioun that I have iseide, and tolde there myne concluciouns. For the concluciouns and other thinges that I there seide, ffreres, thei [= though] hit torne hem to a jape, appelede to this court.

Other audiences in the metropolis besides that which met at the "Cross" listened to the archbishop's eloquence. In 1356 he harangues a London congregation within the cathedral of St Paul's itself, and later "in aula episcopi Londoniensis." A year previously he had paid a visit for a similar purpose, on the feast of Corpus Christi, to the church of the nuns "ad partem orientalem,"[5] and in 1357 "at the New Church of St Mary" he expounds the appropriate text of the Ave Maria in the Feast of the Annunciation. Finally, there is a sermon in the parish church of Coventry in 1356, near the scene of his earlier ministry. This, like the others just mentioned, may have been the outcome of special invitations from those anxious to hear the prominent controversialist of the day[6].

[1] Another is marked "apud pontem" (fol. 56, in 1348). With this compare my reference to Thos. Richmond in Chap. v.
[2] Cf. fols. 97, 112, 119, 124 b.
[3] Nov. 8th, 1357.
[4] MS. Add. 24194. (Latin text in MS. Lansd. 393, fol. 248 et seq.)
[5] This I take to be St Helen's priory, Bishopsgate.
[6] Also two others—at "Datyngton" and "Dacmexton" (?).

Such then, in brief, is the record of this interesting sermon diary, for diary it would appear to be from such typical entries as the following, which concludes a sermon note, for the year 1354, "apud Acrum Dei" (God's Acre):

And all the matter of the rest of this sermon was the matter of the two preceding sermons, namely, concerning those who tithe falsely, against whom we have published statutes, and concerning usurers and those who accept interest, against whom we have also published statutes; further against those who impede the judges of Church courts from investigating any vice that ought to be amended, for the one purpose of making amendment of the soul, and in a method appropriate to the Church, against all of whom a Constitution has been issued to the effect that they should be excommunicated *ipso facto*, together with all who give them counsel, help, or favour; further against those who hinder women from freely making their wills, or Irishmen, as in the second of the two preceding sermons. This sermon dealt with others too, against whom Statutes were framed at the last General Council, a little while ago[1].

It discloses by no means an overwhelming programme of preaching apart from other duties, as thus spread out over the years. But there is good reason for considering it to be merely a somewhat random collection of the more representative and important discourses of the preacher's career, gathered up perhaps at odd moments in his all too infrequent leisure. Of the seven or eight "Paul's Cross" sermons that were mentioned, for example, only four make their appearance in the volume before us; while remarks such as the "sicut potui ad memoriam revocavi" which occurs above one of them[2] disclaim any pretence of systematic reporting. Common-sense, too, would not allow us to suppose that the one example provided of a "Collatio brevis...in sua capella, ad suam familiam in die Pasche" (1356)[3], for instance, was the only collation ever given to that household of his. In days when bishops' retainers earned a reputation, even in the pages of sermon books, for the most

---

[1] MS. Lansd. 393, fol. 80. Cf. again, e.g. fol. 54 (Dundalk, 1348): "Duplex causa fuit assignata quare volui orationem illis predicare dominicam [here his text, 'Paternoster qui es in celis, etc. usque ad finem orationis dominice'], sicut in sermone alio supra de hoc; et tertia ratio fuit adjecta, quia exemplo Domini nostri, qui judeos de sanguine suo...? illam orationem primo docebat, volui eos de sanguine meo illam orationem primo docere. Cetera sicuti in illo sermone."

[2] Ibid. fol. 97.   [3] fol. 97.

iniquitous conduct, are we not bound to believe that so eloquent a prelate as Fitzralph, pluralist though he may have been, gave them more freely of his rebukes and exhortings? Behind the eighty sermons and more that have survived, there must lurk phantoms of at least as many others now lost and forgotten for ever. Preaching once at Avignon of the duties of bishops, he had declared, in the phrases of St Chrysostom:

And Jesus went about all Galilee, as a zealous physician goes about among the sick, administering suitable medicines for any and every complaint. The Lord Jesus indeed went about each region in turn; but we [prelates], who are pastors of a single region each, have not the necessity "to go about the regions." Nevertheless we ought to go about and examine the several complaints of our people, and diligently attend to those among the people who are afflicted with the disease of avarice, that we may make some sermon concerning the evil of avarice, to the restoration of health[1].

This call to fellow-bishops of the great succession from St Augustine of Canterbury "who converted England" and showed a noble example to his successors, is still more characteristic of the prelate who is now to engage our attention, Thomas Brunton, of Rochester[2]. The traveller from Armagh, in north-east Ireland, to Rochester, upon Kentish Medway, might well prepare himself for contrasts in the change of scene. Yet, so universal is our mediaeval Church and its institutions, when the Kentish prelate came to his own see[3] about thirteen years after the Irish archbishop's death, he had much the same variety of congregations to exhort as he whose bones were now said to be working miracles among the good folk of Dundalk. The

[1] fol. 145 b [from Chryst. *Omel.* viii]. Dr Workman takes exception to this sketch of Fitzralph as the model preaching prelate. He has evidence that the king actually ordered him back to his Irish province. Yet, surely this latter injunction may have been the act of one who feared the archbishop's fearless denunciations. (See here later.)

[2] Cf. MS. Harl. 3760, fol. 60 b: "Et certe nos prelati Anglie debemus esse valde solliciti circa curam animarum, si attenderemus sollicitudines et labores precedentium nos prelatorum et maxime sancti Augustini et ejus sociorum qui Angliam convertebant, de quibus non dicunt cronica quod in Angliam venerunt pompatice cum phaleris et equis, ut sibi multiplicarent privilegia, beneficia, et honores, sed venerunt cum letaniis et processionibus, jejuniis et orationibus ac predicationibus, ut ostenderent se esse sollicitos circa animas lucrandas pariter et salvandas. Quorum exemplis nos eorum successores in onere et honore eorum facta deberemus continuare et viriliter confirmare, viz. orando, visitando, corrigendo, predicando...," etc.

[3] 1372 or 1373 (d. 1389).

headings in Bishop Brunton's series of sermons[1] are unfortunately as meagre as the known facts of his history when compared
with those of Armachanus. Yet it is still possible to trace from
them the same kind of visits to friaries and to synods of clergy,
the same kind of Visitation addresses in parish churches of the
diocese[2], the cathedral preachings, above all the same picturesque
London crowds that await the chosen orators of the day at that
famous pulpit-cross—"apud sanctum Paulum, Londonii," as
his own manuscript puts it. Further types of the episcopal
homily now make their appearance in the shape of funeral
orations, and sermons for ordination[3], and for the election of a
new head of the monastery. Unfortunately, however, there is
not a single date to guide us throughout the series, save the
mention of an occasional festival or fast-day; and the majority
of the sermons give no hint, apart from internal evidence, of the
circumstances of delivery.

On the other hand, there is great compensation in the rich-
ness of political and social allusions in these discourses. Brunton
himself appears to have begun his career as a Benedictine monk
at Norwich[4]. His love for brethren of the common cloister
continues to burn brightly even after he has been raised to the
dignity of the bishop's throne. Addressing the monks of the
priory of Rochester, from the pulpit, upon the joys of brotherly
unity, and loading them with compliments, he concludes thus:

"I and my Father are one," that is to say, "I, monk of Rochester,
and my father—namely, the bishop—are one," in the unity of the
religious life, of our profession, of our dwelling together, of our
affection, and in the truth of a true love. Such is the oneness of me,
the head, with you, the members, that, because I have obtained this
comparatively small and modest church, not by prayer, nor by price,
not by letters, nor by my own endeavours, but from God and the

[1] MS. Harl. 3760. These I take to be the *Sermones Solemnes* mentioned by
Bale. Bale, who describes Brunton as "penitenciarius papae," mentions
further "Sermones coram pontifice Romano factos."

[2] Among the names mentioned we recognize Dartford (Derteford),
Pembury (Pepinbery), Wrotham, Hoo and Cobham.

[3] fol. 120 b (in celebratione ordinum). With this should be compared the
ordination address incorporated by Bromyard in his *Summa Pred.* (under
"Ordo Clericalis"): "Secundo prosequenda sunt quaedam themata per
modum collationum ad ordinandos et ordinatos specialiter pertinentium."
A synodal sermon of Rypon's follows the pattern of Bromyard here.

[4] Cf. Bale, *Scriptores*, s.v.: "Thomas Brynton (qui alias vocatur Briton)...
monachus Benedictin. de monasterio Nordovicensi, episc. Roff."

Lord Pope alone, never do I intend to procure for myself a richer benefice, but to stay with you for ever, repeating with truth that passage of the Psalms: "One thing have I desired of the Lord, that will I seek after; that I may dwell in the house of the Lord all the days of my life."...And you are not merely sons to me, as are others in this diocese; but you are friends, intimates, and brethren [amici intimi, et confratres]. Therefore I can say to you that word written aforetime for my theme: "Behold how good and how pleasant it is for brethren to dwell together in unity!"[1]

For the rest, Brunton lives even nearer than Fitzralph to the centre of stirring events in the general life of his times. John Balle, the revolutionary, is actually preaching in his very diocese, during his episcopacy. The Peasants' Revolt of 1381 with its disastrous results in the capital is a matter of immediate concern to him. At Canterbury, Edward, the Black Prince, that mighty warrior, is laid to rest, not far from his cathedral. London itself, with its streets decked for coronation in 1377, as the bishop saw them, London with the court where as confessor to King Richard II he must have learnt much of the current vice and corruption—with Blackfriars, where he was destined to take his place in the famous Council of 1382, which condemned the doctrines of Wycliffe, lay but a mere thirty miles away. The atmosphere of all these happenings hangs thick about the volume of sermons he has left us. Few of them seem to have escaped some notice in the pulpits which he honoured with his fiery presence. Fiery he remains to the last, in his unsparing denunciation of every kind of wickedness in the high places, spiritual and temporal alike. His fellow-bishops he will reprove again and again for their evil example, and their silence amid great abuses of State. The royal counsellors he warns and admonishes in an age of favourites and greedy self-seeking, knowing well the risks of such plain language in the pulpit. The immorality, injustice and oppression of the nobles is his constant theme[2]; likewise the falsity of the middle-class merchants[3], who throng the city. Politely, yet firmly, he suggests, on more than one occasion, that the king and his court would do well to set the example of penitence and devotion by

[1] MS. Harl. 3760, fol. 31 et seq. (Sermo ad Religiosos.)
[2] Cf. fols. 122 b, 124 b, 125, 128 b, 152, etc. In the sermon of fol. 187 et seq. he deals with all three classes of offenders.
[3] Cf. fol. 124, etc.

taking their place in the intercessory processions in London streets[1]. For him Ash Wednesday, with its mood of pessimism, of the tragic sense of sin and failure, of prostration and tears, is the typical occasion for a sermon[2]. His is the spirit of the great Florentine Savonarola, ever calling men to repent and reform lest even worse disasters fall upon them from heaven: "Non sic, karissimi, non sic!"[3]

Yet in spite of all this outspoken criticism of those in office and high dignity in the State, "magnates"—as he often calls them—seem to have continued to form part of his pulpit audiences. Men felt secretly proud of the grand old warrior, doubtless, even while they flinched before his courageous attack. When he goes down to preach to the Carmelite friars of "Eylisforde" (Aylesford), on the banks of the Medway, we are carefully informed in the sermon rubric that it is "coram domino de Grey," descendant, no doubt, of the Lord Grey de Codnor mentioned in Dugdale as founder of their house[4]. One event more in his life, recorded this time not in the sermon manuscript, but in the entries of chroniclers, illustrates the esteem in which he was held by his contemporaries. Both Walsingham's *Historia Anglicana*[5], and also the *Liber Custumarum*[6] among the London Guildhall documents tell how on the morrow after the coronation of Richard II, that is, on Friday, the 17th of July, in the year 1377, a general procession was formed at St Paul's, to pray for the king and the peace of the realm. All the archbishops, bishops and abbots who had taken part in the ceremony of the previous day, together with the temporal nobility and a crowd of others, were in its ranks. According to the *Liber Custumarum*, the sovereign himself stayed in his palace, while the stately cortège made its way through the

---

[1] fol. 114 b and again on fol. 189 b.

[2] Cf. actual sermons, "in die cinerum," etc. on fols. 73, (166 b), 288 b, 299, etc.

[3] Cf. on fols. 128, 187: "Non sic, domini reverendi!" etc.

[4] fol. 93 et seq. The descendant is John de Grey (d. c. 1392). There is a "Narratio" here, concerning monks of Westminster and Chertsey (fol. 94), which should interest collectors of "exempla." On fol. 300 we may indicate another, about a certain queen of Scotland ("vix credenda!").

[5] Walsingham (Rolls S.), vol. i, pp. 338–9. The sermon is wrongly ascribed by the editor in his index to Thos. Trillek, Brunton's predecessor, who died in 1372.

[6] *Munim. Gild. Lond.* (Rolls S.), vol. ii, p. 481.

heart of the city—"humbly and devoutly uttering fervent prayers for the king's welfare, and the happiness of his rule, and for the soul of the said noble lord, Edward, the king lately deceased, and other faithful dead." At the close of it (Walsingham says, "in progressu"), Thomas, Bishop of Rochester, preached a sermon —"ad beneplacitum et nutum, ut creditur, Regis Regum." Since the St Albans chronicler is good enough to make some note of the gist of its contents, we might well try to identify the discourse with one of the many left unidentified in our manuscript. Meanwhile, the present writer has given his reasons for believing that in the so-called B. text of *Piers Plowman's Vision*, referred by Skeat to the same period, we have in the "angel of hevene" that "lowed to spake in latyn," a portrait of this great prelate himself, arguing like Langland's "Resoun," "with a crosse, afor the Kynge," of truth, and righteousness, and judgement to come[1]. Conjecture this must remain. But in a genuine passage of one of his own discourses, at once intimate and pathetic, Thomas Brunton, aged and broken in spirit, reveals to us the moral grandeur and integrity of his soul. Mere empty greatness of reputation in the pulpit might satisfy men of a lesser breed. But, like George Whitefield in another age, popular triumphs there leave him strangely cold and undeceived, as he looks back with an open mind at the actual fruit of so much "honest talking." He is repeating the story of Jonah and the men of Nineveh:

If any man had preached, before these times, of the ills which have fallen upon England, and of the open vengeances of God, even of the slaughter of the mighty, the famine, the mortalities, the storms of winds, the internal feuds, and wars without, who would have believed him, or made repentance with the men of Nineveh? I say for myself, with sorrow, that continually have I preached to these Christians against the sins that flourish in my diocese. None the less I do not see that any arises effectually out of sin; but for the greater part they are like to the dead man whom Simon Magus boasted that he could raise to life. For by means of his incantations, as it appeared, he only moved his head; and these, when they hear good counsel, move their heads, but do not put away their sins. For what adulterer has put away his concubine, and now adheres to his legitimate

[1] See my article "The 'Angel' and the 'Goliardeys' of Langland's Prologue to *Piers Plowman's Vision* (B. text)," in the *Modern Language Rev.* for July, 1925.

spouse? What usurer has restored what he unjustly took? What unjust "maintainer" [manutentor] or false juror restrains himself from his crimes? What user of false measures, by means of which he deceives his neighbours and poor strangers, is now breaking or burning them up? Who from his heart puts away an ancient hatred, instead of revenging himself when he sees his time? Nay rather, of all these cursed uprisers ["surrectores": I take it he is referring back to the *exemplum* of Simon Magus, again], whose peril I have so very often exposed in my own sermons, who is smitten with remorse, who makes a true confession, or in any way makes satisfaction for his wrong-doing?[1]

Here at least there is no false illusion of the triumphs of sacred oratory, such as not a few have entertained in Protestant times[2].

Passing now from the faithful prelate to his *curati*, we shall seek for evidences among the manuscripts of the "salutary barking" of these humbler watch-dogs of the country parishes. Dr Bromyard, the learned Dominican, by no means always free of the charge of self-contradiction in his great preaching manual, had remarked on one occasion that no prelate is more objectionable than the upstart from the lower ranks of society. Be that as it may, for once he is prepared to state that of all ecclesiastics, those of aristocratic birth and upbringing are the worst.

"Who are these," he asks, "who spiritually speaking will have to say (at the Doom), 'My vineyard I have not kept'? Assuredly they who in heart and blood are nobler and of superior rank. For, as hounds that are called 'noble'—such as greyhounds, and the like— commonly do not guard but rather devour, not watching at the poor man's house, but rather snatching and consuming his bread from off the tables of lords, so do the men of noble birth, elated by their blood and pride....For they leave the flocks, and elect to spend their days in the courts of the mighty, to eat the flesh of fat beasts. So, too, as rural and simple hounds are set to protect house and flock, thus to the guardianship of the flock of God must be elected simple men in their humility. And Christ, indeed, appointed fishermen to keep His church...."

---

[1] fol. 287 b.

[2] Bp. Brunton died in 1389. A modern rubbing of the indent of what was once a fine contemporary canopied *brass* to his memory, in Rochester Cathedral, is to be found, I note, in MS. Add. 37954 (B). An engraving of this rubbing, with a short article on the Rochester indents (Sedgwick, T.E.), is in the *Home Counties Mag.* vol. v, 1905, p. 301. Brunton was succeeded at Rochester by another distinguished preacher of the day, the Dominican, Wm. Bottlesham, like Brunton, appointed a royal confessor.

Mention in Registers and other ecclesiastical documents of the preaching activities of these great ones is sparse enough. How much more natural it is to find that such references in them to the ordinary parish clergy are rarer still! If the evidence of their delinquency, their incompetence and idleness did not abound, on the other hand, "no news" here might well be taken as the sign of "good news," and a general healthiness in the body clerical. Chaucer's faithful "persoun," however, who, though called a "lerned man" in the *Prologue* to the *Canterbury Tales*, flatly disclaims such learning later on in his own prologue— "of clerkes I am not textuel"—probably would have been the last to think of issuing a volume of discourses of his own. In this respect, at all events, his case must be considered typical of the preaching *curati* as a whole. The elementary sermon manuals do not represent their own work: they are usually written for them by others. Hence while bishop and monk, friar and anchorite, will leave behind them the monuments of their pulpit eloquence in homily book, in tract and "summa," for our inspection, the preaching of the humbler seculars escapes us practically unrecorded.

One of the rare and notable exceptions among sermon writers of this latter category, thus voices the inferiority of his class, in a quaint homily of his own:

And [= if] a bishoppe or a doctoure stond up to preche the worde of God, muche pepull will drawe thetherwarde to here hym; and ȝiff he repreve vices and synne, the peple will not gruche never a dele aȝeyns hym, ne thei will not forȝett is wordes. But lat a sympull preste as I am seth the word of God to you, and ȝe sett no price thereby....Thus ffareth grett mens wordes now adayes, thei ben taken grett hede of, and pore mens wordes ben sett on syde[1].

This quotation occurs in just such a manuscript as would seem to be the work of the unpretentious homilist we are seeking. Diminutive, unadorned, unrubricated, in faded brown ink upon no vellum, but paper stained and coarse, inwardly in its vernacular subject-matter as outwardly in its appearance, the little "de tempore" series proclaims its true origin and character:

[1] MS. Roy. 18. B. xxiii, fol. 75. Cf. later, also (fol. 75 b), "and another man had done so, as I am, whos holynes had not be knowon...," etc.

" . . . inasmuche as ȝe fynde not in me thise iii auctoritees (i.e. of a doctor)," continues the preacher, "nother grett state of worldely wurshippe, ne holynes in lyvynge, ne hie sotelte in connynge, ne state, ne degre of scole have I none, but purpose to say Goddes worde,—therfore it is nedeful to me to praye to you to preye with me to almyghty God to sende me myght and grace. . . . "

It is the naïve confession of one whom Bromyard would compare to an uncouth nurse, able herself but to chew up the more solid food of instruction before giving it to her charges.

Here is a group of discourses then—"after myne sympull connynge"[1]—of the simplest and most practical pattern, save for an element of the marvellous scattered here and there in some miraculous legend or warning tale. But even Myrc, one or two of whose "Festiall" sermons are recognizable in the same volume, was simple and superstitious enough, and he was no less than a prior of Austin canons in his day. In the case of the former, however, the charming modesty and self-distrust of the unknown author, as expressed particularly in his ante-themes, disarms all criticism. When he prays in a *Sermo pro pace*, that God "will of is gracious goodnes ȝeve me grace in this harde mater som wordes to speke. . . ffor I knowe myselfe unabull and not sufficiente for to do this dede," we are silent, in our sympathy with this most gentle speaker. By a quaint coincidence, on more than one occasion he actually uses Chaucer's famous phrase about the saintly parson, thus: "For so dud Criste hymselfe; for first he lyvyd holyly inward, and afterward he tauthe it forth."[2] Let this, then, in itself be our justification, that search in the dust-laden homilies of the past will not be wholly vain. The "curate" of Chaucer after all is no idle creation of the poet's mind; lost and obscured we have found him among the despised treatises, once dead he lives again, and speaketh here for evermore. His glory shall be in the words of our fifteenth-century English version of the *Gesta Romanorum*[3]:

I have bene a preste this fourty wynter and more, and have fastid,

---

[1] MS. Roy. 18. B. xxiii, fol. 124.
[2] fol. 67 b, and again fol. 75 b: "So that Crist may sey to all tho that preche well, and dose evill the wordes of David the prophete, in the sawter boke. . . ."
[3] E.E.T.S. Ext. S. No. 33, p. 389.

waked, and prayde, gone on pilgremage, *and prechid*, and by the mercy of God I have tornyd many soules to God.

But by no means every rural priest would be of this humble and unsophisticated type[1]. Doctors of Divinity from Oxford like Richard Ullerston, or Simon Alcock, whose treatise on sermon composition will be described in a subsequent chapter, or again compilers of hand-books like the author of the *Oculus Sacerdotis*, William de Pagula, who knows all the rules about preaching, were parish clergy. Yet this, of course, did not mean that they necessarily favoured their people with the benefits of their pulpit knowledge and gifts. So many of the wealthier and more privileged rectors were non-resident pluralists. Furthermore, as the *Cilium Oculi Sacerdotis* itself reminds us, they were explicitly allowed by the Church to hand over the tasks of the pulpit to others, provided that these were approved by the responsible bishop. Nor need we imagine that amongst the numerous temporal vicars thus placed in the churches by episcopal authority, to do duty for some minor, for some incompetent still away "at the schools," for the careless absentee, there would be very many of the "Doctores in Theologia," whom Dr Lyndwood suggests[2] as so eminently suitable for the post.

On the other hand, if the countryside be quitted for the great city, there is every likelihood that here where crowds will assemble, and distinguished reputations may be made, some learned rector or vicar will be found occupying his own pulpit at least on the greater festivals. "At Seint Marie Spitel, in Estir Weke, the ʒeer of our lorde, a thousand, four honderd, and sixe," in London, for example, you may enjoy that "worthi clerk, maistir Richard Alkartoun," a real prophet of terrors and despair, who refers you in the course of his lucubrations to

---

[1] It is worth noting that even deacons were allowed to preach, if rectors. "Et licet rector fuerit tantum diaconus, id potest, et etiam idem officium in propria persona..." in *Reg. Anim.* So Lyndwood: "etiamsi fuerint diaconi tantum...."

[2] The *Cil. Oc. Sac.* suggests: "...scil., alium rectorem, et magistrum in theologia, vel de supradictis religiosis" (i.e. friars) (MS. Harl. 4968, fol. 41 b). In the same connection see the interesting entry *re* Chancellor. Peter Partriche of Lincoln Cathedral, in *Visitations of Relig. Hos.* (Linc. Rec. Soc.) vol. i, p. 175, who obtains an indult in 1427 to reside at Biddenden "to recreate his parishioners with preaching."

what "I seide late in a sermon at Poules cros."[1] Like many another, of whom nothing appears to be known, save what is furnished by a stray sermon or so, he was doubtless a vivid enough personality in his own day, and among his own flock.

As a specimen of the kind of fate that has overtaken the mighty among our ancient preachers, the instance of Dr William Lichfield might be mentioned. Rector of the church of All Hallows the Great, in London ("ecclesia omnium sanctorum, Londoniis"), described by Dr Gascoigne as one of several "predicatores, famosi in vita et scientia," who dared to attack the abuses of the time[2], he is reported to have died in 1448, leaving behind him 3083 sermons, "written in English with his own hand," besides a collection of materials for sermons, entitled "Mille exempla." All that the present writer has been able to trace of his composition so far in surviving manuscripts is a little "tract on the Five Senses," which is to be found attached to a copy of John Waldeby's sermon treatises[3]. Obviously incorporating some of his pulpit utterances, it reveals a vigorous emotional spirit, with a touch of mysticism[4], and that relentless scorn of evil-doers which would account for a reputation gained in the metropolis, where pulpit thunders roll unceasingly, to the days of the Puritans. Wherever such manuscript survivals are concerned, an exception in any case must be made for John Felton[5], perpetual vicar of the parish church of St Mary Magdalene "extra muros," at Oxford. Copies of his *Sermones Dominicales*[6], apparently finished in the year 1431,

---

[1] MS. Add. 37677, fols. 57–61. A Latin version of the same is said to be in MS. Trin. Coll. Oxford, 42. The *Brit. Mus. Add. MSS. Cat.* admits the unlikelihood of identification with Rich. Ulverstone (cf. *D.N.B.*); but with interest I notice Miss Deanesly's reference to a "clerk Alkerton," who attacked a Lollard sermon preached at Paul's Cross, in 1407 by Peter Payne, from Pollard's *Fifteenth Century Prose and Verse* (*The Lollard Bible*, p. 292).

[2] See *Loci e Libro Veritatum* (Rogers).

[3] MS. Roy. 8. C. 1, fols. 122 b–143 b. Some verse of his also survives.

[4] Cf. his exposition of a mystical theme from the Song of Songs (Cantic. 2), ibid., fol. 128, etc., and see further in Chap. III, below.

[5] I find further notice of a "perpetual vicar's preaching" in Bp. Rede's Register (*Sussex Rec. Soc.* vol. viii, p. 100), where a certain discreet man, Master Peter, perpetual Vicar of the parish church of Eastbourne ("Estborne") delivers "a noteworthy address" at a visitation ceremony in the cathedral church of Chichester.

[6] MS. Linc. Cath. Libr. A. 6. 10, fols. 1–227, a collection of Latin sermons "de tempore" is attributed by Dean Honeywood to the "vicar. de Mawdelyn, Oxon."; but so far I have not been able to look into them.

abound in the libraries, as Gasquet and Cutts have already pointed out. Of his career, beyond a word or two of reminiscence in the preface to this work, there is practically nothing of certainty known[1]. Bale states that so great was his reputation that after death his tomb was visited by the people in hope of miracles. But very few of the makers of these homily books in any order of the Church seem to have been makers of history.

Thus far it is the faithful prelate and the faithful "curate" that have engaged our attention exclusively, in their joint response to the great preaching task. But what now of the other side of the picture? A good deal might be said, it is true, against reviving the dry bones of an old controversy over the extent of pre-Reformation preaching in England. Yet no sketch, however fragmentary, could claim even the shadow of faithfulness were no hint given of the mass of evidence in sermon literature itself of the failures, the negligences and ignorances. This same controversy reaches back at least to the seventeenth century when Henry Wharton, writing as "Anthony Harmer," championed the Catholic side of the argument against Bishop Burnet's attack[2]. Roughly two centuries later Cardinal Gasquet may be said to have reopened it, with an article in the *Dublin Review*[3] which was the declared fruit of his researches among English mediaeval sermon collections. His main contention may best be summarized, perhaps, in a reply made to Bishop Hobhouse's assertion that preaching was then no "regular part of the Sunday observances as now." To the question whether the Peckham Constitutions dealing with preaching were faithfully carried out by the clergy, and rigorously enforced by the bishops in succeeding centuries, he replies with an emphatic affirmative: "I think there is ample evidence that it was."[4] Elsewhere he repeats: "in pre-Reformation days the people were well instructed in their faith by priests who faithfully discharged their plain

[1] Prof. T. F. Crane (footnote, *Exempla of Jacques de Vitry*, Folklore Soc.) and the *D.N.B.* (Rev. Ronald Bayne) repeat an old error, already noted in one of the manuscripts, in calling him a "Fellow of St Mary Magdalene College."
[2] See Wordsworth's *Eccles. Biog.* vol. i, and Canon Nolloth in the preface to E.E.T.S. (O.S.) No. 118, p. xvi. (*Lay Folks' Catech.*)
[3] Reprinted in *The Old English Bible, and other Studies*. Similar statements are reproduced in his *Parish Life in Mediaeval Engl.* (*Ant. Ser.*), and Dr J. C. Cox's volume on *Pulpits* (Milford, 1915).
[4] *O.E.B.* pp. 187–8 (ed. 1897).

duty in this regard." Here it is clearly no question of the pulpit activities of friars or monks. From the other side Dr Coulton has made effective rejoinder[1] by exposing some of the hidden flaws in his opponents' armoury, and bringing up fresh weapons of his own, particularly in the shape of contemporary evidences for the ignorant state of the clergy. A recent monograph by Miss Deanesly tends to confirm this side of the argument[2]. Most, if not all, of the sermon manuscripts put forward by Dr Gasquet, however, seem to have remained in the state of neglect in which he found them. It is to these, then, that the present writer intends to turn, the very authorities upon which the Cardinal has set, as it were, not merely his "Nihil obstat," but an enthusiastic "Imprimantur"!

Certain remarks in John Bromyard's *Summa Predicantium* might appear to the superficial reader to confirm an impression conveyed by familiar passages in Chaucer or Gower that the English world of the later middle ages was indeed all too full of preaching[3]. Full of the preachings of the Mendicants it may well have been, especially in populous centres. But this is beside our present point. Even if we have recourse to the better-known writers, to Gower, the "moral poet," for example in his *Confessio Amantis*, where the mood is by no means violent, comment upon the attitude of bishop and "curate" is found to be most unfavourable. Clerks of his own day he contrasts with those of "the daies olde," whose

> lust was al upon the boke,
> or for to preche or for to preie.
> . . . . . .
> —And now, men sain, is other wise!

As for the prelates, they cry:

> Let knightes winne with her hondes
> For oure tunge shal be still,
> And stande upon the flesches will.

---

[1] Appdx. I, *Mediaeval Studies*, 1st Series (2nd. ed., pp. 103–114).

[2] *The Lollard Bible, and other mediaeval Biblical versions* (Camb. Univ. Press).

[3] Even a vernacular homilist, late in the fifteenth century, says to his simple audience, "*So many* prechors, and so few ȝevers of good ensampyll of good lyving saw never man" (MS. Linc. Cath. Libr. A. 6. 2, fol. 184 b). Cf. this with the earlier remark of "Piers Plowman."

> It were a travail for to preche
> The feith of Crist, as for to teche
> The folke painim.

How these shall blush, continues the poet, at the last great Day of Account, when, before Christ the Auditor, they have to compare their own "voide hondes" with those of Peter and Andrew, Thomas and Paul, so richly laden! Turn to Hoccleve, and the complaints are the same:

> The oynement of holy sermonynge
> Hym loth is upon hem for to despende;
> Som person is so threde-bare of konnynge
> That he can noght, thogh he hym wys pretende,
> And he that can, may not his herte bende
> Therto, but from his cure he hym absentithe[1].

In like fashion, the author of *Piers Plowman*, before him, had told of the amusing but scandalous parson of "passing thirty winters," who could track hares in the field so very much better than Latin case-endings in his Psalter-Book[2]. Without proceeding further on this line of evidence it is sufficient to say that so far from being a fashionable literary gibe or a piece of individual spite, the verse just quoted from the *Regement of Princes* sums up to perfection the general witness of the sermon writers themselves.

In a quaint comparison, one has distinguished thus between the two attributes which are both necessary for the successful preacher: "Ther is one maner tree that berith fruyt, but it is not aptid to hous bildyng; and this tree bitokeneth a man that is wel araied in vertuouse werkis, but he is not aptid for feblenesse of kunnynge to governe a puple bi wiis defence aȝens wolves, or bi discreet techyng of hooli scripture."[3] More than a chapter would be required to display adequately, from these particular sources, what the lack of actual virtue in the con-

---

[1] *The Regement of Princes* (E.E.T.S.), p. 52, l. 1429 et seq. (Written c. 1412.)

[2] Cf. B text, ll. 424–6. Like nearly all the sayings of Langland this is derived straight from the current preaching. Cf. Nicholas Philip, the Franciscan (in MS. Bodl. Lat. Th. d. i, fol. 89), "swifter to collect hounds, and to track hares"...; *Oc. Sacer.* (MS. Roy. 6 E. i, fol. 24 b.), "parati ad querendum vestigia leporum," etc.

[3] MS. Harl. 2276, fol. 114 b. These are the clergy, who have "conscientia," as Bromyard puts it (*S.P.—Militia*) but lack "scientia."

temporary priesthood meant for the prestige of the contemporary pulpit. Here, however, it is proposed to concentrate solely on the question of "kunnynge" and the way it was employed. Amongst the Homily-collections recommended by Gasquet in a footnote of his article appears the title of a capacious volume by Master Robert Rypon, a sub-prior of Durham[1]. At the end of this volume, which will be found amongst the Harleian manuscripts in the British Museum, there are eight synodal sermons delivered by him, apparently, at the beginning of the fifteenth century, to secular clergy of the diocese. So impressive are the revelations of this outspoken man, coming as they do from one whose zeal and orthodoxy is beyond suspicion, that we shall attempt to give them a little of the prominence they deserve, but have hitherto lacked altogether.

A good life, Master Rypon admits, is the preacher's first essential qualification. But because instruction cannot be rightly given without competent knowledge, "restat quod scientia est curato necessaria."[2] Two further qualifications added, and we have what may be considered the *sine qua non* of this profession: "Knowledge, election, and the continuance of firm, fixed, and immoveable operation are requisite in advance....But few priests possess or exercise these three qualifications."[3] This latter, of course, is merely a judgement that any idealist might pass upon the average man. But to continue, what, in actual detail, is to be comprehended by this "essential knowledge"? Rypon would reply, first, an adequate knowledge of the Scriptures: "*Curati* are required to have a knowledge of Holy Scripture with which they may preach to the people the Word of God."[4] For the rest he falls back upon the books prescribed by the Canon Law, incidentally thus introducing to us the mediaeval

---

[1] MS. Harl. 4894. See here later in Chaps. II, VI, etc. (fl. c. 1401).

[2] Ibid. fol. 197 b et seq. (Sermo 2º in Sinodo).

[3] fol. 202 b: "Scientia, et electio, ac firme fixe et immobilis operationis continuatio requiruntur antecedenter....Sed pauci sacerdotes habent vel exercent ista tria." Cf. below, p. 35, n. 5.

[4] fol. 197. Cf. also: "Hec scientia scripturarum que verius dicitur sapientia"; and, quoting Lincoln (Grossetête): "Ex sollicito studio scripturarum habebis scientiam in memoria quam non decipiet oblivio." Again, fol. 205: "Prudentiam, autem, que est mater virtutum, generat lectio scripturarum et frequens et assidua inspeccio." With these, cf. elsewhere, *Cil. Oc. Sac.* (MS. Harl. 4968, fol. 45 b); *Reg. Anim.* (MS. Harl. 2272, fol. 2), etc.

preacher's essential library: "And this knowledge, according to the Canon (dist. 38), consists specifically in the following—'The books which it is necessary for priests to study and know are the Book of the Sacraments, the Lectionary, the Antiphoner, the *Baptisterium*, the *Compotus*, the *Canones Poenitentiales*, and Homilies throughout the year for Sundays and Festivals [*Homelie per annum dominicis et singulis festivitatibus*].'[1] And if the priest's or 'curate's' knowledge of any single one of these is lacking, hardly is he worthy of the name of priest."[2] "I do not say," adds the speaker, "that he is bound to know all these things by heart; but it suffices that he should know how to read them distinctly, understand them clearly, and expound them plainly as often as it is his duty."

How far then do the pastors carry out such a prescribed standard in real life? As the sub-prior sees it, by their very assumption of the pastoral office "they are binding themselves to feed a flock already in danger of starvation for the word of God, through lack of the food of instruction, true faith, and moral precepts, in which the soul's salvation consists."[3] Yet, "Assuredly, some of them [the pastors] are destitute of this food, *because many know not how to expound a single article of the Faith, nor one precept of the Decalogue*; and—what is worse—when they lack 'this bread' themselves, they neglect to learn what they do not know. Nay, rather, what is worst of all, many of them despise knowledge and teaching, and reject knowledge; or, if by chance they have any knowledge, or a moderate amount of it, by entangling themselves in secular affairs, or giving themselves up to pleasures, they cast that little away in their folly." In yet another sermon he returns to the charge: "But—what is to be deplored—to-day, some (they ought to learn before they teach!), led on by the spirit of ambition, take upon themselves the aforesaid office who do not know how to preach, nor wish to learn,

---

[1] Gratian's *Decretum*, Pars i, dist. xxxviii, c. 5.
[2] Cf. the quaint vernacular version in a "Mirror" of Sermons, in MS. Harl. 5085, fol. 201: "Thes ben the bokes that the prest schal hav and conen—'Libri sacramentorum, lectionarium, baptisterium, compotum, canonem penitencialem, psalterum, omelias of the dominikes of the 3er, and of other festival daies,' and mani other thinges that ben necessarie bothe in the old lawe and the newe...." For a popular account of these works see in Wordsworth and Littlehales, *Old Service Books of the English Church*.
[3] fol. 208. (Quoting freely from Bp. Grossetête.) Cf. again, fol. 194.

whether they be young or old."[1] What, then, is the result of all this clerical "unconnynge"? Rypon replies: "Without a doubt, if each churchman had the knowledge appropriate to his rank, there would not spring up so many errors in the Church as spring forth in these days."[2] In another sermon he goes so far as to suggest that God in his mercy may actually permit the Lollard to flourish "that those fools who have taken upon them the care of souls may be roused to acquire a better knowledge."[3]

But further, how comes it, we ask, if, as Gasquet asserts, "they would have to prove themselves to be sufficiently lettered, and of good life before they would be accepted for ordination,"[4] that such priests as these should ever arrive in office at all? Rypon has no hesitation in declaring that there is no such working system in fact, whatever be the Church's theory. "There are some clergy," he says, "who rise to these grades, and yet they are ignorant of the duties of the same."[5] As an illustration of what he means, he comments thus upon the office of the lector: "And since it is commonly said 'The lector is blamed, if his lesson is not read over beforehand,' in truth most blameworthy are those who aspire to this grade—and *a fortiori* to a higher—and yet have never read the Old Testament, nay rather, scarcely their Psalter-Book through to the end!"[6] As for the efficacy of the test: "The clergy ought to be examined in their duties before they rise to that grade. *And if this were done strictly, assuredly there would not be so many ignorant priests* in the Church." Quoting from Chrysostom[7], he warns the authorities responsible for such admissions that those who ordain the unworthy are liable to the same penalties as the ordained.

---

[1] fol. 216. Cf. also Bromyard, *S.P.—Predic.*: "Fidem predicabunt qui vix unquam unum verbum de Christo vel fide in scholis theologiae audierunt, sicut sacerdotes, qui statim post parvam informationem vel fundationem in grammaticalibus, ordinantur. Oportet quod sicut tales semper fuerunt surdi ab audiendo verbum Dei, ita etiam sint muti ad bene illud loquendum."

[2] fol. 197.　　　　　　　　　　　　　　　　[3] See below, p. 135, n. 2.

[4] *Parish Life* (Antiquary's Ser.), p. 78.　　　　　　　　　[5] fol. 209.

[6] Cf. here the fifteenth-century English MS. (written by a scribe Stillyngflete) entitled: "Exposicio verborum difficilium Temporalis Legende tocius anni, et eciam correpcio et produccio dubii accentus eorundem, ne materia risus audientibus ministretur, vel pudor legentibus aut fatuitas imponatur" (MS. Add. 14023, fol. 1, 128 b, and again on fol. 154).

[7] "In libello suo de dignitate sacerdotali."

If they plead ignorance of the true condition of the latter, let them recall the words of St Paul to Timothy, "Lay hands suddenly on no man."[1] "For thus what was thought to be an excuse becomes an accusation [excusatio fit accusatio]; and assuredly the law requires an examination to be held for four days preceding the celebration of Orders."[2]

Finally, with clerics who could once boast of a competent knowledge and the best intentions, three vices play sad havoc in these days—"sloth, inconstancy and negligence." Oh, the tragedy of the forgotten! "Utinam sacerdotum nostri temporis non obumbraret memoriam in sciendo debite sciencie oblivio!" Parish clergymen can hardly be blamed for bad memories, it is true. Yet Rypon gives more than a hint that they should realize before taking office so lightly that "the activity of preaching presupposes memorized knowledge."[3] What, too, of the poison of actual vice in the matter?—"But, in returning to our theme, let us see how knowledge of any kind is obscured, through negligent forgetfulness. Forgetfulness is caused sometimes through the omission of study, and sometimes by frequent drunkenness, or by some other evil indisposition of the brain." So he goes on with the tale of shortcomings. As soon as the ambitious hardworking clerk gets into his comfortable benefice, the feverish activity in both preaching and study by means of which he had contrived to win the attentions of the influential and secure the prize, ceases[4]. If it is not actually followed by a period of lustful self-indulgence, at least "all here studie is granges, shepe, nete, and rentes, and to gadre togedre gold and sylver."[5] "I am a ferde," comments our simple parson in his

---

[1] I Tim. v, 22.

[2] Cf. also, in this connection, another sermon warning in MS. Caius Coll. Camb. 334: "Ecce quam expresse hic in sacra scriptura Deus homines vetat super se accipere statum sacerdotis, nisi scientiam habeant competentem."

[3] fol. 202 b.

[4] fol. 203 b: "Experiencia enim docet quod nonnulli priusquam promoti fuerint ad beneficia cum cura vel sine cura, nonnunquam gradum sacerdotalem ascendunt, et tunc quasi cotidie celebrant missas suas, *vacant studio scripturarum, devotioni intendunt,* et plerique sufficientem scientiam habentes *plerumque in adjutorium curatorum predicant verbum Dei.* Sed quid?—revera postquam promoti fuerint, hec omnia quasi totaliter praetermittunt, sacerdotes solum nomine, non re...." So again on fol. 166 b: "Sed certe *multi* sunt qui sequuntur verbum Dei,...donec veniant ad pingues promotiones..." So also Bp. Brunton, in MS. Harl. 3760, fol. 125 b, etc.

[5] From the *Gesta Rom.* (Engl. vers.). Rypon himself thus comments on

quaint vernacular sermon, "leste all thre degrees of holy churche arn gilty in this synne of slowth, as well prelates, prestes, and religious." And "slowth" he interprets here as "occupacioun vel ny3 alle to the worlde."[1] Rypon, as a matter of fact, is remarkably broad and generous for an ecclesiastic in his attitude towards worldly knowledge; but he loses patience with these priests who thus forget the wisdom of God. Well may the prophet cry over them, "Non est scientia domini in terra"!—"How, I ask you, shall they, who are either ignorant, or forgetful of the Law of Christ, rightly lead others to their true end or beginning, which is Christ? Or how, I ask, shall they be confident in their deeds who are made drunk by the cups they have quaffed?" With the drunken cleric all is soon lost: "Voice and senses fail, and so from forgetfulness of knowledge, and indirect and uncertain choice, without doubt error occurs in speech, error in sign, error in deed."[2]

Myrc, who befriends the country parson with his handy book of instructions, still finds it worth his while to bid him take care when he may be too tipsy to repeat the baptismal formula properly[3]. We can guess what such a man would be like on the Sunday when he has managed to mount the pulpit stair.

From Bromyard and from Wimbledon we learn that the case of the "curate" who could boast of a University education might be often little better, at any rate as regards that theological and biblical learning which should be the groundwork of every sermon. Both preachers have the same story to tell as Roger Bacon in an earlier century, of the general neglect and decay of theology in the schools, of the general pursuit after more lucrative knowledge which qualified its owners for worldly office in state or on the manor. Both ask the same kind of

a famous passage, often quoted from St Bernard in our sermons: "'Plus student in salmone, quam in Salamone.' Haec Doctor, quasi sic concluderet 'in Salamone,' qui scripsit, 'Libros sapientiae scripturarum non student, sed potius in hiis quae sapiunt voluptatem vel sapientiam hujus mundi.'" Cf. similarly, *Oc. Sac.* (MS. Roy. 6. E. I, fol. 24 b, etc.; MS. Harl. 2276, fols. 107 b–108): "gret occupacioun aboute worldli thyngis," etc.

[1] MS. Roy. 18. B xxiii, fol. 67 b.   [2] MS. Harl. 4894, fol. 204 b.

[3] See *Instructions* (E.E.T.S.), p. 19. B. L. Manning, who refers to this remark in his *People's Faith in the age of Wycliffe*, does not tell us that it is practically a repetition of earlier legislative phrases. See, e.g. Council of Berkhamstead, A.D. 696 (Wilkins, *Conc.* vol. i, p. 60), etc.

question: "Why do men apply their sons more readily to Civil Law, to the king's court, to the work of secretaries and notaries rather than to philosophy or theology?"[1] Or, "Why does the Law School have a hundred or two hundred pupils, where the School of Theology has not even five?"[2] It is a cry not unheard in our own day. And each time the mediaeval churchman replies that it is all due to insatiable avarice, the mad craving for temporal wealth and position which like another Black Death is spreading to every class of society, not least to that of the priesthood. As the earnest evangelist looked out on the seething world about him, he beheld it with the eyes of St Chrysostom poisoned at the very cradle-side. "Mothers care only for the bodily success of their boys in the world. Of their spiritual welfare they care nothing[3]. Some ordain for them great worldly possessions here; but none ordain them to Godward." "For this Hagar hath brought forth temporal profit," cries one English preacher. ("Ex ideo dominam suam sterilem in hac vita, scientiam viz. divinam contemnit.") Cries another:

" Our stars, that is our clergy, have so fallen from the height of clerical dignity, as from heaven to earth, that they have nought but earthly wisdom, loving earth, thinking of earth, speaking of earth.... Behold among them, these days, no tonsure on the head, no garment of religion, no restraint in speech, no sobriety in food, no modesty in gestures, nor even continence in deeds."[4]

The inevitable reaction of this state of things upon the outlook of those who took the duties of the pulpit seriously is not hard to understand. Wherever the homilies of an outspoken prophet of righteousness have survived from this period, a mood

---

[1] MS. Camb. Univ. Libr. Ii. iii. 8, and Engl. versions.

[2] *S.P.—Advocatus.* Cf. Bromyard again, beginning: "Et haec causa est quare tanta multitudo, et quasi omnes, volunt leges audire lucrativas, quare parentes et amici filios et nepotes suos ad legum mittunt audientiam,...." etc.

[3] Cf. also the complaint of the MS. St Albans Cath. (15th cent.) Treatise on the Decalogue, fol. 24: "But alasse, for sorowe, that fadris now a daies, ther thei schulden teche her children Cristis lore,...thei teche hem the devellis lore of helle;...and thouȝ thei seen and heeren her children breke the commandementis of God fro morowe til even, thei chargen not a pese, but lauȝen and iapen, and ioien there inne, and conforte hem thereto. But if thei seen her children have a worldeli schame or velany, thanne thei wepen and maken sorowe ynouȝ...."

[4] Cf. further in this connection MS. Caius Coll. Camb. 230, fol. 35; MS. Camb. Univ. Libr. Ii. iii. 8, sermon on fol. 127 b et seq. (Wimbledon?)

o

of passionate resentment and gloom shows itself, often giving vent to the language of sheer despair. Unless he stood out like Elijah gaunt and forbidding, his god a threatening Jove with lightnings and tempests in his hand, the world would sink to perdition. In the boiling depths of such a cauldron we discern the magic potion which can produce heroes and saints, stern leaders of men, for which our poor hysterical civilization is still crying, after five centuries more. The price to be paid then was the unlovely Puritanism of the reformers; and the Puritan temper of the seventeenth century can only be fully explained by reference to the pulpit message of the later middle ages.

Meanwhile the youthful *curatus* of the future and the already beneficed[1] cleric "ad scholas" themselves gave heed to no one. University preachers in their turn, like William de Château Thierry[2], at Paris, for example, would warn them that they were sent to the seats of learning, the one at his parent's expense, the other at that of his Church, for the purpose of "working in the vineyard of the Lord, that is, in Holy Scripture, and of bringing back with them in due time to their home churches the wine of knowledge." Otherwise they were thieves and robbers. John of St Giles[3], the Englishman, would tell them from the very pulpit that those who prolonged their studies to the neglect of the cures they had left, even when officially licensed, were but licensed for hell. But all in vain. Freed by bishop's license, either from the restraints of an omnipresent schoolmaster's rod, or the boredom of a lonely parish, they found themselves transplanted to a new and fascinating world of gay

---

[1] "Beneficiati, ne dicam maleficiati!" cries the indignant English preacher (MS. Caius Coll. Camb. 230, fol. 35).

[2] c. 1250. See *Hist. Litt. de la France*, vol. xxvi.

[3] This interesting sermon, apparently, from the one extant MS. in the Bibl. Nat. at Paris, is given by Hauréau, *Quelques Manuscrits*: "...Christus scolaris fuit, matrem suam dimittens propter scolas, et non uxorem, i.e. ecclesiam pro scolis dimittere voluit. Immo, intantum eam dilexit quod, licet lacrymas matris suae et Johannis videret, tamen propter sponsam passus est, in hoc dans exemplum illis qui habent curam animarum, quod ecclesiam non debent dimittere propter scholas. Sed tales objiciunt quod in hoc licentiati sunt a suis prelatis. Sic et multi licentiam habent eundi in infernum!..." Cf. also, for our period, the similar warnings of Bromyard, *S.P.—Operatio*: "Contra illos, cum quibus episcopi dispensant quod causa eruditionis scolas exercere poterunt per septennium, vel alium terminum," etc.

scenes and hot-headed young men[1]. So, as even sermons describe[2], together they romped and raged in Oxford or Parisian streets, sat idly mocking the passers-by from their windows, or wasted their goods in riotous living, in the far country. How much of an advance was this, indeed, for Master Rypon's "lectio scripturarum frequens, et assidua inspectio" over the degraded, bookless, ignorant "curate" of Myrc, who spits in church like his modern *confrère* of the Balkans, and may leave foul even the sacred Host and vessels[3]? If Thomas Wimbledon ventures to speak of contemporary clergy as "priests of Nanea in their ignorance,"[4] still more common is his bitter pulpit censure—"For now as the people are, so also is the priest. 'They are mingled among the heathen, and have learnt their works' (Ps. cvi, 35). Now are our priests as dissolute, as greedy, as ambitious—alike of riches as of honours—as are the common people: and would that they were no worse!"[5]

Most of the comments provided so far, come, it is true, from the ranks of those who were often the parish priest's most inveterate enemies and rivals. Moreover, the ecclesiastical, like the political, rostrum is a place where loose and exaggerated statements may always occur. Yet the sceptical reader who prefers to seek the opinion of bishop and rector themselves in the matter will get little comfort from their utterances. So unanimous and unqualified, indeed, is the verdict of all sections against what a simple vernacular preacher calls "the lewidnesse of many personys and vikaris,"[6] that it is no longer possible to

---

[1] Cf. the innumerable cases of such licenses mentioned in Episcopal Registers; and for further *sermon* evidence, Rypon in MS. Harl. 4894, fol. 194: "ut...in Universitatibus...lautius vivant," etc.

[2] See especially the article by Haskins in the *American Hist. Review*, vol. x (1904), pp. 1–27: "The University of Paris in the Sermons of the XIII Cent." Also Brunton, in MS. Harl. 3760, fol. 176. (As given here in Chap. VIII, p. 332, n. 1.)

[3] *Instr. for Parish Priests* (E.E.T.S., as before).

[4] (2 Maccab. i, 13.) MS. Camb. Univ. Libr. Ii. iii. 8, fol. 130.

[5] fol. 145: "Jam enim sicut populus, sic etiam sacerdos. *Commixti sunt inter gentes et didicerunt opera eorum* (in Ps.). Jam sunt nostri sacerdotes ita dissoluti, ita cupidi, ita ambitiosi, tam divitiarum quam honorum, sicut communis populus; et utinam non pejores." Again, fol. 128 b: "jam laicis sunt tenebrosiores, et in omni genere viciorum dissolutiores"; "Sed numquid predicatores moderni et curati has conditiones [i.e. of holiness] observant?—certe timeo quod nunc pauci!" and Rypon (MS. Harl. 4894, fol. 194): "Quod dolendum est quod sicut populus sic sacerdos; populus insolens, insolencior est sacerdos...," etc.   [6] MS. Harl. 2276, fol. 107 b.

doubt its accuracy. Bishop Brunton is not alone in his solemn complaints in Latin against the appointment of so many unfit and unworthy ministers to the guardianship of the temple, blind in ignorance, dumb from lack of eloquence. Neither is the Berkshire vicar[1], who confesses that many are the priests in these days who neither know nor teach the law of God.

But what is sadly true of the "curate," is true also of his bishop. From sermon evidence alone, the former could retort with justice, "like father, like son." This will hardly surprise the student who remembers that we are dealing with the age of the notorious Robert Stretton[2], nominee of Edward III and the Black Prince. Rejected for his utter illiteracy by the Bishop of Rochester, by papal examiners at Avignon, and again by the English Primate, after as many re-examinations more in the effort to promote him to the see of Coventry and Lichfield, nevertheless he triumphed in the end. The Pope yielding to the royal pressure, he was consecrated "sine examinatione," and made his profession of obedience at Lambeth, "another reading his profession for him, because he himself could not read."

In his *Summa Predicantium*, Dr John Bromyard, pillar of orthodoxy both at Oxford and at Cambridge, produces an indictment against the bishops which can only be described as terrific and overwhelming. He who had once sat with leading bishops of the day, to consider the heresies of Wycliffe, can hardly contain himself when he comes to speak and write of the *Prelati* as a whole. Dr Gascoigne's scorn, which Cardinal Gasquet treats so lightly, is as nothing when compared with it. The present chapter is no place, however, in which to set forth from the English Dominican's pages the brutal lust and excesses, the swarm of illegitimate offspring, the fleecing of the poor, the flattering of the rich, the bribes, oaths, insatiable pride and greediness of these incestuous monsters[3]. If the charges

---

[1] William de Pagula, in *Oc. Sacer.*, cf. MS. Ryl. 6. E. l, fol. 24: "propter eorum ignoranciam predictam non exponunt, nec predicant." See further, *Cil. Oc. Sac.*, mentioning the darkness of ignorance in many preachers (MS. Harl. 4968, fol. 45 et seq.).

[2] Died 1385. Cf. others, *Corresp. Bekynt.* (Rolls S.) vol. i, p. 23, etc.

[3] Still more glaring in the sermons of a fellow prelate, Archbp. Fitzralph of Armagh! (MS. Lansd. 393). Cf. the appalling revelations of his sermon (fols. 62–64 b, etc.) delivered appropriately, *in latino*, at the Prov. Council at Drogheda, 1350–51.

be true, and there is a considerable body of current homiletic evidence alone in support of them, they constitute a tragedy indeed. If, on the other hand, they be false, the treachery and insolence of the groups of preachers that made them can hardly be considered less tragic. In either case the Church would suffer the scandal. But, to return to the more immediate questions of episcopal fitness to teach, Bromyard declares unreservedly that in no other profession would such appalling ignorance be tolerated for a moment. This inefficiency, he says, is deliberately preferred if not fostered, alike in prelate and ordinary priest, in the interest of those who wish to see as holders of ecclesiastical dignities lavish and easy-going relatives, boon companions of the table or the chase, flattering dependents, not stern rebukers of evil. "And this is why more insufficient and ignorant persons find their way into this profession than in any other in the world."[1] Similarly, the great Franciscan, Roger Bacon, had told in an earlier age how prelates, "not much instructed in Divinity at the Schools," would borrow, or beg "the notebooks of boys," when they had to preach, discoursing "with an infinite childishness, and a vilifying of the word of God."[2]

A Cambridge manuscript of Latin homilies[3] compares the prelates to sailors responsible for the safe steering of the ship of the Church across a perilous sea into port. But alas! "a great part" of these sailors know nothing of seamanship, and some, even if they know, neglect their duties. Little wonder then, we may add, that it came to be looked upon by some as "the ship of fools." For this same preacher continues: "Thus the ship of the Church left derelict without helmsmen, and beset on every hand by the waves and billows of a tempestuous sea, beyond hope of recovery, is on the brink of destruction; unless the Lord be pleased to rescue her, and all that are within." "Oh, how many souls in these days we believe to be drowned in this sea [i.e. of worldliness]. Assuredly it is to be feared *almost the whole world*, and that chiefly through the failings of the shep-

---

[1] Bp. Brunton (MS. Harl. 3760, fol. 191) speaks of the "inhabiles generosi" among them who win office by influence. Sim., Wimbledon.

[2] Cf. Wood [Gutch], *Hist. and Antiq. of Oxford*, vol. i, pp. 176–181, with references.

[3] MS. Camb. Univ. Libr. Ii. iii. 8, fol. 145.

herds of the Church." Cries yet another, in almost a Lollard strain, that as Christ was once mocked by the Jews in the High Priest's house "with veiled face," even so is He mocked again to-day by modern prelates and priests of the Church, when teaching and knowledge of Holy Scripture is "veiled" by those whose express duty is to preach it[1]. The quaint metaphors which follow can only be reproduced satisfactorily in the original Latin:

Pontifex interpretatur "pontem faciens," et presbyter, "prebens iter." Facerent enim pontes et itinera ultra tempestuosa flumina hujus mundi! Sed prothdolor pons est fractus, et plurimum ruinosus, et via est vepribus et leonibus, i.e. peccatis et malis hominibus, circumcepta. Nam in domibus nonnullorum prelatorum sacra scriptura non exprimitur aut legitur, et plurimum non habetur, aut saltem velatur in codicibus et in archis. Immo quasi tota confabulatio seu locutio est in nonnullis hujuscemodi domibus de curis et vanitatibus hujus mundi[2].

The stream of blazing indignant words pours out from the contemporary pulpit in every direction, as from a volcano. The very heavens seem blotted out from sight; horror and despair is on every face. Men do not hesitate to attribute almost all the ills in Church and State to the "lost understanding and wit" of the episcopacy—heresy, schism, strife, and bad government[3]. He who sat, as we have said, with ten of their number in judgement on the arch-heretic of the day is not afraid to declare openly that "prelates lead more folk to the devil by the corruption of their foul behaviour and example, than ever to God by preaching or holiness of life."[4]

---

[1] Rypon (MS. Harl. 4894, fol. 198). Cf. also *Gesta Rom.* Engl. vers. (E.E.T.S.), p. 368, of the bishops: "Theyr gostly eyen are made blynde and putt oute" (by the devil).

[2] The MS. St Albans Cath. treatise makes the same remark in English (fol. 8 b).

[3] *Dives et Pauper*: "They have lost understanding and wit to teche the peple; and so al ther flocke is disperplid by eresie, debate, division, and discencion." Rypon (MS. Harl. 4894, fol. 197): "Et indubie, si quilibet ecclesiasticus haberet scientiam suo gradui competentem, non pullularent tot errores in ecclesia, quot pullulant hiis diebus." Thos. Wimbledon, at Paul's Cross: "Et haec est causa multorum errorum...," etc. In the opinion of a fellow bishop, in 1326, they are universally detested in England for their sloth, folly, and ignorance (cf. Wilkins, *Conc.* vol. ii, p. 533). It is of the prelates essentially, too, that the text (Hosea, iv) is repeatedly quoted in the sermon literature (cf. Bromyard, Rypon, Wimbledon, etc.): "Quia tu scientiam repulisti, ego repellam te!"

[4] *S.P.—Ordo Clericalis*: "Nonnulli (prelati)...libentius ducunt canes et

But so far little has been said of the actual outcome of this ignorance in deliberate abstention from preaching of any kind. Archbishop Peckham had raised the hue and cry against the non-preaching bishops of England in the thirteenth century[1], while, as the pages of Hauréau show, others were doing the same thing on the continent. 'These cocks which neither crow nor generate shall be swept off to the infernal market, head downwards'[2]. It was only in typical pre-Reformation fashion, after all, that Bishop Latimer pointed out three centuries later to his fellow-prelates how the busy activities of the devil himself in this respect put them to shame. For the chosen centuries of this study, there is no need to have recourse to John Bromyard, and what might appear to be the personal animosity of friars, to show that the bishop was capable of being both "dumb dog," and "dog in the manger" as well. In the first case it is a distinguished archbishop of the day who says that they are for ever crying "Tonde, tonde! Tolle, tolle!"—"et nunquam exercent 'Pasce, pasce!'"[3] It is none other than the indefatigable Brunton himself, with the most dignified conception of the status and calling he represents[4], who is for ever saying, "We prelates are afraid to speak out," when it comes to the further question of denouncing abuses in the pulpits[5]. His explanation of the causes of this muteness, of which he was certainly not

falcones ad venationem, quam Christianos ad devotionem. Et quod pejus est, plures greges ducunt ad dyabolum pravis moribus et exemplis eorum corrumpendo, quam ad deum predicando...," etc. And compare Rypon, MS. Harl. 4894, fol. 196 b: "Vide! inquit [Bernardus], ut in hiis cotidie videtur, meretricius, nitor, histrionicus habitus, et quasi regius apparatus. Plus fulgent calcaria quam altaria. Vide! mense splendide cibis et ciphis; vide, commessaciones et ebrietates; vide, redundancia torcularia et plena promptuaria.... Fiunt ecclesiarum propositi, archiepiscopi, episcopi, archidiaconi, decani, quo facto, quidam citius inveniantur in stabulo quam in choro, quidam citius currunt ad coquinam quam ad missam, plus respiciunt piscem assum quam Christum passum, plus agunt elixum, quam Christum crucifixum, plus student in salmone quam in Salamone...."

[1] See letter to the Bp. of Tusculum aforementioned; also from the De oculo morali (in Martin, C.T., 1884, preface to vol. v, pp. iii–lxxxi): "No longer brazen in eloquence, but iron and clay," etc.

[2] See Hauréau, Quelques MSS. vol. iii, p. 100, and compare with Neckham's fig. aforesaid; also vol. iv, p. 245, etc.

[3] Fitzralph of Armagh (MS. Lansd. 393, fol. 64).

[4] MS. Harl. 3760, fol. 96: "Nos prelati, quia a Christo nominamur sal terrae, et lux mundi, qui ex officii dignitate, habemus primatum Abel, patriarchatum Abrahe, gubernationem Noe, ordinem Melchisedech, dignitatem Aaron, auctoritatem Moysi, potestatem Petri...."

[5] Cf. ibid. fol. 217 b, etc.; and fol. 61 b et seq. (tanquam canes muti).

guilty himself, agrees with that of Gascoigne, Rypon and others. The very "figure" he uses for his Third Reason is to be found again in an anonymous Latin homily series of the century, even the bone flung into the gaping ecclesiastical jaws—that is to say, the lordly gifts, good dinners, and rewards, which effectually stop the dog from barking[1]. In one of his most striking oratorical efforts this Bishop of Rochester again deplores that those who, like columns, should bear the Church upon their shoulders, ready ever to give life itself, if need be, in defence of her liberties, and to rescue the poor and the innocent from their daily spoliation and sufferings, now hold their peace[2]. And all "because they yearn for great offices, or aspire to be promoted to richer sees." Others have spoken, too, besides him, of the swift penalties that awaited the too fearless court preacher, of the inspection of sermon manuscripts by suspicious courtiers, or the oaths extracted beforehand that nothing derogatory of the sovereign, his acts and his ministers might be uttered in the royal presence[3]. A sermon delivered at Paul's Cross thus pictures these episcopal sycophants and idlers at the Day of Doom, favourite scene for both the sacred orator, and the sacred artist who paints upon church walls. A voice is heard questioning them from that awful judgement-seat: "'How hast thou governed the people of God committed to thy charge?...Say whom thou hast converted from his evil way by thy faithful preaching; whom thou hast instructed in the law of God'....In that place

---

[1] MS. Add. 21253, fol. 58 b, etc. Rypon's version is MS. Harl. 4894, fol. 217 b. Cf. also Thos. Gascoigne, *Loci e Libro Verit.* ed. Rogers, p. 41, who speaks elsewhere of their drunkenness, etc.

[2] MS. Harl. 3760, fol. 187. See also his denunciation of unfit bishops as given in Gasquet, *O.E.B.* 2nd ed. p. 68; and cf. also fol. 118. See also Bromyard, *S.P.—Prelatus*, and MS. Harl. 2398: "And specially prelates that sleeth here brother in many weyes. For they scholde preche hem, and teche hem godes lawe; and by neglygence of hem they both gostlych sleye. And thes scholde stonde as postes aȝenst tyrauntes, and telle hem how by Godes lawe they scholde lede the peple. And this is a pryvy synne that prelates reccheth nouȝt...." Finally, see MS. Add. 9066 (15th cent. Engl. vers. of *Gesta Rom.*) in E.E.T.S. p. 178.

[3] Cf. Brunton (MS. Harl. 3760, fol. 187 b et seq.): "Tacent predicatores, quia multi eorum, si ante haec tempora in sermonibus apud Crucem vicia dominorum generaliter tetigerunt, statim isti tanquam malefactores arestati coram regis consilio erant ducti, ubi examinati, reprobati, banniti, vel a predicandi officio perpetuo sunt suspensi...." Also Gascoigne (as above), p. 38.

shall be heard a dreadful charge, and a most grievous allegation."[1]

Though much more remains in the same vein[2], enough has been said to justify both the popular view of prelates, and in particular the outburst of a scholar like Dr Gascoigne, when in 1449 the tireless sophistry of Bishop Pecock sought for arguments in defence of this episcopal muteness, and expressed them in public. Looking back from this episode at the very limit of our period, the Oxford Chancellor sums up for us what he conceives to be the results of an iniquitous piece of legislation, introduced originally to suppress the Lollard. For to his eyes Archbishop Arundel's Constitution of 1409, which enforced a rigorous system of episcopal preaching licenses, was little else than the official seal of approbation upon this policy of silence. The non-preaching bishops had at last their full opportunity, and, according to him, right well they used it. Hardly for great sums of money or gifts would they now concede even a temporary license to preachers, much less preach themselves. Pulpit silence became golden. Worthy and unworthy together were excluded from the privilege of exhortation and rebuke, the word of God was as it were imprisoned and in chains with the prophet, and evil ran riot unchecked. With Brunton Gascoigne bewails the reign of the wicked counsellors; with Bromyard he denounces the absentee; with Wycliffe[3] he agrees that the futility of preaching has become a general argument amongst those who fear and neglect it. Finally, with all three, he attacks the worldliness which keeps shut the mouths of God's spokesmen. As for the bishops' prohibition of others, this, in

---

[1] Thos. Wimbledon. Bromyard posits the same Judgement-Day question of his cleric (*S.P.—Ordo Clericalis*).

[2] In sermons of the time, quite apart from those attributed to Wycliffe, I find the bishops called, for their lack of preaching, amongst other names: "dumb dogs" (MS. Add. 21253, fol. 141; Bromyard, *S.P.* etc.); "the abhomination of desolation in the holy place" (MS. Camb. Univ. Libr. Ii. iii. 8); "blind watchmen" (MS. Add. 21253); "Anti-Christs" (MS. Camb. Univ. Libr. Ii. iii. 8); "manslayers" (MS. Harl. 2398).

[3] Cf. the *Speculum de Anti-Christo*, Matthew's ed. p. 109 (E.E.T.S.). Though their anti-Mendicant attacks may tend to obscure the fact, the Lollard preachers were really as virulent towards the bishops. Cf. MS. Trin. Coll. Camb. 60, fol. 2 b: "And these secular prelates may well be cleped scribes; for they both more and less writen the money that they pilen of the people more busily than they printen in their souls the knowing of God's law." See further here in Chap. III.

effect, springs from a well-grounded fear that their own ignorance and vices may be exposed, and that eventually they will
have to leave their concubines!

Those of us, on the other hand, who live in an age when a
popular press exercises much of the cheap sensational influence
of the mediaeval pulpit, which in more than one direction it has
superseded, may well feel inclined to sympathize a little with
the attitude of Pecock. We have every reason to believe that the
"bawlers," the vulgar charlatans, the "grete and thikke ratelers
out of textis" were just as shallow, just as illogical, just as
offensive then as they have been ever since. Would not able
prelates, like William of Wykeham for example, be far more
useful about the court than busying themselves in their dioceses
with such an inherently "vulgar" occupation? Be that as it may,
however, though we may find it hard to believe Gascoigne when
he says that the bishops' negligence of preaching was prominent
among the grievances that gave rise to the Commons' revolt of
1450, there can be no doubt about Bishop Pecock's mistake.
Around the episcopal palace left silent, or filled only with
ribald sounds, from the empty cathedral chair and rostrum,
the neglected village church, there had grown up in the popular
mind a well-grounded suspicion of luxury, indifference, waste
and extortion in high places. Where was this pulpit champion
of their rights, this publisher of good tidings, this father to his
people, of whom the faithful spoke? Heir of the apostles, "fed
of the patrimony of Christ," to support which they still sweated
and toiled and paid their offering, the bishop, they knew, had
certainly harried the Lollard and tried to suppress the unconventional preachers of the day. But what had he put in their
place? They had seen him ride off with his horses and sumptuous retinue to some palace by the Strand in London. Learned
and responsible churchmen had been known to say openly in
the pulpit that some of his kind were actually squandering that
holy patrimony upon their own sons and daughters, their
prostitutes and bastards[1]. Meanwhile the inferior clergy were

---

[1] Cf. Rypon (MS. Harl. 4894, fol. 216): "*Moderni* ecclesiastici,...qui
patrimonium crucifixi nedum male tractant, sed negligentissime dispendunt
in meretricibus, cum filio prodigo in pompa seculi...." fol. 195: "Nonne
bona ecclesie per insolenciam et superbiam sacerdotum in potentibus seculi,
immo in propriis consanguineis et nepotibus, nedum in filiis et filiabus ac

doing much as they pleased at home, after their own tastes. Our simple village priest, of the Chaucerian model, shakes his head over the painful prospect, as he addresses his parishioners on the Sunday, in much the same language as we have already heard the distinguished London preachers use. "How wolt thise gret clerkes answere, and thise gret persons that dwellen in lordes courtes, that preche not one in thre ʒere or foure?—I trowe full harde!"[1] Once again the student of history listening closely, thinks he hears an ominous sound. It is the early rumbling of that "Mar-Prelate" storm which did not cease in its fury until it had caused the death of one more Archbishop of Canterbury, in Puritan England. For generations it was to be part of the traditional atmosphere in which Protestant Nonconformity grew up, not therefore, we must admit, without certain historic reasons.

What, in closing, may be said more especially of the muteness of the *curati*? Priest and prelate we have seen inseparably linked together in the great pulpit indictment. The foreign pluralist in an English living, whose complete ignorance of the language, and inability or lack of desire to instruct his parishioners figure amongst the abuses mentioned in the Oxford petition of 1414[2], is in no way different from the non-resident prelate; save, perhaps, as Bromyard remarks, that those who drew the highest pay of all in the Church Militant, usually did the least fighting[3]. But the meaner and obscurer class of clergy

concubinis meretricibus *notabiliter* sunt consumpta?" And again, fol. 202: "...Dant, inquam, bona pauperum et crucifixi patrimonium, quidam concubinis, quidam cognatis et amicis, et quidam ea dispendunt in excessibus carnalium voluptatum." The same occurs in Bromyard, *S.P.—Ordo Clericalis*, etc.; in Archbp. Fitzralph, cf. MS. Lansd. 393, fols. 144 (63 b, as before), etc.; MS. Camb. Univ. Libr. Ii. iii. 8, fol. 11; etc.

[1] MS. 18. B. xxiii, fol. 63 b. He adds, further, the typical "Doom" of God upon them: "I deme the, of thin owne mowthe, that kowdest and myghteste teche, and hydest thi kunnynge, and wold not show it." Read also in connection with the above the sketch of a *Sermo ad prelatos* given here in Chap. VI, pp. 252, 253; and cf. the complaints of the Commons in 1397 against bishops at court (*Rot. Parl.* p. 339, col. 1).

[2] "Quidam,...quandoque promoventur in regno Angliae ipsius regni idioma penitus ignorantes, quique ad informandum subditos indisponuntur et muti...," etc. (Wilkins, *Conc.* vol. iii, p. 360 et seq.).

[3] *S.P.—Bellum*: "Et qui plura stipendia ecclesiae militantis, militantibusque ejus a Deo deputatis, recipiunt, *minus predicando* vel bona exempla dando contra vicia et viciosos pugnant. Sed heu! de patrimonio Christi incrassati, impinguati, dilatati, dereliquerunt Deum factorem suum in bello, et fugerunt."

not unnaturally, were just as prone to the same sloth, under the influence of their own special temptations. The Registers and the homilies are equally agreed on that point. Apart from the prospects of a pleasant stay at the University, or a well-conducted living where a certain amount of producing and even trading could be done, there were other attractions from which the work of the pulpit suffered. Some could find more profitable tasks as manorial officials, with the ability to make an entry, or keep an account[1]. Others would stroll off to enjoy the pleasures of the world for a season, in the populous cities and ports[2]. The tavern, the show, the wrestling match, even the brothel, took their full toll of those who went, or those who stayed behind. And when they had had their fill of these, there must have remained the additional inhibition of a guilty conscience[3]. "As the people are, so is the priest. Would that he were no worse!" It is easy to understand what ripe fields the parishes served by such ministers must have been to the sickle of the industrious charlatan, the heretic[4], and the mischief-maker. Towards the end of the fifteenth century, a homilist, alluding to the famous prophecy of St Boniface concerning "the londe of Albany," which he calls a "bye-worde," has a sad confession to make. "Presthode," he tells his audience, on the fourth Sunday after the Octave of the Epiphany, "wᵗ moche pepil is had in grete dyspyte; for seen [since] holy chyrche was firste ordende, presthode was never had in so lityll reputacion."[5]

---

[1] I may take this opportunity to indicate, in connection with one of our preachers, MS. Add. 5666,—"in the Handwriting of the famous John Brakley, Frier Minor of Norwich, Tutor and Master to Judge Paston, whose accounts these are, when he was at the Inns of Court, at London."

[2] The evidence of the Episcopal Registers, of Langland, etc. is well known, but our sermon evidence will be fresh. Rypon remarks, for example (MS. Harl. 4894, fol. 194): "Sunt enim nonnulli, qui raro vel nunquam ad sua beneficia accedunt. Tamen sui cubilis stramenta, hoc est fructus et emolumenta sui beneficii, *ut in curiis, vel universitatibus seu civitatibus lautius vivant, avidius exigunt, et requirunt*." Cf. also Brunton (Harl. 3760, fol. 125 b): "Contra multos ecclesiasticos qui...ad beneficia pinguia exaltati, vix missam audiunt, nullam dicunt, mundum diligunt, carni inserviunt *et magnatum obsequiis occupati, sua beneficia derelinquunt, et ea officiari per mercenarios faciunt et permittunt*." Wimbledon, etc. See further p. 47, below.

[3] This is actually alluded to in one sermon (MS. Add. 21253, fol. 59): "Praeterea conscientia proprii peccati *multos* facit obmutescere a predicatione."

[4] As in MS. Harl. 2276, fol. 108 et seq. See here in Chap. III.

[5] MS. Linc. Cath. Libr. A. 6. 2, fol. 59 b.

The remark is at least typical[1]. If half the allegations of sermons and Registers are true, who could be much surprised at this confession, or, indeed, at the subsequent turn of events in Church and State?

From this point we must sink even lower in the ecclesiastical scale to the level of the temporal vicars[2], and stipendiary clerks. If these proved incompetent, as was likely in mere hirelings or mercenaries, then, as Bromyard argues, the absentee rector shall himself answer before God for every fault or omission from which his flock has suffered. If, on the other hand, they were competent, then, says the Dominican, they are superfluous: "For what can be done by one, reason forbids to be done by many." Nevertheless the rector had certainly the law on his side, if he answered as Rypon tells us that he did, "Licet aliquando non predicem in persona propria, dum tamen alius suppleat vicem meam, satis est michi."[3] There, as we shall see further, at his door stood the itinerant friar, as anxious to take his place in the pulpit, as ever the other may have been to vacate it[4], ready indeed even to strive with him for it, on occasion, if he rejected his overtures[5]. After all, perhaps, it was sometimes better that rectors should *not* return to occupy a neglected village pulpit. Their song on such random visits was apt to be all of one tune and that an exceedingly bad one:

[1] I hope to deal with the widespread pulpit evidences of anti-clericalism in the age, in some later study. Cf. the remarks added in a fifteenth-century metrical treatise based on the *Handlyng Synne* (MS. Arundel 20, fol. 49 b): "To se a prestly prest yt were grete deynte...," etc.

[2] Cf. the provision for preaching supplies as laid down in the *Cil. Ocul. Sac.* (MS. Harl. 4968, fol. 41 b, etc.), beginning: "Item vicarii temporales per episcopos positi in ecclesiis quarum rectores infra aetatem fuerint, vel quia scolas exercent, vel quia absentes fuerint, populis quibus proferuntur predicare licet" (sic).

[3] MS. Harl. 4894, fol. 161. Rypon himself returns to the charge again, relentlessly: "Quero a tali utrum scit predicare, vel non...!"

[4] The *Reg. Anim.* itself reminds him (MS. Harl. 2272, fol. 9): "Quilibet sacerdos habens curam animarum, potest alteri dare licenciam predicandi suis parochianis." Similarly *Cil. Oc. Sac.* (MS. Harl. 4968, fol. 41 b).

[5] Cf. here Rypon (MS. Harl. 4894, fol. 195): (*In margin:* "Nota contra fratres mercenarios non curatos".) "*Omnes qui venerunt comederunt eos,* —hoc est, eorum fructus. Considerate, queso, qui iam propter desidiam, insolenciam, et superbiam curatorum comedunt suos fructus. Nonne quidam mercenarii in domo, immo verius extra, iam officia curatorum usurpant, utpote in confessionibus audiendis, et in aliis sacramentis ecclesie ministrandis? Et quos et quantos fructus diripiunt, vos novistis." [He is addressing the clergy, *in synodo.*]

But ever among al othur nede
His owne erende wol he bede,
That thei brynge heore offrynges
To chirche, and heore tythinges[1].

We are even told that the bishops themselves prompted them to make such topics the subject of discourse, in place of the more dangerous censure of abuses[2]. Master Rypon of Durham, not without a touch of sorrow in his voice, bemoans the rector's lack of sympathy with his flock, and wishes that he would yearn to set eyes on them for the welfare of their souls, rather than for the material gifts they supply[3].

Indications are not lacking in the kind of literature before us that the results of this seemingly widespread neglect of holy instruction were patent enough to the eye of the faithful observer. More than a hundred years after Peckham's elaborate Decrees, it is possible for the writer of a vernacular treatise to declare that none but a few of the common people knew even their Paternoster, Ave or Creed[4]. Little wonder, then, that the same "Ignorantia Sacerdotum" is sounded again with stern emphasis in 1466[5] and even later, at the end as at the beginning of our period: "There be a lawles people entred into thy sanctuarie, that neither keepe in themselfe the law of God, ne konne teachen other."[6] Above the plaint of Wimbledon at

[1] *The Despite* (E.E.T.S., O.S.), 98, p. 348. Cf. also MS. Add. 21253, fol. 145; MS. Harl. 4894, fol. 198 b (quoting Gorham); and Myrc's *Instructions* (E.E.T.S.), p. 11, l. 356, etc.

[2] Bromyard, *S.P.—Prelatus.*

[3] "Et utinam omnes beneficia ecclesiastica curam habentiam occupantes, haberent istam mutuam consolationem cum suis parochianis, ut viz.—desiderarent eos videre potius propter lucrum animarum quam fructum; —ut, scil. eis evangelium predicarent, ut in fide confirmarent, et sic se alterutrum consolarentur,—scil. curati subditos, per bonam predicationem, et bonae conversationis exemplationem;—et subditi curatos, per bonam operationem, et fructuum dationem.... Sed, quod dolendum est de multis ecclesiis potest dici illud lamentabile,...Non est qui consoletur eam (suple ex omnibus curis ejus)." Cf. also the plaint of MS. Camb. Univ. Libr. Ii. iii. 8, fol. 129 b: "Sed multi patres ecclesiae militantis sunt qui hiis diebus non compatiuntur filiis...."

[4] MS. St Albans Cath. fol. 1 (and MS. Land. Misc. 23). Cf. this with Archbp. Thoresby's comment, *Lay Folks' Cat.* p. 41: "And forthi that mikill folke...."

[5] Constit. Archbp. Neville of York. See Wilkins, *Conc.* vol. iii, p. 599 (repeated again as late as 1518).

[6] Wimbledon's sermon, 1388 (printed Engl. text). Latin version in MS. Camb. Univ. Libr. Ii. iii. 8, etc.: "Gentes illegales intraverunt in Templum, qui non in seipsis legem Dei custodiunt, nec alios instruere sciunt." (Cf. Lament. i, 10.)

Paul's Cross, the awful judgement of the sub-prior at Durham rings in their ears:

What punishment therefore do the priests of to-day merit, who enter upon their churches with the cure thereof, and rarely or never preach the word of God? Forsooth, neither do they preach a good life by their actions, which is called the preaching of an examplary life. Assuredly, they are worthy of the everlasting death of the soul, which is the death of Gehenna[1].

[1] MS. Harl. 4894, fol. 214 b: "Quam poenam ergo merentur sacerdotes moderni ingredientes ecclesias cum cura, et raro vel numquam predicantes verbum Dei? Immo nec opere in se predicant bonam vitam, que dicitur predicatio vite exemplaris. Certe merentur mortem anime sempiternam, scil. mortem Gehenne!" Cf. further fol. 203 b: " Sed quidam nec....verbum dei predicant, nec per bone conversacionis exempla ducunt, nec sacramenta personaliter administrant...." etc., etc. Along with these remarks should be read such evidence from the Registers as the following (Reg. Bp. Grandisson, Exeter, Pt. ii, p. 1140, A.D. 1354–5): "Nonulli nostre Diocesis, nomen Presbyteri inaniter defferentes (sic), set tanti nominis affectu inmeriti, prochdolor, et indigni, omissis animarum curis et ecclesiis parochialibus et collegiatis, propter que ad tantum ministerium ordinati sunt principaliter et assumpti, ad Annualia celebranda et obsequia laicorum mercatorum potissime juxta portus marinos ubi calices exhaurire fecundiores presupponunt infeliciter se convertunt, conviviis et tabernis communiter gaudentes pocius quam ecclesiis vel divinis officiis interesse. Quorum exempla perniciosa populum, quem nedum Ewangelii predicacione set vite integritate exhortari deberent ad salutem, ducunt...ad ruinam." Sim., in Reg. Wykeham, Winch., p. 21, A.D. 1367 ("in locis aliis inhonestis evagantes"......"annualia pro animabus defunctorum in locis remotis pro stipendiis excessivis......" etc.). Our preachers, then, do not appear to exaggerate here.

The unpublished Latin *Manuale Sacerdotum* of John Myrc, linked far too closely by Warner and Gilson (*Cat. of Roy. MSS.*; following Bradshaw) with his Engl. *Instructions,* contains *separate chapters* dealing with such topics as the following, in remarkably outspoken fashion:—" Quod moderni sacerdotes magis indulgent mundanis vanitatibus quam divinis exercitiis." " Quod per ignoranciam sacerdotis devocio sacramenti patitur detrimentum." " De prophetia modo completa—' et erit sicut populus ita etiam sacerdos '." " De sacerdote qui plus diligit tabernam quam ecclesiam." " De sacerdote aliatore." " De sacerdote fornicatore." " De sacerdote negociatore." " Quare permittuntur sacerdotes fornicarii celebrare in ecclesia." etc. [MS. York Cath. Libr. xvi. O. 11, described in the *Explicit* as—" Libellus dictus Manuale Sacerdotis Kirkestall," I have found to be another copy of this work. Does this provide an interesting link between Yorkshire and our Shropshire canon, the author, who tells us in the Preface to his *Festiall* that he had cure of souls?] Friar John Lathbury (see below, p. 305, etc.) is reported author of a treatise—" De luxuria clericorum."

CHAPTER II

MONKS AND FRIARS

IF every bishop had been a Brunton, and every parish priest had been like the parson of the *Canterbury Tales*, Master Rypon's sad confession about the excesses of "the mercenary brethren" in the parishes[1] might never have been made, and Jack Upland's complaint about the burden of so many extra evangelists in the land would have been well justified:

> And Crist himselfe was apaied
> With twelve apostles and a fewe disciples
> To preach and doe priest's office
> To all the whole world.
> Then was it better doe than is nowe at this time
> By a thousand dele[2].

The same sermon-writers whose evidence has helped to enlighten such a statement may be expected with good reason to tell us something about those other preachers, "es esglises, et cimitoirs, einzes Marches, Feires et autres lieux publiques,"[3] the itinerant friars. But first a glance will not be inappropriate at the older and less mobile Orders, "the monkes and cannons," who, as the rude satirist reminds his friar opponent, are still a regular part of the swarming clerical throng.

Under the Cluniac and Cistercian revivals monastic oratory had enjoyed its golden age a full century before the successes of the Mendicants. Apart even from its substantial contribution to homiletic literature, its queer mystical and allegoric moods, its unquestioned influence upon the purity and zeal of monastic life, it had had even a series of popular triumphs. For at one time vast throngs had welcomed St Bernard in his missionary campaigns, as later they were one day to welcome the Poverello and his sons. In England, Joscelin of Brakelond's picture[4] of the twelfth-century Abbot Samson, setting up his pulpit in

---

[1] See above, p. 45, n. 5.
[2] See Wright's *Polit. Poems and Songs* (Rolls S.), vol. ii, p. 30. (Date 1401.) Cf. *Oc. Sacer.*—"multi sunt nomine, et pauci sunt in opere."
[3] (1382.) *Rot. Parl.* vol. iii, p. 124.
[4] *Cronic. Josc. de Brak.* (Camd. Soc. No. xiii) (1187, etc.), p. 30.

the abbey of St Edmund from which to address the lay-folk
"in the Norfolk tongue," gives a hint in itself that the activity
knew no mere national or continental bounds. Is there not a
healthy scorn in the question of another: "How can a man who
is unlettered deliver a sermon in Chapter, or to the people on
feast-days?"[1] Here in England, indeed, there had been a
tradition of monastic preaching at least as old as the Venerable
Bede. So in the century of Bernard, Stephen Harding, and
Richard of St Victor, the last two themselves British by birth,
there were other English preachers who made a similar reputation in their own native land[2]. By the time, however, that the
age of Fitzralph and of Wycliffe has begun, all the great names in
the history of monastic eloquence have disappeared, and the
pulpit here seems to share in the general decline of cloister
fame and cloister influence. As in the case of the abbey at
Westminster[3], Palm Sundays and Good Fridays may still have
remained important occasions for a sermon to the inmates of
Benedictine establishments, when some special visitor from the
Universities might be expected to declaim. As at St Albans[4],
there was no doubt another formal declamation in the chapter-
house whenever a new abbot or prior was elected. But vital,
potent interest in preaching, whether to those from within or
from without the sacred cloister, appears to be dead. This fact
may possibly be reflected in the actual dearth of fresh monastic
sermon literature for the periods under our examination.

In the thirteenth century, current "sermones ad claustrales"
or "ad religiosos," of English origin, are exceedingly rare. For
the century that follows they are practically non-existent.
Such a situation indeed is not difficult to explain. In the first
place, such a work as the *Summa Predicantium*, for example,
will probably suggest to the reader, beyond any mere question
of rival authorship, how far out of touch with the contemporary
scene, its characters and its interests, the older monastic ideal

[1] Ibid. p. 9.
[2] Cf. Ailred (or Ethelred) of Rievaulx, Geoffrey of Mailross, Gilbert of
Hoyland, etc. The foreigner Eustachius, Abbot of Flay, preached in England
with phenomenal success, his sermons accompanied by signs and wonders.
See under year 1222, Higden's *Polychron.* (Rolls S.), vol. viii, pp. 182–5.
[3] See Pearce, *Monks of Westminster*, pp. 27, 113, 144, etc.
[4] Cf. Reg. Whethamstede, vol. ii, pp. 30, 146, etc. Also, MS. Harl. 3760,
fol. 276.

had grown[1]. There was now little enough cause for fresh pulpit energy on the part of the isolated monk; little enough inspiration to be got from many in the monkish audience facing him. On the other hand, in the convent library, as contrasted with the homes of secular clergy, lay ready for his daily use a comparatively rich selection of earlier homilies, expositions, "exemplaria," and the like, with all the added sanctity of age and reputation upon them. "We have in oure libraries," says John Capgrave, speaking of the Canons of St Victor in Paris, in a sermon at Cambridge, "many sundry bokes that to [= two] chanones of that hous mad, on of hem hite Hewe, the othir hite Richard; notabel clerkis thei were and men of holy lyf."[2] Such works by the two famous Victorines, by St Bernard, or the earlier Fathers remained the favourite reading of our homilists alike in the friary or the monastery. Why be bothered then, to compile new ones? The old wine was best, and in this case the cloister scribe might be trusted to maintain a sufficient supply on tap.

The Dominican's *Summa* just referred to, expresses doubtless a much wider view than that of his Order, when, not without a touch of malice, it describes the monk as one wishing to lead a quiet life, and escape the sweat and toil of "the preaching men." He is made to say: "I wish to live in peace in a convent; to read and sing. I don't want to rush through the world, with all its wearying labours!" Even the very knowledge and virtues these cloisterers acquire, we are told, are but weapons of defence, not of offence. They resemble that knight who, on asking his squire whether anyone could now hurt him in his new harness received the reply, "No; nor will you be able to hurt anyone else!" One thing alone could really keep active the stimulus for original and up-to-date preaching, and that was an intimate contact and sympathy with the lot of the people, their sufferings and yearnings, their good and evil, such as the friar enjoyed

---

[1] Bp. Browne compares Chrysostom's sermons, teeming with allusions to the social life of the towns, with those of Bede, compiled in the monastery and lacking all such. See Browne, *Ven. Bede* (S.P.C.K.), p. 231. The same applies to the friars' and monks' sermons of our period respectively.

[2] MS. Add. 36704, fol. 119. From "a tretis of the orderes that be undyr the reule of oure fadyr seynt Augustine, *drawe oute of a sermoun seyd be freer Jon Capgrave at Cambridge*, the 3ere of oure Lord a MCCCCXXII." Capgrave was an Austin friar, of Lynn, author of the well-known *Chronicle*.

constantly, but the monk scarcely ever, save in so far as he violated his own Rule. We catch a significant glimpse of this monastic "innocuousness" amid the conflict, in one of the later chronicles of St Albans Abbey[1]. On his re-appointment to office in 1452, that abbot, whom Bishop Bekynton once playfully offered to chastise for his bad Latin[2], questioned his monks on the subject of internal reforms. "And they said there were three things amongst others, which had now been neglected for a long time, and stood in need of great reformation." One of them was "the preaching of the sacred word by the brothers in the pulpit." "Quia jam itaque per annos varios et multifarios vix fuit confrater ullus qui vellet in se assumere illud onus, et verbum Dei ibidem tempore Quadragesimali coram populo declarare." Possibly the recent unpopularity into which preaching had fallen through the Lollard propaganda, of which this same district had had its share, may have had something to do with the matter. But still it is none the less the note of decay that is sounded. One further fact concerning the delivery of sermons in the greater monastic churches may suggest the same disinclination of the inmates to preach. In spite of a historic rivalry it is clear that the Mendicant friar was quite frequently to be found occupying a Benedictine pulpit. As early as the beginning of the fourteenth century a license is granted to the Carmelites to preach at Winchester Cathedral, after the Dominican and Franciscan brethren have had their turn, "provided that none of the monks wishes to preach in person on that day."[3] Similarly, we have record at Canterbury of "the friars who preached in our church on divers occasions this year"[4]; and the same feature applies further to such establishments of canons secular as the collegiate church of Ottery St Mary[5], in Devon.

[1] Reg. Whethamst. (Rolls S.), vol. i, pp. 24–5.
[2] See Correspondence of Bekynton (Rolls S.), vol. i, p. 116. (A.D. 1440.)
[3] 1316/17, Reg. Sandale, of Winch. (Hants. Rec. Soc.), pp. 32–3; 1321, Reg. de Asserio (ibid.), pp. 411, 422–3: "...qualibet tertia vice post fratres Pred., et Minores...."
[4] Cf. 1458, in Woodruff and Danks, Memorials of Cant. Cath. p. 264. See below an Austin friar preaching at Tynemouth priory (Bened.), p. 64.
[5] 1382, 1383, etc. (Domin. preachers). Statutes of Ottery St Mary, ed. J. N. Dalton, p. 102. Cf. here the typical clause of the Statuta "De sermonum provisione per Canonicos": "Provideatur eciam quod per aliquem de collegio, aut alium, sermones solempnes fiant ad populum..."; and below, p. 156, n. 1. [Lincoln, etc.]

Mention of preaching "coram populo" however serves to remind us of one of two interesting branches of monastic pulpit activity for which evidence does yet survive from our two centuries. In the *Rites of Durham*[1] there is an account of the regular sermon delivered by members of the fraternity in their abbey church on Sunday afternoons; also of other sermons on special occasions in the city churches—the "Bowe" church, St Oswald's "in elvett," St Margaret's "in framwelgate," St Nicholas' in the market place, preceded by solemn processions through the streets. At Durham, too, in connection with the Registers of Archbishop Melton in 1327, and Bishop Hatfield in 1346, we hear of the typical forty-days' Indulgence granted to those who attend the preaching of the monks[2]. With merry Lydgate, then, we may believe that for the period: "Sumtyme is a folle (he means sarcastically a monk, like himself!) as good to here as the word of a fryer."[3]

But apart from sermons to be delivered in the monastery, the monk figures as a special preacher for visitations and for synods of clergy. At a synod held in London in 1402, for example, no less than half of the six special preachers mentioned in the report are monks from Canterbury[4]. There, and at the visitation, where he acts as a helpmate for the bishop[5] in the work of the pulpit, the monk is at last officially outside his own cloister wall, a step nearer, as it were, to that "instabilitas loci," so definitely forbidden in St Benedict's Rule[6]. Personal touches are so scarce in this branch of our survey that it is interesting to meet with a letter of the early part of the fourteenth century, from the Bishop to the prior of Worcester, which deals with a

---

[1] *Rites of Durham* (Surtees Soc.), pp. 46, 104, etc. See below, p. 146.

[2] See *Fasti Ebor.* vol. i, p. 419, note. Cf. also MS. Ashmole (Bodl.), 750, fol. 140 b, for mention of similar Indulgences for those present at "the Monasterie of Syon" (Isleworth), "whenne the worde of God is preched by the brethren of this Ordre" (15th cent.), etc.

[3] See *Merita Missae*, in E.E.T.S. (O.S.), 71, p. 148, l.g. (This is undoubtedly a rhymed sermon.)

[4] Wilkins, *Conc.* vol. iii, p. 273.

[5] Cf. *Conc. Later.* (Innocent III), Cau. x (repeated among the Consts. of the Council of Trent): "Unde precipimus, tam in Cathedralibus, quam in aliis conventualibus ecclesiis, viros idoneos ordinari quos episcopi possint coadjutores et cooperatores habere, non solum in predicationis officio...." And in our *Cil. Oc. Sac.* fol. 41 b ("...per parochias suas ad predicandum verbum Dei").

[6] See *Reg. S. Bened. cap. lxvi.*

case in point. "We sent in your absence," writes the bishop, "for T. de B., to come to us for the purpose of preaching on Monday, in the monastery of O., on the occasion of our visitation there. He has now arrived. Pray excuse his absence, as he is upon an errand of piety. He shall return as soon as he has discharged it."[1] With this can be coupled another letter of approximately similar date, written by Archbishop Thoresby, concerning a certain monk of York, "frater J. de G., commensalis noster carissimus."[2] It was an ancient institution that bishops should constantly retain about them discreet and honest men, as witnesses of their life and conversation[3]; and right healthy and laudable had been the influence of this brother beloved upon the archiepiscopal household during his Christmas visit. "Nedum Divini verbi pabulo, sed gestus honesti modestia tam salubriter quam laudabiliter nos refecit." In fact, so far had he become the darling of that prelate, that other members of the convent appear to have grown jealous of him, and to have murmured that he had been publishing abroad in his palace sermons some of the monastery scandals, thus bringing down upon them correction at the visitations in chapter. However that might be, the enthusiastic archbishop is now asking to have him back "about the beginning of Lent"—"nobis ad magnum nostrum solatium assistentem"—in that great preaching and penitential season. Still more interesting would this document be, if, as has been actually suggested, the mysterious initials stand for the name of John Gaytrige, or Garryk[4]. As the archbishop's literary henchman, this monk of St Mary's Abbey, York, at his request, had translated his edition of the Peckham Constitutions into English in 1357, for the benefit of the more ignorant parish clergy. His work, then, brings to notice the further fact that even monks have their share in the great

[1] See *Letter-Book of the Priors of Worc.* (Worc. Hist. Rec.), p. 40.
[2] See E.E.T.S. (O.S), 118, p. xx. (*Lay Folks Cat.*)
[3] Cf. Wilkins, *Conc.* vol. i, p. 382, etc.
[4] His name is spelt in the MSS. in a variety of ways. In addition to the above, I note "dan Jon Gaytryge" (Thornton MS., Linc. Cath. Libr.); "J. de Gaysteke" (MS. Harl. 1022, fol. 73 b, and dated 1357); "J. de Caterige" (MS. Arundel, 507, fol. 50); "J. de Taystek" (MS. Harl. 1022, fol. 80, with date). Other MSS. of his work appear to be MS. Trin. Coll. Camb. B. 10; MS. York Minster, xvi. L. 12; MS. Add. 25006; MS. Lambeth 408 (Lollard vers.). See also Notes in J. E. Wells' *Manual*.

output of vernacular sermon literature[1] which helped to prepare men's minds for the coming era of lay-reading and reformation.

One dignified sermon collection[2], alluded to in the previous chapter, though written in Latin throughout, would yet seem to illustrate both types of monastic preaching that have just been emphasized. These are the discourses of Master Robert Rypon, sub-prior of the monastery of Durham[3], and prior of Finchale in the years 1397 and following[4], of whom nothing further appears to be known. The presence of English words and phrases in the chief group of homilies here collected suggests that they were intended for lay ears, after the Durham practice for Sundays described in "the Rites"; while in addition we have the separate synodal addresses to parish clergy with which the volume closes. In his pages there is to be noted, furthermore, that overwhelming conservatism of the mediaeval preachers of the convent to which allusion has been made. No mere independent statement is good enough for the writer, but above it and below he must quote from "Lincoln," or Bernard, or Gorham, the very commonplaces of doctrine that few men would debate. In the matter of making acknowledgement, however, he is certainly above the average.

Rypon himself[5] brackets the canon with the monk as a typical preacher at the clerical synod; but pulpit references or examples in the case of the former are even more difficult to find than in that of the Orders we have dealt with. Another vague figure, of an Austin canon regular of Lilleshall Priory in Shropshire[6], can stand appropriately by the side of Gaytrige. He is John Myrc, the author of the popular *Festiall*, an English homily

---

[1] Cf. also the earlier *South-English Legendary* (ed. from MS. Laud. 108, in E.E.T.S. (O.S.), 87), the work of monks of Gloucester Abbey (Bened.); and others noted here in Chap. VII.

[2] MS. Harl. 4894. One sermon introduces the date 1401, with reference to a comet, then appearing. See here, p. 208, Chap. V.

[3] For his preaching activities, cf. *Durham Account Rolls*, vol. iii, p. 596: "Item in expensis domini Roberti de Ripon....predicant(is) apud Heghington...." etc.

[4] Cf. *Charters of Finchale* (Surtees Soc.), pp. xxviii, cxix, cxxxiii, etc. (Compotus Dom. Roberti Rypon prioris de Fynkhall).

[5] Cf. MS. Harl. 4894, fol. 161 (sermo *in Sinodo*): "iste monachus sive canonicus sic redarguet."

[6] See article on "Mirk" (or Myrc, J.), in *D.N.B.*; fl. c. 1403 (Pits). His letter to "Sir J. de S., vicar of A." in which he expresses the hope that he will turn his *Manuale* into English, is in MS. Harl. 5306.

collection in which the saint's-day is especially provided for, as common in the libraries as Felton's Latin *Sermones dominicales*, and a good deal more picturesque. A manual of instructions for parish priests also bears his name, which was quaintly compiled by him in the vernacular in easy verse after the pattern of de Pagula's prose. A copy of his Latin *Manuale Sacerdotis* in York Minster Library may suggest an earlier connection with Yorkshire[1]. But that is all[2]. He is a name, insignificant apart from the wider movement with which his works are connected[3].

The reader who has turned to the company of the Mendicants, on the other hand, will feel himself at last amid familiar surroundings. Here, looming from the pages of history are comparatively well-known types and personalities, never more familiar perhaps than when they lean from "pulpitum" and "scaffaldus," in church or open piazza. Who does not recognize such geniuses of the preaching art when he looks abroad at the Italian scene in the fifteenth century, at the Franciscan Bernardino or the Dominican Savonarola, or two centuries earlier, at the great Berthold of Regensburg, in Germany? In England, almost every dispute in which the activities of the friars reach historical proportions—and they were not few—seem to have raged around pulpit steps. They dispute long with the Universities, and the question of the examinatory sermon must enter in[4]. They dispute with the secular clergy, and it becomes a struggle amongst other things for right of way to the parish pulpit. They dispute with prelates and scholars over the subject of evangelical poverty, and a London preaching-cross becomes a strategic point in the campaign. In politics, behind the throng of noisy rebels and discontents, whether in the rebellion of Simon de Montfort[5], the Peasants' Revolt[6], or the risings which

---

[1] See above, p. 47, and below, p. 297. The *Instructions* have been edited in E.E.T.S. (O.S.), No. 31, his *Festiall* in E.E.T.S. (Ext. S), No. 96.

[2] Among special matters to be inquired into at visitations, in a record of Austin canons about the year 1395 to 1404, I notice: "An prelatus...predicat." But this probably refers only to preaching to the brethren. (Appdx. 1, Salter, *Chapters of Aug. Canons*, Oxf. Hist. Soc. 1920.)

[3] Canon Walter Hilton, of Thurgarton, the well-known author of mystical treatises, was no doubt a preacher, but I know no record of actual sermons by him. See also here later in Chap. vi. [4] Cf. Wilkins, *Conc.* vol. iii, p. 400.

[5] Cf. Little, *The Grey Friars in Oxford* (Oxf. Hist. Soc.), p. 32 (quoting Stubbs, in footnote 6, etc.).

[6] There is almost a literature on this subject. Cf. Jusserand, *English Way-*

follow the deposition of Richard II[1], we catch glimpses of passionate eloquent friars stirring men on to resist the tyranny or the usurpation which mars the hour. Finally, their way of preaching with jests and collection-bags had much to do with Wycliffe's general attack on their system. Look where you will, wherever "a flye and eke a frier" fall into the mediaeval dish, there you may be sure to hear a sermon on the matter from one of the Orders. Scarcely a phase of current thought, scarcely a habit, pastime, occurrence, fails to find a place among their homiletical maxims and reflections.

If the monastic preacher in fourteenth-century England could look back to a distinguished past, so also could the Mendicant. Etienne de Bourbon, on the continent, tells how he had seen noble ladies, in days of early enthusiasm, so affected by the word that they donned the vilest garb of poor women, to follow with greater freedom the steps of the preachers as they went, far and wide, from town to town, themselves like beggars on foot[2]. But the unknown author of a Franciscan *Liber Exemplorum*[3] too, had seen great crowds flocking after a "most famous" evangelist of the Order in Ireland in much the same fashion; and there were tales still told of the signs and wonders that attended the efforts of others who preached the Crusades in this country. The *Speculum Laicorum*[4], a work of English origin, narrates how when a certain friar (in Anglia) was busy thus with his message, one in his audience, who had been to the Holy Land, attempted to dissuade the others. He was a "cementarius" by trade, and paying no heed to a warning vision that night, but continuing his evil detraction, he fell one day

---

faring Life, pp. 302, 306, 308, etc. and *L'Épopée mystique*, p. 158, etc.; Ch. Petit Dutaillis, in a series of *Essays offered to A. Monod*; Powell and Trevelyan, *Peasants' Rising*, pp. 45, etc. For original sources see Walsingham, *Hist. Angl.* (Rolls S.), vol. ii, pp. 10 and 13; *Fascic. Zizan.* (Rolls S.), pp. 292–5, etc.

[1] See *Eulogium Hist.* (Rolls S.), vol. iii, p. 392 et seq. (For a further case of the political preaching of the friars, see letter of Archbp. Greenfield to the Dom. prior of York, 1315, in *Letters from Northern Registers* (Rolls S.), pp. 238–9.)

[2] Begin. "Item vidi ego nobiles mulieres amore verbi Dei sic affectas ut, assumpto pauperum mulierum habitu vilissimo...." See *Anecdotes Hist.* ed. Lecoy de la Marche, p. 75.

[3] Ed. A. G. Little (Brit. Soc. Franc. Studies). A work of c. 1275.

[4] Ed. J. Welter (Paris, 1914).

to the ground from a height and bit through his tongue[1]!
Matthew Paris[2] describes how in 1235 a compassionate Franciscan restored whole a paralyzed woman who had punctuated
his address with her groans; while versions in the sermon
literature are not uncommon of the story of a wanton woman,
some say in Northumberland[3], which bears rich testimony to the
speaker's power. So moved was she by his words that she died.
On being restored to life to make her confession, the words
"Ave Maria" were found inscribed upon her tongue. Tales such
as these, it is true, have often been used by later critics to mock
the men who spread and maintained them in their preaching.
But, for our present argument, they at least bear witness to a
great tradition in the minds of those credulous enough, if you
like, to believe in them then. They came from an age rich in
the emotions and that "suggestive" power which kindle men
to do great things for the Faith, even if mountains were never
removed beyond the mountains of vice and selfishness in human
hearts[4]. Master John of St Giles, John of St Albans, as Matthew
Paris would proudly acclaim him, was surely no phantom of the
imagination. Royal physician, learned doctor of the schools of
Paris, sometime Treasurer of Salisbury Cathedral, about this
time, he had not feared to step down from his pulpit in the
midst of a sermon on holy poverty, in a Dominican house, to
receive the lowly habit of a friar[5]. Little wonder that such a
man converted Alexander of Hales by one of his discourses[6],
and became "a master perfect in theology," "discreet and holy"

---

[1] One MS. version localizes this story near Cambridge (MS. Harl. 2385,
fol. 95 b [Contigit in partibus Cantebrigie]).
[2] *Chron. Maj.* (Rolls S.).
[3] Sic MS. Harl. 2316 (14th cent.), fol. 59.
[4] Cf. the miracle of the old man, a sermon-goer, transported over a mountain, or hill, and other miracles of sermon-goers, in Etienne de Bourbon
(*Anecdotes*, as above, pp. 74–5).
[5] Doctor of Medicine to Philippe Auguste: returns to England from Paris,
1235. See references in *Chron. Maj.* and *Grossetête's Letters* (both Rolls S.),
pp. 60, 62, 131. This incident in Quétif et Echard, vol. i, p. 100, quoted from
N. Trivet's *Chrons. of the Kings of England*, p. 573: (*Annales?*) "...Joannes
in Domo Fratrum Predicantium sermonem faciens ad clerum, cum suasisset
paupertatem voluntariam, ut verba sua exemplo confirmaret, descendens de
ambone habitum Fratrum recepit, et in eodem regressus ad clerum sermonem explevit."
[6] Besides the former references, see *Hist. Litt. de la France*, vol. xviii, p.
397.

for the work of the Gospel, even in the estimation of a Bene
dictine monk none too friendly to the new Orders.

Biographical incidents of this nature are again all too infrequent for the later mediaeval centuries, in the history of our
Mendicant pulpit in England. The numerous entries of sermons
by friars, "coram rege," among the Rolls and Accounts of the
Record Office, the long lists of sermon-writers in Bale or Pits,
even the great Latin example-books themselves, are all calculated to mislead the student who hopes for vivid material from
which to reconstruct their careers. The actual sermons themselves that can be identified with a particular author are very
few and far between. The stories are drawn from extraneous
sources; while the writer's own personality lies hidden usually
beneath a mass of orderly tradition and a laborious *réchauffé* of
earlier expositions. Of the thousand "exempla" and more
which fill the *Summa Predicantium*, only one or two here and
there could be recognized as drawn from the personal reminiscence of the learned Dominican chancellor, who is otherwise so
free with his comments on the general life of his day. It was the
literary industry of the friars themselves, as seen in their
weightier compositions, doubtless, which had much to do with
this extinction of that naïve realism and vivid self-expression
which had inspired the verse of Jacopone da Todi and the
painting of Giotto. They still think and speak of the sufferings
and sin of the world in which they preach, but only in general
and unoriginal terms. Their very "jests" are now at second or
third hand.

Meagre and unsatisfying though they are, we must again
fall back on odd headings and notes upon the sermon page, if
we would revive from contemporary record the activities of the
brethren, as they "travayle from towne to towne in the Sunday
and greate festes, to teche the people goddes lawe."[1] In the
library of Caius College, Cambridge, is a diminutive manuscript
of outline addresses[2] which might well have lain open before
some Dominican missioner in the pulpit, and reposed on the
journey in his tippet, where the unfaithful, as Chaucer reminds
us, carried their fascinating "knyves and pinnes." Most of the
sermons are unlabelled, as if suitable for any kind of audience.

---

[1] *Dives et Pauper*, Prec. iii, cap. xvi.   [2] MS. Caius Coll. Camb. 233.

But a few proclaim now and then, as if with a pardonable pride, some particularly honoured occasion of delivery. Here, for example, is a "sermo in cathedrali Sancti Petri," and another— "ad predicatores in Oxonia." Others bear the rubricated notes —"in synodo," "in electione prelati," "in dedicatione ecclesiae," "ad claustrales," and so forth. Two more, entitled "secundum fratrem Hugonem (or H.) predicatorem," given at much greater length, suggest instances where our preacher, now one of the audience, is noting down with especial care, for future use, the inspiring words of another. The actual contents of these out-lines, however, prove quite disappointing to the modern reader. Another manuscript which partakes of the nature of a sermon diary as well as of a sermon series is to be found in much-defaced condition in the Bodleian Library at Oxford[1]. From the frequency with which the name occurs, it would appear to contain the discourses of one Nicholas Philip, a Franciscan, and records visits to Newcastle ("quod Phelip Novicastri, 1433," etc.), Oxford ("sermo quam predicavi Oxon." etc.), Lynn, Lichfield, and Melton. Besides these we note a synodal address[2], a processional sermon[3], several more at visitations of the brethren[4] and one at the profession of a novice[5]. His in-flammatory attacks on the wealthy, the lawyers, the clergy and others have been noticed by Dutaillis in connection with a study of clerical influences upon popular agitation for social reforms[6]. The present writer has also inspected a sermon note-book among the Caius College manuscripts at Cambridge[7], which was kept on even more systematic lines, probably by some un-known Austin friar of the district, who regularly jots down place and season above the sermons, whether of his own or of others, that he enters[8]. So illegible is his writing, unfortunately, that little or nothing can be deciphered at any casual examination of the work. Dr James calls attention in his *Catalogue*, however, to a sermon here by the Chancellor of the University ("sermo

[1] MS. Bodl. Lat. Th. d. 1.   [2] Ibid. fol. 83.
[3] fol. 141.   [4] fols. 98, 102 b, etc.
[5] fol. 151 (In professione novitii).
[6] Other dated entries in this MS. are: "Oxon. 1432" (fol. 51), and "Lechefeld, 1436" (fol. 113–14).
[7] MS. Caius Coll. Camb. 356. (Late 15th cent. (?).)
[8] Among churches mentioned are Bury, Colchester, Melbourn, Coton, St Botolph's and St Mary's, Cambridge.

cancellarii")[1], a processional oration—"pro belli victoria in francia"[2]—a funeral sermon for the Master of King's Hall, and a sermon "in the feast of Relics, at Bury," amongst others of a more usual type.

If, with the itinerant preacher, we take the road which leads from the eastern University town to London, that road of which Richard Whitford, the monk of Sion, has memories, as he writes his religious treatise for householders[3] a century later, there awaits us now in the possession of the Society of Gray's Inn a little treatise on the Decalogue[4] which incorporates a few personal reminiscences in the text. Once part of a library of Greyfriars in Chester, it claims to be the work of "brother Staunthone," whom from internal evidence we gather to have been a Franciscan in the early part of the fourteenth century[5]. The place-names he mentions, "Frawisham," "Ravenyngham," and Hale, seem to indicate a special connection with Norfolk. Scattered in the pages of this treatise are a number of illustrative anecdotes which for once would seem to have been gleaned not from the pages of other writers, but from the lips of contemporaries, his friends and acquaintances. If we proceed further to put side by side with Staunton's tract a group of five manuscripts in the British Museum containing collections of sermon tales by English Dominican and Franciscan friars, then submit to careful analysis all narratives which claim to have been derived in a similar way, some interesting results may accrue[6]. In the majority of such cases, which are introduced by the characteristic "Retulit mihi quidam religiosus," or equivalent phrases[7], we behold the animated talk, the intimate exchange of confidences and experiences between Religious, in the convent, or

---

[1] Ibid. p. 38.

[2] p. 70. There is also a sermon "at the city of London" noted, with this charming comment: "Item homines London. sunt newe fangul." Did he feel a little boorish and out-of-date on his visit?

[3] *A Werke for Housholders* (W. de Worde, 1533; 1537; 1538; etc.).

[4] MS. Gray's Inn Libr. 15 (15th cent.).

[5] See my article, "Some Franciscan Memorials at Gray's Inn," in the *Dublin Review*, April 1925, pp. 278–80.

[6] These are MSS. Roy. 7. D. 1 (by a Dominican of the Cambridge district (?)), Harl. 2316 (Domin. (?)), Harl. 2385 (Dominican of Cambridge district (?)), Add. 33956 (Franciscan (?)), Burney 361, pt ii (Franciscan (?)).

[7] Cf. numerous examples in MSS. Roy. 7. D. 1; Add. 33956, etc. (similarly "Sicut a quodam religioso didici," etc.); or MS. Gray's Inn. Libr. 15, fols. 5 b (religiosus Gilbertus de Massingham), etc.; MS. Burn. 361, fols. 149, etc.

in the open world. Safely returned from some preaching tour, or some journey to the bedside of the dying, the brethren have ever their little tale to narrate of things seen or heard upon the road. Brother John of Chester, the Dominican, has been told of a lady's pet monkey that strayed into church, swallowed the Host and was burnt by its mistress. With his own eyes he has seen that same Host which was rescued from the animal's stomach unchanged[1]. Brother Ralph of Swyneland tells brother Staunton[2], on his return from London, how when he and the companion friar travelling with him had entered a certain village at nightfall on their route, the good woman who gave them lodging for the night had recounted a domestic tragedy. It was the old story of a disobedient son cursed by his mother, and carried off by the devil. Did they rise next morning before dawn, we wonder, to turn aside into some pleasant meadow and enjoy the prospect of nature, there, like two other friars, once on a preaching tour, to behold an apparition of their own[3]? Master Robert of Burwell will speak of what once befell him by the way[4], or the writer himself perhaps "of what I heard in Essex by the Thames-side."[5]

Journeys abroad to foreign parts will bring, as is natural, many fresh marvels to enrich the conversation and the common stock of anecdotes for the pulpit. Thus Master Robert Cursun, "while travelling about as legate to preach the Crusade" in France, is a welcome raconteur on his return[6]. Peter of Juynesfeld, and his fellow, brother Adam, are naturally full of the wondrous miracle that occurred while they were passing through Rimini, in the year 1268[7], likewise others "from parts beyond

---

[1] MS. Harl. 2316, fol. 12 (Joh. de Cestria, fr. pred. vidit istud).

[2] MS. Gray's Inn Libr. 15, fol. 31: "Item frater Radulphus de S., cum socio suo semel veniens Londoniis, intravit villam quemdam...." The recurrence of a similar tale to this in another MS. collection of this group, and a further parallel noted here later (with MS. Harl. 1288, see p. 63, n. 11), shows the connection of this Gray's Inn treatise with the B.M. MSS. indicated.

[3] MS. Roy. 7. C. xv, fol. 10 b: "...summo mane surgentes ante auroram, putantes tempus illis esse diluculum, deviaverunt, gradientes per quoddam pratum."

[4] MS. Roy. 7. D. 1, fol. 124 b ("Hanc narrationem retulit Mag. Rob⁸. de Burwelle de seipso contigisse...").

[5] MS. Add. 33956, fol. 85 ("Narratur sicut simile egomet audivi in Exsexia juxta Thamisiam").

[6] Ibid. fol. 84 b; cf. fol. 85. His *Summa* is in MS. Roy. 9. E. iv.

[7] MS. Sloane, 2478, fol. 14 b (Two Franciscans).

the sea."[1] Such foreign adventure, however, will be only for
the few. But even at home the pleasing narration may be introduced in a variety of ways. Some noble knight, perhaps,
falls into a reminiscent mood over the guest-chamber fire, like
him who once "coming to besiege the castle of *Kenelworth*,
on the king's behalf,...related a story to the brethren of the
convent, asking them to publish it in their sermons."[2] Those
who come fresh to the cloister have memories of their native
place[3], marvels of the outside world now forsaken, which will
be welcome enough in times and places unenlightened by the
newspaper. Brother Hugh of Hereford has not forgotten yet a
certain horror of his earlier days as a layman, the very sight of
that toad which fastened itself to the face of an undutiful son
for two whole years[4]. The brother, who writes, has chatted
more than once with those who have information of old mutual
acquaintances now passed away[5]. Nor does the tale told by the
Lombard Hubert de Lorgo of his own squire die with him, when
he is buried among the Friar-Preachers of London[6].

Some story has been received at fourth hand. But the friar
narrator can still trace its long journey: "A certain trustworthy
man of religion, a great preacher and a dependable witness, who
learnt this same story from the priest who heard the confession
of the woman mentioned, in her last infirmity, related it to me."[7]
All and sundry in that richly-varied world of the middle ages
bring grist to the Mendicant homilist's mill. Brother tells tales
about brother[8]. Rectors and village priests[9], friendly Cistercian
monks[10], the Visitor of the Order when he comes[11], religious of

---

[1] Cf. MS. Burney 361, fol. 153 (Fr. Walterus narravit de London, quod
contigit in partibus transmarinis); similarly fols. 149, 156, etc.; MS. Roy.
7. D. i, fol. 96 b (ab hospite suo); cf. Add. 33956, fols. 24, 84 b, 85; etc.

[2] MS. Add. 6716, fol. 39 b (Canons of Kenilworth, Warwickshire).

[3] Cf. MS. Add. 33956, fol. 82; and MS. Roy. 7. D. i, fol. 84 b.

[4] MS. Burn. 361, fol. 152 (Fr. Hugo de Hereford laycus audivit, qui vidit
bufonem in facie ejus).

[5] Cf. MS. Roy. 7. D. i, fols. 107 and 113.   [6] MS. Add. 6716, fol. 5 b.

[7] MS. Roy. 7. D. i, fol. 76; cf. fols. (77), (107), 137 b; MS. Add. 33956,
fol. 88; etc.

[8] Cf. MS. Roy. 7. D. i, fol. 107.

[9] Cf. MS. Gray's Inn Libr. 15, fols. 36 b, 38; MS. Roy. 7. D. i, fols. 67 b
and 139 b; MS. Add. 33956, fol. 86 b.

[10] Cf. MS. Harl. 1288, fol. 44 (ut dicit quidam sisterciensis ordinis, A.D.
MCCCCIIII°, in comitatu Cantabrigie...); MS. Roy. 7. D. i, fol. 104.

[11] MS. Burn. 361, fol. 149 (Item quidam frater visitator ordinis ejusdem
retulit).

every kind, the nun, the layman, the gossiping housewife acting as host, even the midwife[1], divulge the little tragedies or successes of the family circle or the group of their intimates[2]. With interest we observe how the speaker frequently requests here the name of a witness, or a place, there the name of the chief character discussed, to be kept secret. The sufferer may be living still[3]; or if not, at any rate to name him would cause scandal for the dead man's friends[4]: "He who told me the foregoing wished that the place where these things befell, and the name of the aforementioned woman should not be disclosed, for a time."[5] Then there are the tender revelations of the confessional[6], and of the last shrift of the dying[7]. Well may the busy Dominicans of Cambridge make use of them discreetly to warn the stubborn, and encourage the good[8]. Finally, much will be gleaned from the hearing of others' sermons[9]. When some distinguished preacher fills the pulpit, there is often a harvest for the eager story-collector in his audience[10]. But our preacher himself, on occasion, returning home from his own preaching, brings fresh illustrative material with him for the next. Friar Walter of Raveningham had thus to relate how a certain cleric interrupted his discourse, contradicting the preacher's argument, only to repent later, when sickness drove him to his bed[11]. Friar Baudellzinus tells the assembled brethren, surely not without a laugh, how once he was due to preach on Sunday, in a Lincolnshire church, six miles from Stamford[12].

[1] MS. Add. 33956, fol. 5 (ut dixit mihi illa matrona que obstetricandi causa presens erat).

[2] Cf. MS. Roy. 7. D. i, fols. 93 b, 113, 137 b; MS. Add. 33956, fols. 82, 86 b; MS. Gray's Inn Libr. 15 as before, etc.

[3] MS. Add. 33956, fol. 82 b (...qui adhuc superstes est...); MS. Roy. 7. D. i, fols. 114 b, 119 b.

[4] MS. Add. 33956, fol. 82 (propter scandalum amicorum defuncti).

[5] MS. Roy. 7. D. i, fol. 119 b; cf. similarly, fols. 122, 137 b; MS. Add. 33956, fols. 82, 86 b; etc.

[6] Cf. MS. Roy. 7. D. i, fols. 75, 76, 77, 82, 92, 119 b; etc., etc.

[7] Cf. MS. ibid. fol. 108 b and MS. Add. 33956, fol. 14; etc.

[8] Cf. MSS. ibid. passim.

[9] Besides references in note following, cf. MSS. Add. 33956, fol. 28 (in publico sermone), Harl. 273, fol. 175 (en sermun).

[10] Cf. Cardinal William of Savoy, at Cambridge (MS. Roy. 7. D. i, fols. 87, 87 b); "Linc. dixit in sermone" (i.e. Grossetête), (MS. Harl. 2385, fol. 120), etc.

[11] MS. Gray's Inn Libr. 15, fol. 10 b (also in MS. Harl. 1288, fol. 56, without name of preacher).

[12] Described as "juxta Scholthrop" (Sculthorp?).

A kinswoman of his who lived at that place, very naturally requested her husband to come with her to the sermon. But he refused, preferring to spend Sunday, in the open, with his bow and arrows. On entering a wood to enjoy the chase, who should face him but the devil himself in the form of an immense hare. He shot; the devil vanished; but the arrow rebounding pierced his clothes. How well deserved a shock for the ill-mannered, impious vavasor, Robert![1] Thus does the pulpit secure its "examples" for the morrow.

John Waldeby's prologue to his homilies on the Creed introduces us to a fragment of contemporary autobiography from the life of a distinguished preacher and Oxford doctor of the "Friar Hermits of the Order of St Augustine."[2] In contemporary records he appears to be occasionally confused with his brother Robert, Archbishop of York, and member of the famous anti-Wycliffite Council of 1382, who retired eventually to the same peaceful Yorkshire friary at Tickhill. The dedication of the work is appropriately made to an Abbot of St Albans[3], since the monks of Tynemouth ("ubi regis Oswini martyris sunt ossa venerabiliter translata"), at whose request the writing was undertaken, belonged to an ancient cell of the great abbey[4]. They had invited him to preach to them, and had been impressed by his eloquence. Waldeby then, who calls himself "ordinis Sancti Augustini minimus, inter sacrae paginae professores indignissimus" in the fashionable University style[5], provides an interesting example of an Austin friar in the pulpit of a Benedictine priory[6]. It reminds us that in spite of the bitter things which a son of St Albans could say of the objectionable behaviour of the friars, and of the contempt which the latter

[1] MS. Add. 33956, fol. 82: "Hec narravit fr. Baudellzinus Cubaud (?) *coram multis fratribus.*"

[2] MS. Roy. 7. E. ii, fol. 50; MS. Caius Coll. Camb. 334, fol. 150, etc. MS. Bodl. 687 is described as a Latin set of sermons on the gospels, throughout the year, by John de Waldeby, and is stated to have been written in 1365 (*Western MSS. Bodl. Cat.* Madan and Craster). This I have not seen as yet. His order is that generally known as the Austin friars. (MS. Roy. 7. E. ii, calls him in the explicit, "ordinis heremitarum.")

[3] This will be Abbot Thomas de la Mare (1349–96).

[4] Granted to the abbey in 1093.

[5] Rev. H. S. Cronin's attempt to read a special meaning into similar phrases used by Roger Dymmok at the opening of his *Liber contra Errores...Lollardorum*, just published for the Wyclif Society (1922)—see p. xii—is quite mistaken. [6] See above, p. 51.

could show in return, it was yet quite possible for happier relations to exist between them. These twelve sermons, as the author tells, had been delivered originally to lay-folk in York. Hence the good monks of Tynemouth may have wanted to make use of them from the manuscript for a similar kind of audience in their own convent church. Waldeby explains, at all events, that he had not forgotten to do their bidding. When on his return to the friary at York he found himself overwhelmed with the crowds, he fled away to "Tikkille, our solitary place," and there amidst a peace suited to contemplation, drew up from scattered notes "in cedulis et membranis," what he calls "a serious tract." A Cambridge manuscript of the treatise contains, in addition to this and companion expositions on the Lord's Prayer and the Ave Maria, a dozen extra sermons on independent themes, which reveal an ascetic mind of even more than the usual morbidity and pessimism. Such texts as "Better is death than a bitter life,"[1] "It repenteth me to have made man,"[2] "Be not conformed to this world,"[3] and that unending cry of the mediaeval preacher—"The days are evil!"[4]—suggest a veritable Jeremiah in the midst of the city. There is certainly nothing of the popular dealer in "fablis or flaterynge" about this friar. In one of these discourses[5] Waldeby himself repeats an old pulpit warning against over-emphasis of the mercy of God, and neglect of the terrors of future punishment. It is a justification of his own favourite method. "Wherefore," says Bartholomew (*On the Properties of Things*), "that bells sound better when a North wind is blowing, than when it is a South wind."[6] "Note further, that if the master is away, boys in school fail to apply themselves to their books. But as soon as they hear his stern voice, their eyes are on the page. So is it with the frightening of sinners, who at present do not study the Commandments of God, which are their lesson-books." A brief note upon a

---

[1] MS. Caius Coll. Camb. 334, fol. 188 b.   [2] Ibid. fol. 185 b.
[3] fols. 176 b and 193.   [4] fol. 195; cf. in Bromyard, *S.P.*
[5] A sermon on preaching (fol. 177 et seq.). Text, simply "Jhesus." This sermon contains English phrases, as do some others, cf. his opening: "Tria me movent accipere hoc thema, viz. dede, nede and spede. Primo dede, scil. predicationis...," etc.
[6] "Sic in proposito, ventus Borialis est frigidus, et asper, et significat verbum predicationis asperum contra vicia, et talis aliquando ad correctionem viciorum melius sonat." See further in Chap VIII, below.

manuscript in the British Museum records the year and place of the author's death: "Johannes Waldebeius obiit Eboraci, 1393."[1]

John Bale's manuscript catalogue of Carmelite writers[2], may serve in the place of actual sermons, to remind us here of the one remaining Mendicant Order of importance. For the years 1350 to 1450 there may be reckoned from it roughly no less than forty names of sermon-compilers, many of them responsible for more than one collection. Cardinal Gasquet is surely right when he argues that if such lists survived for the other Orders, especially those of the Preachers and Minors, the total output would amount to a figure considerable indeed. To-day it is difficult to trace any of these Carmelite productions among the manuscripts that are left. The authors and their work are alike forgotten. But here and there Bale himself preserves a note on some great pulpit reputation of the past. William Badby, Richard Maidstone, John Swaffham, for example, were once distinguished preachers of the court. Two of them are declared to have been the especial favourites of John of Gaunt, "time-honoured Lancaster," while the last-named appears to have won a bishopric on the strength of his abilities in haranguing before these great men of the realm[3]. Another, Robert Mascall, excellent "in reproof of vice and dissemination of virtue,"[4] likewise attained to the see of Hereford in 1404. In the light of such triumphs it is easy to understand the ceaseless warnings of others against pulpit pride and pulpit flattery, against those who are the very devil's own horns in his hunting after souls— "blandientes in predicationibus suis, et querentes ab hominibus gloriam."[5] Bromyard, the friar doctor, knows as well as any man the cunning hypocritical ways by which the unscrupulous rise to power and dignity in the Church. On the small scale Rypon's unbeneficed clerk had preached so lustily for the parish

---

[1] MS. Roy. 8. c. i, fol. 1. With Waldeby compare Thos. Scrope, the Carmelite recluse, as described in Chap. III here. Another sermon by an Austin friar of the period, one Mag. Walter Herdeby ("in ecclesia virginis," i.e. St Mary the Virgin, Oxford) is reported in MS. Digby, clxi, fol. 2, which I have not seen (cf. *History of St Mary the Virgin, Oxford*, 1892, p. 149).

[2] MS. Harl. 3838.   [3] Bangor, c. 1376. Ibid. fol. 83 b.   [4] fol. 90.

[5] MS. Add. 21253, fol. 54: "Tales predicatores lactant homines lacte adulationis."

"curates," until with the coveted living won, he lapsed into silence and idleness for the rest of his days[1]. So now others, "whose duty it is to be harsh as lions against sinners, are fawning hounds that wag their tails, not faithful sheep-dogs but lap-dogs, eating up the luscious tit-bits that lords and ladies throw to them."[2] Some were only willing to preach to the rich, not to the poor. Some made especial point of rebuking and exaggerating the vices of the lower classes, while keeping a tactful silence about the sins of more favoured aristocrats[3]. Woe to the fashionable sycophants of the pulpit!

In contrast to this mood Bale mentions a characteristic feature of a good deal of Mendicant preaching when he says of John Thorp, 'a very frequent preacher to clergy': "He did not fear to reproach even the bishops for their sins and short-comings." In the *Summa Predicantium* of the English friar preacher we have remarked already upon the full blast of the trumpet against the monstrous "regiment" of prelates, and these outspoken denunciations are amongst the most curious phenomena of the mediaeval pulpit. Of all examples in our sermons themselves, none is more striking and unexpected than one which occurs in a vernacular homily collection of the fifteenth century.[4] A preacher, presumably of quite inferior rank, if not the humble priest of the parish, acting as substitute in the pulpit for the bishop on an emergency, ventures to criticize the conduct of both Pope and prelates before lay-folk, in the very presence of the same visiting bishop himself. From the speaker's own remarks we happen to know that this was the case. Similarly, though in less spectacular fashion as we read it to-day, Brother Staunton, aforementioned, in his discussion of the Sixth Commandment, summarily consigns to the gallows of hell "the bishops and other prelates," who refuse to correct their people's sins, adding that this will be the just judgement of the Lord[5]! However well-justified such statements may have been, there can be no doubt that with the friar especially there was also a bitter personal feeling in the matter. We have only to listen to Bromyard's account of the kind of treatment meted

---

[1] See above, p. 31. [2] *S.P.—Predic.*
[3] Bromyard adds here: "Non sic Johannes, qui arguebat Herodem."
[4] MS. Roy. 18. B. xxiii. [5] MS. Gray's Inn Libr. 15, fol. 47.

out, for example, to his fellow-preachers by those holding the keys which could unlock to them the diocese, to discover that. Human wolves like the usurer and the prostitute, he asserts, find in the bishops supporters rather than enemies. As for the faithful dogs, in their attempts to keep such away from the flock of Christ, these they will "assault, restrict, expel." "More willingly would they keep a thousand usurers and as many prostitutes in their own city than twenty friars." In spite of its obvious malice, Matthew Paris' description of the friars' preaching does seem to have a certain resemblance to the facts that have just been cited—"in predicationibus suis vel adulatores, vel mordacissimi reprehensores!"

Enough has been said already to make it clear by now that if the author of the ponderous *Summa* just quoted, will tell us nothing about himself, his book will prove a veritable "speculum vitae" from the point of view of the Mendicants of his time[1]. The ascertainable facts of John Bromyard's own life, apart from his writings, are soon exhausted[2]. The tradition of his early associations with the county of Hereford, in which lies the village whose name he bears, can now be substantiated by reference to the Ordination Lists in the Episcopal Registers of the diocese. His reputation as a formidable opponent of John Wycliffe[3], together with the fact, already noted, of his presence at the Second Session of the famous London Council at the Blackfriars in 1382, is important when his revelations on the state of the Church are in question. So, too, is his tenure of the Chancellorship at Cambridge[4], about the year 1383.

[1] MS. Roy. 7. E. iv, originally belonging to Rochester priory, is the great Brit. Mus. MS. of this work. MS. Harl. 106 contains numerous odd excerpts (cf. fols. 34, 75, 263, 313, etc.). For the numerous printed editions see my note in the opening of Chap. VI, here. MS. Roy. 10. c. x is a fine copy of his Tractatus Juris Civilis et Canonici, apparently identical with the printed *Opus Trivium*, which seems to be a shortened compendium, with extra subject-headings, of the *Summa Pred.* (ed. Paris, 1500 etc.).

[2] Oudin (*Comment. de script. eccl. antiq.*) gives the best account, I think. See also Quétif et Echard. Bede Jarrett (*Engl. Domins.*) confuses him with a Robert de Bromyard, an earlier figure (see *Roll of Household Expenses of Rich. Swinfield* (Camden S.), vol. i, p. 145), D.D. Oxon. 1289, Prov. 1304, died 1310.

[3] It is worth noting that Bromyard occurs amongst the distinguished opponents of Wycliffe given in J. Hurter, *Theologiae Cathol. Nomenclat. Lit.* vol. ii (1906), col. 680.

[4] Appointed c. 1380–90. See Fuller, *Hist. of Univ. of Camb.* (ed. 1840), pp. 69, 122 (he suggests Bromyard was sent to Cambridge from Oxford

Mr Fletcher, in a sketch of the Blackfriars of Oxford, mentions that "when the Fifth Visitation of the English Dominican province was made, by cutting off the dioceses of Bath and Wells and Exeter from the old Oxford Visitation, John Bromyard was appointed vicar in 1397."[1] Finally, the date which is given on a manuscript of his work in the Bodleian Library suggests that he was still active in the year 1409[2]. With the *Summa* in hand let us now review the more general features of the situation as presented to the sight of this distinguished son of St Dominic.

First, the life of the faithful friar evangelist remains an arduous one. He need not even set out with Robert de Braibrok or John de Stone on an expedition to distant Saracens[3] to realize that, as long as some bishop's license throws open to him an English diocese. If that fails he might yet turn his attention to the Jews, who since the first days of Dominican enterprise at Oxford had been the especial care of that Order, so well fitted by its learning to wrestle with the arguments of "blinded"

"on design, to ferret out the Wicklivists (to whom he was a professed enemy)"). Wood (*Athen. Oxon.* vol. i, p. 161) states that Bromyard was also sometime Chancellor at Oxford; but there seems to be no foundation for this tenure which Wood calls probably unique. See also Bale, Pits, etc. For the Blackfriars' Council of 1382, see *Fascic. Zizan.* (Rolls S.), p. 289. As this describes him as "fr. Praed. Joh. Bromyerde, *Cantabrigiae*," Fuller's date (c. 1390) for his transference to this university is probably too late.

[1] *Blackfriars of Oxford*, p. 11.

[2] MS. Bodl. 859, fols. 44–227 (Distinctiones mag. Joh. Bromyard, A.D. 1409). I believe that I have now traced Fletcher's mention of the year 1419 as a last date connected with the career of Bromyard, to its probable source, in W. Eisengrein's *Catalogus testium veritatis...*, ed. 1565, p. 160. Oudin refers to "Eisengrenius" for mention of this date. When, however, we turn to the *Catalogus* in question, we find that it is the habit of the compiler to group his writers "before the year so-and-so," and under the particular heading "ante...1419" occur the names of Rich. Rolle, Thomas Netter of Walden, and John of Bromyard, in this order. Now since Rolle lived c. 1290–1349, Netter c. 1380–1430, and Bromyard would come somewhere between them, this date 1419 can have no claims to any precision. My final reference to the Bodleian MS., date 1409, therefore still holds the field for the present. The Dominican writers in *The English Dominican Province* (Cath. Truth Soc.), 1921 (cf. p. 75, etc.) have obviously taken their reference blindly from Fletcher's article in the *Reliquary*.

[3] Close Rolls (Record Off.), 14 Edw. II (c. 1321), p. 326. Cf. *Reg. Anim.* (MS. Harl. 2272, fol. 9): "(Religiosi) de licencia *suorum* prelatorum,... possunt licite accedere ad saracenos pro verba Dei predicando." Cf. *Cal. of Pap. Records*, vol. iv, p. 106, for a license to an English monk and twelve others "to go and preach the Word of the Lord in the lands of the Infidels," in 1373, etc.

children of the synagogue[1]. Bromyard himself, who reckons preachers amongst the seven classes of good labourers in the world, seems to speak with personal acquaintance of the toils of worthy religious, "attenuati et vexati laboribus et infirmitatibus," true followers alike of the Man of Sorrows and their own indefatigable Founders. Passages like that which discusses with an intimate knowledge and sympathy not unworthy of the best type of modern social worker the problem of the prostitute[2], compel us to believe that there were still friars of the noblest pattern, consecrated to holy service amid the mediaeval slum and its outcasts.

> 'Twas August, and the fierce sun overhead
> Smote on the squalid streets of Bethnal Green.
>
> . . . .
>
> I met a preacher there I knew, and said—
> "Ill and o'erworked, how fare you in this scene?"
> "Bravely!" said he; "for I of late have been
> Much cheer'd with thoughts of Christ...."[3]

Among their number there would be those who might complain with justice that they had toiled all night and gained nothing but kicks and blows, and insults:

> Messangers to bid men come to heven, as doctors and prechers of the word of God, as thei do now daye by daye, but ʒe sett not by hem, the more harme is. Som go yn to youre citte, that is to youre unclene felishippe, as to the taveron, and to other unhoneste place. Som to youre unthrifty merchandize, full of usure, okre, and other falsenes. Some taken is prechers and punyssh hem unto the dethe. But what shall the kynge do thereto, this kynge of kynges? Certeyn, sir, as Criste hymselfe seid, he shall lat slee hem, and brenne the cite of hem[4].

Though Bromyard, in common with his fellows, speaks more than once of the heavenly pilgrim fleeing through the pestilent scenes of earth, his mind stopped, as the cautious traveller

---

[1] There is interesting evidence of this in the *S.P.—Fides*, where Bromyard developes lengthy arguments for the benefit of their conversion, doubtless intended to be used in sermons addressed to them. For the London "Domus Conversorum," given by Henry III, in 1233, see M. Paris, *Chron. Maj.*

[2] Cf. *S.P.—Luxuria*: "...Aliae dicunt quod si peccatum illud dimitterent, non haberent unde viverent cum prole sua, quia, si homines illos, qui eas propter illud exhibent, vel munera eis dant, derelinquerent, paupertate deficerent....Aliae, quod vi opprimuntur...," etc.

[3] Matthew Arnold, *East London.*

[4] MS. Roy. 18. B. xxiii, fol. 56 b. Cf. the Vernon MS. poem in E.E.T.S. 117, p. 684; and *Gesta Rom.*, 15th cent. Engl. vers., E.E.T.S. ed., pp. 30, 31.

stops his nose, from the noisome places, yet he knows also the value of the good life in a naughty world, lived out "inter malos." "As the brightness of stars and candle is better seen and shines more brightly by night than by day," he says, "so are they who dwell in the midst of a perverse people."[1]

The obstacles and counter-attractions that beset the preacher's path and made it thorny enough, were many. There were the smartly-dressed ladies who with bewitching looks led onlookers away to the dances[2]. Not even the twelve apostles themselves, says Bromyard bitterly, would have held the attention of an audience in their presence. There were the shows, the miracle-plays, the taverns, the witches and magicians, Sunday dinners and Sunday sports, the summer joys of the open-air, and many things more, permanently arrayed against them[3]. Hark to the devil's bell calling the worshippers to his evil sanctuary, the merry beat of the drum, the ribald songs of the dancers, the tempting wares and dainties of the world's great Vanity Fair! "...Thei taken noon of goddis word; thei rennen to interludes with gret delijt; ʒhe—that is more reuthe!—to strumpetis daunce. The preest for hem mai stonde alone in the chirche; but the harlot in the clepyng [chepyng? = market-place] shal be hirid for good money to tellen hem fablis of losengerie."[4] But even within the pale of the Church itself was another foe, the hostile parish rector, who could often bar access to the very pulpits the friar was most anxious to command. So formidable became the struggle between them that it passes into the pages of contemporary literature as a byword of the times. The author of *Piers Plowman's Vision* repeats Fitzralph's complaint about the rival popularity of the friar confessors, and describes

[1] *S.P.*—*Conversatio.*

[2] Cf. the earlier story told by Etienne de Bourbon (see *Anecd. Hist.* p. 161) of the dancers who interrupted an open-air sermon with their songs—developed into a favourite sermon *exemplum* of later times.

[3] Such references are most numerous, especially in the *S.P.* (cf. *Audire*, passim): "Loquitur trufator, loquitur vetula, loquitur detractor, loquitur sortilega de his quae ad damnationem pertinent animarum, et multos habent auditores;...loquitur Christus, et ejus ministri,...et dicunt 'quis est hic?' (Eccl. 13)." "[Diaboli] volentes ire ad verbum Dei ducunt ad tabernam vel spectacula...." Cf. Brunton, MS. Harl. 3760, fol. 176: "Isti tamen ad longam dietam libenter vadunt ad luctas, nundinas, et spectacula, ad vanam recreationem corporum, ubi vix ad unum miliare laborant ad audiendum sermonem."

[4] MS. Harl. 2276, fol. 37.

the ravages of Wrath in terms of the ensuing contest between them and the outraged parsons. In the "Crede," the arch-enemy of Mendicants tells how "thei comen in to combren the chirche by the coveiteise of his craft, the curates to helpen. And now they haven an hold, they harmen full many."[1] Chaucer's friar of the *Somnour's Tale* must repeat the well-worn charge— "Thise curats been ful negligent and slowe."[2] By the time John Skelton is reached, the application of friars to hold forth in the parish churches furnishes a whole episode of humour for a "Merrie Tale."[3] Even bishops' Registers are not without their side-light on the matter. Laymen explain at a parochial visitation, for example, with regard to the preaching of their vicar, that whereas his predecessors had been wont to call on friars for the purpose, the present incumbent did not care for them, and gave little encouragement if they happened to appear on the scenes[4].

Into the general history of this unhappy struggle, it is im-possible to enter fully. The main issue at stake can be traced with ease in the records of Conciliar and Papal decrees[5]. It is concerned with the question as to whether friars had the right to preach, and, incidentally, to hear confessions, without the special leave both of the bishop of the diocese and the particular "curate" concerned. Before our special period has dawned, however, an elaborate body of legislation has made its appear-ance, to safeguard the situation[6]. The Mendicant preacher must not preach in the parish church itself without the rector's per-mission. Neither may he preach to parishioners in some other spot, when the rector or his chosen substitute wishes to address them. This was even made to apply to conventual houses in the neighbourhood, except where situated in University towns[7].

---

[1] Skeat's ed. (E.E.T.S.), l. 461, etc.
[2] *Cant. Tales, Somn. Tale*, l. 1816.   [3] *Merrie Tales of Skelton*, No. 8.
[4] Colyton, Devon, 1301. (Reg. Bp. Stapledon, Ex. vol. ii.)
[5] Cf. in our period a mandate of Simon Langham, Archbp. of Canter-bury, "contra fratres mendicantes," 1366 (Wilkins, *Conc.* vol. iii, p. 64). Also the limiting Bull of Pope Martin V, in 1418; and, for the earlier Papal privileges granted, relevant Bulls of Gregory IX, Alexander IV, Boniface VIII, etc.
[6] Cf. *Cil. Oc. Sac.* here (MS. Harl. 4968, fol. 40 b, etc.).
[7] "...[nec] in habitaculis suis juxta parochiam ipsam constitutis, nisi loca ipsa in studiis generalibus fuerint. Tunc enim licet eis in loco et tempore consuetis ad clerum facere publicam sermonem sine licentia rectoris." (Ibid.)

If, furthermore, the prelates have convoked their clergy for the same time of day, then must the friars desist also. At other times, it is true, they may preach lawfully in public streets, in their own houses, at funerals, and at their own celebrations. "Yet this restriction must be observed, that wherever they preach, they shall not disparage the 'curates,' nor draw away their parishioners from the churches, nor say anything calculated to discourage them from payment of tithes or other ecclesiastical dues, nor otherwise corrupt their minds."[1] Behind the careful summary, as a matter of fact, there lay a world of violent speech and opposition. On the one side, Fitzralph of Armagh, arguing fiercely in London against those who deny that "the ordenary persoon is more worthy to be chese than any freris person" as the parishioner's shrift-father[2], is followed by a line of successors. Over fifty years later, indeed, a prominent doctor like John Whitheyd, S.T.P., copies Fitzralph in a Sunday sermon at Dublin, and gets summoned before Convocation for his pains[3]. On the other side, the reminder to friars that "alle men of religion beeth acorsed that speketh in sermons other elliswhere aȝenst payenge of tythinges" might only appear to have inflamed them to fiercer opposition. Mr A. G. Little, quoting from Anthony Wood, describes how "in the years 1423 and 1424 there were nothing but heart-burnings in the University occasioned by the friars, their preaching up and down against tithes."[4] The same scholar gives us, in his study of the Oxford Greyfriars, the story of William Russell[5], Warden of the London House, of William Melton[6], and others, arrested now by the archbishop, now by the University itself for a similar offence; finally of the Graduation oath at Inception imposed on all faculties at Oxford, explicitly disavowing the views of Russell.

---

[1] Further: "...Alioquin, si presumant aliquid dicere in sermonibus contra solutiones decimarum, ipso facto excommunicati sunt."

[2] See MS. Add. 24194, fol. 8.

[3] See Wilkins, *Conc.* vol. iii, pp. 324–5. He seems to have spoken of the friars, "qui dicunt subditis non teneri confiteri eorum curatis," as "thieves, wolves and robbers." He may be called "prominent," as he appears among the archbishop's special "consiliarii et ministri," who conduct the trial of Sir John Oldcastle for heresy, in London, 25th September, 1413. (See *Fascic. Ziz.* (Rolls S.), p. 443.)

[4] See *Grey Friars in Oxford*, especially pp. 85, 86 and 257.

[5] For the sermon of 1425 see Wilkins, *Conc.* vol. iii, p. 434.

[6] See also *Bekyng. Corresp.* (Rolls S.), vol. ii, p. 248 et seq.

The Mendicant campaign, however, had not been without its effect. Says a contemporary document:

There has arisen in the province of Canterbury no little scandal, and serious revolts against the clergy have appeared. Many there are who are striving to withdraw such tithes; many have already actually withdrawn them; and in truth it is feared that more will be hindered from payment of such tithings, to the very great impoverishment and obvious injury of curates and particularly of vicars[1].

Armagh's own description of the kind of propaganda referred to had been clear enough:

And so dooth, as we seith comounliche, confessoures of freres, and telleth openliche that ȝevers of almes in tythinge, of wynnynge of chaffare, beeth nouȝt i-holde to paie tithynges of breed, of wyn, of ale, and of other smal thynges[2]....

That the homiletical attacks of the friars do often throw grim light on the unquestionable vices and degradation of the seculars will have been gathered from an earlier chapter. The heretical theme of brother Thomas Richmond of the Friars Minor of York is an example, only too well justified indeed by accumulated evidence of every kind. Preaching in the vernacular in the year 1426, to a vast concourse of clergy and laity in a picturesque spot on the outskirts of the city, he had declared in Waldensian fashion: "A priest fallen into mortal sin is not a priest. Again I say that he is not a priest; and thirdly I say that before God he is no priest."[3] His attack, which broadens into

---

[1] See Wilkins, *Conc.* vol. iii, p. 452. (Prov. Conv., London, 1425.)

[2] MS. Add. 24194, fol. 9 b. With this compare the interesting warnings of the fifteenth century vernacular homily collection *Jacob's Well* (E.E.T.S., O.S. No. 115, p. 33): "...And all religious persons that in preaching or in any other place say any words to make the people of evil will to pay their tithes" (from *Extrav. de poenis*, Clem. c. 3, de pp. 5, 8). Again: "And all religious men that stir not them that are shriven of them to pay their tithes, if they preach afterwards—'till they have stirred their consciences to amendment." Similarly (in Latin) in MS. Harl. 4968, fol. 40 b: specifying—"scil. jᵃ dominica, iiijᵃ, et ultima Pasche, et in festis Ascensⁱˢ Domⁱ, Pentecostis, Nativitⁱˢ Sᵗⁱ Johⁱˢ Bapt., Assumptⁱˢ et Nativitⁱˢ Beate Marie, studeant expresse informare audientes ut decimas persolvant, ac etiam sibi confitentes similiter instruant...." Notice how the monk Rypon, at Durham, in his sermon (cf. MS. Harl. 4894, fol. 109 b) does his duty in this respect, warning his congregation against depriving the Church of "decimas, oblationes, possessiones, cantarias, vel talia debita."

[3] "Sacerdos in peccato mortali lapsus, non est sacerdos. Iterum dico quod non est sacerdos; et tertio dico quod non est sacerdos coram Deo."

a developed argument for the right of secular judges and lay-folk to cleanse the Church of its immoral priesthood, by laying hands on the offenders and clapping them into jail, may savour of Lollardy, but it is only one step, a logical and practical step, beyond the denunciations of the eminent anti-Wycliffite Brom-yard. Of incontinent priests the latter had himself asserted that the "swinish life" ("vitam porcinam") many of them led, had infected the whole Church, and threatened its downfall. Although such proposed violation of the Rights of Clergy as Richmond suggested would not have commanded his assent, yet Bromyard, like other orthodox, turns sometimes with a wistful eye, as Wycliffe and the Reformers turned, to the civil princes[1], hoping that with their aid it may be possible to achieve what a vice-ridden, demoralized prelacy could never do by its own effort. The pulpit relations between *curatus* and itinerant fill him with dismay. Many rectors and "curates" care little enough about the spiritual welfare of their folk. They think only of what profit may be made out of them.

And this is clear from daily example and experiment. For, the dogs who are willing to guard the flock, that is to say, the poor Mendicants, they restrict, because they fear that their own emoluments will be less. But "there were they in great fear, where no fear was." Because the richer gain would have been theirs, as much through the instruction as the good example of the preachers. This is obvious in their action, however, that more do they fear the loss of moneys than of souls. And thus, contrary to the practice of good shepherds, they neither cherish nor support such dogs, that is, the preachers, but rather hinder and harass them[2].

---

[1] Cf. *S.P.*—*Juramentum*: "Si principes et domini moderni talia (punishments) nunc ubique terrarum contra turpiter jurantes ordinarent, citius ipsi quam predicatores corrigerent; quia citius metu poenarum sensibilium quam metu poenarum eternalium quas predicatores eis minantur talia dimitterent...," etc. See also under *Nobilitas*. For the same in other sermon collections, cf. MS. Roy. 18. B. xxiii, fol. 146 b: "...And trewly this gret wronge and myscheff may not be amended withouten he[l]pe of temporall lordes,—as, wold Jhesu, that thei wold do here besenes to amende it. And ʒiff thei see prestehode defawtiff, or unclene of lyvynge, and thei wold compleyne to the bishoppes, I wene fully that itt shuld be amended; for I wene the faders of the churche wold punysche as the law wold, iff thei were spoken thus to, and trewly....And iff it so happe that anny of the prelatis wold be negligent, and not amende thise defawtes, me semeth, an oure soneraygne lord of is goodnes wold bid them take hede to suche defawtes, I have no dowte that it shuld sonne be amended."

[2] *S.P.*—*Custodia*. Cf. above, p. 46 (Rypon, etc.).

A Cambridge manuscript, containing sermons and a short "Ars Predicandi," will be found to provide an illustration of the arguments on the other side[1]. They are embodied here in an interesting Petition of the Rectors of London against the Mendicant inroads, undated, but belonging apparently to the early fourteenth century. From its clauses we may gather that "the said friars in their public preachings maliciously slander the rectors of the churches in the aforesaid city, with evil reports of their vice and folly; and frequently in hateful manner they preach foul and scandalous things about them, to their prejudice, no little hurt, and annoyance." Some of these Mendicants are suspected of having no proper preaching license from their superiors[2]. Moreover, they are accused, in addition, of tacitly deluding their audiences into the belief that they possess special authority to give a general absolution[3] beyond anything in the power of the ordinary "curate." Finally, when haranguing, or hearing confessions, they fail to warn the people, as indeed they are bound to do, to confess to their own parish priest at least once in the year; and this to the imminent peril of their souls. Another anonymous tractate, now in the British Museum, of about the year 1383, "against the friars' license to preach,"[4] calls to witness the gentle advice of St Francis himself in his Rule[5] and Testament[6]. The writer then proceeds in a similar spirit:

After all, are not the friars linked with the priests in the preaching office to be their helpers? And if so, then the latter still remain the true pastors and principal labourers, nor has any man the right to take from them that preaching office. But they alone are the reapers in the Lord's field and the brothers are there to collect the ears that

---

[1] MS. Camb. Univ. Libr. Gg. iv. 32, fol. 124 et seq.

[2] Cf. the warning of the Council of Salzburg, 1386 (Labbe, S. Conc. vol. xxvi, col. 729): "Volumus tamen quod nequaquam dicti rectores ipsos (i.e. mendicants) invitent, vel admittant, nisi de proponendo verbum Dei a suis superioribus licentiam habeant."

[3] Cf. here Reg. Bp. Brantingham (Exet.), pt. i, p. 567 (entry for 1384–5); and pt. ii, p. 711 (entry for 1390): Chaucer, Cant. Tales: James the Cistercian in MS. Roy. 6. E. vii, fol. 162.   [4] MS. Roy. 7. E. x, fol. 63 et seq.

[5] Reg. ii, cap. ix (ed. Quaracchi, p. 71): "Let the brothers not preach in the diocese of any bishop, when he shall have forbidden it."

[6] Ed. Quaracchi, p. 78: "If I had the wisdom of Solomon, and I came upon poor priests of this world in the parishes in which they dwelt, I would not preach against their will."

escape the reapers' hands[1]....As often as the priest, then, is as sufficient to preach in his own person as the friar, I do not see that the latter ought to interfere with the preaching, thrusting his sickle into another's harvest.

We may be still left wondering at the end which party was the more justified in its complaints[2]. But in the *Summa Predicantium* there is manifest at least in one place a wiser tone, even as in the above quotation from the side of the rectors. Its Dominican author confesses of his party, "there are some who preach with hatred in their hearts towards others. Let them avoid all such hatred and contention (ne rector ecclesiae, dum soli sibi jus predicationis vendicat, etiam aliis recte predicantibus invidia se mordente contradicet)."[3] A letter from Thomas Netter of Walden to the prior and brethren of the Carmelite house at York shows that even a friar superior was prepared sometimes to correct such hostile attitude in a brother of his own Order[4].

Of pulpit controversy between the friars and the older monastic Orders in the Church, one instance must suffice[5]. In the year 1445 a certain leading Franciscan of Coventry, John Bredon, S.T.P.[6], preached a sermon, on the Sunday before the Feast of St Andrew, in the parish church of St Michael, attacking a jealously-guarded privilege of the prior and convent of the cathedral church ostensibly in the public interest:

[1] "Ut dicitur in figura, Ruth v."
[2] See also, in connection with the controversy over Confession, the opinions of Henry Crump in *Fascic. Ziz.* (Rolls S.), p. 351.
[3] *S.P.—Predicatio.*
[4] c. 1426, Epist. Waldensis, in *Mon. Hist. Carmel.*, pt v, pp. 474–5 (ed. 1907). (Thos. Walden to Mag. Jo. Bate, etc.): "...Communis plurimum patrum nuper ad me pervenit querela, de verbo quod predicando Doncastriae in conventu frater Joh. Leysingus, in Purificationis festo elapso, protulit in prejudicium ecclesiae parochialis, dicendo oblationes ejusdem festi ad arbitrium offerentis equa licentia posse fieri in aliis ecclesiis sicut in parochiali, ut aliae oblationes votivae... (etc.). Et sequitur, debuit filius noster eo cautius previdisse et vitasse periculum, quo audivit presentius constitutionem capituli nostri jam ultimo Oxoniae celebrati, contra tales in prelatorum prejudicium predicantes...." (These Chapter Acts mentioned (Oxford, 1426) are now missing, see note, p. 475.)
[5] This should be read in connection with Mr Little's *Studies in Engl. Franc. Hist.* Chap. iii, upon which it throws some fresh light.
[6] He appears again, reported as "cursing" the preaching of the hermit John Grace, at Coventry in 1424. See reference below, p. 127, n. 1.

Hyt is not unknowen that where the prior and covent of the church Cathedral of our lady seynt Mary of this cite of Coventre, persones proprietaries of the parishe chirches of the same, and their predecessoures have had, posseded, and used to have as in rygth of the seid chirche, of time that no minde of manne is the contrarie, th^t what person dye w^t in this seide cite, suburbes, and hamelettes of the same hath ben first brought to the seid cathedral chirche w^t apparail of wex, ther to a byde tille the masse and other observaunces to cristen pepul perteynyng be complete, and had the corps ther of then to be beried other at the same Cathedral chirche, or elles at on of the parishe chirkes or chirche 3erde wer the person of the dede corps was conversant, or ther wer in his live he chase his sepultur, the seid apparail of wex remaynyng w^t the seid Cathedral chirche to the use of the same with taile and possession,—is gode as wele be the lay (*sic*) spirituale as by the lawe temporal.

Against what may have seemed to some of the laity merely a tiresome habit of the past involving unnecessary expense, and to the Mendicants of the city the unfair advantage of rivals, friar Bredon now thundered in no measured language, as we shall see. Enemies from the convent itself were amongst his audience, ready to snatch at his words. On the Sunday following the feast, he repeated his challenge in the church of Holy Trinity. Masters John Wardale and Richard Newport, we note, are again present to witness against him, along with others.

Bredon's subsequent recantation which records the principal statements of his two harangues is sufficiently interesting and suggestive to justify further quotation at length:

"I frer Jhon Bredon," he confesses, "of the convent of this same cite in the time of the holy advent of our lorde last passed [last], in the parish chirches of this same cite, a3ennes the seid custom and titul, as our soverain lorde the king, and the lordes spiritual and temporal ben a certed, opunly prechid and affermed th^t all maner offeringes owed to be geven al only (to) theam that ministren the sacramentes to the parishones. Also th^t nether the pope, ne all the world may compelle any man to offer any thing in the seid Cathedral chirke. Also th^t neither the pope, ne all the world may make but that a fre man in his laste wille may dispose the lightes perteynyng to his cors wher so ever he wille.

"And so I, inducing the parishons of the seid parishe chirches to excute my purpose, bot that thei schulde boldely ber the lightes of the cors fro that tyeme forward to their parishchirke or whether thei elles wolde, not wythstondyng any contrare use, promitteng my self to defende thaem th^t so did, seyng that in Englond was not so leude a cite as this cite of Coventre is, in keping and observyng the seid customme, and promiteng my selfe to make this same cite free, so th^t the said prior and covent schuld not prevale to have theire said customes, wich seyng mygth cause the pepul to turne their hertes fro the seid prior and covent, and fro observyng the seid lawful custom. And also that I seid that in Englond was not so covetous a plase as was the priory of Coventre. Also that I, impugnyng the seide custom by a nother unlawfull mene, seid and affermed that any custom how long so ever hyt be, thogth hit be a hunderth ʒeres, if hit (be) in preiudice of comune wele, it is unlawfull. And that the seid custom is in preiudice of comune good, by cause hit is preiudiciall to the parish chirkes of holy Trinitee and sent Michel of Coventre, and therfor that hit is unlawfull. Also that I seid that all onely thei that ministren the sacramentes and ministren abowte the cors, as vicaris and parish preestes schuld have the obevenciouns and profetes of the cors, and not the monks of the priory which may not minister the sacramentes. Also that I in my billes that I made to be sette upon the chirke dores in the seide cite promised to deliver the pepul of the same cite fro the thraldom of Pharoo, the whiche sownyth aʒaynes the seid Cathedral chirke and the lawful custom of the same.

"In all theis promisses by the lordes spiritual and Temporal, by the commawment of our seid soveran lorde the king, duly examined, is fownden mater upon the which mygth swe grete inconveniences aʒaynes the lawes of good, and of the chirke, and of our saide soveran lorde, and also preiudiciall to the seid prior and convent.... "[1]

The heavy hand of the temporal authority was evidently ready this time to descend with that of the spiritual upon this would-be liberator of the people. The outraged monks appealed to the sovereign with success. Like the majority, when the heat of the pulpit is over, Bredon recants, and "Pharaoh" triumphs again for a season. But even this did not save the condemned from the penalty of banishment from the town. John Lawerne, S.T.P., monk of the convent of Worcester, not far away, whom we shall meet again preaching his doctor's sermon at Oxford, proceeds to enter the friar's recantation in his commonplace book[2], not perhaps without some inward sense of jubilation.

[1] The above is taken from a transcript of MS. Linc. Cath. Libr. A. 4. 16, generously supplied to me by the Rev. Canon R. M. Woolley, of Lincoln. The recantation alone is printed in Leland's *Collectanea*, vol. v, p. 303. See also in M. Dormer Harris, *Life in an old English Town*, pp. 326–27, with reference to the Coventry Leet Book, etc.

[2] It is from this Bodl. MS. that Leland has taken his copy of the Recantation. See here again later, in Chap. vi, below.

Finally, the story of this preaching rivalry has to be carried one step further. For there is actual evidence that the friars quarrelled among themselves, over "the limits" assigned to their houses—"for the purpose of making procurations of alms, or preachings."[1]

But enough of controversies and rivalries! It is to the glory of the Mendicant preachers of all the Orders that, as champions of the poor, they attacked the tyranny and oppression of lords, the weaknesses of knights, the ravages of retainers, the cunning and extortion of merchants, the corruption of the law, in short, every conceivable form of injustice in the land. With passionate violence they arraigned the social frivolities of the age in high and low alike, the amusements men preferred to the holy services of the Church. Nothing escapes their notice. To set forth the details would require a volume as large as the present. Nor, in very different vein, do we miss evidences of that more frivolous, jesting element in their sermons, which, with the elaborate theological "divisions," and hair-splittings over a debased Scholasticism, was pilloried by Wycliffe, and has passed into history, perhaps, as the chief feature of their preaching, to the prejudice of the rest. This element, as might be expected, however, is anything but characteristic of the Mendicant sermon literature as a whole. Like the tombs and inscriptions that perplexed the youthful Charles Lamb when in church, the manuscript homily collections are naturally apt to be recorders of the good, and let the evil be forgotten. Yet indeed few English orthodox moralists of the age failed to incorporate their own rebuke for the preacher of "fablis and lesyngis" and indecencies in some section of their written sermons[2]. If we are inclined to associate such offences rather

---

[1] From a Papal Inhibition of September 1395, drawn up "at the recent petition of the custos, guardian, and brethren of the House of Friars Minor at Cambridge," complaining of their impoverishment "by a certain small House of the Order" at Ware, in Herts., "whose brethren extend the bounds of their procurations so far toward Cambridge" that very great loss to the former results. See *Cal. of Papal Letters*, vol. iv, p. 517.

[2] E.g. Bromyard, *S.P.* (*Audire, Predic.* etc.)—("Aliqua grossa, et foeda, et putrida, sic paleas, et hujusmodi": "apertam fatuitatem": "curiosa et vana (et jocosa) quae aures demulcent auditorum," etc.) Rypon, MS. Harl. 4894, fol. 84 ("Non linguas turpia loquentes;...frivolas sive vanas..."). MS. Add. 21253, fol. 54 ("Trufas et fabulas"). MS. Harl. 4968, fol. 46 ("avertent ad fabulas"). MS. Roy. 18. B. xxiii, fol. 150 b ("fables and tryfuls"). So, too, the writers on Sermon Construction, like Walleys, mentioned below, in Chap. VIII, q.v.

with the pardoner than with the friar, it was at least the latter who systematized the collection and preservation of the witty and improper stories on a grand scale. Moreover, there is the contemporary witness of the Council of Salzburg (1386) to support the Wycliffite assertion: "religiosos, precipue fratres mendicantes."[1] In a world devoid alike of the newspaper and the printed book, of the means of rapid communication by land or sea, the itinerant orator had surely an opportunity which any man of ambition might envy. The sermons themselves show, it is true, that there were plenty of active sports, shows, folk-dances, jugglers, to amuse the holiday crowd. But while the rich could enjoy in the leisure and comfort of their own hall the more substantial provision for the mind of minstrel's songs, the wonders of costly romances, the actor's miming, if they cared, for the poor there was little or nothing but the coarsest fare in this direction. The bard of the courts had himself degenerated. But the "joculator's" jokes and comments were unspeakable for decent ears. He who would escape, in an age of mental awakening, from the narrow round of daily manorial duties, from the mere idle chatter of the pedlars and the inns, the obscenities of the street entertainers, into a wider, more fascinating world of interest and of wonder, might find it as he listened to the Preachers. Here was a man trained in the schools who could tell him of all the marvels of creation, from Bartholomew or Cantimpratanus, in earth and sea and firmament[2], mighty "gestes" of the Romans, wondrous miracles of the saints and martyrs. Modern preachers, eyeing the spoilt children of the modern pew, may well envy the prospect that lay before our mediaeval friar. Traveller, friend of the outcast, master alike of the ecclesiastical and the popular tongue, with intimate knowledge of the world as well as of books, he could mingle in his discourse the latest "narration" with the mysteries of nature, "to please in method and invent by rule"—"joculator

---

[1] " ... Saepe divagandi et dissolutionis materiam mutuantur, ad scandalum aliorum, et tanquam pseudo-prophetae fabulosis praedicationibus audientium animos plerumque seducunt."

[2] Cf. Bromyard's own confession (S.P.—Predic.): " ... curiositates et declarationes et rationes philosophorum, et dubias naturas animalium, quae omnia literatorum aures demulcent ... vel praedicantium gloriam querunt...," etc.

o

Dei" of St Francis and sacred pedlar rolled into one—for ever bringing forth out of his treasure things new and old[1].

The age of Bromyard is actually an age when manuscripts of the Travels of Maundeville can challenge the popularity of almost any other work and come off triumphant, at least in surviving numbers. Quite naturally, then, it is also the period when great English versions of the preachers' "exemplaria" are undertaken—such as Bartholomew's standard *De Proprietatibus Rerum*[2], the *Gesta Romanorum* and the *Alphabetum Narrationum*. The very fact that the Church itself was driven to combat both actor and acrobat in the open, would have suggested to her in time the way in which to compete with them for the ear and eye of the idle onlooker. Our learned Dominican himself, who disapproves most heartily of all "light and shameless persons," like the "mimi et trufatores" (whether in the pulpit or out of it)[3], and with charming satirical humour likens the idle prattler to a draughty vacant barn[4], yet uses hundreds of fables, anecdotes and "figures" natural and domestic in his sermon book. Now and again the reader pictures the awakened congregation, eagerly leaning forward to catch some fragment of a traveller's reminiscence, as he describes the perils of Italian roads, a vineyard custom in France he has observed, or some game which is "commoner in parts beyond the sea."

John Bromyard belongs to a race of preachers who, for all their learning, yet live close to life and nature beyond the pages of books. They know all the everyday sights of the streets, the ways of simple folk, even of domestic animals[5], and can reproduce them by way of illustrating a point with astonishing charm and vividness. If, however, the *Summa Predicantium*

---

[1] This very phrase of scripture is applied to the preacher's task by Odo of Cheriton, in the Prologue to his *Fables*: "Paterfamilias debet proferre de thesauro suo nova et vetera verba et exempla, quibus reficiatur fidelis anima." (See Hervieux, *Fabul. Lat.* vol. iv, p. 174.)

[2] Translated by Trevisa, 1398–9. Examples are MSS. Add. 27944, Harl. 614 and 4789. For the other works mentioned see here in Chap. VII, below.

[3] Yet, characteristically enough, is not above recommending their methods in his hints to preachers, elsewhere. (*S.P.—Predic.*: "sicut ergo mimus....")

[4] "Grainge voide venteuse"; apparently a French proverb ("sicut venti plus abundant in grangia vacua quam plena,...ita ventus verborum...").

[5] Bromyard actually mentions some disease of sheep, and describes the altered habits of the pet monkey in its old age.

and the *Gesta Romanorum* represent the least harmful side of this concession to the popular taste, there is also a worst. The scandalous sermon parodies reproduced in the *Reliquiae Antiquae*, the famous Sermons Joyeuses on the continent, would be almost pointless if they had not had some kind of a real counterpart in the contemporary pulpit. As a matter of fact we have better reason to know that they did. There are even a few sermons in English collections that remain[1] which would fully justify the rebuke of a fifteenth-century English preacher for those who play to a vulgar gallery in the churches, "si come le cordeller fesoit devant-hier."[2]

Maybe such specimens are in a very marked minority in the manuscripts; yet so important for the subsequent history both of preaching and of the Orders is this disastrous outgrowth of vulgarity in the wider sense that its prevalence cannot be doubted. This need not necessarily take the form of what Higden calls "puerilis scurrilitas."[3] Wherever in any age the spirit of genuine piety and true learning is at a low ebb in the Church, there is a tendency for the preachers to become mere charlatans, masters of cheap emotions rather than of the arts, with eyes set on the face of the crowd instead of the Crucified. This was eminently Pecock's complaint of the preaching of his day:

For manye, which nevere leernid ferther in scolis than her grammer, kunnen suche textis bi herte and bi mouth, and kunnen, bi textis, and by narraciouns and parabolis, and lijknessis, preche ful gloriosely into plesaunce of the peple, and into profite of the peple, and semen therfore and therbi ful wise. And if thei were weel

---

[1] Cf. one or two sermons of the *Festiall*; Nich. Philip's Synodal sermon in MS. Bodl. Lat. Th. d. i; etc. For the far more numerous foreign examples, cf. *Hist. Litt. de la Fr.* vol. xxvi, pp. 407, etc. (prédic. bouffon.); Méray's *Les Libres prêcheurs*, vol. ii, chap. xi; Coulton, *From St Francis to Dante*, p. 358, n. 7 (Appendix A).

[2] From MS. All Souls Coll. Oxf. 182, quoted in *Revue Crit. d'hist. et de litt.* (1870), vol. ii, p. 405. (A few lines are in P. Meyer's edition of Bozon's *Contes*, p. xxviii, n.): "Mon amy, il m'est avis que un precheur ne devroit mye parler si ordement devant le comon peuple....Car combien que n'en parle le plus honestement qu'ils pourront, il en y a encores des aucunes qui le vueillent espondre malveysement; et pour cela il s'enfaut estre bien avysee qui parlera devant les gens. Mieulx vault par raison fortune attendre, que hastyvement ramper et sodoynement descendre."

[3] MS. Bodl. 5, fol. 2.

apposid in any of the textis, and parabolis, and othere precheable processis, thei couthe not defende and meyntene eny oon of hem.

If, however, the opinion of such a man be held suspect, we can match it from the other end of the intellectual scale with the regret of our simple non-graduate preacher that "doctours and wyse men of holy scripture" are so scarce. "ʒiff suche men were now adayes that the pepull myght fynde suche truste in, than myght thei well say as holy scripture seyth—'Magister, scimus quod verax es, et viam Dei in veritate doces.'"[1]

Time was when the University friar had bid fair to be the only serious champion of Biblical studies left. But the neglect which in its hold upon the seculars had once given Adam de Marisco and Roger Bacon their great opportunity to distinguish themselves, together with this fatal attraction of "fables and flattering," had now gripped the friars also. The great tradition was allowed to perish, as we saw in discussing the clergy, at the expense of more lucrative sciences. Richard de Bury's words, in the first half of the fourteenth century, form a solemn indictment of the Orders and the lack of adequate preparation for their preaching task[2]. Books they now count as superfluities, except for the few treatises of little worth on which they rely for the "strange heresies" and "apochryphal imbecillities" they scatter, "not for the refreshment of souls, but rather for tickling the ears of their listeners." This same Holy Scripture, he declares, is treated as though it were a commonplace, known to everybody, though in reality its depth can never be probed by lifelong study. Mere boys who have been attracted to the Order are sent out on offensive preaching-and-begging expeditions, without any proper instruction at all. Hence those who have learnt least are often to be found the most aggressive in their instruction of others. "For there grows up among your promiscuous flock of laity a pestilent multitude of creatures, who nevertheless the more shamelessly force themselves into the office of preaching, the less they understand what they are saying, to the contempt of the Divine Word and the injury of souls." ("Resipiscite, pauperes Christi, et libros inspicite studiose!")

So doubtless the abuse spread, as the moralized story-books,

---

[1] MS. Roy. 18. B. xxiii, fol. 75. (Text, Matthew xxii, 16.)
[2] *Philobiblon*, cap. vi (now attributed to Dominican authorship).

and the little sermon manuals (Bury's "quidam quaterni" perhaps), multiplied. "Wax-Doctors," in the open pulpit, would after all look precisely like other doctors, with the pillion of authority on their heads, however little of real knowledge there might be under it[1]. Judicious use of those gentle arts of "showing off one's own knowledge" to advantage[2], or of pleasing the crowd with "vanities and curiosities," as described by Thomas Walleys and others, would be almost sure to produce the desired impression. So alas! "grees groon on out of gree, and prechingis rennen arere, as hereof experience is over ofte in my daies at Poulis Crosse takun."

There is sufficient evidence to suggest that even an element of skilful stage-craft has its place along with the low-comedy of the narrations or the high-flown phrases of the schools, in the developed preaching of the friars in the open air[3]. Be that as it may, the fact remains that judged by worldly standards it had become at length a paying profession, capable of stimulating any pride or avarice that its successful exponents might possess:

> Certes many a predicacioun
> Cometh ofte tyme of yvel intencioun[4].

What clearer justification could there be for the poet Chaucer's comment on "alle tho that prechen for to get worshipes, honour, and richesse," or for Wycliffe's complaints of the friar's pride, than the Austin friar preacher's own revelations in one of his sermons[5]? Many, smitten with this most hidden disease, he admits, will study nowadays not to serve God and their neighbour better, as they ought, but to acquire a solemn name for themselves, to "make themselves great," display their person,

---

[1] See especially in this connection, (beside R. Pecock), *Close Rolls*, 13 Rich. II (Record Off.), p. 217, dated 1390, *re* false degrees purchased at Oxford and Cambridge.

[2] As Bromyard puts it (*S.P.—Predic.*): "commiscendo cum semine Dei subtilitates philosophicas, et vanitates...," etc. (See also note, above, p. 81.)

[3] See here in Chap. v, below.

[4] Chaucer, *Cant. Tales* (Pardoner's Prol.), l. 407, and *Romaunt of the Rose*, ll. 5763–4.

[5] Dr John Waldeby. MS. Caius Coll. Camb. 334, fol. 187: "Hec enim occultissima pestis [temptatio vanae gloriae], ut arbitror, multos studiosos viros latenter invadit et decipit, qui obtentu laudis aut favoris humani aliquam scientiam seu doctrinam vigili studio querunt, non ut de se ipsis humilius sentiant, nec ut magis in Dei et proximi dilectione proficiant, ut deberent, sed ut solenne sibi nomen adquirant, ut se magnificent et ostendant, et alios ibi in honore precellant" (cf. also MS. Harl. 2276, fol. 119, etc.).

and to be esteemed above other men. It was a day when the devil could tempt men even to boast about their pulpit prowess[1].

THE "PREACHING FOX"
(Christchurch Priory, Hants)

Worse still, apart from fame and promotions, there was wealth too to be made out of the business. Again, it might surprise

---

[1] MS. Add. 21253, fol. 52 ("quando temptat hominem ut glorietur de sua predicatione"); cf. also Rypon, MS. Harl. 4894, fol. 196 b ("ambitionem,

many to discover how often in a single composition Chaucer refers to the ease with which friar and pardoner managed to extract money and gifts from the credulous poor by their unscrupulous eloquence[1]—"prechinge the peple for profyt of heore wombes," as Langland called it. Friar Bromyard and the anonymous author of a Lollard tract entitled "Contra mendicacionem fratrum propter predicacionem verbi Dei" (probably Purvey's) amongst the manuscripts of Trinity College, Cambridge, use virtually the same phrase: "Preachers must not preach for the gain of money, but for the gain of souls."[2] A vernacular sermon-compiler, no friend of Lollards, repeats the typical warning that "he that will not preach God's word but he be paid for his travail" is guilty of simony[3]. For the rest, a clause in the Petition of Oxford University to Henry V, presented in 1414[4], bears out the direct statement of Wycliffe that it was the Mendicant here who was the prominent offender.

In the picturesque language of his vernacular homilies the fearless Reformer tells how friars "prechen the peple fablis and falshede to plesen hem. And in tokene of this chaffare they beggen after that thei have prechid, as who seith—'Gyve me thi monei, that Y am worthi, bi my prechyng.' And this chaffare is selling of preching, however that it be florished."[5] It was,

gulam, et inanem gloriam inhiant et affectant"); Bromyard, *S.P.—Predic.* ("ut piscarentur...laudes humanas;...gloriam propriam querunt, etc."); Higden, MS. Bodl. 5, fol. 2 ("fabulosa vanitas"); Walleys, MS. Harl. 635, passim; MS. Harl. 45, fols. 70, 136, etc. ("As when a man precheth goddes word to that entente to have worldliche mede or worschip therfore" (especially mentions "mendinantes" later) etc.). Also *Piers Plowman*, A Text, l. 55 et seq.; *Ploughman's Crede*, ll. 497, 574, etc.; Gower; Chaucer.

[1] I have noted casually half a dozen in the *Cant. Tales.*

[2] Bromyard (*S.P.—Audire*). Anon. *Lollard* (MS. Trin. Coll. Camb. 333, fol. 65 b). Cf. the Cistercian James (MS. Roy. 6. E. vii, fol. 157[b]): "Fratres mendicantes predicantes propter lucrum seu ad ostentacionem, et se commendantes in suis predicacionibus, vel detrahentes prelatos...."

[3] *Jacob's Well* (E.E.T.S., O.S. 115), p. 127. Cf. also Higden's warning for the "Dei Venditores," in his *Ars Comp. Serm.* MS. Bodl. 5, fol. 1 b.

[4] Artic. 35 (concerning friar preachers). (Wilkins, *Conc.* vol. iii, p. 360): "Quia verbum Dei, ut venale, contemnitur; dum plerique predicantium sine mora et medio post sermonem mendicant, igitur, ut vitetur scandalum, expedire videtur ut a mendicatione in ecclesiis fratres abstineant in futuro."

[5] *Vernac. Sermons* (ed. Matthews, E.E.T.S.), p. 282; *Latin Sermons* (ed. Wicl. Soc.), vol. ii, pp. 57–58, etc. Cf. also *A Poem on the times of Edw. III* (Wright, *Pol. Songs*, Camden S. p. 331): "freres,...that wolde preche more for a busshel of whete, than for to bringe a soule from helle." Jack Upland (as before), p. 30: "Freer, what charite is this, to overcharge the people by mightie begging, under colour of preching?"

then, but one natural step further for the worldly preacher who had succeeded, to adopt a deliberately "lucrative" style of preaching. This is half the secret, no doubt, of the ceaseless warnings against pulpit flattery, flattery not only before lords but the common people also[1]. "Pauper" indeed, in the celebrated dialogue attributed by some to Franciscan authorship, goes so far as to suggest that the stern, health-giving element of moral censure in the contemporary pulpit had thus been actually driven from the scene altogether. With money-changers and evil merchants in the midst of Holy Church[2], the cry of the faithful few grew louder and hoarser—"as friends cry to their friend when they see fire or burglars threatening his house."[3] The world, to them, was staggering on the brink of Doomsday and final destruction, while everywhere, even in the very pulpits, men scrambled madly after the gold that perisheth.

But to return from the circumference to the centre: it is common knowledge how the Mendicant fell from his lofty pinnacle of holy poverty, and how great was the fall thereof, whether in respect of his character, his friends, his house, his methods, or his organization. Difficult would it be to overestimate the effects of this calamity upon the reputation of the Mendicants' preaching as a whole. Here, after all, was a fundamental discrepancy between word and action which no amount of glossing or argument could conceal. In England the glaring contrast was at least as old as the day of Matthew Paris, who with malicious zeal recalls the lordly buildings erected but a bare twenty-four years after the first Dominicans had set foot on English soil. Even Eccleston, the Franciscan chronicler, gives his strange witness to the fact that, through the worries of house building, more than one gifted spokesman of his Order

---

[1] MS. Add. 9066 vers. (c. 1440) of the *Gesta Rom.* (apparently added to the original) has: "Prelates and prechours that in thise daies dare not, ne wille not sey the trouthe, but flattre the peple. Wo shall be to such at domesday" (E.E.T.S. p. 178). *Dives et Pauper*, prec. 5, cap. v, has: "I daresay that flateringe of false prophetis and prechours, and of other spekers that blynde the peple with plesaunt lesinges, ne wyl not undo to them ther wickednesse, s principal cause of destruction of many realmys, and londes, people and cetyes into thys day; as we might se at iye, if flateringe and lesingis blent us not." See here, especially, the passage from MS. Salisb. Cath. 103, fol. 143 (unpublished *Jacob's Well*) as given on p. 189, Chap. IV, below.

[2] MS. Harl. 2276, fol. 119.

[3] Bromyard, *S.P.—Predic.*

had lost the inclination to preach, or at any rate to speak of the more spiritual things[1]. From thence the contagion had spread to their rich clothes and haughty mien, the company they aspired to keep, even to the very trappings of their steeds. So fastidious had the Mendicant become that the satirist of "the Order of Bel-Eyse" hints that he might now object to any preaching that involved exposure in the open air, or the risk of an empty stomach[2].

With the reopening of the long controversy over "wilful beggary" in the heart of our period, whether in Oxford schools or London church-yard, the prestige of friars in the pulpit must have suffered a tragic blow. They might almost be said to be ventilating their own hypocrisy. "Oon of that ordre (i.e. Minors) prechede on al halowenday, as hit was reported to me, and discreved foure degrees of povert, and seide that the fourthe degree is of most parfitȝnes of the gospel, and is to have nothing in this world in propre nother in comyn, but begge with Crist."[3] What if even Roger Conway, Minorite, "in concione Londini nuper habita," or Richard Maidstone, Carmelite, elsewhere, were theoretically right in their wearisome "conclusions"? The noble proportions of a Greyfriars tower at Richmond or the pillared splendour of a Blackfriars church in Norwich, all the little details of elaboration carefully noted down by the shrewd author of the *Ploughman's Crede*, were further proof enough, then as now, that: "thai preche alle of povert, but that love thai noght."[4] Yet as late as the year 1464, we find the Carmelite Henry Parker, with curious persistency, still joining issue with the seculars over the same old problem, from the cross at St Paul's. Actions, however, as even friars are ready to admit, speak as loud as words, especially with the unsophisticated layman. There can be little doubt, therefore, that the somewhat overdrawn Lollard picture of Mendicant hypocrisy represents none the less a very formidable widespread impression made by this blatant inconsistency[5]. Apart from lofty

---

[1] See *De Adv. Minorum*, cap. ix.

[2] From MS. Harl. 2253, fol. 121, as quoted in Wright's *Pol. Songs* (Camd. Soc.), p. 146 (cf. Chaucer, *Romt. of the Rose*, ll. 6486–88).

[3] MS. Add. 24194, fol. 15 b.   [4] In *Reliq. Ant.* vol. i, p. 323.

[5] Cf. Chaucer, *Romt. of the Rose*, ll. 6181 et seq.; ll. 6482 et seq.; also Jack Upland (p. 23, Rolls S., as before): "And in this minstrels ben better

towers and sumptuous convents, the sermons give us hints of
growing partiality for the rich, in confessions and burials, in
letters of fraternity, in hospitality, and the like. More particularly in the habits of the preacher, men noted that the so-
called preaching expedition began to look dangerously like a
triumphant progress from house to house, and court to court,
"aȝenst cristes owne sentence that sente his disciples to preche
the gospel, and seide 'passe ȝe nouȝt from hous to hous.'"[1]

> Quant il vont par le pays
> Al chief baroun ou chivaler
> Se lerrount il herberger,
> Ou a chief persone, ou prestre
> La, ou il purrount acese estre.   [acese = à s'e
> Mes, par seint Piere de Romme,
> Ne se herbigerount ou povre homme,—
> Taunt come plus riches serrount
> Ostiel plustost demanderount[2].

This gibe was intended for the friars Minor. But Dr Bromyard of the Blackfriars, also, has some very significant things to
say of Religious "who love rather to be with those reclining at
the court tables along with Herod, than in the prison-cell with
John."[3] He is speaking, in particular, of the friar who fawns
upon the rich for the good dinner he gets from them—"as
many do still."

than ye. For they contrarien not to the mirths that they maken. But yee
contrarien the gospell both in word and deed." (See, too, Wright, *Pol. Songs*,
Rolls S. vol. ii, p. 251.)

[1] MS. Add. 24194, fol. 13 (Archbp. Fitzralph of Armagh).

[2] *Order of Bel-Eyse*, as before. (Wright's *Pol. Songs*, Camd. Soc. p. 145.)

[3] Cf. again, Chaucer, "to haunten other mennes table" (*Romt. of the Rose*,
l. 6600). In ll. 6171 and following, the poet is almost repeating Bromyard's
criticism:

> "I dwelle with hem that proude be,
> And fulle of wyles and subtelte;
> That worship of this world coveyten,
> And grete nedes cunne espleyten;
> And goon and gadren greet pitaunces,
> And purchase hem the acqueyntaunces
> Of men that mighty lyf may leden;
> And feyne hem pore, and hemselfe feden
> With gode morcels delicious,
> And drinken good wyn precious,
> *And preche us povert and distresse,*
> *And fisshen hem-self greet richesse.*"

For though in that place, namely at court, he may not behold the head of John (i.e. the Baptist), yet he sees the widow's cow and the poor man's pig. The poor man is imprisoned and spoiled for the benefit of his master's table, and while the religious eats of the poor man's substance, and flatters the master, the rich man is lying in wait to plunder the poor again.... And a flatterer of this kind sits with the rich in secret, and slays the innocent while he is in agreement with the slayer. But, in truth, better it is to go to the house of weeping than to the house of such a banquet[1].

One of the few "exempla" at first hand in the *Summa* deals with a certain conversation which arose when in the writer's presence a fellow friar was seeking hospitality for the night from some man of property. If, however, the rich repelled him, as on this occasion, the itinerant orator stood a reasonable chance of sleeping in one of the "courts"—as the critic now called them—of his own Order, so numerous had friaries become[2]. These were the "Caim's Castels" so vigorously denounced by Wycliffe, in which the newer Orders had now entrenched themselves in comfort, as we have seen, almost like any Benedictine or Cistercian in his country retreat. Chaucer, contrasting the apostles' practice with this luxury of the modern preacher, in the *Romaunt of the Rose*, says sarcastically:

> They neither bilden tour ne halle,
> But leye in houses small withalle[3].

Once again, then, the sorry tale has to be told, as in the case of bishop and "curate," of decline, negligence, and corruption. But the very voice of the Mendicant prophet crying of sin and judgement to come, amid the failure and desolation, reminds us that there were still able and fearless champions of virtue left—

> preching dayly sermondys inough,
> with good examples full graciously[4],

after the best traditions of their art.

[1] *S.P.—Adulatio*. Bromyard here seems quoting from some tractate: "de 12 abusionibus." See also A. G. Little, *Stud. in Engl. Franc. Hist.* pp. 128-9. (Jo. Wallensis, *Ordin. Vitae Relig.*)

[2] Jack Upland, as before, p. 20: "And yet ye have more courts than many lords of England; for ye now wenden throgh the realme, and ech night will lig in your own courts; and so mow but right few lords doe."

[3] l. 6571. For Wycliffe, see passim, especially *Vernac. Sermons*, ed. Matth., cf. pp. 58, etc. ("leve her heye housis that thei propren unto hem; sith Crist hadde no propre hous to reste in his hede...").

[4] *God spede the Plough* (MS. Lansd. 762), ll. 62-63 (E.E.T.S. ed.).

The learned biographer of Bunyan, writing apparently under the influence of Brewer's then newly-published *Monumenta Franciscana*, hazarded a suggestion that the friars might be considered the pulpit-forerunners of the nonconforming Puritans of the seventeenth century[1]. He was writing even better than he knew, without the added evidence of the sermon manuscripts themselves. In the chequered romance of mediaeval preaching, the Orders provide a remarkable link between the first great mediaeval heresy which did much to prompt their own founding, and the last great heresy before the Reformation which was born in England; a link, if you will, between the Poor Men of Lyons, and the so-called Poor Priests of the rector of Lutterworth. The history of the Christian pulpit, indeed, will be found to take wondrous little heed of the great historic cleavages in doctrine and order which loom so prominently in the history of Christendom as a whole. Of all weapons this "liberty of prophesying" was clearly the most dangerous to entrust to those whose learning and enterprise were to be the match of any Order in the world. Freer, in effect, than any sectary to wander abroad, gathering unlimited impressions of men and things beyond a mere episcopal or baronial domain, to-day in a University in England, to-morrow they might be lecturing or studying at Paris or Padua. If to-day they shared the poor man's lot in his hovel, the next day they might be guests in the very castle of his feudal sovereign. It is nothing less than a panorama of these proportions that stretches before us in the chapters of the *Summa Predicantium*. Looking back now across the years at Giotto's portrait of the somewhat diffident Pope before whom the Poverello stands preaching, with his companions, at that first appeal to Rome, we may well see wisdom and foresight in the frown on that papal brow. For the time being the friars may have rescued the tottering ecclesiastical edifice from the Albigensian attack. But, what of the future? Once planted firmly in every quarter of the civilized community, with the world for their parish, and almost the width of God's heaven for their pulpit-canopy, there was no privileged class they might not dare to assault, no private folly they might not expose, no sacred dogma they might not dare to

---

[1] J. Brown, *Puritan Preaching in England* (Lyman Beecher Lect.).

discuss "before all the people." If some churchmen in authority
were continually complaining that there was not enough preaching by the seculars, others indeed might well complain that
from some other quarters there was a great deal too much. In
view of this outspoken attitude of the friars, therefore, it is
hardly possible to doubt the immense significance of their
preaching, at any rate in England, for the future movements
toward Reformation and Dissent. For, Englishmen, then as
now, illogical in the average, and inclined to be contemptuous
of mere theory, would probably choose to remember the
practical criticism, the daring abuse, and let the more subtle
doctrinal arguments go. Even Wycliffe and his followers owed
a good deal to the very men they abused the most; and it would
be interesting to know how many adherents the Mendicants
did actually supply to his party of reform[1]. At any rate, had
not these very friars cried aloud from the house-tops, what every
man felt in his heart to be the truth, even if he was afraid to
confess it—that the bishops were a curse and a scandal, that
avarice and lechery were ruining the life of the clergy, and
imperilling the health of the Church? So, where these had
preached through fields and streets, at market crosses, perhaps
in the "natural amphitheatre of Gwennap,"[2] there later could
others—Bunyan, Fox, Wesley, Whitefield, and a host of the
nameless—preach freely too, especially when once more the
parish pulpits were to be closed against the unconventional
itinerating evangelist. The lesson was obviously never forgotten. For here we deal with no mere external coincidence
of history, but rather with a potent, undying influence.

In the first place, individuals among the friars, directly
anticipating Lollardy, had adjusted the balance between Mass
and sermon in the services of the Church, had sometimes even
ventured to give the latter a place of distinct superiority[3]. In

[1] Cf. Nicholas Weston, "fryer Carmilett, apostate, and Lollard," at
Northampton (Powell and Trev. *Docs.* p. 45); Peter Pateshul, *ex* Austin friar
(Wals. vol. ii, p. 157; and Foxe's *Acts and Mons.*); (cf. also Thos. Richmond,
Minor, of York (Wilkins, *Conc.* vol. iii, p. 487)).

[2] *Diary of John Wesley* (Sunday, 14th of September, 1766, etc.).

[3] Cf. S. Bernardino of Siena (quoted in Ferrers-Howell's *Life*, p. 219);
Dives et Pauper, which *may* be a Mendicant work, prec. v, cap. x. Others in
G. G. Coulton, *Five Centuries of Religion*, vol. i, p. 124. (One not mentioned
is brother Whitford, monk of Syon, in his *Werke for housholders*: "Let them
ever kepe the prechynges rather than the masse.") Mr Coulton reminds

94 MONKS AND FRIARS

that position it has remained to the present day in the systems of Protestant Dissent[1]. Secondly, they accustomed the ears of the laity to open criticism of the bishops, and other dignitaries of the Church, who might be identified with her authoritative voice in all matters of religion and conduct. That criticism is most characteristic of Brownism and all the more violent forms of Puritan faith from Tudor times onward. A bishop of Rochester, or a sub-prior of Durham, in the middle ages, might denounce clerical vices with perfect propriety before suitable audiences. That was one thing. It was quite another matter when some less dignified preacher essayed to do the same before a mixed congregation which included lay-folk. That this was a frequent enough occurrence, the explicit warnings in the sermons and manuals, in episcopal licenses, in official condemnations of heresy, are all sufficient to testify. Again, thirdly, our comparison applies equally to the political sermon, with its constant discussion of governments and much-needed reforms. "Paul's Cross," as will be seen subsequently, was no innovation of the Reformers in this respect. Nor need the modern "Nonconformist conscience," inclining heavily in the pulpits to the Liberal and democratic side, fail to find its counterpart among the Mendicant supporters of popular liberties in mediaeval times. If the friars did not actually preach communism, some of their remarks might easily have been taken to recommend it. Ancestors, too, of those unfortunate heads of State, assize-judges, mayors and aldermen, and the rest, who were compelled to listen to harangues and exhortations from the Commonwealth preachers at unendurable length, had themselves suffered a like fate, we may be sure, whole centuries before, at the hands of Dominican and Franciscan. Further, all that that unpopular word "Puritanism" has ever stood for, to the minutest detail, shall be found advocated unceasingly in the preaching of the pre-Reformation Church[2]. The long face, the plain diet, the

me further that it begins with Gratian's quotation from Augustine, long before the friars appeared.

[1] One might almost consider the Puritan "Lecture-courses" foreshadowed by such a fifteenth-century homily series as that of *Jacob's Well*, MS. Salisb. Cath. Libr. 103.

[2] For a single example, cf. MS. Roy. 18. B. xxiii, fol. 153: "to worship thy God...in ffastynge and in wakynge, and almes dede doynge, in levynge of swerynge, and in syn blamynge, in symplenes of clothynge, and in sylence holdynge in etynge and drynkynge, and from worldly conformyng...," etc.

plainer attire, the abstention from sports and amusements in company, the contempt of the arts, the rigid Sabbatarianism, the silence at meals, the long household prayers, the stern disciplining of wife and children, the fear of hell, the heavy mood of "wanhope," are typical of the message of the faithful friar, as it may be read to-day. Finally, unenlightened Catholic partisans of every shade may have good reasons of their own for still proving to the world that Puritanism and the sects are wholly abnormal outgrowths of religion. The student, however, who knows his sources at first hand must be allowed to smile a little to himself, when he hears them. For, claim though she might in theory a seamless robe, what unhappy feature of the later warfare of the sects, we may ask, did the Church of the middle ages lack, within her own ranks? Members of different Orders, as jealous[1], bigoted and self-centred as any Particularist sectaries, damned each other in sermons, even struggled with each other in church, for possession of the pulpit. Has the history of Nonconformity itself anything worse to show us in this respect?

---

[1] Cf. further the remarkable sermon *ad clerum* of MS. Camb. Univ. Libr. Ii. iii. 8, fol. 128, which describes "our clergy" as—"invicem invidentes et alterutrum detrahentes," etc. to the utter confusion of the Church : similarly the vivid passage in Rypon's sermon given below, Chap. VI, p. 250.

A LEARNED DOMINICAN
(*MS. Fitzwilliam Mus., Cambr.*, 164)

CHAPTER III

"WANDERING STARS"

IN the great fourteenth-century fresco of the Florentine Capella degli Spagnuoli[1], the Dominican preacher stands in fair white tunic and black cloak amid the architectural splendours of the city, pointing the way to heaven. In the chapterhouse of San Marco, not so far away, the visitor sees the founders of all the four great Mendicant Orders, with St Bernard, prince of monastic orators, and many more, in glory around the Crucifixion scene, each with his own genius vividly portrayed by the brush of the more spiritual Dominican painter. In the ranks of the English clergy, secular as well as regular, we have found at the least a few worthy to be called sons of these prophets, personalities that we can just recognize upon the wall of history, with spiritual garments perhaps as little stained as those of Fra Angelico's heroes. But in the great procession to the pulpit there are behind them, Italians and Englishmen alike, a host of the unnamed and unremembered, lacking sometimes even the distinction of a famous habit upon their shoulders. There are men as eccentric as St Francis, without his gentleness or his genius; wild, restless spirits whose vision shifts and fades in an impatient age. The mere villain and the heretic will be among their number, too, worried as in Andrea di Firenze's picture by the Hounds of the Lord, whether the inward preacher of conscience, or the outward "preachers" in the ecclesiastical courts. With such homilists, misunderstood as often by the modern historian, as by the ancient disciplinarian, the present chapter will be mainly concerned. An English sermon-writer of our period sums up the types for us in caustic fashion:

But it is to be known that there are some preachers who sow nothing but oats, which are the food of horses, that is to say, words stirring to lechery. Others too, there are, who sow barley, that is to say, swelling words, haughty, and stinging. There are others who sow only for the sake of vainglory. Of such speaketh Hosea, viii: *"They sow the wind, and they shall reap the whirlwind."* There are

[1] I.e. in the Dominican Church of S. Maria Novella.

others who sow tares, that is to say, the seed of infidelity.... All these are the preachers of the devil."[1]

To the faithful son of the Church, looking out upon a stormy and perilous age, all irregular ministries good or bad doubtless would be of the devil. But though nothing will be too bad for some of the "libres prêcheurs" we shall have to consider, our criticism in an age of psychology and detachment can hardly be so sweeping as that. They have but one vague feature in common, these pardoners, heretics, and "Gyrovagi"—"who call themselves hermits,"[2] and that feature is their abnormality, their "extravagance." Yet, as little is said to distinguish the aberrations of genius from those of mere insanity under certain conditions, even so here, more especially among devotees of the last-named class, we shall find a few rare examples of the sublimest devotion and the most heroic self-sacrifice. It is from the pages of Bishop Grandisson's Register that this threefold group stands out together, a queer medley of preachers. To the eye of the writer they are the woeful heralds of Anti-Christ[3]. No official enterprise blessed by the authorities has called them forth to labour, it is true. None the less their number and influence are an undoubted sign of the times, and the call of men's hearts. Sparse as the contemporary records are concerning them, it is not difficult to account for their presence in an age in some respects not unlike our own. In the aftermath of a war the cry of the noisy desperate agitator is being heard again. Many, on the other hand, have promptly set about the task of making their own profit out of the cheap credulity and emotions of the hour; while yet others feel called away in brokenhearted despair of humanity and of the Churches to the solitary place, and the practice of contemplation. For the men of the opening fifteenth century, and earlier, there had been pesti-

---

[1] MS. Add. 21253, fol. 43.
[2] "Secta Gerevagorum (sic!) qui se heremitas nominant, et questorum, qui se pardonistas vocant...," etc. (Reg. Grandisson Exeter, pt ii, p. 1198). And again (ibid. p. 1208): "Nonnulli habitu religiosi nostrae diocesis mendicantes...."
[3] 1358. Reg. Grand. (Exeter), pt ii, pp. 1197–8. He mentions first the heretical sects now abounding, and amongst others those who, "per dulces sermones et benedicciones seducunt corda innocencium" (i.e. Rom. xvi, 18): "...quos supra generaliter designavimus Anti Christi precones," especially the Pardoners, and "Gerevagi" aforementioned.

lences, famines, tempests, comets[1] enough to terrify the stoutest hearts, in the world of natural events. In the world of politics there had been ceaseless foreign wars, internal risings, great social wrongs and oppression, corrupt and incompetent government. Against these, and against the equally disastrous corruption and decay in the Church we have already heard the thunder of the preachers. Yet even with them it is the tale of despair, of worse horrors to come, of impending judgement, not of hope, that the most fearless of all has to tell. What is likely to be the result then upon the minds of the ecclesiastical rank and file? For the careless worldling bent on his own interests there is money to be gained by the pulpit, if one can satisfy the popular demand, especially where others have failed. A world that is over-wrought calls like the individual for sudden diversion from time to time, in which its sorrow and disappointment may be cheerfully swallowed up. The peasant too needs even more his charm and his wonder-working relic-monger to overawe the powers he cannot move by appeal or by effort. Here is a chance for the successful "tub-thumper," indeed. But to the earnest and highly sensitive man of religion, on the other hand, the situation will probably seem at first too deep for word or action of any kind. He is tortured by the suffering he sees around him, by his very knowledge that if an adequate message could be found, the world would be in no mood to receive it. At all events he will have to find his place in one of the established Orders of Christendom. But in which? If he has already entered, he knows better than anyone their disappointments, their hypocrisies, their formalities. He becomes introspective, moody, isolated—as they called Rolle in his day, "self-centred"—inevitably unbalanced, like the overwrought prophet of Israel—"I have been very jealous for the Lord God of hosts: for the children of Israel have forsaken thy covenant, thrown down thine altars, and slain thy prophets with the sword; and I, even I only am left." Under the spell of such

[1] The preachers themselves refer to these terrors. Cf. Bp. Brunton, MS. Harl. 3760, fol. 191 b, etc. ("Haec pestilencia"; "certis planetis et constellationibus," and those who ascribe the disasters to them, etc.). Also Robert Rypon's mention of the warning comet of 1401, in MS. Harl. 4894, fol. 116 b ("stella comata"). Pestilences of the period are frequently mentioned in the Episc. Registers (cf. Wykeham (Winch), for 1374, 1375, etc.). See below in Chap. v.

a crisis as this, little wonder that the most timid and orthodox churchmen have flung every ordinance, every recognized means of grace to the winds, and dared to speak direct to the Almighty upon his mountain, that at such a moment eloquent preachers have learnt an eloquence of silence, in some tremendous mystical vision of their own. This is indeed the genuine glory and transfiguration of the Dissenter in history, though but few boasting that name have been found worthy to receive it.

The pardoner is our first type to be dealt with, more properly the "questor," and as the official pen describes him—"vulgariter vocatus *perdoner*"[1]—often indeed as unlicensed in his general behaviour as in his offices. So familiar is he in the pages of Chaucer or Langland, so easily may his spiritual descendants be recognized to-day at Islington Market, or Barnet Fair, still declaiming from open-air platforms, "with many quaint subtle words, and with false behesting," the potency of magic cures, that the type needs little explanation. The charlatans indeed, like the poor they deceive, are ever with us. If, however, it is a matter of surprise that he should be included among the mediaeval preachers, the reply is simply that to the contemporary eye such an one he invariably was[2]. With confidence it may be said that no entry in Episcopal Registers concerning him ever omits to speak of this side of his activity, and in the usual terms[3]. In addition we are informed that, along with parson and friar, he would share the very pulpits in parish churches, at the regular sermon-time—"intra missarum sollempnia." In this respect as in every other, Chaucer's famous picture in the *Pardoner's Prologue* is to be verified fully by the official declarations of the Church. But not unnaturally, in modern record, the actual relic-mongering and begging have been allowed almost to eclipse the rest. Since, for one reason, the ways of tricksters are safest when kept secret, the pardoner has not obliged us, apparently, by leaving any manuscript of his discourses behind him.

---

[1] Wilkins, *Conc.* vol. iii, p. 429, and cf. in n. 2, p. 97, above.
[2] Cf. *Cil. Oc. Sac.* MS. Harl. 4968, fol. 40 b (De Predic.): "Item sunt alii predicatores scil. questores, i.e. pardoniste..."; and *Reg. Anim.* MS. Harl. 2272, fol. 9 b: "Quid juris de questoribus qui discurrunt per ecclesias cum literis remissionum, et predicant abusiones...."
[3] "Predicatio," "officio predicandi," "Sermones," etc. In at least one entry they are distinctly referred to as "predicatores questuarii."

In the majority of cases, at all events, the "questor" appears on the scene as a "special preacher" for what might be called a "Hospital-Sunday sermon"; and the collection that follows in due course is as natural a part of such proceedings as it would be to-day. A passage in the *Summa Predicantium* itself, the more valuable because quite casually introduced into the discussion, puts this beyond doubt. "We see," says the writer, "that messengers come round to the churches [per ecclesias], from diverse hospitals, and preach that they have many weak and impotent inmates, and display large Indulgences, and many things are given them—in truth, rightly enough."[1] They were the proctors (procurators), or in modern parlance agents and "organisers of appeals" for such establishments, charged primarily with the agreeable task of collecting "broche, rynge, poke, belle, candell, vestimente, bord clothe, towelle, pygge, lambe, wolle, peny, or penyworthe," and the other offerings of the faithful, for their dependents[2]. How little need we be surprised that their reputation fell so low as it did, when, in an age notorious for its avaricious and lustful clergy, as the sermons bear witness, there were many "faire wyves" to appreciate the rings and brooches, besides others who might bestow them, and extensive clerical appetites to make use of the good fare:

> But, sirs, o word forgat I in my tale;
> I have relikes and pardon in my male
> As faire as any man in Engelond[3]!

The appearance of relics is easy enough to explain. "Relikes," explains one of our preachers, are "to the...profite to man, bothe bodily and gostily."[4] Hospitals were their natural repositories, particularly since the former seem on the whole to have enjoyed a far better reputation than the doctors for effecting a cure. Moreover, they attracted the wealth from visitor and pilgrim, as in the better known instance of the monastic and cathedral shrines. The pardoner himself, therefore, was only acting on the business-like principle that if the money will not come to Lourdes, then Lourdes must go in search of the money. The sacred collection became a travelling peep-show, and the

[1] *S.P.—Mors.*
[2] Cf. Miss Clay, *The Mediaeval Hospitals of England*, p. 189, etc.
[3] Chaucer, *Cant. Tales*, Pard. Tale, ll. 919–21.
[4] MS. Harl. 2247, fol. 169 b.

proctor, leaving the hospital gate, went on tour in the provinces. With relics as numerous as they were already, a few more in his wallet could hardly create a scandal. The method was that of an up-to-date advertiser, it is true. But there was one difference which made the pardoner even more "modern" and "commercial" than ourselves. Understanding as well as we the power of an appeal to the eye, he did not shrink from making good use of that piece of knowledge, when in the pulpit[1]. As for the pardons or Indulgences, these had had already a long and perhaps none too honourable connection with the ordinary sermons of bishops and Mendicant friars. Archbishop Fitzralph preaching in London himself alludes to their abuse by the latter, and is inclined to shrink from bestowing them at his own sermon's end[2]. However, most people in the "ages of faith" were no more anxious to give their money for nothing in return than they are to-day. Hence the pardoners' Indulgences were granted in effect to stimulate generosity; and how little the question of theology entered into the matter can easily be seen when we observe how the generosity of their terms was increased as the world grew older and less willing to give[3].

The pardoner might be licensed, in the first instance, either by papal bull, or episcopal letters[4]. The mandate of a London

[1] For the further association of relics with preaching, see below, in Chap. VIII, pp. 349–351.

[2] MS. Lansd. 393, fol. 112: "Indulgenciam quasi vereor conferre penitentibus, quia non nisi pauci dies sunt lapsi cum, meis quibusdam ibidem astantibus, unus de istis ordinibus mendicancium concessit audientibus suum sermonem centum dies, et alius die altero octoginta et plures, et puto quod prudenter et caute attendendum esset ab eis numquid in impetratione huius potestatis symonie labes non mediet. Indulgenciam tamen exhibere, quam nos prelati conferre valemus omnibus vere penitentibus, vel qui infra viii dies fideliter penitebunt, vobis concedimus, in nomine patris et filii et spiritus sancti qui est benedictus in secula seculorum—Amen." There is an interesting illustration of Canon Wordsworth's point about "unscrupulous or ill-advised persons, too often adding up the grants of pardon by all the prelates collectively, and parading them before the ignorant, as if the sum total were available to any of the faithful" (see *Yorkshire Arch. Journal*, vol. xvi, p. 376) in a *Preaching* indulgence "of the monasterie of Syon" (Isleworth) in MS. Ashmole, 750, fol. 86. See below Appdx. III. Canon Wordsworth himself kindly supplies me with a notice from his own MS. Transcripts of the Regs. of a forty-days' Indulgence for those hearing the Canons' sermons (c. 1319–20) at Salisbury. Cf. sim. at Durham, etc. above p. 52, n. 2.

[3] Most in our period are for forty days; cf. W. Streche, 1419, as below.

[4] Cf. MS. Harl. 4968, fol. 40 b, again: "quidam per bullas pape, quidam per litteras diocesani, episcopi, vel metropolitani constituuntur...."

Convocation for the province of Canterbury, in 1424, grants recognition to the representatives of three hospitals alone— "Domus S. Johannis Jerusalem in Anglia, vulgariter dicta *Le Frary*, S. Antonii, aut hospitalis S. Thomae Martyris in urbe Romana." Although these have special prominence of their own in the entries of Registers[1], especially the last-named which was devoted to the needs of English pilgrims in the Holy City, the names of hospitals in this country occur as well. Among such licenses or letters of protection granted by individual prelates, we may notice one—"pro procuratore leprosorum de Romesie"[2]—another for a forty-days' Indulgence bestowed on Walter Streche, "proctor of the master and brethren of the Hospital of Saints Wolstan and Godwal of the City of Worcester."[3] Apart from hospital needs altogether, the pardoner might be making his special plea, as a bishop's diocesan emissary, "for the fabric of our cathedral of Exeter, in Lent, when other quests cease for the time being,"[4] for the fabric of York Minster[5], for the maintenance of lights in Winchester Cathedral[6], for the repair of a parish church in Herefordshire[7], or even for the support and repair of the great bridge of the city of Exeter, and the chapel of the Blessed Mary situate upon it[8].

The ordinary license takes the form of a request to local clergy,

That you set forth [exponatis] in good faith, and permit the same persons (proctors or messengers) to set forth to clergy and people committed to your care, the Indulgences and privileges duly granted

---

[1] For the first, cf. the Bull of Pope Urban V, 1369 ("contra questores hosp. Jerus. in Anglia") in Wilkins, *Conc.* vol. iii, p. 84. For the Hosp. of St Anthony, cf. Reg. Archbp. Melton, in *Fasti Ebor.* vol. i, p. 421 (1334–6), Reg. Grandisson, Exeter, pt ii, p. 1179 (1355–6) and Reg. Spofford, Hereford, p. 25 (1422), etc. For the Hosp. of St Thomas the Martyr, at Rome, cf. Reg. Episc. St David's, p. 69 (1398); and see an interesting article in the *Dublin Review* for April 1904, p. 274 et seq. With the latter is often associated the Hosp. of the Holy Ghost, also at Rome; cf. similarly, Reg. Brantingh, Exeter, pt i, p. 566 (1384–5); Regs. Grandiss. ibid. pt ii, p. 1178 (1355–6) and Melton, Archbp. of York, in *Fasti Ebor.* vol. i, p. 421 (1334–6).
[2] Hosp. of the Blessed Mary Magdal. and St Anthony, 1316–17. (Reg. Sandale, Winch. p. 268.)
[3] Reg. Lacy (Hereford), p. 59 (1419).
[4] Reg. Brantingh. (Ex.), pt i, p. 566 (1384–5).
[5] Wilkins, *Conc.* vol. iii, p. 227.
[6] Reg. Wykeham (Winch.), p. 12 (1367).
[7] Reg. Spofford (Heref.), p. 49 (1424). Richard "Byschope," procurator.
[8] Reg. Grandisson (Ex.), pt i, p. 351 (1328).

to the said hospital, during the solemnization of Masses, on Sundays and Festivals, and at other places and times, where, and as often as a great number of the faithful shall be present; minor Masses, and preachings of friars, with other businesses and briefs ceasing in the meantime until the said business be plenarily set forth....[1]

In some cases the actual right of exposition appears to have been restricted to the local clergy alone[2]. In others it is left a matter of option, for the visitors to decide according to their own preference[3]. The parish parson, if popular, we can well believe might succeed better than a stranger in exciting the generosity of his flock; while such a restriction as the first-named would be a wise safeguard against scandals in the pulpit, for which pardoners were all too notorious in their day[4]. Of the three most prominent abuses connected with them, little need be said of the first, the counterfeit pardoner in person, "cum falsis et fictis literis, sigillis fabricatisque, quae nostra esse mendaciter asserunt, sigillatis." Nearly every properly authorized license seems to contain its own warning against such pests, and almost every Register and manual repeats some mandate insisting on the more careful examination of credentials before admission is granted to the applicant[5]. The indefatigable

---

[1] Besides Regs. Sandale (Winch.) and Brant. (Ex.), as given above, cf. also Reg. Lacy (Hereford), (Cant. and York S.), p. 59. (Hospitale degentium); Reg. St David's, 1398, and 1402 (p. 273: "Hosp. of Bl. Mary of Bethleem withoute Bishopsgate, Lond."); Melton in *Fasti Ebor.* vol. i, p. 421; (Hosp. of St Thomas the Martyr, Eastbridge, near Canterbury, 1336), etc.

[2] Reg. de Asserio (Winch.), p. 423 (1321—St Leonard's, Bedford).

[3] Reg. Wykeham (Winch.), p. 12 (1367): ("...populo per se permittatis, vel vos, si hoc voluerint, exponatis").

[4] This is stated specifically in the Decrees of the Synod of Exeter (Quivil. 1287), in Wilkins, *Conc.* vol. ii, p. 137, cap. 47: "Wherefore we forbid our subjects to admit any collector of alms without our letters; and even then let him not be permitted to preach, but let the parish chaplains faithfully expound to the people his business." Cf. also the *Summa Angelica,* under "Questuarii."

[5] Cf. Reg. Grandisson (Ex.), pt ii, p. 1198: (1359). Let them not be admitted—"absque literis nostris manu nostra subscriptis, sigilloque nostro, cum impressione anuli in dorso, more solito consignatis: nec ipsis aut ipsorum alicui ultra ea quae in literis nostris hujusmodi continentur fidem adhibeant aliqualem." Also in *Reg. Anim.* MS. Harl. 2272, fol. 9 b: "Questores eleemosinarii non debent ab aliquo admitti nisi exhibuerint literas episcopi diocesis nec licet eis populo predicare,...et debent episcopi dioc. diligenter examinare literas apostolicas, ne quaequam fraudes committi valeant per easdem." *Cil. Oc. Sac.* MS. Harl. 4968, fol. 40 b.

Grandisson lays bare, in a document glowing with indignation, the system he has detected at work in his diocese, by which a whole army of false *questores*, many of them mere laymen, were being encouraged by the archdeacon's officials, who pocketed the proceeds that came their way from this monstrous invasion of the preaching office. Thus had the laymen actually succeeded at last in reaching the pulpit, with the support of ecclesiastics in office, a pulpit that was forbidden even to the sub-deacon[1]. Well might the Lollard complain in future of the iniquity of prelates, who prevented the simple priest from proclaiming the Gospel, only to promote the endeavours of such lay scoundrels as these. Meanwhile the unauthorized pardoner, in evidence at least as early as the first half of the thirteenth century, flourishes to the end of our period, in the words of the Neville Constitutions of 1466—"licet ex statutis concilii generalis et Clementis papae prohibitum sit expresse."[2]

But not only might seals and letters of authority be abused. The preacher might deal equally falsely with the Indulgence, expanding its efficacy in his predication,—"to deceive the simple, and the better to extort from them their gold and silver."[3] Here was a fine field for the bombast and exaggeration of the popular orator. The friars themselves had been held guilty of such a trick, at the expense of the seculars. An article of the Oxford Petition of 1414[4], entitled "contra falsas predicationes quaestorum," will explain the method adopted, in typical long-winded fashion:

[1] Ibid. p. 1178 (1355-6): "Nos tamen, non sine gravi cordis inquietudine, ex querelis, denunciacionibus, et clamoribus plurium et facti quasi notorietate, intelleximus et in parte ex inspeccione cedularum hujusmodi experti sumus, quod vos archi-diaconorum officiales, vestrive commissarii et registrarii, saeva cupiditate dampnabiliter execcati, pecunie sic collecte vel verius seductoris 'totam' vobis pro iniquo labore sub colore infidelis feodi reservantes, questores hujusmodi tam Hospitalis Sancti Spiritus, St Johannis, quam aliorum Privilegiatorum, ut dicunt, *nedum fratres aut clericos, set multociens laicos aut conjugatos, ipsorum negocia diebus sollempnibus, intra Missarum solempnia, predicandi officio, (quod) non inferioribus diaconibus est permissum, tenore presumpto publice exponere non tantum permittitis, set ipsis nephandissime assistitis, consulitis, et favetis....*"

[2] York. Wilkins, *Conc.* vol. iii, pp. 602-3.

[3] Reg. de Asserio (Winch.), p. 474 ("...questores in suis proponunt predicacionibus ut simplices decipiant, et aurum vel argentum subtili vel fallaci pocius ingenio extorqueant ab eisdem...," etc.). A "Monicio facta ne questores admittantur ad predicandum...," 1321–2.

[4] Artic. 39. (Wilkins, *Conc.* vol. iii, pp. 360 et seq.)

Whereas the shameless pardoners purchase their vile traffic in farm with Simon, sell Indulgences with Gehazi, and squander their gains in disgraceful fashion with the Prodigal Son: but what is more detestable still, although not in holy orders, they preach publicly, and pretend falsely that they have full powers of absolving both living and dead alike from punishment and guilt [the technical "a poena et a culpa"], along with other blasphemies, by means of which they plunder and seduce the people, and in all probability drag them down with their own person to the infernal regions, by affording them frivolous hope and an audacity to commit sin: therefore, let the abuses of this pestilential sect be blotted out from the threshold of the Church[1].

This is strong language, even for the University petitioners, who would be specially interested, no doubt. Yet the Concordat of Pope Martin V to the English Church, five years later, proclaims that England had an evil notoriety for such pests, and that her people were becoming contaminated[2].

If we seek further details of their method, something may be gleaned from the *Regimen Animarum*[3] and the *Cilium Oculi Sacerdotis*[4], which reproduce phrases to be met with again in the Register of Bishop Brantingham of Exeter (1385–6)[5], and in papal decrees. Besides granting Indulgences to the people "motu proprio" to the manifest deception of souls, they dispense with vows, absolve those who confess to them from the worst kind of sins, even perjury and homicide, and in return for sums of money remit the third or fourth part of penances enjoined by others. The souls of parents and friends, whose

---

[1] The Quivil Decrees (Exeter, 1287) are even more emphatic in their charges: "Amongst other errors, they mendaciously assert that they have many more and greater Indulgences than they really have, that thus they may induce simple persons to give more generous alms."

[2] "Whereas in consequence of divers Indulgences granted by the Apostolic See...and the number of pardoners, who at this time abound more than usual in England, persons frequently become hardened in vice..." (Wilkins, *Conc.* vol. iii, p. 391). Cf. also London Convocation, in 1424: "Nonulli pretensi questores...populum decipientes *plus solito*, per provinciam Cantuar., transeunt hiis diebus." These reports throw an interesting light on Chaucer's famous portrait.

[3] De Questoribus, MS. Harl. 2272, fol. 9 b et seq.

[4] MS. Harl. 4968, fol. 41 ("asserunt se posse indulgentias concedere vel super nota dispensare a perjuriis...").

[5] Reg. Brantingh. (Ex.), pt ii, pp. 607–8. The following provide shorter variations of the same: *Cil. Oc. Sac.* (MS. Harl. 4968, fol. 41) and the Neville Constit. of York (Wilkins, *Conc.* vol. iii, p. 602).

relations have given them alms, they profess to rescue from the pains of Purgatory, translating them to the joys of Paradise; and those benefactors(!) who provide them with places in which to carry on their craft, get a plenary remission of all sins— "a poena et culpa," as they say. Finally, in addition to the falsely augmented Indulgences they offer from Popes and bishops, they do not fail to contrast the sweeping absolutions they confer on their supporters with the 'curate's' power to absolve his folk, in general, but once in the year[1]. Gascoigne recalls the fragment of a sermon from one of them, "that I heard lately in the year of Christ, 1453."[2] "Know all of you here present," the preacher had declared, "that if any one of you shall give a penny [unum denarium] to me or to any member of my house, he is freed from all penance[3] enjoined on him by his 'curate,' or by any other priest."

The third outstanding offence lies in the disturbance and conflict they created with the other candidates for the Sunday sermon. This ended sometimes in nothing less than a most unedifying scramble for possession of the parish pulpit itself. John Heywood's scandalous interlude[4] in which a pardoner and a friar each struggle for the privilege of addressing one and the same audience, and come to blows within the sacred edifice, is surely no mere dramatic invention. Careful and repeated warnings in the licenses that preaching of friars and others must stop meanwhile, "that no other questor is to be admitted"[5] at the time when the licensee makes his visit, are in themselves suggestive of the danger, had we not the more explicit statement of such an entry as that concerning the Dominican brothers of Guildford (Guldeforde). They "are in no wise to be *impeded from preaching the word of God by collectors of alms, or by begging*

---

[1] See also a letter of the Archbp. of Cant. 1378, "contra questores," in Wilkins, *Conc.* vol. ii, p. 131 (deceptione multiplici...ac elusione...).

[2] *Loci e Libro Veritatum* (ed. Rogers), p. 125.

[3] Cf. (e. 15th cent.) MS. St Albans Cath. fol. 141; (ibid. in MS. (Bodl.) Laud. Misc. 23): "Many men weenen if thei ʒeven a peny to a pardener, thei schulen be asoylid of the brekinge of alle the commaundementis of God for the takinge of that peny."

[4] "The Pardoner and the Frere," printed in Pollard's *Engl. Miracle Plays*, pp. 114–125.

[5] Cf. Reg. Wykeham (Winch.), p. 12 (1367). Read also the situation in Heywood's instructive play, e.g.: "(Pard.)...'Mayster parson gave me lycence before the, and I wolde thou knewyst it!'"... etc.

preachers."[1] More pointed still is the official injunction else-where, that "if, while making a sermon, the pardoners are warned to keep silence and yet are unwilling to do so, the inquisitors have power to suspend them from that office."[2]

If the friar had thus to suffer one more competitor, the secular parson of the place was even more liable to further insult and annoyance. The Church had once urged upon parsons the duty of giving sustenance to travelling preachers[3]. But under stress of subsequent abuses she had eventually released them from it. Now no prelate nor rector need supply hospitality or bodily provisions to the pardoner when he came[4]. Nor again were they bound to summon their parishioners to listen to his exhortations, even if the pardoner's letters made reference to that duty[5]. Yet from the written complaints of rectors and vicars in London, Exeter, Norwich, and elsewhere[6], it is clear that when the clergy failed to satisfy the visitor's own require-ments, or were too strict in their examination of his letters and seals, the infuriated man was still not above open retaliation. He would proceed to excommunicate those not to his liking, or else take up a position in their churches particularly at offertory time, on some feast-day, there by his vociferous begging, and reading out of the names on his bede-roll, to hold up the

---

[1] Reg. Rig. de Asserio (Winch.), p. 406 (1321). Cf. also the warning, 1424: "tali tempore omnino quod divinum servitium ex hoc seu predicatio verbi Dei in aliqua ecclesia *non impediatur ullatenus, vel turbetur*" (Wilkins, *Conc.* vol. iii, p. 429).

[2] *Cil. Oc. Sac.*, MS. Harl. 4968, fol. 45: "Quodsi quicumque predicatores *vel perdoniste* sermonem facientes moniti ipso tempore silere noluerint, ipsi inquisitores eos ab hujusmodi officio suspendere possunt."

[3] Cf. Peckham's Constitutions, 1281 (De hospitalitate tenenda): "Et ut qui ibidem transeunt et predicant verbum Dei necessaria recipiant corpori alimenta...," etc. (quoted in Lyndewood, *Prov.*).

[4] Cf. *Reg. Anim.* (MS. Harl. 2272, fol. 9 b): "Statuitur quod prelati, rectores, et alii clerici curati non tenentur eos recipere in hospiciis, nec eis in necessariis providere, etiam cuiuscumque religionis sint aut condicionis"; and *Summa Angel.* § *Questuarii.*

[5] MS. Harl. 2272, ibid.: "...nec tenentur facere convocationem populi ad sermones vel exhortaciones eorum, etiam si de tali convocatione mentio fiat in litteris eorum, quia papa revocat."

[6] Cf. Bull of Pope Urban V, 1369 (Wilkins, *Conc.* vol. iii, p. 84). The London complainants included the Rectors of St Dunstan's in the West, and St Mary's "Wolnoth." See also *Reg. Anim.* (as above): "si propter hoc, alia sentencia excommunicationis vel interdicti promulgatur, irrita est et inanis," etc.

service, until it was too late to celebrate Mass for that day[1].

Than adew to the devyll, tyll we come agayn![2]

The "ensamples many oon of olde stories"[3] seem to be further reflected in an episcopal reference to "nonnulla frivola et mendacia" in the contemporary pardoners' preaching. Their exhibition of false relics finds a place in our *Cilium Oculi Sacerdotis*[4]; while the fondness of Chaucer's particular hero for "the licour of the vyne" seems to derive fresh emphasis from a passage in the *Regimen Animarum*, again, which tells—"de questoribus"—of drunkenness and sojourning in inns and places of evil repute[5].

Signs are not wanting that in course of time our preaching fox did not always get away so smartly with his prey. The later papal legislation swept aside a mass of the privileges thus abused, and insisted that all his irregularities should be punished by the bishop of the diocese, "privilegio quocunque non obstante."[6] In a letter of Archbishop Sudbury in 1378, we find that prelate ordering all pardoners who have misused their privileges to be cited[7]. Bishop Grandisson of Exeter issues a mandate in 1328 requiring all goods which remain in the hands of any of them, within his diocese, to be sequestrated, save only in the case of those who are collecting for his bridge over the "Exse."[8] The Council of the Province of Cashel, in Ireland, in 1453, enjoins that all pardoners shall pay tithes of all their gains to the parish in which they happen to reside[9]. Finally, their relics were no

---

[1] "...Ibidem questuare, seu nomina fratriae seu fraternitatis suae legere incipiunt, et continuant usque ad talem illius diei festi horam qua missa ibidem pro illo die convenienter non potest celebrari." Surely the "Ragman's rolles" of the Pardoner in Heywood's play, refer to these "nomina fratriae seu fraternitatis," and *not*, as Dr A. W. Pollard suggests in his notes (p. 212), to "a long unintelligible story."

[2] Heywood, as above.   [3] Chaucer.   [4] MS. Harl. 4968, fol. 41.

[5] MS. Harl. 2272, fol. 9 b: ("Illi questores vacantes commessationibus et ebrietatibus"; and again: "...non in tabernis et aliis locis incongruis hospitari debent, nec inutiles aut sumptuosas facere expensas, nec habitum false religionis portare"). Similarly MS. Harl. 4968, fol. 41 (*Cil. Oc. Sac.*).

[6] MS. Harl 2272, ibid. ("Dominus papa volens huiusmodi abusus abolere, per quos vilescit ecclesiastica censura et auctoritas clavium ecclesie deducitur in contemptum, expresse revocat omnia et singula privilegia...") MS. Harl. 4968, fol 41: ("Nam omnes bulle super articulos predictos quibuscunque vel quomodocunque facte revocantur et dampnantur.").

[7] Wilkins, *Conc.* vol. iii, p. 131.

[8] Reg. Grandiss. (Ex.), pt i, p. 351.   [9] Wilkins, *Conc.* vol. iii, p. 567.

longer to be revered without the seal of episcopal approbation upon them[1]; while, in the official order which prohibits their bestowal of blessings, we are forcibly reminded of Langland's shrewd impostor again[2]. Even more galling than the laughter over a certain Canterbury pilgrim, rebuked by mine host, must have been the jeers of a London crowd at the expense of the "falsifier" John Watte, riding in disgrace through Cheapside, with his face to the wrong end of his horse, in tall paper hat suitably inscribed, the forged Indulgences dangling about his neck.

Of the pardoner, so it seems, few had a good word to say. The almost complete silence with regard to him in sermons, otherwise so full of the current abuses, may be only another indication of the general disdain. He was too bad even to be denounced. He wears the "dunce-cap," as well as the devil's horns amongst the preachers. His efforts are beneath contempt[3], even the contempt of the none-too-squeamish mediaeval pulpit. When the friar preacher in the *Ploughman's Crede* starts to ridicule the claims and methods of the Augustinians, he has nothing worse to say than, "It is a pur pardoner's craft!" To the plaint of the Petition of Oxford that he was often not even a clerk in holy orders, may be added that of the synod of Exeter which pointed out that "with a presumptuous audacity they usurp the office of preaching, whilst totally ignorant of the Word of God."[4]

In a vernacular sermon collection[5] there is one slight reference, after all, which may be worthy to take its place alongside the more witty and elaborate portrait of the *Canterbury Tales*. The writer is busy enumerating the types of thieves, and has come to his third division:

Sothell theves beth the men that slyly can robbe men with many queynt sotell wordes, and with fals behestynge; and sum with fals letters and seeles, with crosses, and reliques that thei bere abowten

---

[1] MS. Harl. 4968, fol. 41: "Item prohiberi debent populi ne reliquias eorum revereantur nisi sub testimonio predictorum prelatorum mittantur."

[2] Ibid.: "Nec benedictionibus eorum populus se prosternat."

[3] Cf. MS. Bodl. 5, fol. 1 b (Higden's *Ars componendi sermones*): "sicut faciunt principaliter questores...." Cf. also Mine Host's outspoken contempt for his relics, at the end of the Pardoner's Tale in the *Canterbury Tales*.

[4] (Quivil), 1287, Cap. 47. (Wilkins, *Conc.* vol. ii, p. 137 et seq.)

[5] MS. Roy. 18. B. xxiii.

them, and sei that thei be of seyntes bones or of holy mens clothinge, and behoteth myche mede that will offre to hem, and hire the letters of pardon, ichon of other, as a kowe or a nox that men lat to hure; the wiche thei sell all for the penny, and fo no mans mede, with many fals lesynges, as the feend here maister techeth hem, for to robbe the pore pepull sotelly of ther goodes. And therfore said Crist, "*Beware of false prophets...*," etc.[1]

From the extreme of folly it is now time to turn to the extreme of zeal. If the increased brutality and chaos of the world had hastened men in the last days of the Roman Empire into an ascetic and anchoretical life, the voices of the pulpit towards the end of the middle ages, heralding another world cataclysm, might be expected to coincide with its revival. "Dies mali sunt." This stern impression—that on earth they are fighting a losing battle after all, that the powers of evil are too powerful, that the world must soon come to its end in horror and confusion—gives a prevailing gloom to the utterance of bishops like Brunton, or friars like Waldeby. In the body corporate there appeared to be now no healthy member to provide a rallying point from disease, and the preachers speak as men who expect that at any moment the great Physician may pronounce life extinct. At the outset of our period stands Richard Rolle, an English Jacopone, clad in his sister's frock. Towards the close of it we catch sight of strange, boding figures that flit about the court of King Richard II's successors, prophesying fresh disaster. The age of hermits has returned. We need not believe that all those irregular "habitu religiosi mendicantes" in Grandisson's Register, all those "eremytes on a hep, with hokide staves" cursed by Langland[2], were necessarily of the evil sort. Even if the majority were out to enjoy the indolency and vagrancy of the tramps' life, there must have been others, like Rolle, to whom the return to nature, to quiet, to simplicity, was something at least as genuine as the piety of him who in his solitary vigil at Northaw had once objected to the very songs of nightingales. One of our noted London preachers already referred to,

[1] Cf. also in a Lollard Collection, MS. Trin. Coll. Camb. B. 14, 50, fol. 65 b: "Quidam enim sunt mercenarii munera querentes per mendacia et falsas reliquias, sigilla, litteras, et per falsa miracula, ut homines deludant, et eis bona sua furentur."
[2] *Piers Plowman*, Prologue (A. text), l. 50; also B. text, pass. vi. l. 190: (An heep of heremites), etc.

Dr William Lichfield, describes the two types thus in a quaint, picturesque exposition of the text, "The foxes have holes"[1]:

> ...And, that mor is to sorow, sum crepen in to holis of the erthe, as Saul enterid in to a cafe—1° Regm. 24—for to do his filȝte therin, and to defoule that stede. Thus sum entren to presthod, sum to religion, *sum to be ankers and ankereses*, qwech maner of states shold be not of comyn lufyng of the worlde, bot as contrary to the worlde, and hid fro the world, as folke that dwellens in cafes. And ȝit many prestes, many monkys, chanons, ffreres, ankyrs, and ankeresses, nunnys, and heremytes are more worldly, lifen more lustily, are more delavy[2] in curiose talkyng of the world, an(d) luken more after worldly reverense and honour then thay shold have done, dwellyng stil in the state of the world that they were first in, or ellys in any worldly state that ever thay shold have comen to. In such private astates may thay do many privey unleveful thinges, more then thay myȝt do if they were in myddys the world. Nethles aȝeynwarde, many a man takys the ordre of prest, many ytaken the state of religioun, or of recluse, as David entred in to the same cafe in to wiche Saul entred....[He] fled theder to defend hym selfe fro the tyrauntith of Saul that porsewed hym. Thus sum enteren into Degre or State before-rehersed for ease and lust; and thes defilen her astate. [But others enter for the highest motives]—for to lyf in chastitie, in penaunce, in prayeres, in holy redynges....These devout men and wemen are no ffoxes in condicions; bot thay may be called brydes of heven....They forsaken the erth, and fly in the eyre, and fer fro the erthe most parte of briddes maken her nestes....They desiren hevynly thinges....Thouȝ they sit and syng on grene bowes, ȝit most hem, for ned of mete and drinke, liȝt downe to the erthe. But whiles thay are upon the erthe, they ben besy lokynge on ich side of (hem), for enmyes and caching of harme....

Yet, especially as it concerns our study, this movement may have been one deliberately turned as much away from the ordinary pulpit as from the other haunts of men. If we lacked the testimony of Hampole there would be still the statement of Wycliffe that this "feigned contemplatif lif," as he called it, was definitely inimical to the preaching of God's law. No better understanding of the issues here involved could be obtained than by listening to these two great prophets of righteousness, the mystical and the more logical thinker, respectively.

Richard Rolle of Hampole has been described more than once

[1] MS. Roy. 8. C. i, fols. 130 b–131. For Dr Lichfield himself, see above, p. 24. Here he is quoting from the *Ancren Riwle*.   [2] =immoderate.

in modern literature as the typical hermit-preacher, by those writing doubtless too hastily under the influence of the early scene of the *Officium*[1]. Rolle himself is not above the minor inconsistencies, perhaps characteristic of the religion of his age. His own career suggests many restless changes of mind. But if he is to be taken at his word at all, we must believe that, after the first phase of youthful enthusiasm, such a title would hardly have pleased him.

"Sum for soth," he argues, "gaynselland, says, 'Active lyfe is more fruytfull, for werkis of mercy it doys, it prechis, and slike other dedis wyrkis; qwharfore more meritory it is.' I say nay; for slyke warkis longis to accidentale rewarde, that is, joy of thinge wroght.... Als oft tyems it happyns that sum of les meed is guyd and preches; another prechis not, that mikyll more lufys. Is he not this bettir for he prechis? No, bot he this that more lufys hyar and bettir is, thof he be les in prechynge."[2]

This enthronement of the contemplative life of love has been spoken of as a reaction from the wearisome logic of the schools[3], in one who had actually left them in a fit of disgust. With no great stretch of imagination and with equal truth it might be described as a reaction from the japes and learned fatuities, perhaps the idle denunciation of the contemporary pulpit[4]. Miss H. E. Allen, indeed, whose researches have gone far to relieve Rolle of the authorship of a more or less commonplace homiletic treatise, believes that this view of his need not be inconsistent with the preaching of "mystical discourses" which would have little in common with the ordinary sermon. Be this as it may, however, we trace in his attitude a definite phase in the history of the pulpit, when "the foolishness of preaching" becomes apparent again after two centuries of the most brilliant efforts, if not by the seculars, at least by monk and Mendicant. It had promised so much; but now, apart from the merely spectacular, it was achieving so little that men turned in despair

[1] Cf. G. G. Perry (preface to *Engl. Prose Treatises of R. Rolle*, E.E.T.S. (O.S), No. 20); and Miss R. Clay, *The Hermits and Anchorites of England* (Antiquary's Ser.), p. 161, "Certain hermit-preachers."

[2] From *The Mending of Life*, p. 48.

[3] Cf. Horstmann, *Yorkshire Writers*, vol. ii, p. xxxv.

[4] Cf. in "a notabell tretys off the ten comandementys drawene by Richerde the hermyte off Hampull" (ed. Perry, p. 10; and Mätzner, p. 129): "new prechynge *that es vanyte and undevocyone*."

to look for a better way. Instead of seeking crowds, they sought the wilderness; instead of a vapid, bookish knowledge hastily acquired and fluently delivered amid bustling scenes, they waited alone for the still small voice that never shouts or hurries for any man, for the slow leavening process of personal contact, so "unbusinesslike," so individual, often reticent indeed like the God that hideth himself, patient with the eternal patience of His universe "groaning and travailing in pain together until now."[1] "Behold my servant whom I uphold; mine elect in whom my soul delighteth. I have put my spirit upon him: he shall bring forth judgement to the Gentiles. He shall not cry, not lift up, nor cause his voice to be heard in the street."

In the Latin *Melum*, Rolle himself seems to take a further step. Having declared in favour of the mystic life of contemplation, he now decides that it is actually incompatible with that of the active preacher:

Good it is to be a preacher, to run hither and thither, to move about, to be wearied; but it is better, safer, and sweeter to be a contemplator, to have a foretaste of eternal bliss, to sing the delights of the Eternal Love....If any one could attain to both, moreover, so much the more praiseworthy would he be. But this would not happen unless he first became a contemplator, before a preacher. And, without doubt, when the sweetness of the divine Love shall have absorbed the mind, the flesh fails, and will now no longer be strong enough to sustain outward labours.

The busy church-going Protestant of our own age, viewing for the first time some Quaker meeting, without previous knowledge of their social service, would be inclined to condemn this rejection of the preacher's activity and the practice of Quietism as a waste of time and opportunity, if not offensively egotistical as well. This, significantly enough, is the attitude of John Wycliffe towards the mystical recluses of his day. "What

[1] So vivid and charming is Dr Horstmann's description of this method on its active side, that I make no apology for quoting from it: "He appeared in the manor-houses of the neighbourhood, made friends with the lord, chatted with the women, knacked jokes with the girls, but all with that intent to preach his love, chastity, and charity....He appeared in the villages and mixed with the people, *colloquially* (as Socrates) *not from the pulpit*, inculcating love, loving-kindness, peace. He formed connections with clerics —one of his epistles (*Cupienti mihi*) is addressed to a young priest...." This is only Rolle's own confession from the *Melum* (see *Yorkshire Writers*, vol. ii, pp. xvi-xvii).

charite is it," he asks, "to a kunnynge man to chese his owene
contemplacion in reste, and suffre othere men to goo to helle?. . ."
Priests nowadays "close hem in stonys or wallis for al here lif,"
or else, "wolen alle be wommen in ydelnesse," when the times
cry out for prophets "to schewe to the peple here foule synnys."[1]
Indeed, we must believe that he has Rolle directly in mind
when he describes how they say concerning the respective
merits of contemplation and preaching, "sith it is the best, and
thei may not do bothe togidre." To Wycliffe no less than to the
dreamer of Hampole it was high time to reject the note of formalism and unreality in the pulpits of the day. But for him the
immediate alternative to be undertaken was the preaching of a
simple vernacular message to the people, based on the text of
Scripture.

It can hardly be considered our duty here as mere historians
to decide which policy was right. Yet it is impossible to overlook the fact that whereas the attitude of Wycliffe became the
attitude of the Protestant Reformers, and has been tried upon
the grand scale in history, that of Rolle remained, as indeed was
only too natural, the ideal of a few isolated spirits. Apart from
the numerically small but conspicuous success of the Quakers
it has scarce been tried by Churches at all. Looking back again
at the Reformation across three centuries of Evangelical
tradition one cannot but feel perhaps that, like most "cruel
necessities" of history, in its turn it was clever with the sword,
but clumsy enough with the ploughshare. "Simple gospels"
of the literal pattern, once in the people's hands, soon become
much as the commoner mediaeval sermon hand-books, the
matter of a few crude ideas and favourite quotations, oft-
repeated and almost as often misapplied. As catchwords for
revolutions and mass-movements, indeed, they may even prove

---

[1] See *Tract on Feigned Contemplative Life* in Matthew (E.E.T.S., O.S.,
No. 74, p. 187 et seq.). Cf. also the attitude of Langland in *Piers Plowman*:
    "Ac Robert Renne-aboute shal now ʒte have of myne,
    Ne 'posteles,' *but they preche conne*, and have powere of the bisschop."
                                        (B. text, pass. vi, ll. 150–51.)
    (For all Prof. Skeat's anxiety (in his notes) that "posteles" = apostles
should not be confused with "postills," there is no reason, to my mind, why
Langland should not intend the word here to be a pun upon Rolle's "*postillator*" (see below, p. 116), in *characteristic* mediaeval fashion. N.B. Skeat's
own confession in the Glossarial Index: "the reason for its use here is not
clear.")

fraught with a deadly explosive energy, fit companions for the dry powder in the soldier's flask, as Cromwell discovered. But there their potency ends. The acute mind of Pecock in the fifteenth century had already noticed this about the Lollard, who could be just as "clamorous" and shallow as the friar in his pulpit[1]. Moreover, the later spokesmen in our churches, too often lacking the mellow scholarship of Wycliffe or Calvin with their somewhat narrow zeal, have continued to rely upon the little "hand-books" along with their texts. So short and fussy is our life; so long and difficult to master is the real art of the Spirit; so exciting and popular are the party cries and creeds, ready-made for the pulpit, for the jaded religious nerves of our modern "men of business." What, on the other hand, we are tempted to wonder, would have happened, if instead of the noisy aggressiveness of Geneva, the Wartburg, and Mr Burnet's chapel, bristling cities, castles, conventicles, pulpits, the Protestant era had chosen the unsacerdotalism of Rolle? His gentle contact with those around him, his independent spiritual life, lived in the peace of the open country, with time and taste for reflection, for the quest after beauty[2] and truth, as well as mere "goodness," all these, no doubt, are things far too aristocratic, too slow, too unobtrusive, and too individual for the industrial plutocracies, bureaucracies, democracies of to-day. "Ego dormio, et cor meum vigilat,"[3] the hermit's favourite watch-word, rings sadly "out-of-date," like bells of rustic England in summer-time, a dreamy sweetness that is passing, too, for the majority of men.

Yet in further justice to Rolle, his type of religious mysticism was to be as fruitful and as active for others as that of earlier visionaries of the Church, like St Francis or St Bonaventura. There is a mysticism which merely aggravates the condition of the diseased and the weak-willed. But in the healthy spirit it can breed so divine a discontent with the things of earth that

[1] "Clamatores in pulpito!" he calls them.
[2] It is necessary to bear in mind, however, that Rolle retains the harsh mediaeval view of womanly beauty, and indeed of the sex as a whole, from the earlier churchmen (cf. Horstmann, as above, vol. ii, p. xi). But see later, also, on p. 123 below.
[3] "I sleep, and my heart keepeth watch," Cant. v. 2, a text frequently used by Rolle. Cf. too, the quaint English drawing in MS. Add. 37049, fol. 30 b, which illustrates it.

only the most active labours will satisfy the mystic. Such was Richard Rolle of Hampole. By somewhat of a strange paradoxical turn of fortune, the hermit who may have declined to preach was destined to become through his writings one of the greatest influences in our history upon the development of the vernacular sermon. Horstmann declares that there are indications that he did still occasionally exhort the people; after the manner, we may imagine, then, of Dürer's John the Baptist, who preaches to his visitors amid the forest trees. Nor is there wanting in some of his works that denunciation of wanton prelates, or of popular vices and frivolities, that championship of the poor and needy, that sense of an approaching end to evil times, that has been noticed elsewhere. In the *Form of Perfect Living* or in his translation of St Edmund's *Speculum*, there is not a little homely practical teaching of the Puritan kind. Pressure of circumstances, after all, may have had something to do with his decision not to deliver regular exhortations[1]. "Non sum episcopus, nec prelatus, nec rector ecclesiarum. Tamen sollicitus sum pro ecclesia Dei, si possem, aliquo bono modo quidquam facere aut scribere quo ecclesia Dei augmentum capiat in divina dilectione."

So the mystic sets out, in his own words, "Probatus postillator (strictam scripturae masticans medullam, ut degam delicate dulcoribus divinis)," to write expositions, homilies, postils, and commentaries—"for you who have need to preach."[2] As enriched and multiplied by the co-operation of other pens, they were destined "to make the North a literary centre for half a century." The extraordinary extent of that influence will be better realized when we come to deal with the actual sermon literature. For what Wycliffe himself proposed to do with the Latin Scriptures, Rolle and his followers did with the Latin treatises of the friars, until hardly an English homily of the new century lacked some affinity with their work. In the wider history of religion, as elsewhere in life, diversity of tongues and

---

[1] "Hi qui praeferunt (i.e. prelati) maxime me odiunt." "Putant quod non potui pure praedicare nec sapere ut ceteri qui sancte subsistunt," etc. See Horstmann, vol. ii, pp. xxiii and xxiv. (The bishops may actually have prohibited him at one time.)

[2] In the *Cupienti mihi*: "ut, quod ego nondum in publico predicando cogor dicere, saltem vobis ostendam scribendo, qui necessitatem habetis predicare."

diversity of gifts may go to the enrichment of the one body. May we not believe that these two literary branches—to change a metaphor—grew together as part of the great tree of Reformation piety, blossoming afresh in Bunyan and in Fox?

If some left preaching alone with the world, other hermits would choose the life, realizing with Waldeby[1], "that solitarines

THE HERMIT PREACHER
(*From MS. Roy. 14. E. iii, fol. 9ᵇ.*)

is profetable to contemplacioun, where a man may geder by prayer, study, and meditacioun, what he schal sey to the peple in sermonyng."[2] The hermit moreover was not enclosed like the anchorite[3], and his wanderings and haranguings in the twelfth century had for a time almost rivalled those of the subsequent friars. Such had been the Frenchman, Vital of

---

[1] See here in the previous chapter, from the Prologue to his Treatise.
[2] MS. Roy. 8. c. i. (Lichfield).
[3] Yet even these may have left their cell to preach, apparently. Cf. the cases of Scrope and Swinderby following.

Savigny[1], who had addressed audiences in England divinely
assisted, as in that other case described by Gerald of Wales[2],
to understand his Latin. It is a Lollard who complains that
"heremites and pardoners, ankerers and strange beggars are
licensed and admitted of prelates and priests for to beguile the
people with flatterings and leasings slanderously[3]." On the
other hand, Rolle had complained of precisely the opposite—
"heremitas abjiciunt"; and such an episcopal prohibition as
that which concerns friar Henry Staunton, in a York Register[4],
under the year 1334, would seem to bear him out. The situation
turned, no doubt, on the kind of message they were ready to
proclaim. Of more value and interest than any scattered
references, however, for a true estimate of the hermit as preacher,
are certain biographical details recorded of these who for other
reasons figured more prominently in the life of the times. In the
story of Thomas Scrope on the one side, and of William Swinderby on the other, re-told, though only in outline, by writers
of recent date[5], we are provided with an arresting contrast in the
careers of two ascetical men. The former succeeds to a suffragan
bishopric—indeed he might have enjoyed higher dignities still
if he had liked—with a universal reputation for holiness, which
survived to his death-bed. The latter, spurred on by a restless
excitability, ended his days in ignominy and heresy, that particular heresy with which the present survey closes.

Scrope, or Bradley, to call him by the name of his birth-
place, the first of the two mentioned, though of noble parentage[6]
and happier fate than his fellow, seems to have been equally
extravagant in the words and actions of youth. Indeed, he is said

---

[1] See Bourgain, La Chaire fr. p. 181.
[2] Giraldus Cambrensis Opera (Rolls S.), vol. vi, p. 83.
[3] From Thorpe's Testament (see Foxe, Acts and Monum.).
[4] Reg. Archbp. Melton, in Fasti Ebor. vol. i, p. 421. An order forbidding
anyone to listen to the preaching of friar Henry de Staunton, hermit. Cf. also
the action taken at Coventry against the preaching of the hermit John Grace,
1424. (See M. Harris, Life in an Old English Town, p. 141 and footnote
references.)
[5] For Swinderby, see Gairdner, Lollardy and the Reform., vol. i; for Scrope
(or Bradley) see Miss Clay, The Hermits and Anchorites of England, p. 163 et
seq. and D.N.B. My own account is written from original sources.
[6] "Ex nobilissimo Scroporum genere natus, relicto patrimonii jure cum
ceteris fortunae dotibus, in Carmelo Nordovicensi anachoritam professus
est." Bale in MS. Harl. 3838, fol. 107 b.

to have called down upon himself the wrath of the cautious Netter, his Carmelite provincial minister. George Fox's famous appearance in the "bloody city" of Lichfield, when "the word of the Lord was like a fire in me: so I put off my shoes,...and went into the market-place and to and fro in the several parts of it,"[1] is the dark shadow of our Whitefriar in the streets of Norwich about the year 1425. In sackcloth and chains he goes, crying that "the new Jerusalem, bride of the Lamb, would shortly come down from heaven, and be prepared immediately for her spouse," adding "that with great joy he saw her in the spirit." "Apart from his singular doctrine, he was assuredly a most kindly, affable, modest man, and worthy of much veneration," says Bale, who speaks later in glowing terms of his "incredible sanctity of life, and his profound learning." In spite of such eccentricity, and Netter's rebuke, after fourteen years of inclusion[2], somewhere about the year 1446, or subsequently, Pope Eugenius IV compelled him to leave his anchorite's cell, and become Bishop of Dromore in Ireland. But "this most humble man" named a substitute of his own Order[3], and managed to get free of the unwelcome dignity in a very short time. Nevertheless, for twenty years he was constrained to work as suffragan bishop in the diocese of Norwich, an honour, however, which in no way damaged the beauty and simplicity of his character. The last picture of him, which Bale supplies, before his death in 1491, "non sine magna sanctitatis opinione," is that of a venerable figure, going the round of his native district, "with bare feet, after the apostolic practice," preaching the commandments of God to the common people. The fact that a collection of *Sermones de Decem Preceptis* is specifically mentioned by Bale amongst his compositions, together with this curious devotion to the Decalogue on the part of ascetics[4] which applies to his case, might prompt us to

---

[1] 1651. (See *Geo. Fox's Journal*, under date.)

[2] Miss Clay says that Bale speaks of 20 years, but he says clearly "post xiiii inclusionis annos." This must be her mistake for the 20 years, which he mentions later, for his tenure of the suffragan bishopric.

[3] According to Bale, Richard Misyn, Carmelite, possibly the same as the translator of Rolle's *Incendium Amoris*, see here, n. 3, p. 226.

[4] Cf. MS. St John's Coll.; Oxford, 94. (Printed by J. F. Royster as *a Midd. English Treatise on the X Commandmts*; No. vi of *Studies in Philology*, Univ. of North Carolina.) Written by a Northern recluse, c. 1420–34

identify with his name one of the several surviving vernacular tractates on this subject. One group, which has come under the present writer's notice more than once, contains passages which recur again and again in the several versions, thereby suggesting that behind them there must lie unquestionably some common source. In proximity to one of these tracts, which may well be the actual *De Decem Mandatis* of Scrope, there may be found references to the life of the "contemplatyf men, that delyteth hem in contemplacions, and in devotions, and delyteth hem onlyche in God, and in none other thyng, ryȝt as it were an aungel of hevene." Not without intimate acquaintance with its perils, the holy man, whoever he be, warns the ordinary layman that he "be nouȝt to muche alone in solitarye lyvyng, in musyng to muche, and to feer of Godes myȝt and his privetees." He is not called like Lichfield's anchorite to be a lonely bird upon the tree-tops. Let him "drawe to wyse and devout cumpanye," when tempted[1]. On the other hand, the writer insists on the "privy place from al maner noyse, and tyme of reste, without eny lettynge" for the practice of prayer. Posture matters nothing but to free the senses—"Sytte ther or knele as ys most ese!" Whether it be the voice of the kindly old Carmelite friar or not that speaks, here surely we catch the sighing of gentle winds, the rustle of trees, the silent passage of the clouds about some hermit's cell. Appealing descriptions of the sacred Agony recall at once the language of the mystical Yorkshire school[2]: "Behold with thy gostly eyȝe, his pitous passion!" In the sufferings of the Virgin, "the teers of Maudelyn, and of hure other frendes," the preacher

Domin.; (cf. fol. 101 b: "Preyeth for the saul of frere Jon Lacy, anchor (fol. 1 adds 'de ordine fratrum Predicatorum') in the New Castell upon tynde, the wiche that wrooth this book . . ." (fol. 1 adds "A.D. 1434"). May we identify the friar Staunton, hermit, of the Melton Reg. (see n. 4 above, p. 118) with the author of MS. Gray's Inn Library 15, "Staunthone de Decem Preceptis" who was almost certainly a friar Minor? (see here, Chap. 11). As for *Scrope*, his name actually occurs twice in an "Orate pro anima" added to a MS. (Harl. 211, fols. 174 and 191 b), containing one variety of the Tract on the Decalogue here referred to.

[1] Cf. MS. Harl. 2398, fols. 182, 186; cf. also fol. 69 b ("a woman recluse and solitarye . . ."). (The Tract on the Commandments is on fols. 73–106.)

[2] We must not forget to add to the same group of writings by hermits the much shorter "notabill Tretys off the ten Comandementys: drawene by Richerde, *the hermyte off Hampull*," in MS. Thornton (fol. 192 ff.) printed in Horstmann, vol. i, pp. 195, etc.

reaches his emotional climax: "And I trowe amonges alle these thou shalt have compu(n)ccioun, and plente of teerys. Whenne ther cometh suche devocion, than is tyme that thou speke for thyn owen nede, and for alle othere lyves quyke and dede, that tristeth to thyne prayer. Caste down thy body thanne to the grounde, and lyft up thyn herte on hy, with dolful chere thanne make thy mone...."[1] But it is the Mosaic Decalogue above all else, stern, forbidding, self-controlling like the hermit's own life, that must be preached: "Prestes scholde teche thes commandementes of God, and publissche hem with al here my3t to the commune peple....But I drede me that we beo bailleys of erroure for thes commandementes."[2]

With William Swinderby we reach what Carlyle called "the fierce lightning of the Reformer." "No wild Saint Dominics and Thebaid Eremites, there would have been no melodious Dante."[3] We do well to remember this fact, however unfashionable the bitter Lollard and the somewhat morose Reformers may be in these days. The long story of Swinderby's picturesque, stormy career opens in the pages of Henry Knighton's Chronicle[4], and closes, for us, in the Hereford Episcopal Registers of Bishop Treffnant, from which Foxe took the greater part of his narrative in *The Acts and Monuments*[5]. Allowing for the fact that Knighton naturally liked him as little as the good wives of Leicestershire whom he insulted, or the bishops, troubled with his heresies, we see at the least a brave impetuous man of the typical stuff of which "obstinate heretics" are made. Acquainted alike with the solitude of hermit's cell and forest clearing, with the ways of the world whether in town, or country, or monastery, he burns un-

---

[1] MS. Harl. 2398, fol. 186. Cf. too the Passion scene in the St Albans Cath. MS. Treatise on the Commandments, fol. 20; also in MS. Laud. Misc. 23 (with the "litil processe" for prayer (fol. 46[b]), as above).

[2] MS. Harl. 2398, fol. 74. Some of these tracts have been quite groundlessly ascribed to Wycliffe, at all events no friend, as we have seen, to the "contemplatyf men." See further in my article in the *Transactions of the St Albans and Herts. Archaeological Society*, for 1924 ("A 15th-century MS. in St Albans Cathedral"), and on p. 281, et seq., below.

[3] *Heroes and Hero-Worship*," Lect. IV, "The Hero as priest."

[4] Under 1382 (see Rolls S., Chron. Knightn. p. 189 et seq.).

[5] The reference to the account of *Proceedings before Bishop Trefnant against William Swinderby, the heretical preacher*, is from Reg. Treffnant (Hereford), pp. 231, et seq. (publ. Cantilupe Soc. and Cant. and York Soc.).

ceasingly with a genuine passion over the corruptions of Church and State, without ever being able to hold his peace about it. If ever clamour could save the world, the pulpit Swinderbys might be justly hailed as its redeemers. "Cry aloud and spare not; lift up thy voice like a trumpet, and show my people their transgression!" Silenced in one diocese, he breaks out in another. Expelled from the churches, he appears upon the highways or in the fields. Hustled and rejected by one crowd to-day, he has a new following by to-morrow. In short, his whole life is at once a lesson in the growth and development of Lollardy, and a curious foreshadowing of the Dissenting type of Tudor and early Stuart times.

A certain mystery seems to hang about his very origin, obscure like that of so many later sectaries. "There was in those days (c. 1380) at Leicester," says the chronicler, "a certain priest William de Swynderby, whom men called William the Hermit, in that he had practised the heremitical life for some time in that place. But when he came hither, or from whence he derived his origin is unknown." Restlessness seems to have been the one certain feature of his early life. Many occupations he had tried; but none satisfied him. Here is the roving inconstant mind of the heretic-preacher at its first stages, as seen by an opponent[1]. He is an undisciplined man, possessed of that fatal spirit of "curiosity" and enquiry, which will always be the foe of religions of authority. His first recorded preaching topic —"de mulierum defectibus et superbia"—merely alluded to by Gairdner, is of interest to us in view of its regular occurrence in every type of contemporary sermon:

Nam ornatum mulierum multum despiciebat, superbiamque, et actus earum aspernabatur, lasciviasque earum aspernabatur; et quamvis bene agebat, tamen nimis importune de hac materia tracta-

---

[1] There is an interesting passage in Dr Lichfield's *Tractate* which throws a quaint contemporary light on the psychology of men like Swinderby (MS. Ryl. 8. C. i, fol. 124 b): "Mich peple that are bonden to cylence, as religyouse folke, *ankyres* and ankereses, are like to floode ʒatys of a mylne, wyche long tyme withstandith the water and kepith it, that it flow not. Bot wen the flowdeʒatys ar opened, then shotys the watir oute at onys. Thus many suche peple kepyn silence for a tyme in certen places. But wen the place or occacion of spekyng comith, *then they speke to myche* and veyn. Thus did the frendes of Job, that were comen to confort hym. They sate still vii dayes; but wen they begonnen to speke, thay couthe not stynt her tonges."

bat, quia finem facere nesciebat, sicuti nec in quacumque alia materia quam in predicatione tractabat.

That was the whole tragedy of his career. Others, we know for certain, denounced unsparingly the wanton fashions, the wigs, the paint, the "horns," the long-flowing trains, the rich furs and wasteful sleeve-lengths, as well as womanly pride and passion. They "did well."[1] But he "never knew when to stop." So heavily did these rebukes from the pulpit weigh upon the minds of the townswomen, good, bad, and indifferent, that they actually proposed to stone him out of the place. But scenting the danger in time, says Knighton, he turned his attentions instead to the wickedness of merchants and plutocrats, "frequently asserting in his sermons that no one could enjoy the riches of this world, and affluence of temporal goods, and attain to the kingdom of heaven." This, again, is only one step beyond the accusing language of Bromyard himself, who, like others, would well nigh damn the merchant and his kind with charges of lying, perjury and the basest forms of deceit chiefly at the

[1] It is only possible to give one or two illustrations from orthodox preaching here. Dr Bromyard makes most amusing reading; cf. *S.P.—Bellum* (The devil's Amazons): "Adducens...militissas suas,...habentes, pro galea, cornua, et capitegia, et frontalia; et sic de alia armatura,—intantum quod a planta pedis usque ad verticem capitis, nihil in eis invenies nisi sagittas diaboli acutissimas...Mulieres in habitu meretricio, ludentes seu choreizantes, vel cum signis levibus incedentes...Tripudiatrices et fatuae mulieres ...," etc. *S.P.—Luxuria* (The devil's incendiaries): "In muliere namque impudice ornata ad capiendas animas, sertum in capite est quasi unus carbo vel titio inferni pro igne illo accendendo, sic cornua alterius, sic collum nudatum, sic firmaculum in pectore, sic de omnibus curiositatibus totius corporis...." (The devil's Apostles): "Sic diabolus eas ad hoc ornat, et per villam, tanquam apostolos suos, mittit, repletas omni iniquitate, malitia, fornicatione...," etc. Rypon, MS. Harl. 4894, fol. 181: "Sed quid dicam de modernis mulieris (sic!)? Certe nedum quod 'mulier *erat* in civitate peccatrix,' sed quod mulier *est* in civitate peccatrix...," etc. MS. Add. 21253, fol. 45 b, etc. ("de muliere fatua, garrula, et vaga, quietis impatiens, nec valens in domo consistere, pedibus suis nunc foris, nunc plateis...," etc.). Ibid. fol. 54 b: "Isti insidiantes, et aucupes, et venatores sunt demones; laquei eorum, discipulae et pedicae sunt malae et fatuae mulieres, quae in apparatibus suis et deceptionibus suis capiunt homines et decipiunt...." The writer actually speaks here of the "many sermons" which deal with this subject. MS. Harl. 45, fol. 96, also calls them "the develis grenes" or snares, even if the wearers are not lecherous themselves. MS. Harl. 1197, fol. 1 b: ("women that arayin hem nycely to be seen of foolis"). MS. Roy. 8. C. i, fol. 123: ("strumptes aray, to gret boldenes,...nyse japynge, nyse cherynge, and sych othere"). MS. Harl. 2398, fol. 9 "Jacob's Well" (ed. E.E.T.S. p. 150, etc.).

expense of rustics and the unsuspecting poor[1]. So far, then, the actual content of Swinderby's message is strangely faithful to the directions for preaching laid down by the great orthodox manuals. It is at least a tribute to his pulpit forcefulness that the chronicle pays, when it informs us that certain honest souls in Leicester were well-nigh driven to desperation by his indictment.

Next follows a period of solitude, first in a hermitage on the Duke of Lancaster's estates, afterwards in a cell within the precincts of Leicester Abbey, set inside or against the conventual church[2]. There is further proof that there was no heresy about his utterances, when we read that the canons received him as a holy man, and continued to supply him with the necessities of life ("victum cum pensione")[3]. This period coincides with a spell of village preaching, and would lead us to suppose that even recluses sometimes could be active to this extent. From the chronicler's lines, one would gather, further, that it was this missionary contact with the outside world that brought him into touch with the Lollard movement, then rapidly spreading through the district. At all events he fell under the spell of one William Smyth and other Wycliffites, dwelling "in a certain chapel of St John the Baptist near a Leper-house," and so became one of their modest company[4].

Little imagination is needed to understand how restless, dis-

---

[1] Bromyard (S.P.—Mercatio) accuses the merchants of profiteering in corn; of using false weights and measures; tricking the balances with the hand; mixing goods with sand, or wetting them to increase weight; mixing new goods with old; miscounting coin, or including bad coin with good; tricking the rustics; selling goods in "locis obscuris" to disguise their real quality and colour, etc. So Rypon, MS. Harl. 4894, fol. 68 b: "Nonnulli mercatores committunt furtum, qui per falsa pondera, per falsas mensuras, per falsa mercimonia circumveniunt populum...." Cf. also ibid. fol. 36, etc. MS. Harl. 45, fol. 71: "lienge" and "forswerynge," "false-schewynge," as in Bromyard: "as doth drapers, mercers, and many other suche," etc. MS. St Albans Cath. fol. 36: "weiȝtes and mesures ben yvel weied and fillid; as tapsteris don"; false weights and measures again in MS. Caius Coll. Camb. 334, fol. 178 b (Waldeby); MS. Harl. 2398, fol. 100 b; Jacob's Well (E.E.T.S. ed.), pp. 133, 118, 212, etc. (Also here cheating the rustics again, and forcing up prices, etc.) I hope to deal with this subject in a subsequent study of "English Society in the Sermons."
[2] "In quadam camera infra ecclesiam."
[3] Cf. Clay, The Hermits, etc. p. 104 et passim, for other examples.
[4] For another interesting case of a recluse (this time female) suspected of Lollardy in this very district, cf. that of the anchoress Matilda, in the churchyard of St Peter's Church, Leicester (mentioned by Foxe, Acts and Monums.), see Knighton's Chron. (Rolls S.), vol. ii, p. 312. (1392.)

satisfied preachers, like the Leicester hermit, found a fresh and welcome rallying point in the new sect, if such it can be called. Knighton himself, speaking of the situation, tells us so greatly was it multiplied, by now, that of every two men that you might meet on the road one would be almost certainly a follower of the Oxford reformer. Dissatisfaction, indeed, is sown broadcast over our sermon literature, as well. No sinister motives therefore from Knighton are needed to explain the adhesion of such a character. The patience of many churchmen might be long. That might only prove how passive if not positively indifferent they could become under the yoke of familiar evils. Less tolerant souls, however, writhing under the same rotten and foetid ecclesiastical system that bishop and friar had cursed, would grow tired at length, and have none of it. Why then should they not welcome with outstretched hands the first signs of this "reformacion without tarying for anie"?

With Swinderby, as we should expect, the new move was to be the signal for a fresh outburst of preaching. How should he contain himself? The new theme was "contra libertates ecclesiae, et contra ecclesiasticos personas," continues our indignant narrator, "to blacken the reputation of the church-men, by asserting that they lived a shameless life, appropriated church goods in evil manner, and expended them in worse." Indeed! Dr Gairdner may be a little shocked and impressed; but we can hardly be deceived at this stage by the crafty Knighton. Was there a single eminent preacher of the day on the side of orthodoxy who was not speaking, even writing for the future instruction of others, in precisely the same strain[1]?

[1] See here, in Chap. I. For the rest I can only take that orthodox enemy of Lollards, Master Rypon of Durham, to illustrate further (MS. Harl. 4894, fol. 213): "Quod dolendum est, nonnulli, et forsan sacerdotes et clerici, potius voluptati quam castigationi corporum inherentes in dicto bello per gladium carnalis concupiscentie miserabiliter sunt devicti, et in carnalibus peccatis, presertim in gula et luxuria, quasi bestiales effecti, in tantum quod de gulosis sacerdotibus verificatur illud prophete—'Sacerdotes pre ebrietate nescierunt,' et de luxuriosis sacerdotibus...(Bernardus)—'In multis sacer-dotibus regnat fornicatio....'" Page after page can be found in the same strain. So Bromyard, Waldeby (see especially MS. Roy. 7. E. ii, fol. 31: "wicked and lascivious priests expending church possessions in fornication and other uncleanness," etc.), Wimbledon, Lathbury, and a host of others. Archbp. Fitzralph's accounts of his fellow prelates ("tam majores quam minores") beggar all description. Cf. also here, in Chap. I, pp. 35, 42–3, and Chap. VI, pp. 248–253, etc.

However, it was certainly one thing for the doctor and the prelate to make such remarks before suitable congregations, and quite another thing in Swinderby's case to cry them from the house-tops. Matters grew far more serious, when he and his associates proceeded to tell their lay audiences that old heresy that the priest who lives contrary to the law of God is no priest at all, and that it is a positive sin to give tithes to the immoral, to the absentee, to the ignorant and non-preaching curate[1]. For it was this and not the clerical condemnation that constituted the ravings of a heretic. The message[2] was proclaimed alike to the citizens of Leicester, and to the country-folk of Melton and "Loughtborowe," in hospital chapel, in parish church, and cemetery. For once his historian bears eloquent witness to his successes: "He captured the affability of the crowd, and attracted their friendship to such an extent that they would say that never had they seen or heard anyone expound to them the truth like him; and thus he was revered as another god among them." Strange contrast to earlier results in the same district!

Notoriety of this kind naturally attracted the attention of the Bishop of Lincoln, and at length led to an injunction of silence and ostracism. Then occurred that amazing scene, as dramatic surely as anything in the annals of covenanting Scotland, or Puritan England, when the preacher seized upon two mill-stones which lay for sale in the high street, outside his chapel, and setting them up for a pulpit, summoned the crowd, and preached in defiance of all bishops "that he was able and willing to preach in the king's high-way in the teeth of a hostile bishop, if only he retained the good-will of the people." "Then you should see the throngs of people from every quarter, from town and countryside alike, flock to his preaching in number twice as great after this inhibition and sentence of excommuni-cation as ever before it." What a theme for Carlyle to have conjured with! "He is the warfaring and battling Priest, who

[1] Yet as regards the first statement we find Master Rypon saying in his sermon (MS. Harl. 4894, fol. 207 b): "Tales ideo mali sacerdotes sunt solum nomine tenus, et non realiter sacerdotes, quia nec bene vivunt, nec bene docent." (*But* here in a sermon to the clergy themselves only, *not* "ad populum"!)
[2] Cf. also his advanced views on the subject of debtors: "Item predicabat quod homines possunt debita sua cum caritate petere a suis debitoribus, sed nullo modo aliquem propter debita implacitare aut incarcerare."

led his people, not to quiet, faithful labour, as in smooth times, but to faithful, valorous conflict in times all violent, dismembered: a more perilous service, and a more memorable one, be it higher or not."

Unfortunately in Swinderby's case the note of triumphant leadership was not to last. He was only rescued, after fresh citation and examination, from the fate of burning, by the kindly offices of the aforesaid Duke of Lancaster, and was forced to make an ignominious recantation of his heresies and errors. In later years he told how the false witnesses arrayed against him then were "five friers or more, that some of them never saw me before, ne heard me, and three lecherous priestes opanlie knowen, some living in their lecherie twenty yeare, men sayden, or more, as by their childer was openly knowen." Space forbids that we follow him further afield with the same precision as hitherto. There is another period of silence and retirement, like that of Luther after Worms perhaps, when he dwelt at the old Leicester chapel again—"sad and mournful, to such an extent that those of his friends who formerly saw him in his prosperous days, now left him as it were desolate, neither visiting, nor consoling him, nor ministering to him his wonted sustenance." That is the tragic fate of the preacher whose triumphs have been achieved on the strength of pulpit reputation alone. Now out of his throne, too broken in spirit and hedged about with enemies to maintain further resistance in the open, the spell is broken and the reputation blasted. His friends forsook him when the old defiance perished. The tale of his recovery, of his flight to Coventry, "where in a short time he was held in greater honour than before by the laity, and preached for about a year" with striking results, of his subsequent alarms and incursions in the diocese of Hereford, all can be read in the pages of Foxe, of Gairdner, or of the original Registers themselves[1]. Nor is it within our present scope to consider the character of his erroneous opinions.

---

[1] With Swinderby cf. further the case of Jo. Grace, and the popularity of his preaching in the Little Park, at Coventry, in 1424; first monk, then friar, then recluse. For references to the *Leet Book*, etc. see Harris, *Life in an Old English Town*, pp. 140–41; and Clay, *The Hermits...*, p. 164. Cf. further MS. Harl. 6388, fol. 16, "A Hermit preached in the Parke and there was a great audience."

The actual style of Swinderby's preaching may be gathered
from what, though called *A Letter to the Nobles and Burgesses
of the Parliament*, is obviously compiled from a typical discourse
of some kind[1]. Its tenor agrees well with the spirit of the
hunted man. Picture him, now in "a desert wood cleped
Derwaldswood," "and there in a certain chapel not hallowed, or
rather in a profane cottage,"—"accurset shepheardes hulke,"
some called it, now "in an unhallowet chappell that stonds in
the parke of Newton[2], besides the towne of Leyntwarden of this
same dioces"; now, on his own confession, "preaching to the
people in the church of Witney of your dioces." He cries to the
Parliament men: "This land is full of ghostly cowards, in ghostly
battaile, fewe dare stand. But Christ, the comforter of all that
falleth (to that his heart brast for our love) against that fiend,
the doughtie duke, comforteth us thus, *Estote fortes in bello*. . . .
'Be ye strong in battaile,' he saies, 'and fight ye with the old
adder.'" The speaker knows there is little need to describe the
abuses of the times. No one would deny them. Rather does he
challenge the secular arm, in characteristic Lollard fashion, to
defend the right: "Awake ye quickly and slepe nought, and
stand now strongly for God's law," even as "Judas Machabeus,
that was God's true knight, that comforted hartely God's true
people to be the followers of His law." The whole is couched
in the most violent threatening language as we should expect, of
fierce penalties from God[3], of impending vengeance on those
"that breake his bidding, and dispiseth his lawes and his domes."
The thunders of the persecuted sectary are added to those of
the erstwhile hermit. His regular denunciations after the old
prophetic manner, his solid array of Israelitish heroes well
foreshadow that element of Old Testament Judaism which was
to permeate alike the preaching and the practice of the Reformed

---

[1] See Foxe, *Acts and Monums.* bk. v (*Ch. Hist. Ed.* 1855, vol. iii, pt i,
pp. 128–30).

[2] Swinderby himself seems to have denied preaching in this chapel
("Truely I wot not where that place stands"). From W. H. Summers,
Our Lollard Ancestors (1906), it would appear that remains of both these
chapels survive, the former (Deerfold Forest, W. Herefordshire) known as
"the Lollard's Chapel" (pp. 51–2).

[3] "If that ye wenden against me and will not heare me, I shall adde hereto
seven fold woundes for your sinnes. I shall send amongest you beestes of the
field that shall devour you and your beestes. I shall bring you into a field, and
wayes shuln be desart. . . ."

Faith for centuries to come. But, as we have seen, it is no exclusive cry of the disappointed fanatics. The great churchmen
of the court and the Universities, judges and opponents of
Wycliffe, were equally disappointed in their way, certainly
equally violent and threatening with tongue and pen. Such is
the last word of too many, be they high-placed, or low, for a
world that snuffs out their fond enterprise, that rejects their
little plan of salvation. With it go the vision and the hopes too
often built like those of the petulant child upon a here-and-now,
an outward manifestation, an external *Civitas Dei*, that is
soon denied them. For all their talk of a future life, Heaven to
Bromyard or Waldeby is little better than a welcome vindictive
triumph over an evil generation and a perverse world that
opposed them. Such it has remained to a large extent in the
old-fashioned Protestant theology.

Once more we are brought face to face then, in the history of
our pulpit, not with mere picturesque trifles of antiquity, but
fundamental issues of life, that cannot be relegated to any
"dark ages." For hard it is in every period to find the correct
mean between an excessive tolerance, and an excessive out-
spokenness. This impetuous believer, to whom the religious
solution and its God seem clear as daylight, stark realities,
imperative and intimate as the moral law within, will fight all
the braver for his narrow creed. He may succeed to a "crowning mercy" of his own, and beyond it. Sooner or later there
comes the moment when his little arrogant schemes may be
shattered at a stroke. Who was he to set right the world, and
pose as the champion of the Almighty? This other, a scholar,
large-minded, patient, diffident, a respecter of institutions,
shrinks and does nothing aggressive—"*waiting* for the consolation of Israel." Who shall choose between them, for a despairing world? Too seldom at all events has the disappointed
preacher—like Milton, or an almost forgotten liberal Germany
—had wit and courage enough to break forth into singing, when
outward hopes were destroyed. If we mistake not, it is here that
the "Incendium Amoris" proves its vast incomparable superiority over the theology and the ethic of the "Dies Irae." For
the "idly contemplative" Rolle, with his steady glow, continues
to warm and cheer our spirits, long after the flaming Lollard

and Anabaptist have burnt themselves and their propaganda—
not their enemies—to ashes. To the perspiring Swinderbys
the time is so short, the day of the Lord is always "at hand";
not some gentle day of inspiration leading to long summer
moods and mellow autumns, but a sudden violent act of destruction, a storm designed to suit a peevish temper, and a petty
grievance against the creation: "And therefore, sith our time
is short, how short no man knowes but God...." The real
seer and man of faith, soothed and uplifted by the majestic silences
and travailings of God and Nature, will leave to the future in
song, in poem, in sonata, or in the fragrant memories of his few
intimate friends what the present refused to hearken to, or
understand. "And now I have told you before it come to pass.
...Hereafter I will not *talk* much with you."

But what of the Lollard, and his place in the English pulpit,
now that we have come to him? When Dr Gairdner wrote his
learned study from a ripe acquaintance with almost every kind
of document that might be associated with ecclesiastical and
public Records[1], it is safe to say that the rich contemporary
evidence of great orthodox sermon collections in this country
had not lain open before him, nor probably before anyone else.
Though a peep into this other chamber would certainly not have
intoxicated him, it could hardly have failed to enhance that sense
of "much moral evil," in the Church, "which the best men in
her knew not how to remedy."[2] However exaggerated, however
antiquated in its forms of speech, this particular literature has
an intimacy not merely with outward facts but with the inward
thoughts and feelings of reputable churchmen of the day which
cannot be ignored[3]. In the light of it therefore the deeper

[1] Except the Registers, I understand, which he confessedly had not
studied.

[2] See *Lollardy and the Reform.*, vol. i, pp. 36, 37.

[3] See especially above in Chap. i. Here is another sample from Rypon
(*Syn. Serm.* MS. Harl. 4894, fol. 198): "...Omnes gradus ecclesiae militantis, quorum quilibet indubitanter Christum male vivendo *in multis
personis* illudit. Sed quilibet conqueritur de alio dicens, 'Vath qui destruis
templum Dei!' Clerici imponunt defectus regnantes in ecclesia laicis, et
laici clericis econverso, superiores inferioribus, inferiores superioribus. Sed
certe possum vere dicere illud, quod dixit mulier de infante in presencia
Salomonis, 'Nec mihi, nec tibi, sed dividatur!' Nullus gradus in ecclesia se
potest totaliter, *ut estimo,* excusare. Sed comparando laicos clericis, *timeo*
quod clericorum peccata sunt graviora criminibus laicorum...," etc.

history of such movements for reform will have to be re-written or expanded. With the witness of these English preachers of eminence before us, now supplementing the evidence of the Registers, it is certainly quite impossible to dismiss the Reformation as any mere act of wanton cupidity or destructiveness, from without. Meanwhile, we are faced, roughly speaking, with three groups of new material; first, the utterances of men whom we can recognize directly as the outspoken enemies of Wycliffe or his party—Bromyard, Brunton, Rypon, Myrc, Lathbury[1], and others, whose words make clear confession of their attitude; secondly, the equally indubitable homilies and tracts provided by the Lollards themselves. But between the two, as it were, there appears a third group of manuscripts, written in the vernacular, whose authorship may be a matter of some debate. Hitherto usually attributed to the reformer, when noticed and attributed at all, by reason of their demand for more scriptural preaching, and their independent criticism of abuses, they reject none the less what the records of trials and sentences declare to be the characteristic Lollard attitude towards images, lay-reading of Scripture, veneration of saints, and so forth. These will be discussed and explained in a subsequent chapter, but for the present we may safely discard for them a heretical authorship. All three groups are remarkably unanimous upon one point, the disastrous corruption in the Church. There is little attempt to hide any of it, and many of the statements have a similarity which is positively arresting. In favour of Lollardy, then, viewed as a first deliberate attempt to *do* something practical[2] and immediate to remove abuses, where others merely threatened and denounced, they constitute a very formidable argument. Yet with drastic proposals for reform, however well-grounded, there must always be the further question of

---

[1] Although in the case of Rypon, and Myrc, practically nothing is known of their careers, their writings contain definite attacks on the Lollards, as heretics of the day (similarly with the unknown author of *Jacob's Well*). This is especially marked in the case of Rypon (cf. p. 138, n. 1, below).

[2] This essentially *practical* aspect of their religious view is well brought out in the Lollard preaching. The homilist of MS. Add. 24202 contrasts with the idle folly of pilgrimages what to him are the real religious duties: "to kepe Goddis hestis, and mayntene oure lawe, and help faderlis and moderlis children and pore widowis, and to releve hor tenauntis of chargis and taxis that thei may not wel bere...," etc. (fol. 28 b).

appropriate means. Here the follower of Wycliffe seems to have proved himself as prone as any reforming agent of history, to that excessive insolence and tyranny which so often ruins the success of the cause. There are preaching scenes, indeed, as vivid as those of Swinderby which testify to that fact. A mayor of Northampton and his friends, for example, are not above arresting a vicar by armed force in his own church, in the middle of the service, to compel a hearing for the Lollard preacher they have introduced, "the said maior remaining in the pulpit hard by the preacher, till he had finished his sermon." And now "the whole town is become Lollardes, no man dareing open his mouth against theire likeinge for fear of the said maior and Lollards."[1] Moreover, once outside the schools, it was so subversive a movement from below, that who, amongst persons of any responsibility[2], recalling the Peasants' Revolt or the murder of Sudbury, could fail to be suspicious of the results? The task of a Treffnant was unenviable indeed, when further "stirring up of schism between clergy and people" might well provoke a revolution. But when all is admitted, Carlyle's dictum about the Reformation has to stand for the historian, however little to the liking of the ecclesiastical "clothes-philosophers" of to-day: "When Hercules turned the purifying river into King Augeas' stables, I have no doubt the confusion that resulted was considerable all around. But I think it was not Hercules' blame; it was some other's blame!"

The first point to be noticed in the general contribution of Wycliffe to English mediaeval preaching is his insistence on "the naked text," or exposition of the Gospel message "per nudum textum," freed of the accumulation of foreign matter from without. On the one hand, the ignorance and silence of parochial clergy, on the other, the scholastic refinements and

---

[1] See Powell and Trevelyan (*Docs.* re Peasants' Revolt), p. 46. The whole account is worth reading (c. 1393). Cf. (after the fray): "The said maior gat him up into the pulpit to incourage the said preacher to goe forward with his sermon, etc. and commaunded the people to keep silence, and give heed to the sermon uppone the paine of death...."

[2] Cf. Letter of the Archbp. of Canterbury, 1382, in *Fascic. Ziz.* (Rolls S.), p. 272: "...per predicationem suorum et sibi (Wycl.) adherentium, qui semper dissencionem pretendebant, et plebem ad insurrectionem provocabant ita ut vix aliquis eorum predicaret, quin ad pugnam inter se audientes provocarentur, et schismata in villis fierent."

analogues of the doctors and friars had made such a demand
sooner or later inevitable. "Sermones de tempore" in manuscript will prove how widely the reformer's challenge was to be
taken up. Furthermore, from it can be traced each successive
step in the Lollard conception of the pulpit. Though neither
his Evangelicalism nor his Puritanism were by any means
original, as we have seen, this adhesion to the scriptural phrase
as ultimate standard of religion itself, revived and maintained
the superiority of pulpit evangelism over ceremonial, and with
it every element of mediaeval Puritanism which had flourished
in the past. True theology, argues Wycliffe, needs no "Forma"
for its presentation. "Goddes Law" alone has power of
regeneration. "Debet evangelisator predicare plane evangelicam
veritatem."[1] Therefore very naturally it follows that "this
veyn novelrie" in song and Use and furniture, this "deschaunt,
countre note, orgon, smale brekynge," these prayers and
Masses "withouten cessynge," and the rest, are as superfluous
and as evil a concession to the sensuous spirit of the age as the
japes and "glosing" and "argumentis that foolis maken," in
the pulpits. Nay, rather they are all hindrances abominable
to the proclamation of the Word. If, further, with Sautry, for
example, "I say that each deacon and priest is held to preach
the Word of God rather than to say matins and canonical hours,"[2]
why should not worship of images, places, and relics, "processions, genuflections, inclinations, censings, kissings, oblations,
kindling of lights, pilgrimages," and the rest go the same way
eventually as the canonical hours? So with regard to the actual
manner of sermon delivery, there were other simplifications to
be made. Preachers "shulden preche opinli...and drede no
worldeli muk in houses." They should "algatis beware that
the peple undirstonde wel, and so use comoun speche in ther
owne persone." They must not fail to speak to audiences,

---

[1] *De Off. Pred.* II, c. 3. Cf. here also MS. Trin. Coll. Camb. 60, fol. 4 b
(Lollard sermons): 'For Christ's preachers should cleanly tell God's law,
and not meddle with man's law that is troubled water. For man's law con-
taineth sharp stones and trees by which the net of God is broken.... For
virtues and vices and truths of the Gospel be matter enough to preach to the
people.' See further Loserth's Introd. to Wycl. *Serm. Lat.* (Wycl. S.) vol. i.
[2] See his Conclusions, No. 3, in *Fascic. Ziz.* (Rolls S.), p. 409. Wycliffe
makes the remark that Christ says nothing of these things in the Gospels, but
only of preaching.

"for thei be fewe, and oure fame shulde be litil." Did not
Christ himself go to "smale uplandishe towns, as to Bethfage,
and to Cana in Galile," while "he traveilide not for wynnynge
of moneie"? They must be set free for the work of the ministry,
from taint of simony, from benefices, and—here we reach what
is perhaps the crowning heresy of the Lollard position—from
episcopal control and interference: "Crist was not lettid thanne
bi feigned jurisdiccioun to preche amonge the folke, al if he
wrathide the prelattis; for this use in jurisdiccioun was not yit
brought in by cautel of the fiend, as it now is, to lette trewe
prechinge." This sentiment, expressed thus in a sermon of
Wycliffe, became a challenge in the mouth of every follower
after him, to flout the episcopal license, and preach, like
Swinderby, "withouten leefe of byschoppes."[1]

Now much in the new programme might find a parallel in
the work and life of the early friars. In its Puritanism it recalls
the tone of St Bernard and the primitive Franciscans. The independence and stern moral teaching of its spokesmen reminds
us also of the hermits[2]. But this last persistent attitude erected
into a doctrine was an innovation indeed. In the long history
of the pulpit it was the bishop who by his apostolic rank, his
primal cure of souls, was from the first looked upon as chief
preacher of all. It was only at his will and pleasure that the
Mendicants, in all their glory, had been allowed to exercise
that privilege in the dioceses. The defiance of the Lollard, then,
we must consider as a last word in that long pulpit condemnation of prelacy, its utter incapacity, its foul behaviour, and its
negligence of this same instruction. Heresy, with support from
the civil arm, was now to attempt what friar and hermit would

---

[1] Cf. e.g. also Wycliffe, *Lat. Sermones* (ed. Loserth), vol. ii, Sermo
xxxviii, etc.; *Fascic. Ziz.* passim; the *Lanterne of Light* (MS. Harl. 2324, is
a copy of this, ed. E.E.T.S., O.S., No. 151): "Sacerdotes simplices et fideles
contra prohibitionem episcoporum, et absque predicandi licentia possunt
predicare cum voluerint" (quoted in Wilkins, *Conc.* vol. iii, p. 374), etc. Cf.
also Swinderby's typical argument: "I say that no bishop oweth to let a true
priest that God hath giffen grace, wit, and cunning to do that office; for both
priestes and deacons that God hath ordained deacons or priestes bene holden
by power given to them of God to preach;...for this is due to the people
and the parisheners to have it, and aske it."

[2] Their fondness for the Commandments (see above, p. 119) descends to the
Lollards. See MS. Add. 24202, fol. 32 [rather even than *paternoster*, or
bileve, etc., "it is most nede to teche hem the hestis of God"]; also Wycliffe's
De Mandatis, recently published by the Wyclif Society.

often have done themselves if they had dared. It was to attempt, it is true, but to fail—until the Reformation. In similar fashion, that other great innovation, the gift of vernacular Scriptures direct to the laity, might be looked upon as an equivalent sentence passed upon the notorious failure of the parish clergy to instruct. Finally, if according to the original Lollard plan, deacon and unbeneficed priest might preach as freely as any "curate," what should stop an extension of the privilege to the very layman himself? This, as we know, is where the daring enterprise ended[1]. No testimony is more fresh and impressive in its way perhaps, than that of a Latin homily in an anonymous collection of the period. The speaker beholds in the lay evangelists another warning sign of the times:

> Behold now we see so great a scattering of the Gospel, that simple men and women, and those accounted ignorant laymen [laici ydiote] in the reputation of men, write and study the Gospel, and, as far as they can and know how, teach and scatter the Word of God. But whether God would appoint such, as the world grows old, to confound the pride of the worldly-wise, I know not. God knoweth![2]

In closing, we can only afford to glance at the Lollard preacher, as his opponents see him, and at the practical outcome of his propaganda. Knighton's account of their discourses as opening with much sweetness and devotion, and closing with much subtle ill-will and detraction, does agree on the whole with the great doctor's own method as set forth, for example, in his vernacular homilies. Wycliffe's Gospel expositions develope, almost invariably, into some censure or other of current abuses, before they end. Sometimes the reader is left to amplify it himself: "Here the preacher may touch upon all manner of sins, especially those of false priests and traitors to God." Not unnaturally this feature of abuse grows rather than diminishes

---

[1] E.g. cf. the famous case of Walter Brute, "a lay person, learned, of our diocese," etc. See Reg. Bp. Treffnant, pp. 278 et seq. (1391).

[2] MS. Camb. Univ. Libr. Ii. iii. 8, fol. 149. The preacher goes on to refer to the Abbot Joachim of Fiore (c. 1145–1202) "in expositione Joann." (i.e. the *Expos. in Apoc.* or the pseudo-Joachite additions). Rypon, speaking of their activities, as "Lollardi," adds (MS. Harl. 4894, fol. 77 b): "Et forsan Deus misericorditer hoc permittit, ut illi insipientes, qui super se curas animarum assumunt, ad perquirendam meliorem scientiam excitentur." Cf. also *Jacob's Well* (ed. E.E.T.S. p. 276): "But some laymen kun better knowen hem-self in governaunce from sin than some gret clerkes...," etc.

in the sermons of his followers[1]. Hence what we have seen
illustrated in the career of Swinderby became the regular complaint of those of responsible position in the Church, who saw
in every Lollard an active centre of dissension, even of popular
revolt, in the towns. As Bishop Brunton reminds us again, the
middle and lower classes with their strong anti-clerical bias were
all too ready to give ear to his sweeping accusations[2].

Political and social revolt was bad enough; but what of
revolution in theology? From what has been said so far in the
present chapter of the characteristic message of Lollardy, and
indeed from a more prolonged study of Wycliffite literature, the
impression will be gained that this movement was in its own way
as completely dependent upon traditional authority and the
influence of the past as orthodox Catholicism itself. The infallibility of the Scriptural text had merely taken the place of
the infallibility of an inspired organization, which further professed to hold the one key to its correct interpretation. This is
true. But modern historians of the Church in their portrait
of the Lollard as a narrow "Evangelical," are sometimes too
apt to overlook another side to his appeal. It was a side of
which neither he nor his opponents were able to miss the
significance in their own day. The Lollard preacher himself
cries, like the prophetic Joachim, that it is now high time for
men to put away childish things, the external machinery of
worship, and develope a more inward and spiritual religion:
"And now men shulden be more gostly."[3] Though in almost
the same breath he proclaims his challenge a return to the
golden age of the Church—"as dyden the apostlis of Crist,"
it involves none the less an advance towards the spiritual

---

[1] Cf. e.g. MS. Trin. Coll. Camb. 60, its bitter attacks on the Pope, etc.:
fol. 5, prelates and "new religious" are "the fiend's church," etc.; fol. 112 b,
"Pope is Anti-Christ, and cardinals are his 'wicked limbs,'" etc.

[2] MS. Harl. 3760, fol. 217 b: "Immo mediocres et populares citius audiunt
clamores docentium errores, quam veros predicatores." See here above,
p. 132, n. 2.

[3] MS. Add. 24202, fol. 26 b (a Lollard sermon treatise on Images). Cf.
also the significance of the statement a line or two later: "for oure lord God
dwellis by grace in gode mennes soulis," etc. This is the interesting MS.
purchased by the British Museum from Archbp. Tenison's Library at the
church of St Martin-in-the-Fields from which Halliwell printed the sermon
"of miraclis pleyinge" (fol. 14 et seq.) in *Reliq. Antiq.* vol. ii, p. 42 et seq.
(copied by Mätzner, *Altenglische Sprachproben*, pp. 222 et seq.).

independence of the future. To go back was but to go forward. It is in the sermons of opponents, however, that he is made to appear as the veritable champion of what to-day might be called "modernist" opinions. Of all his heresies the most grievous lay in his attitude toward the Holy Mysteries of the altar. Here he is heretic indeed, eternal type of those accounted proud in their own conceits, who put reason before revelation, and take sides with "Science" in her notorious conflict with Religion. Says the orthodox homilist:

Bot this luf and drede [of Christ in the Sacrament] wantes many gret clerkes, the which leven so mich upon ther owne kindely resoun, and the princepales of philosophi th^t is mannes wisdom groundede onely in kindely resoun of man, th^t thai wil not leve [i.e. believe] the trew feith taght be holy chirch of this blessed sacrament. And therfore thai fele not the sothfast confortable effecte of the mervailes and miracles before saide, neither opun nor privey, toching this holi sacrament. Wherfore mich folk is deceyvet in that party, th^t rather ʒiven credence to th^t a gret clerk teches acording to kindely resoun, then to th^t holy chirch teches here of onely in bileve above resoun.

For ther may no man soner erre in bileve of the sacramentes of holy chirch, and specialy in this hie wonderful sacrament of cristes precious flesh and blode, then may gret clerkes, bot thai have grace of trew mekenes and luf drede, whereby thai leve ther owen wit and kindely resoun, and submitt thaim lowly be trew bileve to the doctrine of holy chirch. That grace god graunt us specialy of his gret mercy in thees last dayes, th^t bene as it semes nihe the commyng of anticrist and his disciples, the which shal princepaly founde to destruy the trew feith of this blessed sacrament....

We have sene in our dayes how the disciples of anticrist that bene clepede lollardes hase made mich dissensione and divisione in holy chirch and puttes many men in to errour of this blessed sacrament be the fals doctrine of ther maistre, the which thurgh his gret clergy and kunnyng of philosophi was deceyved, in that he ʒafe more credence to the doctrine of aristotel th^t stant onely in naturele resoun of man then he did to the doctrine of holy chirch and the trew doctours therof, touching the precious sacrament.

ffor aristotel teches, as kindely resoun acordes, th^t the accidentes of brede or wyne, th^t is (to) say the colour, the savour, and so forth of other, mowe not be bot in substance of brede or wyne after ther kinde. Bot the doctrine of holy chirch is th^t in this blessed sacrament, be special miracle of god above kinde, the colour, the savour, and other accidentes of brede and wyne bene ther w^t out the kindely subjecte, th^t is to say w^t out the substance of brede and wyne th^t

was before the consecracioun. And for als mich as this doctrine of holy chirch is a3eyns the principals of philosophi th^t is naturele science, therfore the forsaide maister of lollardes repreved it, and so he erred himself, and many other made to erre touching the bileve of this holiest sacrament, the whech 3iven more credence to him for the opinion of his gret clergy than to the trew doctrine of holy chirch[1]. And thus 3it in our dayes have anticrist wroght in the first maner before saide be this fals maister of lollardes and many other of his disciples into destruccioun of trew cristeen bileve touching this blessed sacrament of cristes body, and many other poyntes a3ens holy chirch....[2]

Five hundred years have passed; but the speaker's sad complaint, here uttered without malice, is uttered still, where the disturbing "modernist" raises his head. How small the gulf that divides us in some matters from our pre-Reformation ancestors!

Perhaps the commonest portrait of the ordinary Lollard preacher as drawn by orthodox hands with less restraint is that of the hypocrite, who feigns piety in order to indulge his secret pride or become the darling of the people. Thus Walter Hilton, Canon of Thurgarton, in a tirade against boasting and pride, supplies a quaint illustration of Pecock's comment upon the ignorant preachers, which, had it not been for a marginal note[3], we might hardly have identified with the followers of Wycliffe at all. In its light we seem to be looking at the notorious

[1] Thus Rypon, discussing *Superbia* (MS. Harl. 4894, fol. 77 b): "Quidam sunt increduli, ut pote in fide multipliciter aberrantes, et simplicem populum faciunt varie aberrare, utpote Lollardi, qui contra constitutiones patrum et oppiniones antiquas de sacramentis ecclesiae, praesertim de sacramento Eucharistiae, confirmatas, contrarias asserciones et opiniones publice et privatim docent pertinaciter et affirmant" (and ibid. fol. 32 b, etc.).

[2] MS. Add. 19901, fol. 84 b et seq. (e, 15th cent.). From "a short tretis of the hiest and most worthi sacrament of crist(es) blessede body, and the merveiles there of." Another copy in MS. Arundel 364, fol. 204 et seq. adds that it is written "to confusioun of alle false lollardes and heretykes" (fol. 204 b). Also in MS. Arund. 112. [It usually follows the Engl. transl. of the *Spec. Vitae Christi*, attributed to S. Bonaventure, a translation made (perhaps by John Morton, Austin friar) by a friend or admirer of "Maister Walter Hylton, the Chanon of Thurgarton."] Cf. also with the above, Rypon, as before; a sermon "de solempnitate Corporis Xti," in MS. Linc. Cath. Libr. A. 6. 2, fol. 167 b (truths of the Sacrament "denyed by Eretykis"); *Jacob's Well*, E.E.T.S. ed. p. 19; (also pp. 59, 156, etc.); and the elaborate arguments of Bromyard. Lathbury, in MS. Roy. 11. A. xiii, fol. 236^b.

[3] "Contra ypocritas et Lollardos."

preaching laymen of Bunyan's day, or the democratic orators of a still later period:

> Thare er some that semes as thai had forsakene the werld, bot thai hafe na cure ne bysenes aboute the clensyng of thaire conscience.... Bot all thaire stody es outward for to seme haly to the sygth of the werld; and thai er besy for to visete haly men and wyse men and see thaim, and for to here of thaim some gud wordis of edificatione, that thai mygth preche and telle the same wordis that thai have herd to other men with avauntynge and vayne glory of thaim, that thai can sai sa wele. And perchaunce some of thaim when thai hafe herd or rede a litele of haly write or has gettyne a litele cynnynge of techyng of holy faders, alstite thai make thaim-self doctours and wille teche other men, nogth that thai hafe fulfilled in werkes, bot that thai haf herd and sene in bokes. And sa thai presome of thaire aghene [i.e. own] connynge and despice other that er synfull; and thai covete state or prelacy, that thai mygth teche all men[1].

Equally illuminating is the account of them given at greater length in a manuscript of vernacular homilies on the Sunday Gospels, which themselves exhibit a renewed enthusiasm for the simple exposition of Scripture[2]. The author says much of their "feyned holiness," of their "shepes clothynge," and their pursuit of "symple men that ben as sheep." In a striking analogue he lays stress on those very Lollard features which we should have expected to see condemned by moralists on the other side. He describes how the wolf takes advantage of the sleeping watch-dog and the absentee shepherd in the night, like the heretic with "his false turnyng of hooli scripture":

> But he is aferd to openli come among stedfast men in bileve, and therfore he awaiteth whan men berken nouȝt aȝens synne and false techyng, but slepen in synful lustis of flesshe, and if he se shepardis slowe either absent from trewe techyng of her sheep....

Impatience and ill-temper, especially in the evil day, are other well-marked traits suggesting the unbalanced, nerve-wracked character of the fanatic, now hugely elated, now gloomy and cast down:

---

[1] MS. Rawl. C. 285, fol. 69. See Horstmann, *Yorkshire Writers*, vol. i, p. 123. Cf. again *Jacob's Well*, p. 164 (feigning holiness, to deceive the people by false teaching, "as Lollards do"), etc.

[2] MS. Harl. 2276, fol. 113, et seq. (sermon for the 8th Sunday after Trinity).

Also the wolf in kynde is buystouse[1] and stif in bodi; and so an heretik is strong and stif in falshed,....hasti in techyng.... *With her tunge thei magnifien Cristis martiris, but thei wolen not have her pacience.* And so speciali ȝe shuln knowe hem bi her unstedfastnesse, and unpacience in adversite....Anoon as ony thyng fallith to hem to wordli welthe, thei waxen proude, and thei ben travelid with boost and with veyn glorie. Thei ben hogeli angwisshid in adversite, and unmesurabli ioyful in prosperite[2].

Finally their sharp heresies prick and rend men's consciences "as thornes and breris pricken men, and torenden her clothes."

Face to face, at last, with a situation in which the fundamental notion of "prelatio et cura animarum" was thus being defied by evangelists of heresy and strife, the Church was bound to do something to cope with it, beyond the mere punishment of individuals. Episcopal mandates like that of the Bishop of Worcester issued in 1387—"ne Lollardi predicent infra suam diocesim"—whether openly in churches, or church-yards, streets, or other secular places, or secretly in halls, chambers, gardens or closes ("gardinis")[3], follow the example of Archbishop Courtenay's better-known *Monitio*[4]. But the outstanding measure is that of Archbishop Arundel published in 1409[5]. Three main provisions are set out in its clauses. First, there is to be a rigid tightening up of the system of licenses, by which no secular or regular might now venture to preach under any circumstances, to clergy or people, in church or outside, without prior examination by diocesans, and the subsequent issue of letters of authority. Moreover, there is further stipulation that licenses should be granted "to one specified parish, or more, as seems expedient to the Ordinary afore-

---

[1] boisterous = powerful (cf. Shakespeare and Dryden).

[2] We might see quaint illustrations of this latter point, perhaps, in *Fascic. Ziz.* (Rolls S.), p. 307. The Oxford Chancellor, at Repyngdon's public preaching, "post sermonem vultu jocundo ei applausit"; or (Powell and Trev. pp. 46–7) at Braibrok's preaching at Northampton, c. 1393: "And after the said sermon, the said maior and Lollardes with great pride and jollite ledd the fals preacher to the howse of the maior. And after the said Lollards retourning to the churchyard of the said church, and with haustie wordes threatened bloues to any that would gainsaye in any point touching the said sermon."

[3] Cf. also the warning of the *Cil. Oc. Sac.* MS. Harl. 4968, fol. 44, § 4: "ne suspicio heretici oriatur, non in loco clauso vel occulto."

[4] See Wilkins, *Conc.* vol. iii, pp. 183, 202, 215, etc.

[5] Ibid. pp. 314–19 (cap. I, etc.).

mentioned, according to the quality of the person to be admitted." Henceforth any "curate" who admitted a preacher lacking adequate credentials was to be dealt with severely. Secondly, parish clergy, who continue quite naturally to enjoy the old privileges with regard to their own people, are yet to confine their discourses strictly to the simple topics of the layfolk's faith as outlined by the Peckham Decrees. This may be looked upon as a measure at once checking the more aggressive and speculative spirits among them, and also urging the rest to fulfil their long-neglected duties, from omission of which the cause of heresy had grown and benefited. Lastly, comes that most significant order[1], "Predicator conformet se auditorio, aliter puniatur." That is to say, let him confine his attacks on clerical vices to audiences of clergy, on lay vices to laymen, and so forth. When dealing with matters of doctrine, the sacraments, articles of the faith, etc. he is to keep rigidly within the limits of discussion prescribed by Holy Mother Church ("quod per sanctum matrem ecclesiam reperitur discussum")[2].

Gascoigne's view of this legislation we have considered above. To him it was a cruel death-blow to English preaching[3]. Even if he seems to have exaggerated, there is sufficient in it to account for the decline which did undoubtedly take place. The prelatical enemy of preaching had at least a plausible excuse for his actions; the able spokesman might well keep his mouth closed for fear of violating the new restrictions. Thus the last hope of this particular ministry, its art, its flavour of originality in thought and presentation, its fearless ventilation of public and private sins was doomed. Art, at all events, it could remain no longer, crushed beneath the weight, not merely of that formal tradition and authority which had stifled scholasticism, but now of solemn prohibitions and episcopal threats. A virile pulpit cries out for freedom, for the right of a man to declare the vision that God has given him in His own way, provided he first gives full consideration to the claims of his Church and of other people. Now, however, if popular rumour carried the news of some too outspoken address to the

[1] Ibid. cap. III and IV.
[2] "...quod per ecclesiam terminatum fuerit, aut decisum; nec verba scandalosa circa eadem scienter proferat publice vel occulte...."
[3] See p. 41, and cf. Wycl. *Serm. Lat.* No. lvii, vol. i, p. 377.

ears of the bishop or his officers, there would be a Henry Wynnegode, some Official-Peculiar[1], at the offender's heels. The suspicious prelate might even summon a synod in a neighbouring church, and have up the "pseudo-predicatores" at almost a moment's notice[2]. Who could afford to preach, without thinking twice, and more, in such circumstances? *Sic transit gloria pulpiti!*

Space has prevented all mention hitherto of the individual preaching licenses to be found in bishops' Registers[3], and elsewhere. For the first half of the new century after Wycliffe's death, there is a certain number of such entries, it is true. One, dated 1418, for Lewis Newchirch, priest, bachelor in arts, "nobis testimonio fidedigno multipliciter commendatus," introduces a long and wordy preface on the recent iniquitous scattering of the tares—"per varios ecclesiae catholicae degeneres et privignos, emulosque, et detractores."[4] This is now to be followed by dissemination of the true and divine seed. Another, of the year previous, recommends the celebrated Dr William Lyndewood to the whole area of the province of Canterbury, for preaching in Latin or in English, to clergy and lay-folk[5]. But we judge of the straits to which bishops were put to find adequate missioners, by the fact that the last-named license expressly violates in its scope a principle of the Arundel Constitutions: "Non obstante constitutione provinciali Oxoniensi nuper per bonae memoriae dominum Thomam Arundel Cantuar. Archiepiscopum, predecessorem nostrum, edita," etc. Still more flagrant is the case of a general license to preach in

---

[1] Cf. Reg. Bp. Stafford (Bath and Wells), p. 298. (1412.)

[2] Cf. the Abbot of St Albans, at St Peter's Church, St Albans, in Amundesh. (Rolls S.), vol. i, pp. 222–4.

[3] I have extracted the following number of licenses to preach from the Registr. Comm. of Bp. Lacy of Exeter, between the years 1420 and 1440:

1420–21	...	...	...	6
1421–22	...	...	...	2
1432	...	...	...	2
1436–37	...	...	...	1
1438	...	...	...	2
1440	...	...	...	1
			Total	14

[4] Reg. Lacy (Hereford), p. 25.

[5] Wilkins, *Conc.* vol. iii, p. 389: "Vobis, quem litterarum scientia, morumque laudabilis vitae meritis, aliisque virtutum praeconiis sufficienter novimus insignitum...."

the diocese granted to the four chief Mendicant Orders, *in toto*, by the Bishop of Bath and Wells[1], within a year of the great measure. In like manner Bishop Repyngdon, of Lincoln, himself once a noted Lollard in his youth, but now zealous enough, had granted permission to all graduate and non-graduate theologists of Oxford in the year 1405 to preach anywhere within his jurisdiction[2]. And we are told that Lollardy was by no means extinct in the University!

Under the force of circumstances, one at least of Arundel's safeguards had thus actually broken down already. The same urgency which had brought that situation about, is reflected again in a Papal Bull of 1428. It urges the appointment of special "heralds of the cross," without delay, "in each separate city, diocese, estate, walled town, and village of England," to combat the Wycliffites and Hussites, with no less than a hundred days' Indulgence for those who will listen to them. It was all too late, however, to check the current stagnation, or stave off the Reformation of the future. Benefactions of private individuals toward the work of the pulpit might increase[3]; a bright particular star like Colet might arise in the homiletic firmament, seeming to presage the dawn of a new day in the Church. But it was not to be just yet. When dawn came at length, it was red and fiery, storm-presaging. The star of promise had gone out, doomed to a lonely fate until the hour of its eclipse, like those other stars of our survey—"sidera errantia, quibus procella tenebrarum servata est."

[1] Reg. (Bath and Wells) Bp. Bubwith (Som. Rec. Soc.), p. 65. See also ibid. p. 112, 1411–12, license to the Provost of Oriel College, Oxford.

[2] Reg. Repyngd. (Linc.), quoted in *Ch. Quater. Rev.* vol. xix, art. iv, p. 74. The writer is wrong in speaking here of Arundel's *recent* policy of restricted licensing. It was only framed in 1407, and issued two years later (cf. Gairdner (as above), vol. i, pp. 62, 107, 545, etc.).

[3] Cf. 1446, Bequest of Wm. Estfield, Knt., citizen, mercer and Alderman of the City of London (twice Mayor): "for sermons to be preached at St Paul's Cross, and in the pulpit at the Hosp. of S. Mary without Bisshopesgate; and also to the clerks of the Univs. of Oxf. and Cambr. coming to London to preach the Word of God...." 1486, Another similar (Padyngton). See Sharpe's *Cal. of Wills* (Lond.), vol. ii, pp. 510, 589. 1490, The Recorder of Coventry, Henry Butt, "left land to pay for 3 Sermons to be preached yearly in this cittie for ever" (MS. Harl. 6388, fol. 25). Cf. also the Bequests at Oxford and Cambridge Universities themselves: [1446, Thos. Collage, £40 bequest to preachers of Univs. of Oxf. and Camb. (to encourage Divinity, now at a low ebb, etc.). See Wood (Gutch.), *Hist. and Ant. of Oxf.* vol. i, p. 596; and Cooper, *Annals of Camb.* vol. i, p. 198, etc.].

PART TWO

THE PREACHING SCENE

CHAPTER IV

"INTER MISSARUM SOLLEMNIA"

Hit was uppon an holy-day, in an heiȝ feste of the ȝere,
Muche folk was to churche gon, godes word for to here;
The preeste of the chirche undude the gospel,
And lerede the parischens, as he couthe wel[1].

EVERY preacher, if he be worthy of the name, will have an
audience of some kind. Nor indeed will that audience be
the only thing that casts an influence, for better or for worse,
upon his endeavour. Unless he be a man of unusual obtuseness,
he will respond somewhat to his material environment also; he
will at least be limited by times and seasons and regulations of
worship. Thus the natural curiosity arises, as we proceed, to
see something of these "parischens" and others who hang around
him, something, too, if we can, of the place where he stands,—
all, in fact, that may contribute to what past experience of the
gay company of the middle ages would lead us to imagine as a
picturesque if not actually another gay scene in itself. On this
matter the reader shall now be allowed to make judgement.

The question must first be asked, what of the place of
preaching in the religious services of the day? More than one
ecclesiologist has remarked on the extreme paucity of references
to the sermon in the great ritual books. It has suffered precisely
that fate of being overwhelmed by the grander spectacles of
"ordynall" and "uss," which Wycliffe himself deplores. Yet
with regard to regular Sunday and feast-day, two formal
occasions of preaching can be discerned. The first is that
occurring "inter missarum sollemnia," as the Registers say.
Here the sermon of the period was delivered in England, so far
as we can make out, either between creed and offertory, or else

---

[1] Vernon MS. fol. 288, printed in E.E.T.S., O.S. No. 98, p. 329.

PLATE II

A PREACHING SCENE IN THE XIII CENTURY.
(*From MS. Egert.* 745, *fol.* 46.)

A MEDIAEVAL PULPIT OF WOOD.
(*From a sketch by the author.*)

after the latter[1]. The second occasion is an affair for the Sunday afternoon, a self-contained service following the ordinary Sunday dinner, eaten after "matyns and masse," a little before noon[2]: "After mete loke thou go to the prechynge, ʒif eny beo in toune: lette for no thynge."[3] The characteristically different requirements of these two situations themselves go far to explain the great divergence in sermon length to be found among the written collections of our manuscripts. The five or ten minutes' discourse[4] of him who will let "thus myche of this gospell suffice at this tyme" contrasts in its obvious suitability for the morning Mass, with the lengthy orations of a Rypon or a Brunton. The poet's "ʒif," too, is an important reminder that the Sunday sermon "ad populum" remained none too common even at its most impressive hour. It finds echo in the "si placuerit[5]" of the ceremonial books at the cathedral. Even in the greater churches, indeed, the Durham custom of a sermon for every Sunday in the year would seem to have been the exception[6]. As for the village church, it is enough to repeat that the Peckham Constitutions of 1281, which remained the basis of all future legislation on the subject until the Reformation, required the "curate" to expound his programme of instruction but "four times in the year, that is once in every quarter, *on one solemn day or more.*"[7] Subsequent Constitutions

---

[1] See Appendix i, below. [2] See Appendix ii, below.

[3] Vernon MS., E.E.T.S., O.S. No. 98, p. 351.

[4] Cf. MS. Harl. 1197, "Short Homilies or Postills on the Gospels and Epistles for all Sundays in the year," etc. MS. Roy. 18. B. xxiii, provides examples of very different lengths.

[5] "Fiat sermo, si placuerit" (cf. Sarum Ceremonies, Sarum Pontifical, etc.). For a late example (1522) cf. the "quandoque continget" in Thorpe's *Registr. Roff.* p. 276.

[6] To take two examples: (a) *Lincoln Cath.*, in the older thirteenth-century "Consuetudines," once provided for a sermon "ad populum" each Sunday (*Liber Niger*, p. 284, De officio Cancell. (*Linc. Cath. Stat.*) and cf. pt. ii, pp. 158–9); but in the fifteenth-century *Novum Registr.* pt. i, Sermon Sundays are limited to four in Advent, ten from Septuag. and continuously throughout Lent to Easter, inclusive; (and Ash Wednesday). (b) *Colleg. Ch. of Ottery St Mary, Devon*, in the Grandiss. Foundn. Statutes (1342) (see Dalton, p. 102): Sundays for "Sermones ad populum" are 1st and 3rd in Advent, Septuag., 1st, 3rd and 5th in Lent; (Assumpt. of B.V.M. and Feast of St Edw. the Confessor). Cf. also Erasmus on Dean Colet at St Paul's: "He resolved (*which was not usual in those times*) to preach every holiday in his cathedral." Wordsw. *Eccles. Biogr.* takes it in the above sense. *But may it not mean merely* unusual for *the Dean?* See below p. 156.

[7] So also in Pagula's *Oc. Sacer.* (MS. Ryl. 6. E. i, fol. 27 b, etc.).

do furnish several variations on the original theme here, it is true, some of them in the direction of greater frequency[1]. Nevertheless, a general survey leads to the conclusion that Myrc's own pulpit comment that "each curatour is holden by all the law in Holy Church, for to expound the Pater Noster to his parishioners *once or twice* in the year,"[2] represents the actual state of affairs far more accurately than Cardinal Gasquet's theory of a minimum total of sixteen sermons per annum. Of the continual complaints, lasting down to the time of Wolsey, that the Peckham decrees were not being properly observed, something has been said in an earlier chapter. Special exception certainly must be made for the greater festivals, such as Easter, Whitsunday, and Christmas, and for the processions of Palm-Sunday and Rogationtide, when, as Walleys reminds us, many would be preaching[3]. But there was one season of the Church's year which easily eclipsed all others in this respect. This was Lent, great season of fast and shrift—still pretty faithfully observed from what one gathers in the sermon literature— when it was intended that there should be daily sermons in all the churches[4]. It provided the earnest preacher with his great opportunity to stir the solemn crowds, now haunting the sanctuary, to prepare themselves for the great acts of Confession and Easter Communion which would follow, preaching vehemently—

---

[1] Cf. here, Russell (Sodor and Man), 1350, "Omnibus dominicis diebus, et festivis"; Thoresby (York), 1357, "Saltem diebus dominicis"; Langham (Ely) 1364, "Frequenter predicet et exponat"; Nevill (York), 1466 (back to the original Peckham "once in each quarter"). See Wilkins, *Conc.* vol. iii, pp. 10, 59, 599; and *Lay Folks Cat.* (E.E.T.S., O.S. No. 118), p. 6.

[2] *Festiall* (ed. E.E.T.S.), p. 282. For Gasq. *O.E.B.*, p. 191.

[3] Cf. MS. Harl. 635, fol. 8 b ("Tunc enim quia plures solent predicare..."). Easter sermons are most numerous. Isolated examples are frequently to be found in MSS. (cf. MS. Linc. Cath. Libr. A. 7. 12, fol. 181; MS. Harl. 2398, fol. 175 b; etc.). Cf. also in *Lincoln Cath. Stats.* (Blk. Bk. etc.): Stations and Processions outside the Minster, with sermon, Palm Sunday, Easter, three Rogation Days and St Mark's Day (Greater Litany, see below, p. 201). (Chancellor also to give a month's notice to priors of the Mendicant friars of Lincoln to arrange sermons in *their* churches, if stations are to be held there.) Cf. also *Rites of Durham* (Surtees Soc. p. 104) for similar sermons in parish churches, for these Processions, at Durham (see above, Chap. ii, p. 52).

[4] See Conc. Arl.; Conc. Later. (Innocent III), etc. repeated at Conc. Trident. (Sess. xxiv, cap. iv); sermons "saltem omnibus diebus festis, tempore autem Jejuniorum, Quadragesimae (et Adventus Domini) *quotidie*, vel saltem tribus in hebdomade diebus...."

...as freres doon in Lente,
To make us for our olde sinnes wepe[1].

The work of the Mendicants undoubtedly takes first place where Lenten oratory is concerned. Its greatest monuments are their immense "Quadragesimalia," with elaborately divided discourses for each of the forty days[2]. Examples of unquestioned English origin appear to be now extinct. But the numerous entries in Bale's list of Carmelite writers compel us to believe that once they were as common as the examples surviving from the continent. Signs of a like activity are to be noticed on every hand. The very numerous Lenten sermons surviving, both in English and in Latin, concern themselves naturally with exhortations to come to shrift, and to the hearing of God's Word, to avoid the hiding of sins from the priest, to make amends in prayer and penance, in abstinence and almsgiving, for the evil of the past year:

Good men, the tyme of lenten [is] entred, the wiche tyme we must clense us of all our mysdedis that we have done before; and this holy tyme we shuld absteyne us more from synne and wrechednes than another tyme of the ʒere.... Now shall we strength us to faste, to come to the churche, and to serve God in holy preyours, and to shryve us of oure mysdedis....[3]

Thoresby's "Catechism" for simple lay-folk had made their instruction and due examination in matters prescribed by parish clergy, a necessary preliminary to Confession "in the lentyn tyme." So Bishop Grandisson, granting a year's license for non-residence to a West Country parson, for example, insists that notwithstanding he shall return to his church in Lent, to instruct his parishioners "in those things that pertain to the

---

[1] *Canterbury Tales*, Clerk's Prologue, ll. 12, 13. Cf. in sermons, Rypon, MS. Harl. 4894, fol. 1 b: "(predicatores) movent suos auditores ut poenitendo ad Christum redeant,... *sicut forsan erit de multis in Quadragesima.*" Also in Bromyard, *S.P.*

[2] Among numerous contemporary continental examples, cf. Ambrose of Spiera (d. 1454), a little-known Servite (my edition of his *Quadr.* is Venice, 1476 (Vendelinus)); John Gritsch, of Basel (d. c. 1430), Franciscan; Robert Caraccioli, Franciscan of Lecce, Bishop of Aquino, Italy (c. 1470); etc. Booksellers' Catalogues of Incunabula frequently contain notices of them. The sermon-books themselves include vivid descriptions of social excesses, fashions, amusements, etc.

[3] MS. Roy. 18. B. xxiii, fol. 100. (Beginning of sermon for Lent: Text, "Ductus est Jesus in desertum....")

cure of souls."[1] At Norwich we are informed that out-door Sunday sermons were delivered annually at this season from the Greenyard preaching Cross, hard by the Cathedral—"pro tota civitate Norwicensi."[2] A similar practice holds at Northampton[3]; and the St Albans abbot, as we have seen, makes fresh efforts to revive what was once thus provided regularly for laymen in the nave of his own abbey church[4].

Of ordinary week-day sermons at the great pulpit-crosses outside, we catch but a few stray glimpses in the accounts of Lollard trials. With the possible exception of Friday[5], however, no one particular day seems to have been preferred. Choice was probably determined here by events of special importance in the calendars of Church and State. When Erasmus explains in his *Dialogue*, in a later century, that one of the advantages of remaining in the world, in place of entering a monastery, was that a man might still choose his favourite preacher, or when Dr Bromyard upbraids those who have not troubled to go to a sermon for a month[6], we are forced to believe that in the larger towns at any rate regular preaching-courses were no rarities of the day.

The typical sites of English mediaeval preaching are almost as varied as the different groups of the preachers themselves. If we begin with Religious and canons secular, there is, besides the church, the chapter-house in monastery and cathedral

---

[1] Reg. Grand. (Exeter), pt. ii, p. 827.

[2] Wilkins, *Conc.* vol. iii, p. 282.

[3] "everie Sunday during Lent, at the cros in the churchyarde." Powell and Trev. *Docs.* p. 48.

[4] Whethamst. Reg. (Rolls S.), vol. i, p. 25 (omni dominica Quadrag.). Note too the Ash Wednesday sermons, "in die cinerum," or "in capite jejunii," in Brunton (MS. Harl. 3760); MS. Camb. Univ. Libr. G.g. vi. 16, fol. 51 (see quotation given below, Chap. v, p. 244); Myrc's *Festiall*; MSS. Linc. Cath. Libr. A. 6. 2, fols. 84 b, 90 b; and Harl. MS. 2247, fol. 49 b, etc.

[5] Cf. "A Sermon in the Cathedral, or at the Cross in the same churchyard, on every *Friday* for ever" (1459). See Valentine Green, *Hist. of Worcester*, vol. i, p. 55. A Friday sermon at Paul's Cross (1419) in Wilkins, *Conc.* vol. iii, p. 394. A Friday sermon at Oxford, in Snappe's *Formul.* (ed. Salter, *Oxf. Hist. Soc. Tr.*), from MS. Cotton Faust. c. vii, fol. 128 b, Archbp. Arundel writes: "On this very day, Friday,... I was in the church of St Mary, the University was present, the sermon was begun, the text being 'Come into the garden'...."

[6] *S.P.—Audire (verbum Dei)*. *Jacob's Well*, MS. Salisb. Cath. Libr. 103, (c. 1440) suggests a daily series, on the general outline of Faith, delivered "this hool tweyne monythys and more" (fol. 214 b).

precinct. For the monk and friar, here, as a rule, was the scene of the daily morning "lectio," and the evening "collatio," which, though it may have involved often enough the reading of sermons and expositions, need hardly concern us on that account. Rather we shall turn to behold it at some holy festival when the chancellor is haranguing, or the eloquent brother is expected from Oxford, to provide a homiletic feast at the cost of twenty shillings or more[1]; or again, at the episcopal visitations, or the still rarer election of a new head. Thanks to such entries as those of the recently published Diocesan Registers of Lincoln, the Visitation preaching scene may be conjured up with a certain distinctness[2].

First comes the splendid procession of robed dignitaries— bishop, dean, chancellor, treasurer, sub-dean, archdeacons, canons, prebendaries, or possibly abbot and prior, and all the officials of a monastic establishment, along with the brethren— filing slowly into the "parlement-hous," rectangular and sombre as at Gloucester, or exquisitely polygonal as at Westminster, with central pillar like some great tree-stem branching into a forest of vaulting ribs, and glorious window-tracery. The presiding prelate then sits him down in his "fair stall or seat of stone,"[3] and the rest of the audience follow his example, ranging themselves about the wall in order of seniority, and overflowing into the centre. The chosen preacher of the occasion now advances, possibly one of the doctors resplendent, as a simple preacher had seen them elsewhere, in their furred "tabbardys, hodys, chymerys, and pylyouns."[4] On bended knee and with bowed head before the "reverend father" presiding, he "humbly beseeches of him the wonted blessing, that he might preach the word of God in the beginning of the said visitation."[5] After the

---

[1] Cf. Pearce, *Monks of Westm.* p. 113 (solut. fratri W. de S. veniendo de Oxon. predicando, et redeundo, xxvi. s. viii. d.; Palm S. and Good Friday, 1386); p. 144 (pro sermone in die parasceves...xx. s.; 1440–2).

[2] Cf., as used here, Reg. Bp. Gray, Linc. Dioc. Regs. If visitation takes place in a nunnery, the sermon is made in the vernacular (cf. Reg. Bp. Alnwick, ibid. (1442), pp. 46, etc.).

[3] Cf. the *Rites of Durham* (Surtees Soc.).   [4] *Jacob's Well.*

[5] Cf. Conc. Lat. Sess. xi, ult.; and Conc. Trid. Sess. v. ("Ab (episcopis) benedictionem petere teneantur antequam predicare incipiant"); visitation sermon in Linc. Chapt. House, 1439, Bp. Alnwick presiding (*Linc. Cath. Stat.* pt. ii) before the usual throng: "egregius vir magister Thos. Duffeld, in sacra theologia bacallarius, accepta a dicto Revdo. patre benediccione consueta, juxta actus futuri congruencium proposuit verbum Dei...," etc.

blessing, he moves either to some temporary pulpit, or else, no doubt, to the stone lectern with richly carved desk-head, that stands in the middle of the area, facing the president's chair[1]. Then the Latin discourse begins: "Reverendi patres, fratresque perdilecti, quia ante quamlibet visitationem ordinariam saltem in publico laudabili consuetudine solent visitatores per modum collacionis ad visitandum proponere, igitur ut conformem me aliqualiter eisdem, sit hoc thema...."[2] "The which being ended, the same master...betook himself to the place where he was wont to sit," and the visitation business begins.

Very similar will be the opening sermon before a synod or general convocation of prelates and clergy, as in the case of that held, for example, in the chapter-house of York in 1426, when the "venerable man of rare learning, Master John Roxby, a famous doctor in theology," preached from the text "Vocavit Josue majores."[3] Sometimes the visitation sermon had apparently to do duty for regulars, seculars and lay-folk together, as in the case of Bishop Alnwick's visitation of the Austin priory of Bicester, on the 28th of May, 1445, where there were but eight canons in the house. In this case the parish church was used for the purpose, and the sermon was delivered "in the vulgar tongue...there being present in that place the prior and convent of the said priory, and a throng of clergy and people."[4]

---

[1] Cf. the remarkable examples now in the churches of Crowle and Norton, in Worcestershire, probably originally in the Abbeys of Pershore and Evesham respectively. See *Vict. Hist. Co. of Worc.* vols. ii and iii; and Cox's *Pulpits and Lecterns*. An old discussion in *Notes and Queries* decided, and rightly, that there was no permanent pulpit in the chapter-houses. However, there was certainly one used by the preacher in the chapter-house of Lincoln, in 1432. See *Linc. Dioc. Registers*, as above ("pulpitum ascendit").

[2] MS. Bodl. Lat. Th. d. i, fol. 107 (the opening of Nich. Philip's *Sermo pro Visitatione fratrum*). Notice that sometimes the presiding prelate himself will preach on these occasions; cf. 1314, Beverley Minst., Archbp. of York (*Chapter Act Book*, Surtees Soc.).

[3] Wilkins, *Conc.* vol. iii, p. 487 (the text is apparently from Joshua i, 10). Cf. another series of synodal sermons, in London, in Wilkins, *Conc.* vol. iii, p. 273. (1402.)

[4] Reg Alnwick, *Linc. Dioc. Regs.* vol. xxiv, p. 34 (see also editor's note here). For other sermon notices of this class, cf. *Cathedral Visitation*, Lichfield, 1428, in Wilkins, *Conc.* vol. iii, p. 509 (de modo et negotio visitationis episc.). After the reception of the visiting bishop, and certain prayers at the cathedral high altar, the company is to pass to the chapter-house for a sermon, in the presence of bishop, dean, chapter, vicars and others. Cf. at Claremont, 1283, in Baluze, *Misc.* vol. i, p. 279; here, too, *another*

If we turn to reports of the general chapters of Benedictines or Augustinians in the same century, we shall find that a whole series of official sermons has become formal part of the proceedings; and the task of appointing the special preachers for the next provincial assembly is definitely recorded as a piece of the necessary business. Thus, at the Benedictine chapter-general held at Northampton in 1423, "there were then assigned to the sermons for the next provincial chapter, first, that is to say, for a sermon to clerics and literates, delivered in Latin,"— three Bachelors of Sacred Theology, and the "Prior Studentium" at Oxford. Secondly, "a sermon to be given in the vulgar tongue" was allotted to another Bachelor, to two Doctors in the same Faculty, and to the "Prior of the Students" in Cambridge, making a total of eight in all, for the two groups. Two sermons are mentioned in connection with this particular meeting. One is an opening discourse on the first day, after Mass, to the clergy—"stilo satis commendabili mentales delicias universis presentibus affluentissime propinans verbum Dei ibidem fructuose proposuit Dom. W. Waldens, in Latinis." The other again follows celebration of Mass at the close of the proceedings, this time in the parish church of All Saints, addressed in the vernacular to clergy and people, together[1].

A chapter of Austin canons[2] at Osney, in 1443, is of particular interest as it appears in the character of a model chapter for future occasions, and its regulations for procedure were fortunately noted down at the end of the official report—"ne processus presidentium ruat, vel ordinationes et statuta negligantur." Although no less than three distinct sermons make their appearance in the report, the added "Forma Capituli" mentions only two. Yet even here it is prescribed that persons shall be nominated for three sermons for the coming chapter[3]. After the year 1446, however, subsequent accounts take notice of but the one "in Anglicis." Looking back at "Oseney"

sermon "ad populum," in the vernacular, at the close. The sermon by the Archbp. of Canterbury in 1408, at Paul's Cross (in Wilkins, *Conc.* vol. iii, p. 310), to clergy and people, was probably part of the official proceedings at the close of a Convocn. of the Prov.

[1] Wilkins, *Conc.* vol. iii, pp. 419 et seq.

[2] For these details see *Chapters of Austin Canons*, ed. Salter (Oxf. Hist. Soc. vol. 74).

[3] Cf. also ibid. Appdx. i (c. 1370): "per quos sermones fieri...debeant."

again in 1443, we find first the great opening procession of prelates, procurators, and inferior clergy to the number of two hundred. These make their way on the Sunday afternoon— "ad secundam horam post nonam"—to the preaching cross in the cemetery of St Frideswide's, Oxford, where the presiding Abbot of St Osyth's delivers "a solemn sermon in English" to the assembly. Besides the aforesaid distinguished company of abbots and priors of the Order, there are present the Chancellor of the University and a vast crowd of doctors, masters, scholars and others, a truly magnificent setting, in scarlet and vestments of gold, for the "concionator." Mass follows within the church. On the Monday, "about the seventh hour," in the Osney chapter-house, a canon of Leicester, and scholar in the University, as deputed at the last chapter meeting, bowing before the presiding abbot for his blessing, proceeds to his "very useful" sermon, in Latin, "with some brilliance of style" ("sermonem valde utilem, dictamine non carentem"). Finally, at the same hour of the morning, on Tuesday, and in the same building, the Abbot of St Osyth harangues them again, "refreshing their souls with nourishment of the word of God" most elegantly before they part[1]. It had been a long and doubtless an exhausting session continued from the previous day, with little rest. Were there any nodding heads, we wonder, canons "ponderosi et etiam somnolenti," at sermon-time[2], in the long canonical rows, under that great lord abbot's searching eye? Alas, that the Chapter Acts do not tell us, though our popular sermons will be more generous in this respect:

> A holy man went on a day
> To here here sarmone at ane abbay,
> And als he sat with simple mode
> Him thoght the sarmon wonder gude.
> Bot als he luked in that tyde
> He saw the fende cum him biside
> With a picher in his hand,
> And a cup ful fast birland [= poured out]
> And ilk one that his cop wald kepe
> And drank thar of, sune was in slepe[3].

[1] In the same volume, cf. also Chapter at Northampton, 1446. The earliest mention of chapter legislation *re* the sermon here (apart from a *Sermo Commonitorius*, prior to 1250) is under Newstead, 1356.

[2] Cf. MS. Caius Coll. Camb. 334, fol. 181.

[3] MS. Harl. 4196, fol. 88 b (*Engl. Metr. Homs.*).

Mention of St Frideswide's Cross serves to introduce us to the Universities, as another busy centre of preaching "ad cleros." At Oxford, within the church of St Mary the Virgin, still crowned with its majestic spire erected in the early fourteenth century, the torrent of sacred eloquence has never ceased to flow from that day to our own. The chancellor's and proctor's books[1] of the first quarter of the century following require a public sermon to be given here in Latin on every Sunday during full term, roughly from the Feast of St Denis to that of the Translation of St Thomas, before noon, and in the presence of the Chancellor and University. All students were to attend[2], and in proper academic dress, if they occupied the body of the church[3]. The actual arrangement of this sermon—"ad honorem Domini nostri Jesu Christi et sacrosanctae Matris ecclesiae, necnon ad profectum studii"—to be made by a Doctor or Bachelor of Sacred Theology—was in the hands of the chancellor assisted by two "collatores sermonum" who were to be seculars, if possible[4]. The selected preacher was to receive two months' notice beforehand, and, according to a later version of the rules, if unwilling to perform, was to be deprived of all University privileges for a year. The Cambridge Statutes of the period 1303–1306 relating to this subject were obviously framed on the same pattern. Besides the Sunday sermons they provide in addition for one to be delivered similarly "on the day of the Translation of the Blessed Virgin Ethelreda."[5] These Latin orations, however, seem to have shared in the general decline of pulpit exercises, which, in the country, resulted from Lollard propaganda, and Archbishop Arundel's

[1] See here *Munim. Acad. Oxon.* (Rolls S.), vols. i and ii. The earliest reference to University sermons at Cambridge appears to be of the year 1303 (cf. *Documents relating to the Univ. and Colls. of Cambr.* (H.M. Stat. Off. 1852), vol. i, p. 397, and Bass Mullinger, *Hist.* p. 299 note). At Oxford apparently, from the end of the twelfth century (see Rashdall, *Univs. in Midd. Ages*, vol. ii, p. 344, etc.).

[2] See Rashdall, ibid. vol. ii, p. 625.

[3] Cf. *Anc. Stats. of Univ. of Cambr.* St. 175: "Insuper omnes gremiales ...etiam sermonibus ad clerum, si pro tempore sermonum hujusmodi in corpore ecclesie locum habere voluerint, in suis habitibus scholasticis personaliter sint presentes."

[4] Two "Collatores sermonum in ecclesia Beatae Mariae Virginis," Masters Pray and Herlow, appear in a list of University officers appointed by the Proctors for the year 1457 (see *Munim. Acad. Oxon.* vol. ii, p. 749).

[5] "De Sermonibus ad clerum diebus Dominicis in ecclesia Beate Marie," Stat. 169 (*Documents*, etc. as above, vol. i, p. 398).

policy. For, in the year 1444, we find the sovereign himself writing to the Oxford chancellor, "that ye with ripe and suffisant maturite advise a sure remedy in that party."[1] On certain high festivals or important fasts of the year, on Ascension Day[2] and the Feast of Corpus Christi[3], for example, a sermon in English at the open-air cross of St Frideswide's, for the benefit of "town and gown" together, seems to have been substituted at Oxford. These were special occasions when, precisely as in the case of the cathedral system, the preacher was expected to be one of particular dignity, here at the Universities either the chancellor himself, or one of the Masters Regent in Theology ("tunc actualiter regentem"). At Cambridge a special Statute gives us four such days in the year— the First Sunday in Advent, Septuagesima Sunday, Ash-Wednesday, and the Festival of Corpus Christi—although the audience named is purely clerical, and the place of delivery St Mary's, the University church, as usual[4]. Among the published correspondence of Thomas Walden, the Carmelite, there is a letter of the year 1421, addressed to him as Provincial Minister (or rather "ad diffinitores et provincialem, in capitulo Northampton," to be precise) from the University of Cambridge. It complains that a certain friar of the Order, William Bekle[5], in open violation of the University Statutes, had failed to appear at a convocation in the first year of his regency, when the sermon had been allotted to him ("non obstante sermone sibi assignato"). In spite of the fact that there had been postponement "ex gratia" for a month, the general procession had to take place at length incomplete and sermonless[6]. We can imagine the feelings of those in authority who had been so rudely flouted!

[1] Letter of Henry VI to the Chancellor of Oxford University: "...Forasmuch as We be enformed that the Sermons in latin, which were before this tyme, save now of late, be now gretly discontynued, to the gret hurt and disworship of the same, we therefore...wol and commande you straitly...," etc. See *Munim. Acad. Oxon.* vol. ii, p. 541.

[2] Cf. 1382, Chanc. Peter Stokes nominates Nich. Hereford to preach here, "praecipuum sermonem anni." See *Fascic. Ziz.* (Rolls S.), p. 306.

[3] Cf. 1382, sermon here of Phi. Repingdon. See ibid. pp. 299, 306, 307.

[4] Stat. 168: De sermonibis ad clerum quater in anno.

[5] A short account of him will be found in Bale's MS. Harl. 3838, fol. 97 (d. 1438).

[6] "Ac tandem generalis processio sine sermone...peracta fuerat incomplete...." See *Mon. Hist. Carmelit.* pt. v (1907), p. 465 (Epist. Waldensis).

Besides the "University sermons" proper, there were also the regular Latin examinatory sermons, specimens of which we shall examine later[1]. These were required of all Bachelors proceeding to incept in Theology; other sermons also of the Doctors in the same Faculty upon graduation[2]. At Oxford, indeed, a notable struggle had ensued between the friars and the University authorities at the beginning of the fourteenth century over the place in which they should be conducted. The latter had now decided to transfer the official site from the Dominican and Franciscan convents to the more central University church of St Mary. But the Mendicants objecting to this blow to their power and prestige, argued that the change was to less peaceful and commodious quarters. A long and bitter controversy, however, involving many grievances, and charged with not a little pulpit recrimination into the bargain, ended at last in victory for the University side. It was agreed that each incepting friar, for the future, should preach two sermons in St Mary the Virgin's, "ad clerum," in addition to the examinatory discourse itself[3]. Here the latter continued to be given from the year 1311, until the erection of the famous Divinity School, completed about 1480, which with its fan-traceried roof is one of the architectural glories of this most distinguished nursery of the preachers[4].

Passing now to the scenes of preaching "ad populum," we find that, at the cathedrals served by secular canons, this task is in the hands of the chancellor. When not preaching in person

[1] See here Chap. vi, pp. 259–262, Sermones examinatorii.

[2] *Munim. Acad. Oxon.* vol. i, pp. 307–8; vol. ii, p. 392, etc. and *Camb. Documents*, vol. i, p. 397. Cf. also John Lawerne's "Grace," printed in Leland's *Collectanea*, vol. v, p. 301, from a Bodl. MS. 692 (fol. 36): "Ista gratia conceditur a congregatione prefata, A.D. mill⁰ cccc⁰ xxxviii⁰, eidem Johanni *sub ista conditione*, quod dicat sermonem praeter formam, in ecclesia beatae Virginis *post susceptionem gradus*, et sub hac forma registratur in universitate nostra Oxoniensi." 1438. His "Sermo Examinatorius" has been already mentioned earlier in the same MS.

[3] See also a Letter from the University to the Archbp. of Canterbury, 1421, in Wilkins, *Conc.* vol. iii, p. 400: "quod quilibet frater de ordine Mendicantium taliter incepturus...," etc.

[4] Since the above was first written, Mr Falconer Madan has kindly drawn my attention, at the Bodleian, to two books which will be found to supply some references to this subject: Rev. Ll. Bebb's Preface (History of the Institution) to *Univ. Sermons, Oxf.* (Geo. Allen, 1901) and a *History of the Ch. of St Mary the Virgin, Oxf.* by Rev. E. S. ffoulkes (especially Chap. III, p. 140 et seq.).

on the days carefully specified for such exercises in addition to the sermons "ad cleros," he it is who must usually appoint a substitute from among the canons, or from outside[1]. In the York Statutes, however, it is prescribed that the dean shall occupy the pulpit on Palm Sunday[2]; in the Statutes of Lichfield, he was to preach, if he wished, on the First Sunday in Advent, and on Ash Wednesday, if not, the nomination of the substitute for these occasions lay with him, and not with the chancellor. The *Novum Registrum* of Lincoln prescribes further that the latter shall have the consent of the dean when choosing other preachers for the sermons "ad populum."[3] For the rest, as we have seen already, in the case of monastic cathedral churches, the Mendicant friar might be invited to preach, whenever no approved member of the foundation was found ready to fill the post[4]. For the pulpit scene itself we must be content to allow the practice as described in the case of Durham[5] to illustrate what might take place at these abbey churches and cathedrals of England. "Every Sunday in the year," we are told, "there was a sermon preached in the Galilee at afternoon, from one of the clock until three, and at twelve of the clock the great Bell of the Galilee was tolled every Sunday, three-quarters of an hour, and rung the fourth quarter till one of the clock, that all the people of the town might have warning to come and hear the word of God preached." Furthermore, "adjoining unto the lower part of the great window in the West end of the said Galilee was a fair iron Pulpit with bars of iron for one to hold them by, going up the steps unto the pulpit, where one of the monks did come every holyday and Sunday to preach at one of the clock in the afternoon." Here, then, in this very pulpit, we picture Master Rypon, the sub-prior, whose sermon manuscript has been so fortunately preserved for us after its ejection

---

[1] Cf. in *Linc. Cath. Stats.* pt. ii, pp. 158, 301, at *Lincoln* ("predicare vel per se, vel per alium quem de ecclesia elegerit") and ibid. vol. i, p. 284.; at *York*, ibid. pt. ii, p. 96 ("...et aliis qui predicare debent assignare dies," etc.); at *Lichfield*, ibid. pp. 25–32.

[2] Ibid. p. 92, "per se, vel per alium."

[3] Ibid. p. 301, "per se, vel *de consensu Decani* per alium...."

[4] See above, p. 51 and cf. Lincoln (ibid. pt. i, p. 284; pt. ii, p. 158): "Et hoc fiat vel per canonicos, *vel per alios viros autenticos*, si inveniantur qui velint, et sciant."

[5] See the *Rites of Durham* (Surtees Soc.), p. 46, etc.

from the Durham monastic library. Let us hope he had not to complain, like others elsewhere[1], of many absenting themselves from so edifying an exercise, about the year 1400[2]. In the record of a visitation held by Bishop Alnwick, at his cathedral church at Lincoln, in the year 1437, we are afforded a further glimpse of the difficult task of keeping order and silence amongst the crowds that visit these great churches at sermon-time. Complaint is made that the *vergers* are not fulfilling their duty in this respect. Therefore they are to be threatened with penalties to stir them to action[3]!

Apart from cathedral and older convent, our townsman would be still more likely to find himself at this period in one of the great "preaching-naves" of a friary church, lofty English equivalent of the Franciscan Santa Croce, at Florence, or the church of the Cordeliers at Toulouse. Such are the "large and wyde chirchis whiche religiose persoones, namelich of the begging religiouns, maken, that therebi the more multitude of persoones mowe be recevyed togidere, for to here theryn prechingis to be mad in reyne daies."[4] The cross in the open convent-yard would be used if the weather was fine[5]. Pecock's description suggests at first sight another curious parallel between friar and later Dissenter. Indeed without the striking beauty of St Andrew's Hall, a Dominican fragment left to us in Norwich, and the testimony of *The Plowman's Crede*,—

...wonderly well y-beld,
With arches on everiche half, and belliche y-corven
With crochetes on corners, with knottes of golde

[1] Cf. Evrard du Val, French preacher of the thirteenth century (in Hauréau, *Quelques MSS....*, vol. iv, p. 47): "Contra multos...qui retrahunt se a monasteriis, diebus dominicis, propter sermones."

[2] Cf. however, below p. 216, his complaint of recent laxity in the attendance of clerics at the annual Patronal Festival, with its procession.

[3] "Virgarii non faciunt silencium tempore predicacionis verbi Dei, sicut in sermonibus et predicacionibus, et quia plus timetur quod specialiter injungitur quam quod generaliter imperatur, ideo videtur statuendum et injungendum fore quod sub pena amissionis proximorum obituum post negligentiam commissam diligentius intendant ad faciendum silencium debitum." See *Linc. Cath. Stat.* (Bradshaw and Wordsworth), pt. ii, p. 386.

[4] Pecock's *Repressor* (Rolls S.), vol. ii, p. 553. Cf. also such entries as 1311, Church of the Franciscans, at Oxford: "A vast multitude of people there assembled on the occasion of a public sermon to the clerks," in A. G. Little, *Grey Friars in Oxford*, p. 39.

[5] Cf. the interesting note in the Cambridge friar's sermon notebook: "Die vacat sermo propter pluviam." MS. Caius Coll. Camb. 356, p. 58.

Wyde wyndowes y-wrou3t, y-written full thikke,

. . . . . .

Tombes opon tabernacles, tyld opon lofte—

we might have ventured to compare these capacious halls of sacred oratory to the eighteenth century meeting-house. Very possibly, too, the earlier mediaeval examples, with the narrow tunnel-like crossing to the chancel which remained a feature to the end[1], were of this appearance, in days when "the visitor acted with great severity because of the windows," or some other Franciscan enthusiast "ordered the embossments in the cloister to be scraped away."[2] Now, however, in the centuries before us, those fascinating little coloured shields of arms, those "lovely ladies y-wrought" in alabaster upon their tombs,

In many gay garmentes that weren gold-beten,

raised the homiletical ire of Wycliffe, precisely as similar offences in the monastic cloister had called down the fury of another great Puritan preacher in St Bernard. Both would condemn them as a wanton feeding of the senses[3], and a monstrous hindrance to the attention of sermon audiences:

His si3t schal so be set on sundrye werkes;
The penounes and the pomels and poyntes of scheldes
With-drawen his devocion and dusken his herte;
I likne it to a lym-3erde to drawen men to hell[4]!

[1] Clearly seen in the ruined towers of Greyfriars, at King's Lynn, and Richmond. See also an article by Ian Hannah on Irish Mendicant Houses in the *Archaeol. Journal*, vol. lxxii, 1915, pp. 111–126.

[2] See Eccleston's *De Adventu Minorum*, caps. vii and ix. (The windows were "in the chapel at Gloucester.") There is perhaps no more vivid witness, in its way, to the subsequent ornateness in Mendicant churches than the two little scrolls, of early Tudor date, comprising *MS. Egerton 2341*, which give instructions for "all the Images of Seyntes, th^t shal be made in the V panes of the wyndow in the grey fryers at Grenewych," with other royal figures. Here are actually the notorious "schapen scheldes" of arms, to accompany them, set out for the glass-painter in their colours!

[3] For Wycliffe in our period, cf. *Liber Mandat.*: "Nimis hodie pascunt sensus, ut visum spectaculis ornamentorum ecclesiae sumptuosis...." For St Bernard, see references given in Coulton, *Five Centuries of Religion*, vol. i and Bernard's *Apologia ad Gulielmum*.

Our preachers frequently comment, sometimes disparagingly, on the rich tombs in the churches; cf. Bromyard, *S.P.—Mors.* etc. (painted and fair without, but foul within); Rypon, MS. Harl. 4894, fol. 19 b (the carved figure contrasted with the skeleton within); Myrc's *Festiall*, p. 85; *Gesta Rom.* (especially 15th cent. addition, Engl. vers.), p. 305; *Spec. Laicorum*, § "De sepultura."

[4] The reference here (*Ploughman's Crede*, ll. 560–65) is really to those who

The poet-moralist's soul swells with indignation. Looking the great Dominican Chancellor Bromyard full in the face, would he not have dared him to deny that the lovely ladies and their finery were the preacher's greatest enemies outside, as it was?[1] "Gentes illegales intraverunt in templum!" The churches of the Blackfriars at Norwich or of the Austin friars in London, however, unlike Santa Croce, are probably no exotic Mendicant growth on the national soil. They are one with the huge naved parish churches of the last great architectural style, well-known feature alike of Cotswold hills, Lincolnshire fens, or Norfolk countryside. Some of the earliest of these latter, St Nicholas, North Walsham[2], and St Nicholas, King's Lynn[3], were probably being planned while our *Summa Predicantium*, English culmination of formal homiletic art, was being penned. In the case of the last-mentioned edifice, church-building reaches a point where the distinction between nave and chancel finally disappears but for a wooden screen, leaving one immense broad gallery of stone and glass, but lightly arcaded, which was to be the prototype of many churches more[4]. If, now, we recall the generally recognized influence of ritual upon the much earlier development of the *chevet*, for example, why should we not proudly claim for this new feature the influence of the contemporary pulpit? Unfortunately the architectural experts have explanations of their own. In the case of King's Lynn, a whole volume of quite special, plausible reasons has been advanced, for its adoption[5]. Yet, on the other hand, there are still those very real arguments of Bishop Pecock upon our side, about preaching and about the English rain.

are attending Mass. But I have found among the MS. Sermon Excerpts of M. Hauréau an interesting equivalent for the *sermon-hearers*, in France: "Quando veniunt ad sermonem in quo deberent se speculari, et videre defectus suos, tunc advertunt se et respiciunt marmosetos, et columnas claustri et ecclesiae." (From a sermon before the canons of St Victor, Paris, end of thirteenth century; in Hauréau, *Quelques MSS*. vol. iv, p. 139.)

[1] Cf. above, p. 123.   [2] 1382–1404 (?).

[3] 1414–1418: perhaps planned as early as 1399.

[4] Called by Bond "The Aisled Chapel" type. Cf. St Stephen's Bristol; Gresford, Cheshire; St Andrew Undershaft, and St Margaret's, Westminster, in London; and Long Melford, Suffolk, to mention a few scattered examples.

[5] E. M. Beloe, *Lynn St Nicholas*.

Without giving offence, therefore, to Mr Beloe, or to the architects[1], it may be said that here was the splendid coincidence of a building-plan evolved to do precisely what wealthy clothiers and burgesses wished done with their bequests, for the crowded sermon audiences. With another splendid coincidence we shall content ourselves, and pass on. Churches at Northleach and Cirencester in Cotswold, or Banwell beneath the Mendips, with these stately rebuilt naves, have each their own contemporary pulpit in stone, conspicuous features of the permanent architectural scheme!

Mention of the pulpit as part of the furniture of churches serves to remind us that it too was evolved from earlier forms. "Debet autem predicator in loco eminentiori esse, sicut et evangelium legens," says Durandus[2]. In pointing to the "gospel" ambo as the most suitable spot from which to deliver a sermon in church, he is also pointing to the probable archetype of "pulpitum" as screen and "pulpitum" as ordinary pulpit. Stone and marble ambos, in groups of two and even three intended for the reading of Gospel, epistle, etc. at Mass[3], and said to date from at least the sixth century onwards, are still to be found, as the tourist knows, in earlier basilican churches of Italy. Chrysostom, it has been said, was the first to exchange the elevation of the altar steps, when preaching, for a more prominent place "super aquilam," in the loftier, that is to say, of the two regular ambones ("paulo altior et ornatior, pro evangelio"). This was done deliberately to make himself the better heard. In the land of the Pisani, then, those mastercraftsmen of pulpits, it is easy to trace the great thirteenth-century *cattedra* at Pisa or at Siena in the north, that of Ravello in the south, to this natural origin. But in England[4], where the earliest surviving pulpits date from about the beginning

---

[1] See, however, Prof. E. S. Prior's *Eight Chapters on Engl. Med. Art* (Camb. Univ. Press, 1922), pp. 125–6.

[2] *Rationale* (c. 1286).

[3] Cf. Martène's description (*Ant. Eccles. Rit.*) of the San Clemente Trio, at Rome: one on the right of the chancel, facing the altar for the Epistle, a second facing the people, "pro legendis prophetiis"; a third on left of the chancel, facing the choir, for the Gospel.

[4] The present writer makes no apology for introducing this little sketch, as Dr J. C. Cox's book, *Pulpits, Lecterns and Organs* (Milford), 1915, even apart from its historical inaccuracies, makes little attempt to trace the development of English pulpits.

of our period[1], the capacious ambo type is not to be found. The smaller varieties here, in both stone and wood, nevertheless, would seem to appear appropriately enough at a time when the preaching movement inspired by the friars was at its height. Their present rarity is easily accounted for, in the case of the timber constructions—undoubtedly cheaper and commoner, when the wholesale destruction of carved and painted wood-work in later centuries is called to mind[2]. For the rarer, more permanent erections in stone, a source of development from the monastic pulpit-lectern in the wall, where, as one of our preachers reminds his audience, "men of religion have a lesson read at meat to feed the soul,"[3] might well be looked for. Splendid, indeed, are such structures remaining at Beaulieu, Shrewsbury, and Chester. But as a matter of fact very few of our parish pulpits could be derived from this type[4]. From manuscripts, on the other hand, we get a clear idea from even earlier times, of a simple, light, panelled platform of wood, mounted on legs[5], which could be moved with ease, outside as well as inside the sacred building, as required. This agrees with contemporary descriptions of "setting up" the pulpit in different places, and with the variety of sites necessary to suit the various audiences to be addressed. In the absence, then, of any great decorative scheme, in which the pulpit might participate, this serviceable unadorned pattern would be likely to hold the field. When, however, such interior schemes were developed eventually in the fifteenth century, notably in East Anglia and in the western counties, exactly as we might have expected, the pulpit, whether

[1] Fulbourn, Cambs. (c. 1350), and Mellor, Derbyshire (c. 1360), have been put forward as amongst the earliest. The *pulpit* of Upper Winchendon, Bucks., may well be added to the list of earliest examples (c. 1340). It will be found illustrated in the recently issued volume of the *Ryl. Comm. on Hist. Mons.* for *Buckinghamshire*.

[2] From Mr Keyser's well-known *List*, I have estimated for our period (c. 1350–1450), *roughly* fifteen in stone, and thirty-five in wood, surviving.

[3] *Jacob's Well* (ed. E.E.T.S.), p. 144.

[4] Dr Cox suggests Weston-in-Gordano, Somerset, and others (see p. 32). Staunton, Glos. might be added, perhaps, for the general type. MS. Add. 25089, fol. 79, has a crude illustration, showing a friar preaching "ad populum" from a stone pulpit of this kind.

[5] At least two pulpits thus mounted survive, at Worstead, Norfolk, and Wenden's Ambo, Essex. For miniature illustrations from MSS., reproduced in print, see references supplied by Lecoy de la Marche, *La chaire franç.* pp. 229–32. They are common in the illuminated MSS. themselves.

of wood or stone, shares in the glory of chancel-screen and bench-ends, with only a slight modification of the former plan. The ordinary mediaeval bracket would suggest the replacement of corner-legs by a central pedestal, when the pulpit was now set permanently against pier or wall. Sometimes, even the typical canopy is reproduced above it[1]. For the rest, panels here, as on the screen itself, lent themselves naturally to enrichment with figure-painting and carved work, while mouldings blossomed into foliage. Thus the preacher's rostrum takes its place of honour, as it were, in the general ensemble[2]. Towering above him at a point, in smaller buildings, not so far from his head, is the great Rood itself. From his feet in triumphal procession goes the long line of apostles, martyrs, doctors, saints. Ever about him are the "sermons in stone, books in the running brooks" of vine-trail and beading. God is in everything. What finer background could be sought for the silvery eloquence of preaching?

Stern moralists of the middle ages, however, were no more apt to be deceived by mere outward brilliance in such places than their successors, who talk sometimes as though the middle ages had had no conscience. There was a limit even to church-decoration. When the Lady Meed declares to her confessor, "that ther nis nouthur wyndou, ne auter that I ne schulde maken othur mende, and my nome write," for the admiration of future generations in the holy place, she was giving voice to a common conceit of the wealthy. Dr Bromyard himself wittily declares in his *Summa Predicantium* that in justice these would do better to inscribe thereon the names of the poor they have defrauded in their progress to such ill-gotten magnificence[3].

[1] Cf. Edlesborough, Bucks. and Cold Ashton, Glos. The former is in wood, the latter in stone. Original *bases* to wooden pulpits of the "wine-glass" variety are naturally rare *in situ*. But a fifteenth century specimen from the church of Moreton Hampstead, Devon, will be found among the English woodwork exhibited in the Victoria and Albert Museum, S. Kensington (Exhibit No. 126 [1907]).

[2] In spite of a considerable discussion over the point in *Notes and Queries*, it is easily proved that *either* the north *or* the south side of the chancel arch was used for the pulpit-site here, entirely according to convenience, not according to any rigorous ecclesiastical regulation. The "mediaeval mind" was not so chained to petty points of ritual as some of our modern "ritualistic" minds, nor by any means so fearful of divergence.

[3] This is a common and interesting enough point in our sermon literature to justify further illustration: Bromyard, *S.P.* (as above), *Fama bona*:

Furthermore, if the same practice were extended to the fine apparel they wear, the names of the sheep that provided the material would have to appear. Stains and defacement were the only genuine contribution of the owners. But to return to church memorials. Bromyard and Langland might have referred their condemnations of "suche writynge" to the very pulpits. For more than one of mediaeval date still bears this quaint feature upon it. The height of personal vanity is reached surely in the case of the donors of a remarkable little painted pulpit at Burnham Norton, in Norfolk[1]. Here, apart from the inscription,

"Aliquis opus ab alio factum adornat, vel aliqua de suo addit *fenestram*, forte, vel *vitrum*, vel aliquid tale, ad laudem et memoriam nominis sui; vult nomen suum in opere illo imprimere. Dicit lex quod in titulo illo inscriptionis solum inscribere debent quantam summam ipsi expendiderunt de suo, et quantam ipsi fecerunt; et non totum opus ei ascribere, nec de alieno opere famam et gloriam acquirere. Huic concordat optime sacra scriptura...." A remarkable parallel to *Piers Plowman* as above! He continues as in the text above, concluding: "vix invenirent in operibus et edificiis suis spatium in quo nomen proprium insculperent. Sed satis longa invenirent spatia in quibus nomina pauperum et simplicium, et etiam dominorum quibus serviunt, quos defraudaverunt, inscriberent." See again under *Acquisitio* (*mala*) ("Robbing Peter to give to God," and the story of the devil who claimed a church). Wimbledon, in his Paul's Cross sermon, quoting Hugh of St Victor (who apparently himself borrows from St Jerome): "Poor men are often spoiled to clothe timber and stones." *Jacob's Well*, quoting St Bernard, "Thou makest clad the church walls of dead stone with *painture of brightness,* shining with gayness, and lettest the quick stones of God, the poor, go naked and needy," (E.E.T.S. ed. p. 306); ibid. pp. 203 and 175–6 ("Robbing Peter to give to Paul," (*a*) "*to make therewith churches,*" (*b*) "to *friars, and houses of religion*"). Sermon in MS. Linc. Cath. Libr. A. 6. 2, fol. 198 (The extortionate and the trickster at the market, when "put to examynacion" for their injustice "wyll sey...'I wil gyffe a boke or a chalys to the chyrche, or a bell or a vestment, and so schall I be prayed for every sonday, or ells I wyll do some other good deede lyke to the same'.").
  [1] Other examples, Rossington, Yorks. (15th cent.), "Orate pro anima Ric. Stansall et uxoris ejus"; and Heighington, Durham (e. 15th cent.), "Orate pro animabus Alex. Flettcher et Agnetis uxoris ejus." The Burnham Norton example besides the "Orate pro animis" for John and Catherine, exhibits the words "fecerunt fieri..." along the lower border. On the pulpit at Cranborne, Dorset, on the other hand, an Abbot of Tewkesbury, Thos. Parker (d. 1421), puts but a modest "T. P." Dr Cox dates the Burnham Norton pulpit, c. 1475; but too much credence must not be given even to his archaeological judgements, e.g. (p. 68) of the *Lutterworth* pulpit he objects that "the embattled transom across the centre of each panel" *must* make it of *late* fifteenth century workmanship. But this is a *characteristic* feature of the tracery on the lower stages (particularly at the back) of the St Alban's Feretrar Chamber, at least early fifteenth century work (cf. *Ryl. Comm. Hist. Mon. Report*, etc.), and from detailed evidence probably to be ascribed to the end of Richard II's reign. The tracery is *singularly* like that on "Wycliffe's" pulpit. Mr Patrick, A.R.I.B.A., I notice, states in a volume of the *Brit.*

the figures of husband and wife share its panels with the four
great doctors of Latin Christianity, in equal dimensions.
Preaching from those oaken panels whereon the rustic congregation beholds each holy-day John and Catherine Goldalle
amid such exalted company in glory, could any friar have found

G.R.Owst.

BURNHAM NORTON PULPIT, NORFOLK

ready to hand a more solemn object-lesson for his discourse on
"Superbia"? In the early days of Franciscan enterprise in this
country, a brother had been severely punished for the very act
of "decorating a pulpit with pictures."[1]

Arch. Assoc. (N.S. No. 7 (1901), p. 210): "In the pulpit are preserved all that
remains of the carved panels of what is said to have been the original pulpit
used by Wycliffe; which is quite likely to have been the case, as they are
elegant in design and of the date of the fourteenth century."
    [1] (Though doubtless of saints.) Eccleston, *De Adv. Minorum*, cap. vii.
Keyser's *List* gives forty-one pulpits with traces of painting on panels still left.

If preaching is to be held responsible for the appearance of the pulpit, it may also claim its share in the production of the pew. One thing at all events seems clear from documentary evidence both here and abroad. Whereas kneeling was the characteristic posture of audiences for Mass[1], sitting was the posture for sermon-time. Even at a comparatively early date there is little to bear out the statements made that the majority of the congregation was wont to remain standing. William of Auxerre, a Dominican preacher, about the year 1273, for example, inveighs "against some who when they come to church for the sermon stand, and do not wish to sit down, thus preventing the others from being able to hear."[2] The mediaeval miniatures, moreover, depict listeners as seated, though what they are actually sitting upon may be by no means clear. Turning to archaeological evidences, we possess several fragmentary sets of heavy wooden benches in parish churches which apparently cannot be later than the end of the thirteenth century, and must be distinguished from the priestly furniture of the chancels[3]. In addition there are interior wall-ledges of stone, even earlier in date, which would have been used for a similar purpose, though most likely by the more aged and infirm who were present. Taken together, however, these are sufficient to explain that scuffling after vacant seats and ensuing quarrels in the middle of the service which was sometimes the disgrace of English as well as continental church-going[4]. The clergy, of course, by virtue of office, enjoyed the use of pleasant stalls or sedilia of some description in the sanctuary. But the noble-

---

[1] Cf. Myrc's *Instructions* (E.E.T.S. ed.), p. 9, etc.

[2] *Hist. Litt. de la Fr.* vol. xxvi, p. 429. See some other references in Lecoy de la Marche, pp. 209–10, who does not give the above. Also for Engl. MS. Vernon (E.E.T.S., O.S. No. 117, p. 476), "At a sarmoun ther I *seet*"; *Gesta Rom.* (E.E.T.S. p. 391); *A litel soth sermoun* (E.E.T.S. No. 98), "And sit ye still adown"; Wilkins, *Conc.* vol. ii, p. 140, and vol. iii, p. 434, "continuing on their seats." See also in the text below, p. 167.

[3] See Cox, *Bench-ends* (Milford, 1916), p. 6. But why has he omitted all mention of the *early* specimens at Chelvey, Somerset, a set of ten? (cf. *Bristol and Glos. Arch. Soc. Trans.* vol. xxix, pt. i (1906), p. 41).

[4] Wilkins, *Conc.* vol. ii, p. 140, Synod of Exeter, 1287: "The inhabitants of parishes quarrel repeatedly about seats in the church, two or more persons laying claim to one seat, which is a cause of much scandal, and often produces an interruption in the service." For abroad cf. Hauréau, *Quelques MSS.* vol. iii, p. 125, and examples from the preaching of St Bernardino, in Italy.

men and patrons of churches, too, could claim in true feudal fashion a regular seat as their own. Sir Richard L'Estrange might be seen, for example, in the year 1417, at the sermon in St Dunstan's, at London, in the dignified seclusion of his family (?) pew, "locum sive sedile dictum vulgariter 'Le Closette,'" his mind then innocent enough of that disgraceful outrage which was to follow upon Sir John Trussel later in the day. Likewise Sir John, when he comes in to church at Vespers sits down "super quendam descum," afterwards mentioned in connection with a certain bench (or stool?) opposite ("quoddam scamnum[1] ex opposito ipsius desci existens")[2]. By the middle of the fourteenth century, at least, the wives and widows of *Piers Plowman's* acquaintance were provided with pews of the ordinary sort, as noble dames of former generations had sat in state on their own cushions, brought in for them by the servants. But what would be the lot of the ordinary folk in the rural districts? One of our contemporary treatises in re-telling a popular story from the *Vitae Patrum* may provide a hint. When the "holy Abbot Artemus" sets out with his companions to test the efficacy of the sacrament, "they come alle thre to churche, the Sonday, and sette hem togedere upon a sete of rysches."[3] From the rushes of summer-time, from the straw of winter[4], covering the stones of the rude pavement beneath him, our rustic villager would heap together sufficient to keep off the cold and damp, and mitigate the hardness. There he would squat, as the sermon proceeded, listening or sleeping, or chatting, according to his taste. A few at the back would prefer to defy orders and stand, lolling against a pillar, or strolling with acquaintances, the more devout and well-mannered gazing at the preacher,

---

[1] Mr Hamilton Thompson's explanation of this word as "simply a stool" (cf. Gloss. *Linc. Rec. Soc.* vol. vii, p. 248) is inadequate. Cf. *O.E. Vocs.* (ed. Wright-Wülcker), "bynk," "benche," "bynke"; sim. *Prompt. Parv.*

[2] Wilkins, *Conc.* vol. iii, p. 385. Cf. also the warnings in our Manuals, e.g. *Jacob's Well*, that only priests and *patrons* are to sit in the chancel.

[3] MS. Harl. 2398, fol. 48 b. Mr Coulton calls my attention to evidence in Salimbene's *Chronicle* (sub anno 1248) that sermon audiences then sat frequently on the ground, abroad.

[4] Cf. Church Wardens' Accounts, e.g. All Saints, Bristol: 1408, For one trusse of stree, vi d.; 1427, For rushes at Easter, vi d.; 1427, For straw at Chrystmas, ix d., etc. And see also A. Burton, *Rushbearing*. (For fresh green rushes strewn in the *house*, at Easter, cf. Myrc's *Festiall*, E.E.T.S. ed. p. 129; and again in MS. Ryl. 18. B. xxiii, Easter sermons.)

as we behold them in pictures, over the heads of the ladies seated immediately around his pulpit[1]. The extensive series of pews, sufficient for all, which fill the naves of many churches by the second half of the fifteenth century, reflecting much of the carven beauty of clerical stall, pulpit, and screen, are testimony in themselves to the place which preaching has come to take in the religious life of the people.

With a place for the priest and a place for the people thus provided in our scene, it is time to give heed to the living beings who occupy them. We may follow, indeed, the steps of that pathetic figure, moving—familiar enough to the ears of ancient English sermon-goers—towards the church-yard gate; or "the chyrche style"[2]:

As she wente in the strete, she sawe mych folke go in to a chirche. Thought she, "I wil go wete what this folke do there," and wente here into the chirche, *and sette here downe, as othere didden.* Sone after come a persone into the pullpite and prechid[3].

As likely it might have been the Franciscan "ffrere Henri," that "comeli clerk," with girdle of knotted cord, grey-brown habit, and "come les autres, nuy3 peez." Or equally likely a pardoner, with his sly bag of tricks. "The lewede men likede him wel, and leeveth his speche." Best of all, it might have been that rare and splendid occasion when no less a dignitary than my lord bishop is due to preach in that parish church on a visitation. Thus did Bishop Grandisson come to St Buryan, in 1336, "exercens suam jurisdiccionem ordinarium et diocesanam," in those remote parts of Cornwall, first to absolve the guilty, then to preach, with his sermon finally interpreted for him "in lingua Cornubie," for the benefit of his outlandish subjects[4].

[1] Cf. even such late illustrations as the Woodcut, 1528, reproduced in Méray's *Libres Prêcheurs*, vol. ii, title-page, or Luther preaching (MS. Add. 4727). Also Myrc's warning for Mass-time: "Ny lene to pyler, ny to wal" (*Instr.* E.E.T.S., p. 9).

[2] MS. Linc. Cath. Libr. A. 6. 2, fol. 125 b. Again in MS. Roy. 18. B. xxiii, fol. 108 b.

[3] *Gesta Rom.* Engl. vers. (E.E.T.S. ed.), p. 391. For other versions of this story, besides MS. Harl. 2316, fol. 59, mentioned here in Chap. ii, see *Jacob's Well* (E.E.T.S. ed.), p. 174 and MS. Roy. 18. B. xxiii, etc.

[4] See Reg. Grandiss. (Exeter), pt. ii, p. 820, and cf. *Cil. Oc. Sac.* (MS. Harl. 4968, fol. 45): "Episcopi debent singulis annis omnes parochias sue diocesis visitare, et scrutatis erroribus (sic!) remedia et correctiones adhibere, et *singulis ecclesiis sermonem facere,* aut per se, aut per alium ydoneum...." With this, cf. *re* Bp. Grossetête, above, p. 10.

His train of twenty or thirty mounted clerics and attendants[1] would be as good as a Lord Mayor's show to see. As for the sermon, the ladies, faithful souls, have been in a flutter of excitement over it for weeks. Did not Master Humbert de Romans tell us a story of how a certain noble dame herself once rebuked a corpulent archdeacon, because he dared to disappoint them? He had come, with a brilliant retinue to a certain parish, "sub nomine visitacionis"; really, however, to enjoy the splendid visitation dinners that he knew awaited him there. The first evening passed cheerfully enough, eating and drinking at his host's expense. The intention was to repeat the operation next day. However, certain noble ladies had gathered already in the church that morning, expecting that the visitor would preach them the usual sermon. What was their horror and amazement to find that, when Mass was ended, which he had insisted on being said "sine nota," in a hurry, he was preparing to get back to his table again! Up rose an angry female and addressed him thus: "Behold, lord archdeacon, for a whole day have we waited in silence, expecting you to preach the word of God, and perform your proper office!" His curt reply was profoundly true to type: "We never meddle with such things." But she, noble lady, was not to be put off in that manner. The last word was hers, and a good one: "Little did he care for us that committed the care of our souls to you. See, here you are leaving behind you from your visitation nothing but the dung of your horses!"[2]

That all happened in France a long while past. But the prelate's sermon has still its ancient power of attraction in our own period and country. "For to suche men of grett powere and myȝthe," an English preacher assures us, "men takes hede, and ȝeveth grett audience. To ensample,—and a bishoppe or a

---

[1] Cf. legislation, Wilkins, *Conc.* vol. i, p. 505.

[2] From Etienne de Bourbon (*Tractatus*). Cf. ibid.: "Sunt autem prelati aliqui, cum visitant, magis solliciti quomodo visitentur loca in quibus est abundantia caponum et anserum et gallinarum pinguium, quibus pascantur et impinguentur, quam loca famelicarum animarum, ut verbo Dei reficiantur ab eis." Also Bromyard, *S.P.—Predicatio*: "Contra illos qui non visitant, nec curant infirmos sicut aliqui medici, nisi ubi sunt loca pinguia ubi bene procurantur, et lucrantur." See, too, the story of the greedy archdeacon who eats up the parish priest's substance, on a visitation, in MS. Harl. 3938, fol. 119.

doctoure stond up to preche the worde of God, muche pepull
will drawe thetherwarde to here hym; and ӡiff he repreve vices
and synne, the peple will not gruche never a dele aӡeyns hym,
ne thei will not forӡett [h]is wordes."[1]

> He preched on sa fair maner
> That it was joi for to her,
> And quen his sermoun ended was
> The folc wit mikel joi up ras
> And thankid Jesus in that plaӡ
> That gaf thair bischop sli[che] graӡ[2].

The bishop's visitation address, like all good things, will,
naturally, be rare enough. Even when one of the preaching
sort has arrived in the town, being only human at the best, a
severe cold in the throat may prevent his speaking, when every
arrangement has been made. This seems to be the situation
indicated by one of the most naïve and vigorous little remarks in
all our English sermon literature. At the end of a vernacular
homily with an unmistakeable "visitation" text, the village
parson or some other substitute at hand for the emergency,
strives to allay the general disappointment. They shall have
their special Indulgence all right! "Sirs, my lord shuld have
preched here hym selfe, that is here presente now, but he is a
litill dezezed. And therfore he ordeynt me to preache in is
stede; and he granteth you as muche pardon as thoӡ he had
preched hym selfe."[3] No doubt the attention had flagged. For
the mood is as clear as when to-day the village flower-show is
bereft of its great lady, or the political meeting of its carefully
advertised speaker.

How, then, will our audience behave? Whether within the
sacred precincts or upon the public square, in its motley
character it will probably reflect most of the great feudal
class distinctions and class prejudices which seem to run
deeper in mediaeval flesh and blood than even differences of

---

[1] MS. Roy. 18. B. xxiii, fol. 75.
[2] *Engl. Metr. Homs.* ed. J. Small, Edinburgh, 1862, p. 90. This is from a
curious *narratio* of a bishop (or archbishop), famed for his sanctity, who
eventually confessed in the pulpit, before his people, to an act of gross
immorality committed by him with a nun.
[3] MS. Roy. 18. B. xxiii, fol. 69 b (text, "Visitate..."). For the concluding
grant of the Indulgence itself here, see in Appendix iii, § (1).

nationality. Some of the portraits sketched in our manuscripts
are wonderfully realistic and amusing. The lord and lady of
the manor with their circle will probably be present. They have
a bad habit of sleeping late in those too cosy new-fangled
bedrooms of theirs. By the time my lady has completed her
extravagant toilet, and sets out churchward with her spouse,
the parson and all the people of the parish are weary and
exasperated with waiting for them[1]. There is a sermon story
of a certain lady of Eynesham, in Oxfordshire, "who took so
long over the adornment of her hair, that she used to arrive at
the church barely before the end of Mass." One day "the devil
descended upon her head in the form of a spider, gripping with
its legs," until she well-nigh died of fright. Nothing would
remove the offending insect, neither prayer, nor exorcism, nor
holy water, until the local abbot displayed the holy sacrament
before it. Then it disappeared, leaving my lady cured for ever
of her temptation, we imagine[2]. For the dame who knows
that she is the best-dressed woman in the parish, however, there
is a certain satisfaction in entering late; this too, quite apart
from the flattering thought that God's service has been delayed
out of respect to your rank and person. The eyes of the village
are now centred anxiously upon the south door. "Ther is
most pryde in entrynge of holy churche with pompe, vayne
glorie, with noble atyre, for to be miche yset by amonges the
peple, more than for eny devocion to god. And most in his
festys!"[3] Lords and ladies, they are all alike, these "folke
of grete estate." Says another preacher: "Also grete lordes and
ladies that cometh to holy chirche in riche and noble apparaile
of gold and silver, purles and riche stones, and other worldliche
worschipful atyre byfore oure lord god all mighti, schulde take

---

[1] Cf. *S.P.*—*Ociositas*: "Tales ociosi, qui sunt...in lecto calido, qui tarde
surgunt, intantum quod quandoque sacerdos et missa, immo ipse Deus in
missa oblatus, eos, ultra horam debitam, cum totius parochiae detentione, et
offensione exspectabunt...," etc. (and elsewhere in *S.P.*). This explains
cap. xxxi of *The Bk. of the Knt. of La Tour-Landry*. Cf. the amusing story
in MS. Harl. 2391, fol. 233, of the priest "who often began Mass before the
proper time, so as not to vex a knight by keeping *him* waiting!"
[2] MS. Add. 11284, fol. 64. Cf. also MS. Add. 27336, fol. 70.
[3] MS. Harl. 2398, fol. 9 b. Cf. again, MS. St Albans Cath. fol. 19:
"...*on the holy day*...long ligging in bed, with myche pryde in gay clothing,
myche wast in iaggid [i.e. 'jagging'] and dagging, in late commynge to chirche,
and ovyr this *more to be seen theere, than for ony soule heelthe*...."

ensample of the noble quene Hester." For "sche dede away all hir riche apparaile, and lowed hir mekeliche byfore God," when she came into his house. "Sotheliche so may be grete abhomynacioun to God of thilke that in suche thing haveth pryde or likyng, and of thilke that so attyreth hem to be seie[n] of foles as thei beth hemselfe. And theigh thei seye that thei doth it forto worschipe God therwith in his chirche [Oh! eternal sophistry of women!], thei schulde understonde that God taketh none hede of suche worschip." "And therfore thei schulde at chirche...noght be proude in herte, nother of her astates, ne of her apparaile."[1] Up the nave they go to their seat. How awful is that lordly eye that searches the congregation in its way, whenever "ther come a grett lorde into a churche"; even as he that "loked on ys on side, and saw where a grett gentill [lady] satt on knees, and red on hure primore," according to one preacher's story[2]. The lady at his side "stirring up the dust with her train, makes the good laymen, the clerks, and the priests all drink of it, often makes it fall too upon the altar of the Lord."[3] Oh! the abominable dust of the churches, and the ways of our ancient nobility! Once in her place she may not keep still for long: "But ever as anny man com in to the churche, or wente oute, she loked after hem,...and toke none hede to hur preyours."[4] The preacher will not forget to warn his people again of such haughty misbehaviour: "And therfore, ffrendes, cownte not hem that are absente fro the churche, ne beholde hem now3th that goyth owte. But only, when thou arte comon to the chirche, prey to God of is mercy for thin own synnes and trespase, and loke that thin herte and thi tonge acord bothe to thether!"[5]

But such is human nature, merchant and bailiff, if they be there, even the labouring men, with their "rude minds," as

---

[1] MS. Harl. 45, fol. 113 et seq. (cf. fol. 111: "And also he schulde with glad chere *hyre sermones and goddes wordes*, and in that tyme sette his thoght and his wille to hyre and understonde the wordes of God that there schulde be seide....") Cf. MS. Salisb. Cath. Libr. 103, fol. 125 b (*Jacob's Well*) "Lordys and ladyes schulde for3etyn here ryalte and here powere..." etc.

[2] MS. Roy. 18. B. xxiii, fol. 105 b.

[3] Cf. MS. Add. 21253, fol. 106 (sermon): "Ipsae [dominae] caudis suis moventes pulverem, et illum faciunt bonis viris laicis, clericis, et sacerdotibus bibere; illum faciunt saepe super altare Domini cadere."

[4] MS. Roy. 18. B. xxiii, fols. 105 b–106 (a "Narratio contra ficte orantes ").

[5] Ibid.

Pagula describes them[1], have all their own little faults and weaknesses, in the place of worship, "yvel to be ocupied when thei come in thedir, with myche iangling and iapinge, and many othere vanytees, settynge nouȝt bi prechinge and techinge of goddis word, but wenynge that it is an ydil thinge."[2] It is hard enough to get some of them to the church at all: "Anone he wyll make hys excuse and sey, 'I am olde or sekely, or the wedir is colde and I am febyll.' Or ells he will excuse hym and sey thus, 'I have a grete howsholde,' or ells he hathe some other ocupacion to do, but, for all these excusacions, and a man wolde com and hyre hym, and sey, 'I wil gyffe good wagys,' then wyll thei ley all maner of excusacions a bak and com un to theyre dyvyne service acordyng to theyre dutye."[3] Middle-class wives, too, will ape the grandeur of their superiors, and the Sunday finery of the servants almost vies with that of their mistresses:

Seynt poule techith how women schulde araye hem when thei goo to chirche, for to preye god. Thei schulde have, he seith, clothinge and atyre after that her astate asketh,—that were honeste and with oute to outrageous coste; and that is to understonde after the estate that thei beth of. ffor that that is mesure to one is outrageous to another. ffor more falleth to a queene then to a countesse; and more to a countess than to another symple lady; and more to a lady than to an other symple woman. ffor seynt poule techith hem to be symple in siȝt, that is to seie, meke and schamfaste, and no queyntise seche, ne devise for her hevedes—as tressis, philettis, [as in the year 192–!] and othre suche wrecchidnes, as many foles doth, that strecchith the nekke as an herte, or kambreth the nekke as an hors. And also seint poule seithe and counsaileth hem that thei nogth atyre her hedes, neither with silver, gold, ne purle, ne other riche stones; but that thei cover her hedes with clene veyles, and nameliche at the chirche, when thei beth to fore God, and schewe hem there as good women schulde doo[4].

After all the preacher can afford to take more pains with the

[1] Cf. MS. Roy. 6. E. 1, fol. 28.   [2] MS. St Albans Cath. fol. 19.
[3] MS. Linc. Cath. Libr. A. 6. 2, fol. 197. Cf. Myrc's *Instructions* (E.E.T.S., O.S. No. 31, p. 37): "Hast thou spared for hete or colde to go to chyrche when thou were holde?"; also MS. Harl. 2398, fol. 27; *Jacob's Well* (E.E.T.S. ed. pp. 261, 291), etc. For the counter-attraction of *Sunday Sport*, etc., see my article on "'The People's Sunday Amusements in the Preaching of Medieval England," in the *Holborn Review*, Jan. 1926.
[4] MS. Harl. 45, fol. 113 et seq.

female element than with the male. For Bishop Brunton makes it clear that then, even as now, men were in a minority, and the churches were attended mainly by the womenfolk[1]. The sexes are probably separated, the latter "sitten all a rewe,"[2] as we have seen, and with good reason. For strange things are done in churches[3] and strange folk go there. Gower's lover, like Dante, is amongst those "in chirches and in minstres eke, that gon the women for to seke,"[4] harmless enough, in his case, it is true. But the "lechour" may go, too, as the preacher describes, under an otherwise calm exterior, thinking his evil thoughts, and finding the very journey thither irksome enough: "Hym thynketh the tyme of a myle the space of thre myle weies."[5] Even the heretic, the infidel, and the excommunicate, may enter the church expressly to hear the sermon alone, though on no other account. "For that purpose they ought to be received by all."[6] It is a remarkable throng that faces him who stands in a mediaeval pulpit, disturbing, heedless, vicious, perhaps dangerous—who knows? Men can quarrel and strive, as well as drive their bargains in this "hous of praier."[7]

The sermon has now begun. A busy hum of conversation rises, at times well-nigh drowning the voice of the gesticulating speaker. So common an occurrence is it that hardly an English

[1] Cf. MS. Harl. 3760, fol. 125: "Sed homines, et maxime juvenes otiosi a deo subtrahunt servitium debitum...."

[2] Gower, *Conf. Amant.* bk. v.

[3] Cf. MS. Harl. 2398, fol. 9 b: "*Lecherye* and *glotenye* beth *ofte tyme* ydo in holy places"; MS. Harl. 45, fol. 68: "lecherie in holy chirche"; fol. 120: *do.* "in holy stede, as chirche...," etc.; MS. Harl. 2398, fol. 42 b: "...lygge by a woman in churche"; MS. Vernon, fol. 366, as given in Horstmann, vol. ii, p. 341, a "Forma Confitendi": "disyryng wimmen in chirche"; etc. Cf. with these the Ely Misericorde-carving on p. 177 below. This also explains the presence of such unpleasant stories, as of caps. xxxv and xxxvi, in *The Bk. of the Knt. of La Tour-Landry.*

[4] Gower, as above.

[5] MS. Harl. 2276, fol. 36 b.

[6] Cf. MS. Harl. 4968, fol. 42 b (*Cil. Oc. Sac.*): "Hereticis, et excommunicatis, et infidelibus licet ecclesiam ingredi, ut sermonem audiant *tantum*, et ad hoc ab omnibus recipi debent" (from Grat. Decret.). With this compare the sermon story (originally from Greg. *Dial.*) of the preacher who requested all excommunicated persons to leave the church, before his sermon began (MSS. Add. 11579, fol. 140 b and Harl. 2851, fol. 103 b, etc.).

[7] Cf. MS. Roy. 6. E. 1, fol. 26 b: "seditio, clamor, impetus, contentiones, rixae, confabulationes, negociationes, nundinarum mercata," etc.; MS. Harl. 2398, fol. 91: "merchandyse in the churche"; MS. Harl. 2276, fol. 119: "stryves and debates,...biyngis and sellyngis..."; MS. Add. 21253, fol. 136: "...non litigent, vel rumores narrent, vel res suas ibi vendant." MS. Salisb. Cath. Libr. 103, fol. 158^b. All these are carefully denounced.

sermon collection fails to deal with it. Perhaps he is old and inaudible, and half the village congregation, freed on the holiday from the heavy labours of the week, sleeps fitfully. However rich and impressive the background and the ceremonial of the parish church may be, it is certainly no meekly reverent audience that the English preachers are prepared to reveal to us in their homilies. Awed ourselves by what we may see to-day, we are apt to forget that the response in alert spiritual fashion to what is beautiful in art and ritual is itself largely a modern growth. Intimate quality of soul, it is not to be bred suddenly or automatically by any form of mass-religion, where the first primitive fear has disappeared. Our mediaeval Catholic, the homilies tell us, can snore as heedlessly, gape as incessantly in his Gothic fane, as ever Hogarth's Protestant worshippers amid the horrors of box-pews and cushioned "three-decker."

> Men suld be bowsum [i.e. buxom] in thaire mode,
> And gladly go to gostly fode,
> That es to say to goddes worde
> That prechores gaders of goddes horde.
>
> .   .   .   .
>
> Bot Crist gifes tham no sight perfite [i.e. of himself]
> That in sarmon has no delite:
> ffor many foles will here sarmowne
> With owten any devociowne.
> Devociowne es a luf langing
> That out of a mans hert suld spring
> To ȝerne thc blis that lastes ay
> And put all vanitese oway.
> Sum men at sarmones er to blame
> And war wele better be at hame:
>
> .   .   .   .
>
> Sum other unto sarmon cumes
> Bot in thaire brest no thing it blomes;
> ffor slepe thai may no tent take,
> (Bot at the taverne will thai wake.)
> fful light thai er, ill laykes to lere,
> And hevy sarmons for to here.
> His hevide than may he noght hald up,   [=head]
> But wele he kepes the fendes cup.
> That the fendes cup, call I,
> That makes tham slepe and be hevy[1].

[1] MS. Harl. 4196, fol. 88 b (*Engl. Met. Hom.*). To complete our comparison, Bp. Brunton mentions in a sermon (MS. Harl. 3760, fol. 176) those who go to church, or to sermon, merely "pro forma."

These two old vices of sleeping and talking are an irresistible temptation to the mediaeval sermon-goers. No one knows it better than the father of all wickedness himself:

In dayes that bethe now, prechours may seye Allas! for while they ...speke the wordes of God, there comithe an hisser, scil. the devil, and he whistelithe so swetly that...synners herithe no worde of God, but turnithe hem to dilectacion of synne, to which the devil temptithe hem. For the devil hissithe be mony diverse weyes in the sermon; and how? For he makithe some to slepe that they her not the wordes of God; and some he makithe to chatir faste; and hem that he may not make chatery ne slepe, he makithe hem to have litle swettnesse or non to the worde of God[1].

There is no end, in fact, to his ingenuity, and that of his assistants in this direction. Who has not heard the oft-repeated sermon story of how once a certain preacher, seeing how drowsy and sluggish his irreverent congregation had become, was granted by God to know the cause of their indevotion then and there? Thus it was that he saw with his own eyes the little black fellow that runs around, and puts his fingers over the ears and eyes of the people, making them deaf and sleepy. Asked who he might be, the "Aethiopian" replied he was a devil, and his name "obturans aures et oculos." Had he any friends? Yes, indeed, at work with him there. One called "indurans cor" hardened people's hearts; another, "obturans os," prevented them from confessing; and a third "obturans bursam" hindered the making of amends and restitution due[2]. Old

---

[1] *Gesta Rom.*, Engl. fifteenth century vers. (E.E.T.S. ed.), p. 138. Cf. further, Brunton, MS. Harl. 3760, fol. 124 b, etc.: "sompnolenti otiosi, et ponderosi"; Bromyard, Waldeby, and Rypon, as above, in text; MS. Camb. Univ. Libr. G. g. vi. 16, fol. 49: "*oft* in church jangelling or sleeping"; MS. Harl. 45, fols. 57 b, 58, 111, etc.: "Pledinge and janglynge in holy chirche," "Speke harlottrye, and foule wordes of villany and synne in chirche; (to studie more in brekynge of voyse than in devoute singynge)," "Jangle, lawghe, bourde, and tryfle there, *as many fooles doth*"; MS. Harl. 2398, fol. 3: "Harletrye and unskylful jangelynge in holy churche"; *Jacob's Well*, passim: "Sleepen in church, singen, rownyn, jangelen"; idle play; sleeping in church in time of preachings; idle words, chidings, reprovings in holy church; telling tales, japing in divine service; voice-breaking in church; etc., etc. oft repeated; Myrc's *Festiall*, p. 116: talking, joking, and "chaffaryng," and *Instructions*, pp. 36 and 45: disturbing the priest; MS. St Albans Cath. fol. 19 and Bodl. 5: jangling and japinge, etc., etc.; MS. Linc. Cath. Libr. B. 5. 8, fol. 850: "jangelyng, and trifels"; etc., etc.

[2] Bromyard, *S.P.—Audire (verbum Dei)*; again in Engl. vers. of *Alphab. Narrat.* (E.E.T.S., O.S. No. 126), p. 66 and Myrc, *Festiall*, etc., etc.

Abbot "Macharye" had seen much the same sight when he went into a church. But there the fiends were small as children, and blue as men of "Inde," running all about, and scorning there every man, making faces at them ("making a mowe"), and as they awoke greasing their lips with ointments from a box, until "the folk jangelyd and telde talys" again[1]. Thus does pixie-land re-invade the churches, after fourteen centuries of Christianity in the world[2]. For a parallel to-day we must seek out the peasant churches of Southern Italy[3], or the "Orthodox" folk of the Balkans with their Rain-maiden, and their Yuletide "Badgnak."

When the same preacher comes to recite yet another similar tale, he is rapidly losing patience, and his "moralization" becomes the more violently personal as the din increases. How shall we stop this intolerable chattering? Oh, tell them Voragine's tale[4] about the devils that collect in sacks and record on their scrolls, "the words of the people which they jangleden and rownedyn in church." "Forsoothe then," cries he, getting his thrust in, "I drede me the feend hath a gret book aȝens ȝou, wretyn of ȝoure ianglynges in cherch; & ȝit ȝe excusyn ȝow therein, & seyn 'Me muste speke to hym that spekyth to me'! Bethware, and levyth suche talys for dreed of God, & for rewthe of ȝoure soule!" That devil once had a most strange accident. The audience pricks up its ears again. "The feend seyde: 'I wryte thise talys of the peple in this cherche to recordyn hem afore God at the doom for here dampnacyoun, and my book is to narwe to wryten on alle here talys, thei say so manye.'" And

---

[1] *Jacob's Well* (E.E.T.S. ed.), p. 237. I give this to illustrate two interesting variations of the same "exemplum," originally from the *Vitaspatrum*.

[2] In Bromyard's version of a similar "exemplum" (*S.P.* s.v. *Ferie, seu Festa.*) the devil who busies himself thus with the lay-folk is called Grisillus.

[3] A friend of the present writer who recently visited Palermo, in Sicily, described to him precisely such a scene at a sermon in the cathedral. The preacher was quite inaudible, half-way down the church, from the chattering. Guides were calmly prepared to take one round the building, while the preaching proceeded. Cf. again in Coulton's *Mediaeval Studies*, No. 2, p. 24.

[4] Cf. Bromyard, *S.P.—Exemplum.* This is *his* cure for those who play games during sermon-time: "Expediret forte talia audire exempla quia *terribilia exempla* finis et poenae malorum citius a peccatis revocarent." Caesarius of Heisterbach tells of Abbot Gerard, rousing his dozing congregation at Heisterbach by crying: "There was once upon a time a King called Arthur!" and then rebuking them for awakening to hear "fables"! (*Hist. Litt. de la Fr.* vol. xxiii). Cf. Waldeby quoted below, p. 333.

straightway in drawing out the parchment with his teeth, he struck his head against the church-wall behind him, and made the others laugh to see it. Then the homilist returns to the charge again: "I trowe the feend hath nede to drawe lengere & braddere his rolle here; for it is ellys to lytel to wryten on alle the talys tolde in this cherch. For it is nevere lefte, but it be at sacre, for prechyng, ne shryfte, ne schame, ne dreed of God, ne of the world. But they amendyn hem, thei schull be perysched both body and soule!"[1] That picturesque little "exemplum"—devil's teeth and all—has found its way on to a misericorde among the stalls at Ely[2]; into how many religious treatises it would be hard to say.

THE DEVILS IN CHURCH
(Ely Cathedral)

But if these abominable disturbers could put their noses into Hell, and there learn their fate, they might amend them right quickly:

> And tho that were up to the lippes blak,
> Stryf and jangeling in chirche dude make;
> Uche to othur jangled with scorn,
> To heere godus wordus thei hav for-born[3].

Those that sleep "as a beast, in God's service," may be only an offence to themselves. The worst of the talker is that he may

---

[1] *Jacob's Well*, pp. 115 and 232.

[2] By overlooking the *side* carvings, Bond, in his *Misericordes* (Frowde, p. 166) has missed the full significance of this scene. One devil records on a scroll, while the other, on the left, draws out the parchment with his teeth.

[3] MS. Vernon (eleven pains of hell); E.E.T.S., O.S. No. 98, p. 107, etc.

"let others from the hearing of God's word."[1] And here the
rich and powerful are no better than their poorer neighbours,
when they condescend to be present at the sermon[2]. Worse
yet than either sleeping or chattering, from his lofty position
the friar has actually espied some playing at chess, or gambling
with dice, while he is discoursing. Little use is it to argue with
such. They only retort: "What do we want to listen to sermons
for?" "Each man has five senses, and knows when he has
done what is wrong or right. Well enough does he know when
he commits fornication, or steals, or gets drunk, that he is
sinning."[3] How foolishly they talk, argues the learned Dominican. A craftsman desiring to learn his craft might just as well
say: "I have my senses. I don't need to listen to the master."
Never mind! Those who refuse to give heed to their lesson in
this life, shall receive a worse in the next. Do the village women-
folk bring their needlework with them, we wonder, to beguile
the often weary sermon-time? "Longe me thought the preest
in prechyng!"[4] Alas, how heavily it weighs upon those who have
no "swetnesse,...in heryng Goddys woord, no more than a
beeste, but evyl apayed & wery in...herte therof."[5] Cries
John Waldeby to his hearers: "Oh, how many, in listening to
the word of God...are heavy and even somnolent! For one
hour seems terribly long to them. Yet to dwell for a day and a
night at the tavern, in lust and song, and other vain amusements, does them no hurt; for in these days men like a short
sermon, or no sermon at all, when in church, and long drinking
in the ale-house."[6] Dr Bromyard had protested once that

---

[1] *Jacob's Well* (p. 103); cf. also p. 108: "Letters of others' prayers and
devotions, and troublers of divine service." But even in the era of Protestant
respectability things could be apparently as bad; cf. in a visitation at Lincoln,
of the year 1607: "that the prechers are usuallie much troubled in ther sermons by the prophane walking and talkinge of idle and irreligious persons,...
as also for drunkenes, talkinge, and going out in service time," etc. (*Linc.
Cath. Stat.* pt. ii).

[2] *S.P.—Predic.*: "Sic magni tyranni, divites, et potentes,...si veniunt ad
predicationem, dormiunt vel garrulant, et illam aure capere nolunt."

[3] *S.P.—Exemplum* (begin. "Illis enim qui ad scacos vel taxillos, dum pre-
dicatur, ludunt..."). Cf. *Jacob's Well*, "idle play" in church, etc. (p. 304).

[4] From a contemp. *Forma Confitendi*, in MS. Linc. Cath. Libr. B. 5. 8,
fol. 850.

[5] *Jacob's Well*, p. 280.

[6] MS. Caius Coll. Camb. 334, fol. 181.

Englishmen were the worst sermon-goers in the world[1], and
Nicole Bozon, Franciscan, that "many are more grieved by a
short homily than by six week-days of labour and bodily
affliction."[2]

Not content, however, with merely "passive resistance" to
the preacher's effort, with late coming and scant attention, the
congregation apparently will take matters into its own hands on
occasion, with shocking aggressiveness. That an English king
of notorious impiety should send to the preacher, "demanding
vehemently that he should put an end to his discourse," might
excite little surprise[3]. That ordinary lay-folk should do the
same is a somewhat different matter:

> Sometimes they say to the priest, "Let us out of church quickly,
> because one of our friends is having a banquet, and we have to rush
> off thither!" If, to be sure, a sermon, which concerns the soul's
> salvation, is due to be given, *they strive to prevent it, with various
> excuses*, saying, "The day has gone!" ["Dies transiit"], and such
> like, or, at the least, they are annoyed. In truth, if by no possible
> means they can escape from staying a brief hour in the church,
> then they spend the short time there in empty gossip, and unprofit-
> able chattering, heedless that the House of God is the House of
> Prayer. But afterwards, away to dinner and the tavern; no hurrying
> in this fashion there. Rather do some spin out the rest of the day,
> even far into the night, eating and drinking, as though celebrating a
> feast[4].

"So many solicitations, so many expenses, so many toils, so
many courses to be prepared and so often," with these gluttons,
that "by reason of this they frequently desert the things which

---

[1] *S.P.*—*Audire* (*Verb. Dei*): The Queen of Sheba and "omnes nationes
Xianitatis—in causa ista possunt surgere contra Anglicos, quia vix invenitur
natio Christiana quae ita raro et invite audit verbum Dei."

[2] See ed. *Contes Moral*, P. Meyer (Soc. des anciens textes fr.), § 26. Cf.
also Bp. Brunton, MS. Harl. 3760, fol. 176: "Isti tamen ad longam dietam
libenter vadunt, ad luctas, nundinas, et spectacula, ad vanam recreationem
corporum, ubi vix ad unum miliare laborant ad audiendum sermonem...";
Bromyard (*Aud.*): "Sed heu! Homicida stat per 40 dies in ecclesia ut mortem
evadat temporalem, et vos non libenter statis in uno sermone, ut temporalem
et eternam evadatis!"; MS. Add. 21253, fol. 140 b: "Certe multi sunt nolentes
audire predicatores Christi." B. L. Manning is certainly too sweeping in his
essay, on this subject. (See *The People's Faith...*) and perhaps A. G. Little
(cf. *Stud. in Engl. Franc. Hist.* p. 133).

[3] Kg. John at an Easter sermon by St Hugh (*Mag. Vita S. Hug. Linc.*
Rolls S. p. 293: "Tam materiam quam moram sermonis non aeque ferens,
tertio misit ad eum, flagitans obnixe ut sermoni metas ponat...").

[4] *S.P.*—*Ferie seu Festa.*

pertain unto the honour of God, such as the hearing of God's Word, and the like, saying or thinking that they want to hurry away to luncheon lest the food should go bad, or their belly grow famished and ache."[1]

These great Sunday dinners and subsequent revelry were amongst the devil's worst snares for the ruin of devotion. Robert de Sorbon, an old Parisian preacher of the thirteenth century, says to his congregation, with a merry twinkle, no doubt, when Easter Sunday comes round, "I know well that to-day you want a short sermon and a long table!" But when this gluttony became the habit of every English holy-day, it was beyond a joke.

At her mete, meche more waast, myche cost, myche glotenye, mony idil oothis, lecherous wordis, and othere vycious wordis. Soone aftir at the ale, bollynge and synginge, with many idil wordis, as lesynggis, bacbitinggis, and scornyngis, sclaundris, yvel castingis, with al the countenaunce of lecherie, chidingis, and fi3tingis, with many othere synnes; makinge the holi daye a synful daye. And so it semeth now a daies that the holi daye may be clepid the sory day. For of alle the daies in the 3eer, the holidayes ben moost cursidli dispensid in the develis servyce in dispite of God, and alle his seyntis in hevene....It is wondre that god suffrith the peple to lyve up on erthe[2].

That was no proper sequel for the sermon at Mass.

The subject leads us on to notice a further vice of leaving the church before the sermon had actually finished, or indeed before it had even begun. "Here 3e may se that 3e that heryn no3t full dyvyne servyse in 3oure parysch-cherche, but a morwe-masse, & gon and fyllen 3oure bely,...how 3e have drunkyn of the develys crewettys and arn empoysouned in slowth."[3] That it was the sermon that generally suffered the most, in this respect, is clear from evidence stretching back to very early times. Durandus, at the close of the thirteenth century, repeats a Statute of the Council of Carthage[4], belonging to the fourth, that "he who goes out of the audience in disdain

---

[1] Ibid. *Gula.*
[2] MS. St Albans Cath. fol. 19. Cf. also for Sunday Ale-house scene, MS. St Johns Coll. Oxf. 94 (fol. 123) as printed in *Edit.* Royster, pp. 21–3 (as before), and my art. in the *Holborn Rev.*, as above, p. 172, n. 3.
[3] *Jacob's Well*, p. 116.
[4] A.D. 398. (Here from the *Rationale.*)

while the priest is delivering his homily in church shall be excommunicated." Caesarius of Arles is said to have had the church-doors shut after the Gospel on many occasions to prevent anyone leaving before the preaching had begun[1]. According to M. Langlois, the people of Paris were once in the habit of doing this regularly, only to make confusion worse confounded by returning at the Creed. In this case, however, the thirteenth-century preachers so grossly insulted had a ready retort: "Thus do the toads, when the vineyards blossom. The perfume of the flower drives them off, and kills them, even as the sweetness of the Word of God puts these townsfolk to flight." The evidence for such conduct in the England of Langland and Chaucer is sufficiently plain. "Some," adds a contemporary version of the *Gesta Romanorum* in English, concerning the devil's activities in the churches, "he maketh for to go away from the sermon."[2] Master Rypon of Durham has a whole paragraph dealing with this and kindred behaviour in a theme on the text: "Tempore accepto exaudivi te." These words may well be applied, he argues, to both preacher and hearers, if the preaching is pleasant and acceptable to the latter, and they listen *to the end* ("usque finem; quia haec est 'exaudire,' i.e. *usque ad exitum* audire"). He proceeds to explain further that the reason why the speaker is *not* heard "intelligently, gladly and obediently" to the end may often be traced to faults on his side as well as theirs. Conceivably he may be preaching for vain glory, or for gain, or may even be notoriously vicious himself. His audience, on the other hand, may spend the time chattering or sleeping, or else *withdraw before the end of the discourse*[3]. The "animae rudes," doubtless would excuse themselves, as Bromyard describes, on the score of "being rude, and therefore of not knowing, understanding, or being able to carry away what is being said."[4]

Then, as now, people objected to being "preached at," with this difference, that in the later middle ages they had to put

---

[1] From Martène, *Ant. Eccl. Rit.* (Predicatio).
[2] MS. Add. 9066 vers., E.E.T.S. ed., p. 138.
[3] MS. Harl. 4894, fol. 17 b, etc. Cf. *Jacob's Well*, p. 11: "When thy curate showeth thee the articles of the Curse, go not out of the church, till they be showed, for no cause, but hear them with full will."
[4] *S.P.—Audire (Verb. Dei).*

up with a vastly greater amount of it and were sometimes not afraid to object vociferously in front of the preacher. Confronted by such clearly-defined classes, with corresponding duties and corresponding shortcomings, all equally clear and definite, it was only natural that those charged with the duty of sacred reproof in a less democratic age should be equally direct in their criticism. From the general documentary agreement of the latter we can see that so habitual became this practice of class rebuke that it produced among our sermon-goers certain characteristic reactions and moods on their part, varying from laughter to threats. We can observe the somewhat risky process at work as well in the pages of Rypon, again, as indeed anywhere else:

"Truly some folk to-day" ("nonnulli moderni"), he explains from his pulpit, "are not ashamed to sin. Repentance they despise. But beyond everything else they hate to hear anyone speak of their own vices. If I speak to the ecclesiastics, some of whom are simonists, some lascivious, some greedy, some drunken, some lustful, some avaricious, some men of merchandize, some men of the chase, yea, I should rather say more given up to the world and its pomp than are secular folk; again, if I speak to temporal lords, knights and squires, yes, and to other men, too, how lords oppress the poor, tyrannically robbing them of their possessions in their unbridled greed, how they promote and maintain quarrels with their neighbours, yea, and protect the most abandoned of their officials in causes the most unjust, through their pride defending them; how, too, they are a prey to wrath and envy amongst themselves; yet, again, if I speak to the lawyers, how they defend false cases for sake of profit, and to jurors, how for similar ends, through their perjury, they cause the upright to lose their wealth; how merchants and other men of craft deceive each other with false oaths and fictitious goods; finally, how all the aforesaid, and all the common people also, make abominable use of false swearing, lies, yea, and every kind of mortal sin;...how this realm is in perdition—and who doubts but that the aforesaid sins are the cause?—if I say all this and more to them, he who is accused will instantly complain, he blushes with shame, yea, he is ill at ease, he at once decries the preacher, attacking either his person or his status, thus, 'I have never known worse, prouder, or more greedy men than the churchmen!'"[1]

---

[1] MS. Harl. 4894, fol. 180 b et seq. Also fol. 174: "Audientes sua facinora obstupescunt, et ex hoc predicatori,...aut clam, aut publice obloquuntur." Cf. here MS. Linc. Cath. Libr. A. 6. 2, fol. 129: "He that is a Curate,... soche as ow3te to rebuke synfull pepyll and sey the trowthe un to hem in

As Bromyard says, the whipped horses have kicked out; the cry of the stricken from the crowd tells whose head the stone has struck[1]. The word of the preacher has "gone home," as we say. It has hit the target, and, being human, the target objects.

On the other hand, to behold one's neighbours struck in this fashion created a considerable amusement:

"When their own sins are preached against, they get angry," declares the *Summa Predicantium*; "when it is against those of others, they are pleased. In spiritual 'goods' they consider others' welfare before their own, but not in temporal, for it seems that they would rather that others were healed than themselves, and that all the aforesaid benefits should be the lot of other men rather than theirs. This is obvious enough when the clergy endeavour to get the laity rebuked from the pulpit for wrongful tithing, and the laity try to get the clergy preached against for giving evil example."

So our Dominican proceeds, mingling drollery with satire:

The men are delighted when the preacher harangues against the women-folk, and *vice versa*. Husbands are pleased when their wives' pomposities are denounced in the sermon, how perchance they may spend the half of their wealth upon their own adornment. Wives rejoice to hear the preachers attacking their husbands, who spend their goods upon the ale-house[2]. Those who know that they are guilty of some crime try to get the detractors denounced in the pulpit, because they think that men will talk of their deeds. And so what is preached against others' vices, gives pleasure, but what is said against their own, displeases. Thus when the preacher attacks all vices, everyone is displeased[3].

Rypon, describing the same situation, tells us how he has seen the lay-folk laughing ("tunc rident laici"), when the ecclesi-

remission of theire synnys,...oftentymes he schall be blamyd, and peraventure for his tru sayng he schall be gretely trowbelyd...."; MS. Add. 21253, fol. 64[b] (lapidant eos lapidibus detractionis).

[1] *S.P.—Audire* and *Detractio*. Cf. also Thos. Walleys, in MS. Harl. 635, fol. 7 et seq: "Si aliqui quorum reprehenduntur vicia, irascantur"; and Waldeby, in MS. Caius Coll. Camb. 334, fol. 179.

[2] To complete the picture, the *S.P.* mentions under *Acquisitio (mala)*: "Quando pauperes seu simplices audiunt predicare contra divitum injusta acquisita, inaniter gloriantur...." Finally, cf. Bp. Brunton in MS. Harl. 3760, fol. 176: "Et tales, licet pro forma vadant ad...ecclesiam vel ad sermonem, non tamen student in libro consciencie ut per auditum verbi Dei propria crimina recognoscant, sed ita judicant proximorum crimina et defectus..."; also Gasquet's extract in *O.E.B.* (2nd. ed.), p. 82.

[3] *S.P.—Audire (Verb. Dei)*. Again in a sermon of Bp. Brunton (MS. Harl. 3760, fol. 186). Part of this will be found translated in Gasquet, *O.E.B.* pp. 96–7.

astics are in for a bad time, because they love to hear them
accused of precisely the same vices—greed, immorality, and so
forth. With the more accomplices in the world, the happier they
feel. We are actually permitted to see them storing up the
choice tit-bits of the discourse in their minds, chuckling over
them, repeating them to their acquaintances, when it is over:
"Oh! how truly the preacher spoke, to-day!"... Shame on them,
hypocrites! They ought to be *sorry* to hear such things, as well
for their own wretched condition, as for that of their fellows[1].
Such allusions to the frequency of this perilous method of
address are apt to puzzle the modern reader. Clear it is from
such testimony, at all events, that while a few heretics were
being condemned for it, and licences warned men "that you in
no wise loosen your tongue over those matters by means of
which scandals in some way or other have been able to arise
among clergy and people,"[2] the practice must have continued
almost unabated.

But besides gratifying denunciations, there could be gratifying jokes and trifling. Reference has already been made, in
the chapter dealing with the friars, to "ridiculous old wives'
fables" and obscenities which cause "loud roars of laughter"
("risus cachinnationesque") amongst the audiences. Méray
has attempted to illustrate them in the case of the country
where later met the Council of Sens[3] to condemn all such
scandals. What, however, was true of Dante's Florence long
before[4] will still be true, in a measure, of Chaucer's England.

---

[1] MS. Harl. 4894, fol. 174 b: "Si predicentur eis peccata talium ecclesiasti-
corum bene reportant illa, et rident, et de eis confabulantur, dicentes quod
verum dixit; ubi tamen de ratione verecundarentur et dolerent...," etc.;
cf. MS. Salisb. Cath. Libr. 103, fol. 142 b (unpubl. *Jacob's Well*): "Ry3t
so *whan a preest prechythe trouthe, and truly repreuvythe synne in prelatys*
and in other grete men, other peple no3t gylty in the poyntys arn glad, and
turnyn hem ly3tly to here the trouthe...." Similarly, too, Bp. Brunton,
MS. Harl. 3760, fol. 176 b: "...Semper defectus judicant sacerdotum."
[2] Cf. Preaching License for John Borard, c. 1381, in *Reg. Wykeham*
(Winch.), vol. ii, p. 326. Cf. also Walleys' warnings in his *Forma Predicandi*
(MS. Harl. 635; Lathbury, MS. Roy. II. A. xiii, fol. 188 ("nulla scandalosa,
vel invidiosa.")
[3] 1528. Labbe, *Conc.* vol. xxxii, col. 1199, § xxxvi.
[4] *Paradiso*, Cant. xxix (ll. 88–120). Cf. also *Piers Plowman* (A. text),
pass. xi, ll. 24 et seq. for the friars' popular "harlotries"; and *Cil. Oc. Sac.*
(MS. Harl. 4968, fol. 42): "Predicator debet utiliter docere, *et prudenter
tacere*, ne per defectum sane doctrine errores firmentur."

In the spirit of those careless Athenians who assembled to hear a Christian preacher on Mars Hill, our mediaeval townsmen would stroll off casually to "Predicacion," on the chance of hearing "some humorous remark" ("aliquid verbum jocosum")[1]. Otherwise, well-dressed like the worldly wife of Bath, it was a pleasure merely to see and to be seen, in any such fashionable and highly reputable assemblies[2], where news and mirth might be provided. When they should be like glass windows letting in the light, excluding the tempests[3], they are only wretched sieves retaining, while steeped in the waters of preaching, nothing from without but the filth ("nisi aliqua grossa, et foeda, et putrida, sicut paleas, et hujusmodi"). "If anyone tells some open folly in the pulpit (in predicatione apertam fatuitatem diceret), they retain it in the memory well enough; not so the useful things." "As in the case of those who, lacking appetite, prefer to eat fruit and delicacies in place of the heavier and more solid food which is more sustaining, so these folk hearken with the greater zest for vain, quaint, and laughable matter in the sermon, which may provoke them to mirth."[4] Unlike him whom the devil found reverently pondering "that the prest spake" on his way from church[5], they go home bursting with the jokes, there to retail them at leisure: "The good things they fail to bring away. The remarks that were out of place, they are all too ready to seize upon, to repeat them again and again with glee." Evil generation! Sermons are not to be listened to lightly, like the heroic deeds narrated by actors and heralds, or idle readings from the Romances, cries the preacher. Know you not that "he who listens negligently to preaching is no less guilty than he who lets fall to the ground the Body of Christ."[6]

---

[1] Rypon, MS. Harl. 4894, fol. 119 b: "Illi ergo qui non audiunt verbum Dei bona intentione, sed forte ut audiant *aliquid verbum jocosum....*" Cf. Bromyard: "jocosa, quae eos *ad risum provocarent.*"

[2] Rypon, in continuing the above quotation, I find, actually refers to this motive in sermon-going hinted at by Chaucer (fol. 119 b): "ut ibi cum aliis videantur."

[3] Bromy. *S.P.—Predic.*

[4] *S.P.—Audire.*

[5] MS. Vernon, fol. 288, in E.E.T.S., O.S. No. 98, p. 329, etc.

[6] Quoted by Bromyard, without reference to source (from Pseudo-Augustine, Hom. xxvi in Psalmo, and Gratian's *Decretum*).

Since laughter over sermons apparently was so common[1], since homilists railed so fiercely, and men of the pew were not afraid to check them sometimes with their "Dies transiit!" and even worse, it would be interesting to know how far these obstructions and this personal raillery could be pushed in the contemporary scene. Jacques de Vitry had been wont to rouse his audience with such pointed remarks as: "Do you want me

A FASHIONABLE SERMON AUDIENCE
(MS. Harl. 4380, fol. 20)

now to talk to you about worthy womanhood? I'm going to say something instead about that old dame whom I see asleep over there!...For God's sake, if anyone has a pin, let him wake her up! Those who sleep at sermon-time take good care not to sleep at the table."[2] St Bernardino in Italy, during the early

---

[1] Besides Rypon, etc. above, cf. here also the quaint title of MS. Add. 14023, as given above in Chap. I, p. 30, n. 6 "...ne materia risus audientibus ministretur...." Notice, too, that Master Rypon himself has his own narration, which, in the sermon, he admits is "in parte jocosa"; MS. Harl. 4894, fol. 103 b (marked *Narratio jocosa* in the margin!).

[2] Cf. also (reported by Langlois, etc.): "He who is sleeping over there in that corner will not know my secret!"

fifteenth century could cry: "Come, woman, don't go to sleep!"
or "Drive away that dog!" in the midst of his orations, as
readily as anyone[1]. Mr Ferrers Howell tells a yet droller tale
of the great Franciscan's pulpit experiences. In this incident
the congregation rose from its seats, in the open-air, to stare
at an unhappy usurer sitting beneath the pulpit, who had become the unintended butt of the speaker's scorn. With shouts of
laughter and a buzz of conversation they pointed him out to
their friends, "while he with bowed head and closed eyes
eagerly longed for the sermon to be over."[2] Turning to
Chaucer's Pardoner, it is therefore with interest that we note
how for frankly vicious ends it is now the orator's set purpose to
produce just such another situation:

> For whan I dar non other weyes debate,
> Than wol I stinge him with my tonge smerte
> In preching, so that he shal nat asterte
> To be defamed falsely, if that he
> Hath trespased to my brethren or to me.
> For though I telle noght his propre name,
> Men shal wel knowe that it is the same
> By signes, and by othere circumstances.
> Thus quyte I folk that doon us displesances[3].

Our English poet had obviously seen the practice at work in his
day.

From the side of the listeners, again, rude interruption and
contradiction might break into the sacred discourse[4]. Even
ladies had been known to retaliate in the past, when the pulpit
grew too insolent. A certain lady of rank in the thirteenth
century interrupted a Dominican in the midst of his sermon,
in spite of the fact that he had been invited thither to preach

[1] Cf. Ferrers-Howell, *St Bernardino of Siena*, p. 281, etc.
[2] Ibid. p. 128.
[3] Prol. to Pard.'s Tale, ll. 412–420 (*Cant. Tales*).
[4] Cf. my example from an English friar's "narratio" in the fourteenth-
century treatise, "de Decem Preceptis," in MS. Gray's Inn Libr. 15, fol.
10 b, given in "Some Franciscan Memorials at Gray's Inn" (*Dublin Review*,
April, 1925). Stories of such sermon interruption from the audience are quite
common in *exempla*. Cf. MS. Add. 28682, fols. 210 b (story of the hostile
rustic who sneered at the preacher's remarks on Hell-pains "because the
latter had never been there," to see for himself), 264 b; MSS. Add. 11872,
fol. 88 b; Burney 361, fol. 151 b; etc.

in her chapel expressly against the sins of the opposite sex. Another, we are told, had ventured to "hold up" the preacher for scriptural evidence in support of his arguments—"and he was exceedingly confused!" ("et ipse fuit valde confusus")[1]. With these examples we must be content to compare the story of early Tudor times, believing that it may possibly be typical of other English occasions too. A poor wife had been personally rebuked for her chattering by the friar in the pulpit. Her angry retort rang through the building for all to hear: "Marry, sir, I beshrew his heart that babbleth most of us both! For I do but whisper a word with my neighbour here, and thou hast babbled there all this hour." Such conduct may be implied, indeed, in a passage of the *Fons Jacob*, which has not yet been published, though here one would have associated it rather with the sermon's end. Those who have been stung by his words, "turnyn awey wrothly fro the preest, and defendyn here dyffau3tys, with false colourys, and excusyn, and turnyn to tellyn talys and iapys, *and to deprave the prest, and the woorde of trowthe*."[2] Still more vivid and curious is the suggestion given in the same treatise that the congregation was not afraid to propose sly subjects of discourse to the preacher himself: "So suche folk askyn a prechour *of an other mannys defaw3te, and preyin* [him] *to towche ther of trowthe in his sermon that day, 3if this be gynne on hem.* First thei byddyn hym seyn trouthe, and tellyn hem the truthe of here vyces." Unfortunately, like Pilate, however, they are not prepared to wait for the full answer. "Therfore prechourys hye and lowe arn aferyd to sey the trouthe, bothe seculere and relygious; and stodyin how in here sermouns they mown with flateryng colourys, symylacyouns, and fals excusacyouns, favouryn and plesyn the peple, grete and smale, leryd and lewyd, in here synne, and so excusyn here vyces, wrongys, and here falsnesse"[3]—precisely as we saw elsewhere in the case of the court preachers.

Of applause, shouts and hand-clappings, notable habit at

[1] Given by Lecoy de la Marche, *La ch. fr.* pp. 216–19. The second is of Robert de Sorbon, again. Cf. also Berthold of Ratisbon, in Coulton's *Mediaeval Studies*, No. 2 (2nd ed.), p. 25.
[2] MS. Salisb. Cath. Libr. 103, fol. 142 b.
[3] Ibid. fol. 143. See also the sermon-story, with similar advice offered to preachers by an inhabitant, in MS. Harl. 1288, fol. 56.

sermons in the neighbourhood of Parisian schools[1], borrowed, no doubt, from the scholastic disputations of less sacred character, little need be said. We notice in passing the applause of procurators and chancellor when Nicholas Hereford preached at Oxford in the church of St Mary the Virgin, and Philip Repyngdon at St Frideswide's Cross in the year 1382[2]. These, however, were special occasions when party feeling ran unusually high, as five years later in the case of Peter Pateshul, the Austin friar in London. He had appeared in the pulpit of St Christopher's, to expose the vices of the very Order which he had recently quitted, and his words had drawn excited members from the friary where he had dwelt[3]. When these objected from the body of the audience, as the sermon proceeded, they were promptly set upon by the crowd, and chased ignominiously back to their convent through the London streets. A threat to burn it to the ground was only averted by the personal appeal of two well-known and respected friars, and a city sheriff. It is a scene which illustrates, at all events, the sudden notoriety which a sermon might attract for its author in a city church, and the inflammatory passions to be excited, still hot and threatening from the pages of Walsingham[4]. But excitement might take a different and a less harmful, though not necessarily a less destructive turn. As in the days when the Breton Thomas Couette preached, and French womenfolk, stung to the heart, made public bonfires of their favourite ornaments and vanities[5], so two centuries later their sisters of Italy were wont to do the same in the piazzas of Siena and Florence at St Bernardino's bidding. "Tables, cards, dice, false hair, rouge-pots, and other

---

[1] Cf. Hauréau, *Quelques MSS.* vol. ii, p. 108; vol. vi, p. 257, etc.: "Velut fragores quosdam tonitruorum, clamores in sermonibus et disputationibus, complosionesque manuum emittunt." See also Haskins, in *Amer. Hist. Rev.*, as before. The phrase "cunctis acclamantibus" is used of the end of St Hugh's Easter sermon, described in *Mag. Vita S. Hug. Linc.* (Rolls S.), p. 293.

[2] *Fasc. Ziz.* (Rolls S.), pp. 305, 306, etc.

[3] See Walsingham (Rolls S.), vol. ii, pp. 157, 158; and Foxe, *Acts and Mons.*

[4] Cf.: "Cum furore clamantes, et dicentes—'Disperdamus homicidas, incendamus sodomitas, suspendamus Regis et Angliae proditores!' Cum isto itaque furoris clamore currentes, ignem in habitacula Fratrum injicere proponebant...." See also the Northampton incident I refer to above in Chap. III, pp. 132, 140 (n. 2), above.

[5] *Hist. Litt. de la France*, vol. xxiii, p. 248, etc.

tribulations, even to chess-boards" had been known to enter the flames. But with the enthusiasm of the sermon over, and the preacher gone, they were liable to that same reaction which befell certain remorseful ladies once driven to make good the loss of their horned head-dresses, of whom it was written that "like snails in a fright they had drawn in their horns, but shot them out again as soon as the danger was over." Subsequent "revival" methods in the history of evangelism have never allowed us to forget how deadly can be that reaction, where a shallow excitable oratory and shallow audiences are concerned. The age of the great crusaders and the early Mendicants over, it would seem that the more phlegmatic, calculating Englishmen[1] had grown tired or suspicious of the type. Dr Bromyard, though forceful enough on the subject of warnings and "terrible words," yet, without either M. le Bon or the social-psychologists to inspire him, rejects the "revivalist" in suitable terms. He is an earthen vessel filled all too quickly with hot liquid. Therefore he will be emptied again all too soon, when he has cracked[2]. The Dominican knows, too, the essential difference between the unstable excitable Italian and his own countrymen. The English ladies would never destroy their best bonnets for any man.

Preachers and writers of moral treatises in the nature of things, driven to expose, denounce, purge, are bound to pay more attention to current vices than virtues. It has been ever our aim in the present study, therefore, with this in mind, to do justice alike to the whimsicalities, the confidences, the sad confessions, and the triumphs of the pulpit as they are presented to us, but to emphasize that little in the way of comprehensive, statistical information should be pressed from them as a whole. We are reminded of the fact anew, when we would deal with the happy sermon scene, rich in the fruits of the Spirit; for naturally there is so little about it. She is a modest maiden,

---

[1] Bromyard is always appealing to the "business" instincts of his audience, especially when threats fail. His argument continually is "This does not pay," or "God is not a bad business man, he will have all debts paid," etc.

[2] *S.P.—Conversatio.* Cf. also remarks in Chap. VIII below (such is good *only* as "a beginning dread," it cannot save the man). Cf. also *S.P.* ibid: "Alii sunt qui ad tempus totaliter convertuntur, quia cum magno fervore confitentur, et bona vota faciunt, et quandoque opera incipiunt; sed cito ad peccata revertuntur...."

an unobtrusive Cinderella pushed into the background by her more noisy aggressively-attired sisters[1]. But we shall not forget to wait for her at the homiletic feast. The faithful quiet work has been done, we believe, by more mediaeval preachers than some would believe, though there were none but the angels in heaven to record it. Does not the eminent Dr William Lichfield declare that "a man herynge holy sermonys is ofte by such herynge stired in his herte to repentaunce and gode lyvynge"[2]?

> ffor he that goddes wordes preches
> unto the sinful man, he teches
> sune out of his sin to rise
> and be lastand in goddes service[3].

When the gracious figure of a youthful Rolle steals into the village pulpit, men and women alike will be unable to refrain from tears. "And they all said that never before had they listened to a sermon of such power and efficacy."[4] So was it, again, with the poor woman, whom first we followed into church when our sermon began. "This woman was right sorye and wepte faste,...and longe she thought till the sermone were done. And when it was done, she wente to the prechoure, and prayde hym for the love of God to here a synfull wreche" "Quando predicator descendit de pulpito, totus populus recedit"[5]. The preaching is over then, and "the folk wend homeward." There is the listener who can "with glad chere hyre sermones and goddes wordes, and in that tyme sette his thoght and his wille to hyre and understonde the wordes of God that there schulde be seide."[6] There, too, beside others we have mentioned, is one observed by Bromyard, who knows that the message was

---

[1] For the benefit of collectors of "exempla," I note that this famous story occurs in a sermon of Rypon (MS. Harl. 4894, fol. 27).

[2] MS. Roy. 8. C. i, fol. 122 b (cf. Rypon, MS. Harl. 4894, fol. 174 b: "...quando audientes sua facinora statim compunguntur, et penitent....") Cf. stories of individuals moved by sermons, in MSS. Roy. 7. C. i, fol. 101 b; Add. 11284, fol. 21 b; ibid. 33956, fol. 21 b (women); ibid. 18364, fol. 40 b (nobleman); ibid. 15833, fol. 173 (drunkard); Cotton Cleop. D. viii, fol. 113 b (priest); Add. 27336, fol. 76 (knight); etc.

[3] MS. Harl. 4196, fol. 88 b (*Engl. Metr. Hom.*).

[4] See the Officium S. Ricardi, in *Yk. Breviary* (Surtees Soc.), vol. ii, Appdx. 5: "...ut multitudo audientium sic esset de ipsius predicatione compuncta, ut se non posset a lacrimis continere...."

[5] Rypon, in MS. Harl. 4894, fol. 84.

[6] MS. Harl. 45, fol. 111 b.

good and true, and cries at the end: "Happy is he who can carry that out! This is good food, if anyone can eat it," adding in his heart, "but it is not for me!"

But what savour hathe a synnefull man in prechynge? For sooth litill or noon. No, but as a n]asse hathe in pipynge. *Bartholomeus, de proprietatibus rerum*, seyth, thow that an]asse had ryght good lykynge in ys mete, and he hard a pipe or a trumpe, anone he wille lyfte is hed oute of the mawgere, and be full glad in is kynde as [l]one[g?] as that he hereth itt. But anon as that he hereth that the pipe or the trumpe is sesed, than anon he putteth down is hed aȝeyn to is mete, and thenketh no more thereof. Forsothe ryght so itt fareth by a synnefull man, thowȝ he listen never so well goddes worde and holy prechynge for the tyme that a man precheth. Hope thou that itt fedes is soule goostely? Nay, forsothe; but itt commeth in at the on ere, and goyth oute at the othere[1].

The duty of practice thus follows the preaching, but there is another small duty for someone yet towards the preacher, especially if he be a Mendicant visitor. In the latter case, of course, all should contribute something to his maintenance, if they can: "To the pore prechoure thou owyst to geve (alms), though he axe the nat. And therfore loke that the pore prechoure, goddes knight, nede nat to axe for thy defaute.... For, as the apostle saith, it is due dett to the pore preachour of goddes worde to lyve by his prechyng."[2] One type of almsgift, however, is sure to be acceptable, and that is a good dinner, when the work is done. Some knight or squire of the parish will possibly entertain him on this occasion[3]. From a remarkable

---

[1] MS. Roy. 18. B. xxiii, fol. 110 b (in margin "Asinus amat melodiam"). Cf. the "bacbiters" in MS. Linc. Cath. Libr. A. 6. 2, fol. 130: "ne they take none hede to the worde of God, be it prechid never so often to them; they may well here it wᵗ theyre eerys, but it synkythe not in theyre herttis." Similarly, too, the *figure* of the ass that likes harp-music, yet tramples on the harp, MS. Harl. 1288, fol. 44 b.

[2] *Dives et Pauper*, prec. ix, cap. xv. The Dominican friar, Thos. Stubbs (d. c. 1360), is said to have written a tract, " de Stipendiis debitis Predicatoribus Verbi Dei." For those interested in fees paid to special preachers, examples will be found: for ecclesiastical establishments, at Westminster (see Pearce, *Monks of W.* pp. 27, 113, etc.), at Canterbury (Woodr. and Danks, *Mem.* p. 264), at Ottery St Mary (Dalton, p. 102). Here the editor reckons a sermon fee=2 guineas in modern money. For court preachers see below, p. 219, and for city preachers, *Munic. Records* of York, etc.

[3] Cf. the case of R. Rolle, as above: "Post missam igitur predictus armiger ipsum ad prandium invitavit." Also the case of the Lollard preacher mentioned in Chap. III, entertained thus by the mayor.

little warning in the pages of the *Summa Predicantium*[1], prepared apparently for him who might thus find himself a guest at some noble or fashionable table, we can follow the preacher further into the very place of hospitality. It shows once more how little our human nature changes through the centuries. Freed now from his cares and worries, the man of God throws off his air of pious detachment, and expands rapidly towards his fellow-creatures under the influence of the meal. He is a genial guest, with an ever-welcome fund of news and anecdotes. He has all the gossip of the countryside ("omnes rumores patriae") to narrate to the more select and intimate audience around him. "If there is any strife or warfare about, he will defend the one side, and damn the other," as bravely as any layman. Nor will he fear, when the company rises to his jokes and waxes merry, to poke fun at parsons and preachings too! Beware, my friend! "Frequently those who laugh pleasantly when such are story-telling and jesting in their presence, laugh scornfully *at* them, when they are gone; judging them to be fools, for all the pleasure that their gossip may have given. No wonder! For 'their speech bewrayeth them.'" The quaint warning was apparently framed for a very good reason. Mr Little gives us an anecdote from Eccleston's *Chronicle* about a warden who "after preaching to the people made jokes with a monk, after dinner, in presence of a secular," to his own lasting shame and remorse[2]. More pointed yet is the sermon story told of Master Walter of London, who, "when he was invited to lunch, after his preaching at London, by a certain burgess, was made almost drunk with 'wesseyl' by the master of the house, his wife, and daughters. At length, in taking his leave, he drank 'horssub.'" But, once mounted on his steed and riding homewards, he was to learn that even a horse might preach sermons to its clerical master, by a noble example of abstinence along the road[3].

So, too, let the layman keep serious and fruitful the rest of his Sabbath day, when he has returned. His final task will be to repeat the sermon to such of his household, children and domestics, as could not come to church to hear it[4]. That done,

---

[1] s.v. *Predicatio*.   [2] See *Studies in Engl. Franc. Hist.* p. 127.
[3] MS. Roy. 7. D. i, fol. 131 b–132.
[4] Cf. Bromyard, *S.P.*—*Audire*: "...Et narrabis ea filiis tuis; quia, illi, qui tenentur esse in ecclesia, tenentur remanentibus in domo, filiis suis et

there must be no idle sporting, but errands of mercy and piety, till the bell rings for Evensong[1]:

Aftir ʒoure mete, visite them that ben sike, and in myschef; and speciali tho that god hath mad nedi, other bi age, or bi syknes, as pore feble, pore crokid and pore lame. Hem thou schalt releve with thi goodis, aftir thi power, and aftir her nede, for thus biddith the gospel....So men schulde not be idil, but as besi on the holi day about the soule, as men ben on the werk day about the bodi [2].

familiae, cum rediverint, quae in ecclesia circa predicationes...audiunt, narrare." Cf. in MS. Add. 27336, fol. 61 b, the amusing story of the devout woman who regularly repeated the sermon to her worldly husband. One day he complains that she thus spoils his meals,—and then chokes!

   [1] Cf. MS. Vernon (*Dispute*), printed in E.E.T.S., O.S. No. 98, p. 351:

      "Aftur, whon thei rynge, go to Even-Song.

      .   .   .   .   .

      Whon Evensong and Complyn bothe ben ido,
      Hom to thi soper then wel maiʒt thou go."

   [2] MS. St Albans Cath. fol. 22; cf. also MS. Harl. 2398 (*Mem. Credentium*), fol. 2 b; Ibid. fol. 92 (Tract on the Decalogue); MS. Add. 24202, fol. 14 et seq.; MS. Lamb. 408 (version of Thoresby's Catech.), E.E.T.S. ed. p. 41; MS. Salisb. Cath. Libr. 103, fol. 104b; etc.

CHAPTER V

"AT THE CROSS" AND "IN PROCESSION"

FROM conversation to sleep or to amusement, from eager attention to scorn and to laughter, and from laughter to tears, we have seen the sermon audiences in church pass almost the full cycle of human emotions while the priest was busy with his theme. For his part, however, he might naturally expect to have still more to complain of in the way of disturbance and distraction when the place of his harangue is transferred to the open air, whether of churchyard or market square. How difficult it will be to reconstruct from English sources the chief features of this other preaching scene may be judged perhaps from a recent work, which, though it provides us, amongst other things, with an excellent sketch of the architectural evolution of the Preaching Cross, yet leaves unrealized an ambition expressed in the preface to provide adequate documentary references[1]. With the particular sources at our command, however, it is yet possible to go further than this.

The identification of a preaching station has for long been recognized among the many purposes served by the erection of stone crosses in the open from very early times[2].

"The venerable father and bishop Kentigern," wrote Joscelin of Furness, five centuries later, "had a custom in the places in which at any time by preaching he had won the people to the dominion of Christ, or had imbued them with the faith of the cross of Christ, or had dwelt for any length of time, there to erect the triumphant standard of the holy cross....Therefore among the many crosses which he erected in several places where the Word of the Lord was preached, he erected two which to the present time work miracles."[3]

From such a record, it might be inferred that even when the primitive site of the village cross-roads had become a thriving market-place, and the early monolithic cross had blossomed, as

[1] *Old Crosses and Lych-gates*, by A. Vallance, F.S.A. His statements about the earliest record of Paul's Cross as preaching-place, and about R. Wimbledon's sermon as Wycliffite are incorrect.

[2] Marking burial-places, boundaries, cross-roads, fords, stations in funeral processions, assemblies, etc. Cf. Baldwin Brown, *The Arts in Early England*.

[3] *Historians of Scotland*, vol. v, cap. xli (Life of St Kentigern, fl. c. 600 A.D.).

it were, through subsequent stages of expansion into a market-cross of the full-blown canopied style, they remained the scene of the preachers' activities. Such lofty structures as may be seen at Winchester, or Leighton Buzzard in Bedfordshire, appear naturally suited to such a purpose. But the present writer can find no evidence for any regular use of these civic crosses other than "for the reading of public proclamations."[1] The wandering preacher "in the street" ("in platea")[2], or at the fairs ("ad macellas in publicis mercatis"), may well have climbed its steps to deliver what M. Lecoy de la Marche and others describe as "allocutions improvisées dans une foire, dans un marché, dans une traversée."[3] This, however, would make them but temporary expedients from our present point of view, like any wall upon which brother Benedict might find it convenient to stand when addressing the random crowd. Wherever, on the other hand, we find definite mention of the regular outdoor pulpit[4], it is at a spot "in cimiterio," on hallowed ground beneath the shade of some church or convent. One of the most interesting of such entries combines both sites in its purview, "at the cross in the churchyard, in the market-place of Northampton"[5]; but none the less "in cimiterio" that cross remains, wherever the audience may happen to be.

Fate has left us just two unquestioned examples of the outdoor pulpit of stone with canopy above, as permanent as the lofty cross which once surmounted it: "A curious cros craftly entayled, with tabernacles y-ti3t, to toten al abouten."[6] Strangely

---

[1] I have come across a quaint reference to this in a contemporary sermon, MS. Roy. 18. B. xxiii, fol. 85 b: "Trust trewly iche worde that 3e speke, God hereth hem as lithly as thoo that thei were *cried at the crosse.*"

[2] Cf. MS. Harl. 4968, fol. 45 (*Cil. Oc. Sac.*), § 4: "Ubi predicandum est? In loco publico debet sermo fieri, sive in ecclesia, seu in platea, seu alibi multis saltem congregatis...."

[3] Cf. excerpt from *Rot. Parl.* above in Chap. II, p. 48. See here also below under J. Ball, p. 209, n. 4.

[4] I give what may be a first list of such, from contemporary records casually collected: St Paul's, London; "Le Greneyard," Norwich (1405, Wilkins, *Conc.* vol. iii, p. 282); Hereford Cathedral (1393, Reg. Trefnant, p. 360); Worcester (1459, Valentine Green, *Hist.* vol. i, p. 55); St Frideswide's Priory, Oxford (1268, *Mun. Ac. Ox.* vol. i, p. 6; 1382, *Fascic. Ziz.* p. 306, etc.);

(5) All Saints' Church, Northampton (c. 1393, Powell and Trev. *Docs.* p. 48); Hosp. of St John, Lichfield (1345), and St Mary's Church, Drogheda (1355, both in MS. Lansd. 393, Fitzralph's sermons). Hosp. of St Mary of Bethlehem, St Michael's, Cornhill, and St Mary Spital, London (cf. above, pp. 23, 143, and Vallance).   [6] *Ploughman's Creed*, ll. 167–8.

enough, the one at Iron Acton in Gloucestershire[1] belongs to a parish church-yard; the other stood in what was once the open convent-yard of the Dominican friary of Hereford[2]. Both would

THE BLACKFRIARS PREACHING CROSS, HEREFORD

seem to have been erected in our period, at the opening of the fifteenth century, while Bromyard, himself a native Dominican of Herefordshire, was still preaching. Add to these, then, "the great crosse in the Minstar Cemiteri of Hereforde," as Leland beheld it[3], and we are furnished with the three recognizable

---

[1] Square; stem and cross surmounting destroyed. Illustrated in A. Rimmer, *Ancient Stone Crosses of England* (1875); A. Vallance, as above, etc.

[2] Blackfriars (or Redcoat Hosp.); hexagonal; cross and pulpit restored in 1806. Illustrated in Bede Jarrett, *English Dominicans*, and A. Vallance, etc.

[3] *Itinerary*, vol. viii. Originally a stone-covered pulpit in the centre of the Bishop's Cloister; now demolished. Canon Wordsworth, of Salisbury, kindly sends me a reference to it in F. T. Havergal's *Hand Guide to Hereford* (1863), p. 82.

varieties of sites—cathedral, conventual[1], parochial. Again, it is easy to account for the paucity of survivals, by considering the feelings of Reformers, or of Puritan Dowsing and his kind when they beheld so large and public a cross defying them in the open, even "as the image of the crucifix in the highway by Coggeshall,"[2] that was "cast down" as early as 1532.

Of the most famous example of all, in St Paul's cemetery in London, there is early documentary evidence as to its existence from the year 1241, and to its use for preaching from 1330 onwards. But Mr Baildon reminds us in a recent paper[3] that the form and appearance of the original "crux alta in majori cimiterio," damaged by earthquake and tempest in 1382, repaired in 1387[4], but superseded between 1449 and 1470 by Bishop Kempe's inferior wooden structure, is still quite unknown. In the absence of any discovered miniature illumination it has been suggested that it may have resembled the Edinburgh Mercat Cross. But this theory is quite without foundation[5], and rests on an unnecessary confusion between what is for secular usage in the street, and what is pre-eminently for the preacher in the hallowed church-yard. May we not see rather in such lordly and suitable erections as the so-called "Baptistery" in the parish church of Luton with its fine panels and tracery comparable to the refectory pulpit-lectern of Shrewsbury, or again the splendid canopied pulpit of stone in the collegiate church at Arundel, Sussex[6], so scantily treated by Dr Cox, types of the

[1] To complete my list of contemporary references to pulpit-crosses, I add: In Friary Yards: Blackfriars, Cambridge (now Emmanuel Coll.), 1247, MS. Ryl. 7. D. i, fol. 87, A Sermon by Cardinal Wm. of Savoy: "predicatione sua, dum transiret per *Cantebrigiam, in cimiterio fratrum Predicatorum,* coram multis et magnis"; Blackfriars, Ludgate, London (1411, Will of Roger Jaket, in Sharpe's *Cal. of Wills (Court of Husting),* vol. ii, p. 391).

[2] Foxe, *Acts and Mons.* vol. iv. I notice that A. Rimmer (*Stone Crosses,* as above, p. 197) says of our Iron Acton pulpit-cross, "it has been mutilated designedly...by heavy missiles; there are marks on the upper part where stones have struck."

[3] W. P. Baildon, F.S.A., "Early Hist. form, and function of Paul's Cross," in *Proc. of Soc. of Antiq.* (London), 1918.

[4] See Archbp. Courtney's Indulgence, in Dr Simpson's *Docts. illust. Hist. of St Paul's Cath.* (Camden Soc.), p. 7.

[5] The reference "*super* crucem" put forward in support by Mr Baildon is equally pointless. It occurs in the case of the Minster Cross, Hereford. See Reg. Trefnant, p. 360, as before.

[6] This appears to be equally unique among the pulpits of England. In a Topogr. of Arundel, I read that it was screened off and used as a pew (!) in the eighteenth century, while a more central pulpit of deal took its place.

structure that is being sought? If this be so, then Kempe's fifteenth-century wooden substitute would reflect, however crudely, the general features of the earlier Paul's Cross.

What was said in another connection of the likely preference for light and modest pulpits of wood over the more permanent and costly varieties applies here undoubtedly with equal force[1]. From the days of early Crusading eloquence one may be familiar in the manuscripts with the legged "pulpitum" or the more spacious "scafaldus" placed temporarily in the open to accommodate now a preacher, now a royal party[2]. Thus the miniature paintings of our own fifteenth century show the homilist, perched hard by the sacred edifice itself, within the walls of the church-yard, in the same kind of wooden pulpit as we found him using in the nave[3]. Such, then—and only such—will be set up for temporary occasions, for some Lenten course or other, as when the churchwardens of St Margaret, Westminster, pay 2s. 8d. in the year 1478, "for a pulpite in the Chirche Yerde, agenst the preching of Doctour Penkey."[4]

When would these church-yard crosses and pulpits be most in request? That part of the question which concerns regular Sunday and work-day use we attempted to answer in the opening of the previous chapter. But a word might be added concerning the festival and procession of Palm Sunday, which was perhaps the most typical occasion of all. Even in rural districts, this celebration was likely to involve some kind of an out-door sermon. Martène speaks of it as a feast observed with

[1] The external pulpits of stone, set in the wall, like Refectory pulpits, as e.g. that at Magdalen College, Oxford (c. 1480); at St-Lô or Vitré, in France (15th cent.; external wall of church), or again in the cloister of St-Die (illustrated in Viollet-le-duc, *Dict.*) may be borne in mind, also. It is clear, I think, that the stone pulpit was rare at any time, in the open.

[2] An interesting MS. illustration of the "scafaldus" used in the open, as at the preaching of the Crusades, will be found in the *Bk. of Hours of the Queen of Navarre*, pt. ii, Plate XXVII.

[3] See especially the remarkable scene in MS. Fitzwm. Mus. Camb. 22, reproduced above as Frontispiece: also Chaucer in a pulpit, "in a feir feld ful of folk," in MS. Corpus Chr. Coll. Camb. 61; and cf. the record of brother Berthold's wooden "belfry," complete with pennon, in Coulton's *Mediaeval Studies*, 1st ser., No. 2 (2nd edit.), p. 20.

[4] *Churchwardens' Accounts*, Cox (Antiq. Bks.), p. 155. In this connection cf. also S. Anthony of Padua's moveable pulpit, Wadding, vol. i, p. 24. At the Greneyard, Norwich, in 1405, the recanting heretic speaks, "super quoddam scamnum, seu scabellum ad hoc sibi deputatum in medio cleri et populi" (Wilkins, *Conc.* vol. iii, p. 282).

peculiar care and honour in England[1], where the Host would be carried in procession "to some church or station" ("ad aliquam ecclesiam aut locum"), at which the gospel would be read, a sermon delivered, and the palms blessed. The humbler kind of church-yard cross, with simple stem and base, it has been thought, may have been often the particular "locus" chosen[2]. In the cathedral cities no less a dignitary than chancellor or dean or even bishop would be expected to occupy the pulpit; and sometimes, as at Hereford in the year 1419, he might have important political matters to discuss in his theme[3]. The Palm Sunday sermon in some collections bears distinct reference to its delivery under special conditions. "Hodierna die de more processionem fecimus. Ideo nota de tribus processionibus quas Christus fecit," cries Master Rypon[4]. Do his opening references here to the sepulchres, with their rotting corpses within, reveal the preacher "in cimiterio," pointing to the graves about him? "Dominica in Ramis Palmarum. Sermo super evangelium, *qui est in processione*," is the heading of another[5]. Because the Palm Sunday service is so long, Myrc will "shortly" explain to his country-folk why it is so-called, and the ritual involved[6]. Other processions of a similar kind would take place at Rogationtide, and the patronal festival, or anniversary of church dedication.

Processions held annually in connection with the Rogation Days had at least one feature in common with the more prominent group which follows in our survey. They were designed

[1] *Ant. Eccl. Rit.* vol. iii, p. 202. He refers to Archbp. Lanfranc's Statutes, an ancient Salisb. Missal, and Matthew Paris' account of the rich "vasculum" or "scrinium" used for the host at St Albans on this festival, in the *Bk. of the Lives of the xxiii Abbots*. (Also to Normandy.)

[2] Cf. with this an entry in the *Observances of the Austin priory at Barnwell* (trans. and ed. J. Willis Clark, 1897, Camb.), pp. 150–51: "On Palm Sunday a procession of great solemnity is held, on account of which, if weather permit, a cross is to be set up in the outer court, and the convent are to walk round the cemetery as far as that cross."

[3] Reg. Lacy (Hereford), pp. 63–4. A Mandate received from the archbishop for prayer to be offered for the peace proposed between the King of England and the Dauphin, after the surrender of Rouen: "Quod vero mandatum dominus ipsemet (i.e. episc. Heref.) per omnia ut supra scribitur exsequebatur, in predicatione sua publica, habita die in ramis palmarum in civitate sua Herefordensi."

[4] MS. Harl. 4894, fol. 124. Later he explains the symbolism of the Psalm and the cry of "Osanna."

[5] MS. Add. 21253, fol. 73.   [6] *Festiall* (E.E.T.S. ed.), p. 115.

to ward off specially impending danger, so far, that is to say, as public intercession might achieve that end. A delightful homily, hitherto unpublished[1], will explain:

Good men and women, ʒe schal have this weke that is commyng iii holsome dayes of prayers, that is Monday, Tewysday, and Wednysday, that holy chyrche callythe rogacion dayes, or in ynglysche tong the dayes of prayers. And ʒe schall understonde that holy chyrche makythe ii latynes [i.e. litanies] in the ʒere, a more latyne, and a lesse latyne. And there aʒenste we have ii procescion dayes, the firste is the olde gang day on the whiche we sey the more latyne, when we halow and faste on seint Markis day when it fallythe not in Ester weke, ne on the Sonday. The secunde procession day is on these iii worthi dayes[2], and they be callyd the new gang dayes, and the lesse latyne. A latyne is no more to sey but as a prayer or a besechyng. And whi the firste is callyd the more latyne and the tother the lesse latyne I schall tell ʒow. As for the first th^t is the olde gang day, that day is the procescion that men use on Seynt Markis day, and that is callyd the more latyne for iii skyllys....[3]

In these processions the clergye of holy chirche prayethe in theyre latynes for the helppe of all seyntis; and so scholde all other pepyll do that folow the procession, for many dyverse skyllis. ffirste that God scholde withestonde the batell of owre enmyes bothe bodyly and gostly. ffor in that tyme of the ʒere the devylls and other wickyd spryritis are moste besy a bowte for to drawe a man in to synne and wrechednes. Also holy chyrche prayethe that criste scholde kepe the tender frutis that be done on the erthe to mans helppe, and so scholde al cristen pray for the same....

Also in these processions baners and crossis ben borne and bellis rong th^t the spyritis that flye above in the eyer as thyke as motis in the sonne scholde flee a wey frome us, when they see baners and crossis on lofte, and heryng the bellis ryng[4]. for lyke as a kyng hathe in his oste baners and trompettis and claryons to the drede of his enmyes, Ryʒte so in lyke wyse almyʒtti god that is kyng of all kyngis hathe bellis for his clarions and for his tromppis, and a cros reysed for hys banere. ffor lyke as a tarrant scholde be a drede if he herde a

---

[1] Although the MS. (Linc. Cath. Libr. A. 6. 2) from which this sermon (headed *Dies Rogacionibus*) is taken, is itself a very late fifteenth century production, the style of this and one or two other homilies in it suggests that we have here re-copied some further examples of John Myrc's composition, unknown to the published *Festiall* series. See later here, also, on p. 215.

[2] See above, e.g. in Chap. IV, p. 146, n. 3.

[3] fol. 133 et seq. The explanations that follow here from history (?), are full of interesting allusions to quaint contemporary custom and folklore.

[4] As in the Rogationtide sermon in Myrc's *Festiall*. See E.E.T.S. ed. pp. 149, 150 and 151.

nother lordis clarion, and see a nother lordis banere in his londe, ry₃te so in lyke wyse the devyllis and the spyritis that flyethe on lofte in the eyer dredythe moche more cristis clarions and his tromppytt is that ben the bellis, and cristis baners that ben the crossis a reysed....

Wherfore ₃e schall come to the chirche these iii dayes, as I have tolde ₃ow, that ₃e may go devowtely in ₃owre procession praying to all the seyntis in heven to pray for ₃ow to criste that he wolde have mercy and pite on ₃ow as he bow₃te ₃ow on the roode,... etc. Amen, etc.[1]

The other great class of processions involving a sermon is that which follows some special mandate from headquarters for public intercession. Wars, pestilences, the inclemency of the weather, the health of the king, queen, and royal household, some expedition about to cross the Channel, demanded that the whole nation should signalize publicly its loyalty to the throne of Heaven, repent, and pray upon its knees[2]. The Archbishop of Canterbury writes to the bishops, and they to their principal clergy, that they arrange "solemn processions,... with ringing of bells, and customary chanting....And let them exercise other pious works of devotion, humbly and devoutly, so that amongst other things the nourishment of God's Word may be publicly set forth."[3] In the Register of Bishop Spofford

[1] Ends (MS. Linc. Cath. Libr. A. 6. 2) on fol. 138. Cf. two vernacular sermons for Rogationtide in MS. Harl. 2247, fol. 105 et seq., etc. For Latin examples, with similar explanations of ritual, etc. cf. *Archbp. Fitzralph*, in MS. Lansd. 393, fol. 45, etc. (*feria 2ª in Rogat⁸*.): "...quare rogamus sanctos; quare crucem portamus ante processionem; quare vexillum; quare draconem duobus diebus ante processionem, et tertio die post processionem; quare primis diebus cum cauda plena, et tertio die cum vacua; et quare campanas pulsamus...," etc. Also Rypon in MS. Harl. 4894, fol. 144, etc.

[2] Cf. here the sermon themes suggested by Higden's treatise on the Art of Preaching (in MS. Bodl. 5, fol. 5 b, etc.) for these special occasions: "In processionibus 'pro pace'—*Rogate quoad pacem*; vel 'contra pestem,' —*Domine, salva nos, perimus*," etc.

[3] 1401 (Jan. 14). Reg. Bowet, Bath and Wells (Somerset Rec. Soc.), p. 24. Cf. also, e.g. Reg. Wykeham, Winch. (Hants. Rec. Soc.), pp. 89, 105, 109, etc. (1369, for peace; 1374, 1375, etc. for pestilence; etc.); Reg. Thoresby, York (*Fasti Ebor*. pp. 460, 461, 463), (1361, for removal of wars, pestilences, and other troubles of the kingdom; 1368, for pestilence; 1369, for the king, queen and prince); Reg. Melton, York (ibid. p. 415), (1319, for fine weather, because of the rains); Reg. Zouche, Yk. (ibid. p. 443), (1345, for the king and his army); Reg. de Asserio, Winch. (Hants. Rec. Soc. pp. 576, etc.), (1321, for peace); Reg. Rede, Chichester (Sussex Rec. Soc. p. 75), (1400, for weather, and the king's prosperity); Reg. Spofford, Hereford (1431, for wars, pestilence, and other ills; 1436, for the Duke of Gloucester's expedition to relieve Calais); and many in Reg. Grandiss. Exeter, etc. In Wilkins, *Conc.* vol. iii, note especially p. 42 (1359, on resumption of the war with

of Hereford there appears an interesting example of a Royal Letter of the year 1443, of this kind, written in the vernacular, requesting processions and prayers for the resistance to be made to "our adversary of France, and his oldest son that calleth himselfe Dauphin," who, "with all the myght and puissance that they can and may assemble,...enforcen hem, and maken, and be disposed to make, in this season that now is at hande, unto us as soore and as myghty werre bothe by water and bi lande as they can divise, and namely in our duchies of Normandie and Guienne." The bishops are accordingly exhorted, required, and prayed to

do all the devoir and diligence possible to yow in this behalve, making all thoo that be called ministers of Goddis Chirche, seculiers and reguliers, withyne your diocise, to go openly and devoutly [in] procession divers daies in the weke al this yere next folwyng, and to pray especially for the prosperite of us and of all oure reaumes, landes, and subgects, and especially for the good and gracious spede of all thoo that shal laboure and aventure their personnes to the withstandyng of the forsaid malicious purpos of our said adversari, and of his helpers....

An Indulgence of forty-days' pardon is granted "to induce hem the more effectually and with the more desire to entende to alle the things abovesaid." Finally comes the reference to the preaching: "And to enable hem the more diligently to continue theyr devocion in alle the thynges abovesaide, us semeth that hit shuld be ful expedient that ye ordeyned from time to time good and sturyng precheris of Goddes word to go abrode in your diocise, that might and wold remembre hem and exhorte hem to the said continuance."[1] Acquainted thus with the circumstances of delivery, the reader is now in a position to deal with such sermons as remain in the manuscripts from these occasions.

At one procession, "pro rege et principibus," about the year 1345, we are enabled to listen to Archbishop Fitzralph of Armagh, in London, as he expounds to the people what they

France; mentioning "predicationes"); p. 177 (1383, "for the Bp. of Norwich setting out against the heretics" ("sermonibus")); p. 195 (1386, for the expedition of Lord Arundel, Admiral of England, crossing the sea ("sermonibus")).
[1] Reg. Thos. Spofford, Bp. of Hereford (Cantilupe Soc. etc.), pp. 252–54.

should pray for, and their manner of praying[1]. Amongst other
things let them intercede on behalf of the sovereign, he says,
"that he may live justly and sincerely in his own person." For
sometimes God punishes the nation for its sovereign's sins.
Let them ask that "he be directed with prudent and sane
counsel"; "that he may obtain a just and happy issue in his
military campaigns." With memories of war-time sermons
still fresh, we are driven to confess that the mediaeval preacher
here shows a spiritual discernment, a breadth of vision, and a
self-control, which might have put to shame many another
occupying a pulpit in England but eight years ago. "Wherefore men pray improvidently," he cries, "that he [the king]
may overcome his enemies, and also slay in battle. For those
who pray thus, in their praying offend God, and hinder their
lord the king. They offend God, in acting contrary to his command—'*Thou shalt love thy neighbour as thyself*' (Matt. xxii)....
They hinder the king, withdrawing from him their *spiritual*
petitions." Such men who beseech God "to pour out the blood
of their adversaries" are violating that rule of prayer that insists "that each shall seek and pray for *all* men that which they
would desire to be done to them by others." And "there is no
one who would desire that others would pray for them in the
aforesaid fashion." "But prayer is to be made that [the king]
may obtain a just peace, that we, as the above-mentioned
authority of the Apostle states, may live a quiet and tranquil
life,...and that so we may live piously and chastely....And
indeed less learned men often err greatly when they pray for
the king and his nobles, demanding from God that he give them
corporal triumph in battle over their foes." None the less the
preacher is equally emphatic that "the Law of Nature requires
that we pray for the king, and also support our troops—*in
facultatibus*; for he is the protector and defender of the people."
Is there after all a conflict of loyalties in the archbishop's own
mind, as he preaches?

Interest quickens as Fitzralph goes on to deal with the
"pacifists" of the day. Someone has declared that a war of

---

[1] MS. Lansd. 393, fol. 26 b. See also ibid. fol. 48, for another of his
processional sermons, in London (Text: "Offerant oblationes deo celi,
orentque pro vita regis," 1 Esdr. 6.)

defence is right enough, but this attacking of France across the channel is indefensible. The prelate replies that "according to the judgement of our realm" the territories of England and France are properly one kingdom, the indivisible realm and dominion of the English king. By hereditary right the rule over both devolves upon him and his successors[1]. For all his lofty religious impartiality, our preacher is ever the loyal Englishman at heart. His remarks are interesting evidence for the work of the pulpit in the political sphere, here dealing with the arguments of a peace-party that doubts the justice of the campaign very probably on religious grounds, as in subsequent Lollard days.

Turning to Bishop Brunton's sermons, we find him discussing the topic of the hour in a similar situation, though not in so argumentative a mood[2]: "How the nobles of England but recently sent to Brittany have been besieged by our adversaries," he says, "the news informs us clearly enough. I know of no better refuge for their liberation or defence than to be watchful with one accord in prayers [his sermon-text is "Vigilate," 1 Petr. v, 8] for a twofold reason: first because the prayer of the besieged availeth much, if they prove stable in faith....[3] Secondly, because vigils of prayers kept by us can help them...."[4] Besides the lordly orators of the Church, however, a "good and stirring preacher of God's Word" of the simpler sort has left us his "Sermo pro pace" in manuscript[5]. Nor does a comparison between the two end in his disfavour, for it is full of

[1] "...Si objiceretur quod verum est pro defensione regni sui, non pro invasione regni alieni, responsum fuit quod, juxta judicium regni nostri, unum fuit regnum sive imperium aut dominium utriusque regni. Ex quo utriusque regni jus hereditarium in una persona pro se et suis successoribus residebat. Et ob hoc, licet dua sint regna, non minus unum sunt regnum ipsa dua, et membra unius regni, sive unius imperii aut unius dominii. Et ita in persona sui regis se mutuo sicuti membra unius corporis se juvare tenentur...."

[2] MS. Harl. 3760, fol. 193.

[3] He goes on to give an *exemplum*:—"Hoc patet in Historia Romanorum de Theodosio imperatore...."

[4] Another "exemplum" follows here concerning "Clodovecus, rex Francorum," who, amongst other things, "transmisit litteras ad ecclesiasticos et religiosos, ut pro sua expeditione in orationibus vigilarent," we notice, in the approved fashion.

[5] MS. Roy. 18. B. xxiii, fols. 123 b–126. (Text: "Quis ibit ad rogandum pro pace?" Jer. xv, 5.)

homely, practical instruction, exactly suited to the congregation before him. His report is in the original English of delivery, therefore the more attractive. A brief excerpt which contains the chief topical reference of the address will illustrate the preacher's style. He has been discussing the lustful men, who "whils that thei are in that synne,...are not worthy to be herde to prey ffor the pece." He goes on:

But, I preye the, who shall goye to preye for the pees? Trowly, cristen men, I see iii thinges th[t] god hath take grett vengeaunce [for]; and 3iff we will loke to this londe of ynglonde this tyme, I drede me th[t] thise iii synnes are overmoche reynande in this londe. But what is the cause that we have not these dayes no pees as we were wonte ffor to have? Certenly synne is the cause; ffor ther as this londe was wonte to be plentewous of goodnes and holynes in lyvynge, Nowe is this goodnes growon in to grett malice and shrewdenes, and holynes is turned in to synnefull wrechednes: bot how shall we dryve avey thise iii synnes th[t] I have spokon of?—trewly w[t] iii vertewes....[1]

When, on the other hand, the procession gathers under the cloud of plague, of bad harvests, floods, or warning signs in the heavens, the "Sermo in processione" will naturally make equally significant reference to these ills[2]. Bishop Brunton's own solemn discourse, when the terror of a raging pestilence is added to the anxieties and sufferings of the war abroad[3], gives us some vivid insight into the perplexed, horror-stricken minds of his listeners. He begins by pouring scorn upon those who attribute it to planets and constellations in the sky ("illi qui talia ascribunt certis planetis et constellationibus"), and not to the nation's sins:

Therefore, since the corruption of lust, and designs of wickedness are greater to-day than in the days of Noah—for a thousand fashions of vice which assuredly did not exist then are rife to-day,...since, too, greater to-day is the cruelty of lords than in David's time, let us not impute the scourges of God to planets or elements, but rather to our own sins, saying, "Worthily do we suffer these things, for we

---

[1] Ibid. fol. 125 b. Cf. further, the rare practicality and soundness of the following (fol. 126): "Ryghtso, ho wolde th[u] prey the ffadere of heven for the pees, when th[u] will not latt thi ney3bore be in pees?..."

[2] Cf. in MS. Harl. 3760, fol. 125: "Unde igitur in regno Anglie tanta est fructus diminutio, tam crudelis pestilentia..."; fol. 189 b, etc.: "Quantum ad processiones, si fiat processio pro quacunque tribulatione...."

[3] MS. Harl. 3760, fol. 191: "ex parte nostri imminens est pestilencie periculum, ex parte adversarii malitiosa impugnatio...."

have sinned" ["Merito haec patimur, quia peccavimus"]....But you say, "If sin was the occasion of the aforesaid, by the just judgement of God the notorious sinners should perish, not children, or the just who have not sinned in this way!" I make reply and say that the children are dying not for their own sins, but for those of their parents....The little ones would have wished to follow in their steps, after all; and in truth God does them no wrong, when death may be the way out from the prison-house, the end of exile and toil, the escape from all perils, the return to the father-land, the entrance into glory. Or let us say that God punishes the innocent that he may chastise us who are the worst, and the offenders [nocentes]. For in the manner of the bowman, God who "hath stretched and made ready his bow" sometimes shoots the arrow of death beyond the mark, that is, in his striking of the sinner, whether father or mother, or some older person, sometimes "on the near side of the mark," by smiting son or daughter or someone younger, sometimes on the left side, by smiting their neighbours, sometimes upon the right side by smiting brother or sister. But at length he hits the mark itself, when he carries off the sinner asleep in sin, from the midst, by awful death. Thus it happened to King William Rufus....

The typical *exemplum terribile* follows. Eventually he reaches the immediate problem of the moment: "But someone asks— 'Since sin is the outstanding cause of the pestilence, what are to be the remedies, that the Divine hand may cease?' I reply that the chief remedy would be the confession of the sinners. For how should the scourge of God cease at the people's prayers, while a third part of them are in mortal sin?"[1] The sins of the nation are the one cause of every form of disaster, to the mind of these English preachers. No formidable Jeremiah in ancient Palestine, no eloquent Savonarola in mediaeval Italy ever emphasized this gospel of divine retribution more incessantly. Master Rypon, preaching in Lent of the year 1401, of a certain vice which here shall be nameless, can be as relentless in his expositions as my lord of Rochester. Attention is riveted now upon the appearance of a comet in the sky[2]:

Would that that cursed sin were not subverting the realm of England! And this sin, it is said, has grown to be so much of a habit that it is scarcely reckoned a sin at all. And without doubt, although the destruction of the kingdom has not happened yet, perchance for the merit of certain just persons dwelling therein, none the less a

---

[1] Ibid. fols. 191 b–192 b.   [2] Cf. *Dives et Pauper*, prec. 1, cap. xxix.

certain earnest [quedam arra] of destruction has come to pass, and this is appearing over the greater part of the kingdom, as is well known, from day to day in signs, as for example in the water-floods, in the bad harvests [fructuum paucitate], and in the comet now appearing, viz. A.D. 1401 in Lent. As for this star,—according to the Venerable Bede, in his book, *de ymagine mundi* (lib. i, cap. ult.), "Comets," he says, "appearing towards the North in the Milky Way with flaming tails, and portending revolution or pestilence, or wars, or tempests in summer-time, are seen for a week; if for longer, they portend, according to others, a mortality among the nobles, or barrenness in the land." These things, says he, are certain earnests and signs of the destruction of kingdoms; oh that they may come not to pass in this kingdom! And if they should do,—which God forbid! —assuredly, if the experience of the past according to the blessed Gregory is that of the future, the aforesaid crimes and vices of the inhabitants will be the cause thereof[1].

To deal adequately with the many stirring scenes around Paul's Cross in London would demand something even more than an independent chapter. There might almost be said to be a literature on the subject already. Bishop Brunton himself had urged on all bishops the prime value and importance of preaching in this London pulpit, a century and a half before the Reformation:

At London, because it is the principal city of England, and in that place there is a greater devotion and a more intelligent people, and therefore, it is to be presumed, greater fruit. Moreover, because each bishop of England has subjects or parishioners in London, therefore, when he gives instruction there, it is as though he were preaching to his own people and to the other churches of England in addition, so that in effect, by so doing, each of us may apply to himself that word of the Apostle [2 Cor. xi, 28]—"*that which cometh upon me daily, the care of all the churches*"—of England[2].

The famous church-yard Cross itself is a veritable mirror of mediaeval life and thought, reflecting the many moods and

[1] MS. Harl. 4894, fol. 116 b. Bp. Brunton also is inclined to associate the occurrence of pestilence with the reign of this "peccatum sodomiticum" (MS. Harl. 3760, fol. 191 b) in England.

[2] MS. Harl. 3760, fol. 60 b. For the original Latin see my article afore-mentioned in the *Mod. Lang. Rev.*, July, 1925. I notice the following at the Cross (from Wilkins, *Conc.*): (*in our period*), besides Bp. Brunton, and Archbp. Fitzralph of Armagh (variously, as noted elsewhere); Bp. of Carlisle (1378); Archbp. of Canterbury (1408); Bp. of Llandaff (1419); Bp. of Rochester (1428).

opinions of those who crowded around it. Great processions of rejoicing and of lament as well as great preaching, recantations, sentences of excommunication—like those passed upon "Robert de Brus, and all Scotsmen" in 1318, or the murderous clerics in the church-yard a century later—expositions and burnings of "many bokes of eryses,"[1] unhappy delinquents "with faggottes and tapers,"[2] all figured there during its long history—"in the prechenge tyme." Finally, it would not be fair to omit all mention of cemetery preaching of an irregular kind, with the classical instance of John Ball before us, "a preacher for twenty years,"[3] he who collected his audience as the parishioners came streaming on Sunday from the church door[4]. There rustic and pedlar sit together on the gravestones, in the warm sunlight, as Dr Bromyard must have seen them in his travels, "sicut homines super tale lignum vel lapidem ad solem in estate,"[5] listening to wandering friar, pardoner, and Lollard—"apud crucem in cimiterio," where the rude forefathers sleep, the living among the dead.

In closing it is proposed to attempt a reconstruction of the outdoor scene around the pulpit cross, from current sources, as it would have presented itself in some English town during the fourteenth or fifteenth centuries. Thus may the "certain very religious father William Melton, of the Order of the Friars

[1] Notably of Bp. Pecock, in 1458. Cf. also the case of R. Walker, 1419 (Wilkins, *Conc.* vol. iii, p. 394). Of the former, see the account given in the *Grey Friars Chr. of London* (Camd. Soc.).

[2] Cf. the picturesque little ceremony of a later period, in *Hall's Chron. of the Reign of King Henry VIII* (xxv yere), 1533/4: The guilty (the "holy maid of Kent" and her adherents) are "by the kynges counsaill adjudged to stand at Paules Crosse, wher thei with their owne handes should severally deliver eche of them to the preacher that should bee appoynted a bill declaryng their subtile craftie and superstitious doynges." Which they did, "standyng on a stage at Paules Crosse made for that purpose."

[3] Cf. MS. Harl. 6388, fol. 11; etc.

[4] Froissart, ed. Lord Berners, cap. 381, p. 641 (ed. 1812): "This preest used often tymes on the Sondayes, after masse, whanne the people were goynge out of the minster, to go into the cloister and preche, and made the people to assemble about hym....Thus Johan sayd on Sondayes, whan the people issued out of the churches in the vyllages...." Also, in his "Denunciatio" by the archbishop, 1381 (Wilkins, *Conc.* vol. iii, p. 152, etc.): "...Ibique aliquando in ecclesiis et cemeteriis, praeter et contra ipsarum ecclesiarum presidentium voluntatem, aliquando ad macellas in publicis mercatis, et aliis locis profanis, aures mulcendo laicorum opprobriis... predicare et dogmatizare nullatenus pertimescit...."

[5] *S.P.—Ociositas.*

Minor, S.T.P....a most famous preacher of the word of God"
have delivered those sermons to the people of York which
actually persuaded them to change a pageant-day, and purify
their city[1]. Thus did many a great one of the Greenyard at
Norwich, or of the market-place at Northampton. First, as
likely as not the preacher would arrive on horseback. This is
not always in the mind of our modern "text-book" writers of
social history, but it is too frequent a detail of the original documents to be a matter of doubt. The well-known French miniature of John Ball preaching astride his steed—"palefridus suus
pinguis, et rotundus, et faleratus," as a preacher's mount was
once described,—may be grotesque enough of the socialistic
clerk, but none the less will be a true portrait of the more
fashionable Mendicants of the age. Denunciations of this pompous, spectacular way of arriving and departing about the pulpit
are to be met with from the thirteenth century onwards. Stephen
of Bourbon has a delightful story of "what a little old woman
did to a certain great theologian, who, when he had preached
about the humility of Christ on Palm Sunday, and the ass,
straightway mounted a richly caparisoned palfrey[2]. The old
hag then ran up, and taking hold of his bridle, questioned him
in the midst of the crowd, 'Master, was the Lord's ass like
that?'" But he was silent. St Dominic himself, troubled profoundly over the spread of heresy, had noticed this particular
failing in the case of the bishops who had preached all in vain
to the Albigensians[3]. An English satirist at the beginning of the
fourteenth century could tell how his spiritual offspring rode
the whole day long—

[1] In 1426. His influence here reminds us of a Bernardino or a Savonarola
again. Like them too he seems to have suffered his reverses; see here, p. 73.
The account of his preaching in York in Drake's *Eboracum* (appdx. p. xxix,
from the City Records) tells how "coming to this city," he "recommended
the aforesaid [Corpus Christi] play to the people, affirming that it was good
in itself, and very laudable," then proceeded to rebuke their licentious
behaviour. The sermon for the Procession-Day itself, in the year 1478, was
preached in the cathedral, however. See Davies, *Extracts from Munic.
Records*, p. 77, and cf. p. 43.

[2] "Ipse preciosis vestibus similiter ornatus." See *Anecdotes*, p. 216. Ct.
also Matthew Paris' description of the friars arriving at St Albans in 1247,
their steeds, "sellis deauratis falerati" (*Chronica Maj.* Rolls S.).

[3] See also the similar tale of St Bernard and a heretic of Languedoc, in
G. G. Coulton, *Five Centuries of Religion*, vol. i, p. 287.

Yl purrount, s'il ount talent,
Chevalcher tot plenerement
Tote la jornee entiere.

on the plea that they had sore feet, not like the Minors bare-
footed, but well shod[1]. The complaint of Wycliffe, in one of his
vernacular sermons, brings the practice down to our own particular epoch: "And here thenken many men that siche prechours shulden be war that they come not with myche peple,
ne many hors to preche thus."[2]

Once the faithful steed had been known to prey on its owner's
mind in the middle of his sermon[3]. A certain good man, in this
case no worldling, left the ass which carried him on his preaching tours ("per quem portaretur per parrochias ubi predicare
deberet") outside the church, when he went in. As the service
proceeded, he became unable to shake off a haunting anxiety as
to its fate. Perhaps some thief would carry it off, or some wolf
devour it. With a sudden noble effort of self-renunciation he
mastered his mood. Going outside, he set the animal free to
wander away, remarking as he did so that he would rather lose
his ass than his heart. Not every preacher would have been able
to say that.

But to return to our scene. Before the preacher's arrival, the
church-yard pulpit cross where he will appear has first been
"solemplie decked...with Tapestrie, and other furniture,"[4] for
the occasion. Prominent among these, as in every manuscript
illumination of the kind, is the great embroidered pulpit cloth,
rich and spacious as a cope, covering almost the whole of the
central panel from top to bottom: "in circuitu vero summitatis
pulpiti dependentur panni serici et inaurati."[5] Now he comes
escorted by the mayor and his fellow-clergy, "with great solemp-
netie, arrayed 'en une cloke, une taberd, et une chapon furres

---

[1] *The Order of Fair Ease* (MS. Harl. 2253), in Wright's *Polit. Songs*
(Camd. Soc.), p. 146. For the mounted preacher, cf. also MS. Vernon
(E.E.T.S., O.S. No. 117, p. 784): "The monck rod niʒt and day," etc.

[2] Ed. Matthew (E.E.T.S.), p. 200. Cf. also in the story told of Master
Walter of London, and his horse, above in Chap. IV, p. 193.

[3] More usually the preacher is at prayer in this story, but one MS. version
has "aut predicans."

[4] Powell and Trev. *Docs.* (as before), p. 48, etc.

[5] From "Officia in Coronationem," Rich. II, 1377, printed in Maskell's
Mon. Rit. vol. iii, pp. 68–9.

de pellure,' and with a capp uppon his head, as...a Doctor or Master of Divinitie."[1] These robes are the crowning glory of pulpit pageantry. They are also the outward badge of authority and learning in the speaker. Preachers of the sort that—

> ...loveth in markettes ben met with gretynges of pouere
> And lowynge of lewed men, in Lentenes tyme[2],

—and they are not few—know well their value in attracting and impressing the crowds, "therebie to be reputed of the common people for great clerkes."[3] Repeated comments of the Dominican sermon-writers as well as the notorious traffic in University degrees about this time show clearly how coveted was the honour of wearing them. Thomas Walleys thus warns his would-be preacher—"de predicatoris habitu"—against pulpit robes too brilliant, or too wondrously wrought, such as might induce the people to attribute to him those very vanities of the world which he must bid them avoid. Full of sanctified commonsense are the warnings of these old orators of the Church. Higden declares that such who appear with pompous gesture, elaborate adornment, and superfluous train were better termed "the ministers of Anti-Christ."[4] Bromyard points the absurdity of the richly-decked preacher denouncing, as we have seen elsewhere, the pride of fine clothes in the laity ("vestium religiositas et decentia, quem predicantes contra vestium superbiam illam non ostendant"), likewise of the lover of good dishes "who proclaims the poor man Christ, with a fat belly and ruddy cheeks."[5] Such incongruities did not always pass unheeded by the man in the street:

[1] Powell and Trev. p. 49. In this case the Lollard preacher, Wm. Northwold, is thus accused: "whereas he never took anie degree in scoles." Cf. also the description quoted above in Chap. IV from *Jacob's Well* (E.E.T.S. ed.), p. 276.

[2] *Ploughman's Creed*, ll. 566-7. Cf. Bromyard's parallel to this whole passage, in *S.P.—Avar.*: "...sciunt quod magis sunt in honore, vocantur ab omnibus 'Rabi,' et habent primos recubitus in coenis et salutationes...." (From the Gospel Pharisees, of course.)

[3] Powell and Trev. (as before): "Diverse of which said preachers were faine to borrowe in the said toune of Northampton furred hodes and habites for the time of their sermones"; and later (p. 49): "...repaired again to preach at the said crosse arraied in his furres as before."

[4] MS. Bodl. 5, fol. 11.

[5] *S.P.—Predicatio*," cf. Chaucer's gibe (*Romt. of the Rose*, ll. 6486-8): "fillen...my paunche of gode mete and wyne, as shulde a maister of divyne."

Ye poope-holy prestis fulle of presoncion,
With your wyde furryd hodes, voyd of discrecioun,
Unto your owyn prechynge of contrary condicioun,
Which causeth the peple to have lesse devocioun[1]!

One curious little scriptural comment in a contemporary homily
—"de inani gloria"—is surely a fragment of the writer's own
personal reminiscences of these preaching-cross vanities of the
day. Says Scripture, the devil placed Jesus upon a pinnacle of
the temple. "Where the preachers were wont to ascend, and
where many had inane glory" ("ubi solebant predicatores ascen-
dere, et ubi multi inanem gloriam habuerunt"), explains the
homilist[2].

> And in worchipe of the worlde her wynnynge thei holden;
> Thei schapen her chapolories, and streecheth hem brode,
> And launceth hei3e her hemmes, *with babelyng in stretes*;
> Thei ben y-sewed with whi3t silk, and semes full queynte,
> Y-stongen with stiches, that stareth as silver[3].

With the typical bidding-prayer for "al the clergise, al the
knithhode, and al the gode comenalte, with al tho that ben went
out of this world,"[4] and so forth, the sermon will begin. It
is not our business to give heed to it now, but to take a parting
look at the brave spectacle around with its life and colour. No
wonder the wife of Bath liked such preachings so well. Not to
speak of a city mayor and corporation, the clergy and the burgesses and the ladies, as at "Le Greneyard," in Norwich, on
Palm Sunday of the year 1405 there might be present in addition
a bishop, the prior of a cathedral convent, and some noble
knight of the shire, each with his appropriate body of attendants[5]. How, then, is the distinguished audience seated? Looking at the well-known painting of the Paul's Cross preaching
scene at London, executed early in the seventeenth century, one
would imagine that the long covered gallery-boxes of timber, set
against the transept wall of the great church to accommodate

---

[1] Wright, *Polit. Poems and Songs* (Rolls S.), vol. ii, p. 251. Also Jack
Upland's question: "Why make ye so many 'maisters' among you?" and
Ploughman's Creed, ll. 497, 574, etc.
[2] MS. Add. 21253, fol. 51.   [3] *Ploughman's Creed*, ll. 550 et seq.
[4] MS. Worc. Cath. Libr. F. 19. Cf. other examples given below in Chaps.
VI and VIII. Also Wilkins, *Conc.* vol. iii, p. 440 (concerning a sermon at
Paul's Cross, 1425): "Inter preces et inchoationem processus sermonis."
[5] Wilkins, *Conc.* vol. iii, p. 282.

the royal party, might be the natural survival of a pre-Reformation custom[1]. But this is apparently not the case. The erection of these permanent wooden galleries and pews, which converted the chapter-house at Canterbury, for example, into a regular "sermon-house" for lay audiences in the same century[2], was a device of Protestant and Puritan times. An interesting record of the year 1650, concerning the Greenyard at Norwich above-mentioned, makes clear the distinction between earlier and later practices. First we are informed of the subsequent innovation here, in an account which agrees perfectly with the painter's testimony in the case of London: "The great pulpit was set up, and galleries were made next the walls on the East and South sides, for the mayor, aldermen, common-councillors, liverymen and wives to sit in, and hear the sermon." Now follows the mediaeval custom, agreeing strangely with our account of the contemporary practice in church: "But in old time they had a moveable pulpit, which was carried into the yard, and set up in Rogation-week, as were also forms and benches to sit on. And the ground about the pulpit was strawed with green sedges, the two first days. It was carried back again (into the chapel, I suppose) on Ascension-day."[3] St Bernardino of Siena, it has been stated, was the first "in modern times" to introduce the separation of the sexes in public worship[4]. But if the cord mentioned in connection with Thomas Couette's preaching in the thirteenth century before audiences of thousands in the open air[5] was intended to serve the same purpose as Bernardino's low canvas screen set up between men and women in the piazzas[6], this can hardly be the case. Since we have seen that this separation probably obtained within the churches in this country, it is only likely that it would be the custom here also in the open.

Much that was said about the character of the sermon-goers in the sacred edifice, in the first part of our sketch, will apply

---

[1] 1616. (In possession of the Soc. of Antiquaries, London.)
[2] See Woodruff and Danks, *Memorials of Cant. Cath.* pp. 301 and 323.
[3] See Kirkpatrick, J., *Relig. Orders of Norwich*, 1845, pp. 64, 65.
[4] See reference in Ferrers Howell, *St Bern.* p. 281.
[5] The other theory advanced seems absurd, "that they were obliged to suspend the orator in the air by a cord, that he might make himself heard by everyone!" See *Hist. Litt. de la Fr.* vol. xxiii, p. 248.
[6] Cf. the well-known paintings by Sano di Pietro, and Vecchietta.

with equal force to the new scene outside. Direct information on this aspect of the subject is considerably harder to obtain, for the simple reason that, in the harangues concerned with a wider public than that which assembles at the church, the former intimacy between speaker and hearers seems to have disappeared. One Rogation-tide sermon, however, noted by the present writer whilst at work in the cathedral library at Lincoln, thus prepares its hearers for the coming procession in the open with quaint warnings in the style of Myrc. The preacher bids them

not to come and go in procession talkyng of nyse talys and japis by the wey or by the feldes as 3e walke, or to bacbyte 30ʳ even cristen. Or to go more for pompe and pride of the worlde then for to plese God, or for helpe of theire owne sowlys. Soche processions are but veyne and litill worthe for the helpe of man. but 3e scholde come mekely and lowly wᵗ a good devocion, and folow 30wre crosse and 30wre belles in 30wre bedes biddyng and good prayers, that almy3tty god will the rather thorow3e 30wre prayers stynt the grete perells and mysheves that ben a mong mankynde, and to bryng 30w to the blis[1].

If, on the other hand, we may combine such preachers' evidences as that of Bishop Brunton on the London intercessory processions, "pro tribulatione," with Master Rypon's complaints at Durham concerning the decay of the great annual procession to the minster, it would appear that such gatherings were increasingly avoided by the more genteel classes. Brunton tells us, indeed, that at London only ecclesiastics, religious, and a few middle-class persons take part. The "magnates," who are the worst offenders before God, and therefore the most beholden to show repentance, will crowd to a tournament, but keep carefully away where any public prayer or acts of penitence are concerned. Even the bare numbers attending, these days, are most unsatisfactory:

Does it not seem abominable that, if there should be a duel held to-morrow in the city of London, by every law prohibited, so many

[1] MS. Linc. Cath. Libr. A. 6. 2, fol. 136. Cf. *Jacob's Well* (E.E.T.S. ed. O.S. 115, p. 191): "rounnynges," janglings, idle words, chidings, reprovings ... in processions, etc.; also Rypon in a Palm-Sunday sermon (MS. Harl. 4894, fol. 124 b, etc.)

rich men and nobles would congregate there, that there would scarcely be room enough to hold the multitude of them? But if a procession is arranged at London to pray for the king and the peace of the realm, altho' the bishop may be present with the clergy, yet scarcely do a hundred men of the populace follow him[1].

Turning to Durham, we find that it is the clerical element this time which absents itself from the sacred ceremony in the open. The words of the sub-prior's sermon, hitherto unpublished, are sufficiently vivid and interesting to justify further quotation at some length:

And truly, in this case almost all the rectors and vicars of this diocese are guilty of sin, for this reason. It is well known among you that there was an ancient custom, nay rather, it is a synodal constitution, that all rectors and vicars of this diocese should come in person, or at least send in their place some honest priest and clerk to this monastery—as it were to their chief place of rest—at least once in the year, namely in the week of Whitsuntide, with banners and crosses erect, to march in procession, with a view to more devout prayer to the Blessed Mary, Saint Oswald, and Saint Cuthbert, patrons of this church, for the peace and tranquillity of this realm, and especially of this our own district [huius patrie]. But now assuredly, that devotion is well-nigh wholly swept away. Neither rectors nor vicars come hither, as I have just said they are bound to do in person, but send as intermediaries laymen, sometimes shameful persons [inhonestas], with little or no devotion. And, without doubt, one is forced to believe that the withdrawing of this devotion is the great cause wherefore this district is infested with wars, pestilences and other ills more than it was wont. And little wonder, surely! for these saints—Oswald and Cuthbert—withdraw from us their wonted suffrage. Thus it is commonly said, "Saint Cuthbert sleeps," because he shows forth no miracle, nor lends aid to his people, as formerly he was wont to do. In very truth we are the cause, because we do not lend our devotions in wonted fashion, as we ought. Let us therefore lend to him the wonted devotions and prove that he sleeps not, but will be ready to bring us aid even as he once was, or yet more fully. And you, my reverend lords, who regulate this synod[2], stir up, I beseech you, the incumbents [curati] here present, and absent,

---

[1] MS. Harl. 3760, fol. 189 b: "Nonne apparet abhominabile quod si in civitate Londonii cras fieret duellum omni jure prohibitum, tot ibi congregarentur divites et magnates, quod vix eorum multitudinem vix capere posset locus? Sed si Londonii ordinetur processio ad orandum pro rege vel pace regni, etiamsi episcopus sit ibi presens cum clero, vix sequuntur eum de populo centum viri."

[2] This is the first synodal sermon of this most interesting series.

that they be no longer forgetful of their home [cubilis], I mean, this
monastery, or of their former benefits, but do their proper duty and
service, as they are bound[1].

The great and aristocratic might at least make it their excuse
that the evil behaviour of the processional crowd kept them
away. Clubs, drawn swords, blows and even bloodshed had
not been unknown at such times within the sanctuary itself[2].
The "banners and uplifted Crosses" were themselves on occasion little better than standards of revolt, emblems of local
jealousies and party feeling. Dr Bromyard informs us further
that for one who prays devoutly in the procession there are many
who chatter idly and offensively. For one who sings, beseeches,
blesses with devotion, there are many that laugh, scorn and curse.
Even the very crowd that may come is itself an offence to God,
because it represents a majority of the vicious and the careless,
alien to the true spirit of prayer. He would rather listen to the
pleadings of a few righteous men than this company—"Multi-
plicasti gentem; non magnificasti laeticiam."[3] It is the sorrow
that is increased thereby, not the joy; for these undo the good
which the faithful few might achieve, if they were left unhindered.
Better would it be if they remained at home. Then the true
worshippers would have a chance to make their prayers heard[4].

Of the fine clothes and the pride of the ladies we may be
expected to know something by this time. There was an old
preachers' story on this topic, which, since it is to be found in
the *Florarium Bartholomei* of our English John of Mirfield[5],
we may claim the right to repeat. A certain dame, well past
middle-age, had decked herself to excess for a procession of the
kind we are describing. As it wound its way through the narrow
mediaeval street, she in its ranks, it happened to pass the house
of a certain ecclesiastic who kept a pet monkey. It was a clerical
monkey, and therefore should have known better, except of
course that in the first place it was strictly against the rules for

---

[1] MS. Harl. 4894, fol. 194 b, etc.
[2] Cf. disorders at a Procession, at Southwell, Reg. Zouche (in *Fasti Ebor.*
p. 444), May 11th, 1348.
[3] Isa. ix, 3 (quoted here by Bromyard).   [4] *S.P.—Oratio.*
[5] MS. Camb. Univ. Libr. Mm. ii. 10 (Cat. No. 2305), *De Indumentis.*
This tale appears in another sermon encyclopaedia considered to be of English
origin, the *Spec. Laic.* See MS. Add. 11284, fol. 64; see also Et. de Bourbon
(*Anecd.* p. 229).

such persons to keep any. However, sitting at its master's window, it espied the old lady, and, sliding down from its perch, snatched off her brightly-tinted wig and leapt back again. In the merry laughter of onlookers and marching throng, in her own utter confusion and shame, that foolish dame had her deserts. If, immortalized by the preachers, she still lives on, it may at least be accounted to her righteousness that she has provided a warning to many generations of sermon-goers, if not a little innocent amusement too. Unfortunately, however, such warnings appear to have proved ineffective: "The women of our time," the preacher goes on, "when they are at home with their husbands take no trouble over their adornment, but when they display themselves in public, they wish to go forth adorned; —*and yet they say that they adorn themselves for the benefit of their husbands!*" (et tamen dicunt quod ornant se *propter maritos suos*)[1]. Sadly Dr Bromyard is driven to a similar confession: "As against one who comes and goes to church or procession chastely, humbly and in orderly fashion, there are many, foul within, and proud without, displaying in their garments and all things more of pride than of humility."[2] Who can wonder, then, at tempests, or reverses in war? Who can be surprised that victory comes not in France, with such treachery at home in the camp? Finally, there is the rank scepticism of the day to be dealt with. Those who come to pray, frankly disbelieve in the efficacy of the Church's prayers. The pious they deride, and wish out of their sight for ever. "They say that never were there such evil times nor so many tempests, as have occurred since men of religion, and those who pray for the world were multiplied throughout it."

The preacher whose eye is open to facts has no easy task before him. In the very best of audiences, moreover, there will always be those whose pleasure it is to distort the speaker's words in order to create some new scandal for the dinner-table or the shop. A public sermon of Bishop Brunton illustrates how tactful the reputable preacher must be where such news spreads like wildfire in a great city. He is discussing the processions again: "But perchance some will say—'Rochester intends to prove by his sermon that kings and nobles are obliged

---

[1] Ibid. col. 4.   [2] *S.P.—Oratio.*

to come to procession; but for all that, before these days such a thing was not commonly seen.'"[1] (Ah! Be careful! It is not what Mr Spurgeon thinks of the Gospel narrative, that these mischief-makers are waiting to hear; but what he thinks of the government or the court.) "I reply—'It is not my intention to compel anyone to come to procession, but rather to persuade them to devotion.'" Woe to those who deal falsely with the word of God. "Thei depravyn it, and the prechour also, and mysreportyn it."[2] For the rest, in English towns as in Siena or Florence, ordinary noises and disturbances of the street must be expected to distract both preacher and congregation. Yelping dogs will have to be driven away[3]. Children must be quieted. Even a lordly prelate's discourse might suffer rude interruption at the cross from some artificers' brawl—"in which place because of such conflict, and the wounded fleeing thither, with very great outcry, no little tumult and alarm" could ensue[4].

Church and cemetery, chapter and "chepinge," through them all we have followed the steps of preachers and people in our mediaeval England. Though quite the most normal and important, yet they by no means exhaust between them the places where sermons will be made. Sermons there will be in the private chapels of palaces and manors, royal, ducal, episcopal. Even so, "fr. John Dymmok, ord. pred.," like many another, "did preach before the king in the Chapel within the Manor of Shene at Pentecost, and receive the Royal alms of a mark."[5] Sermons there will be at Westminster, when Richard II[6] or Henry IV[7] is crowned; sermons at the opening of Parliaments[8].

---

[1] This passage occurs in two of his sermons (MS. Harl. 3760, fols. 114 b and 189 b: "Sed aliquis forsitan dicet, 'Roffensis intendit probare per sermonem quod reges et proceres obligantur venire ad processionem, quod tamen, ante haec tempora, communiter non est visum.'"

[2] MS. Salisb. Cath. Libr. 103, fol. 157 b (*Jacob's Well*, unpublished part).

[3] Cf. the Paul's Cross picture, 1616; and remarks in S. Bernardino's preaching.

[4] Thos. de Appleby, Bp. of Carlisle, preaching at Paul's Cross, 1378. See Riley, *Memorials of London*, p. 415.

[5] Lib. de Recept. in *Ryl. Wardrobe Accts.*; 13–14 Rich. II, as quoted in the *Reliquary*, vol. xxii, p. 89 (Palmer): sim. at Berkhamsted Castle, 1384; etc.

[6] By an unnamed prelate. See Walsingham, *Hist. Angl.*, vol. i, p. 332.

[7] By Archbp. Arundel. See Twysden's *Decem Scriptores* (ed. 1652), cols. 2743–62; and Dean Hook's *Lives of the Archbps.* vol. iv, p. 479, etc. (Text of sermon: "Vir dominabitur populo," 1 Sam. ix, 17.)

[8] Cf. Archbp. Sudbury, 13th of Oct. 1377 (see Hook, as above, vol. iv,

A sermon at the very foot of the scaffold, indeed, in Tyburn, long before the days of Protestant and Catholic martyrs. For here in the year 1402, "in the sight and following of many thousands," an aged Master of Theology, condemned to the gallows with eight other friars for preaching treason, actually "made a devout sermon on the text—'Into thy hands, O Lord,' and swore by the salvation of his soul that he had committed no crime against King Henry, devoutly commending all who were the cause of his death."[1] Against this tragic spectacle, set now for contrast the absurd caricature of a "Boy-Bishop" in the pulpit, on St Nicholas' Day, "preaching with such childish terms as make the people laugh at his foolish counterfeit,"[2] when, for example, they "come every Childermas daye to Paull's churche, and hear the childe-bishoppes sermon."[3] Alas! that we lack "all the quires of sermons for the Feast of the Holy Innocents, which in my time [i.e. c. 1300] the Bishops of the Boys used to preach."[4] Who shall now deny an element of romance in the history of our venerable pulpit?[5]

On serious occasions, everything clearly depended, then as indeed ever, within or without the sacred building, upon the reputation and the personality of the speaker. No vulgar tricks of oratory or personal adornment, no immensity of tradition, form, circumstance, could hypnotize men for long, or make what later ages delighted to call "a painful preacher," in the

p. 268). Cf. also MS. Thornton (Lincoln), version of *Morte Arthure*, ed. Banks (1900), p. 18, l. 636, etc.:

"In the palez of ȝorke a parlement he haldez,
With all the perez of the rewme, prelates and other
And *aftyr the prechynge* in presence of lordes...."

[1] *Eulog. Hist.* (Rolls S.), vol. iii, p. 392 et seq.
[2] Puttenham's *Arte of Poesie*.
[3] *Stats. of St Paul's School*, 1512.
[4] From the Will of Wm. de Tolleshunte, almoner of St Paul's, 1328. See an interesting little pamphlet, *The Boy-Bishop at Salisbury and elsewhere*, by Canon J. M. J. Fletcher (1921), to which Canon Wordsworth has kindly drawn my attention. The author describes three late examples of the Boy-Bishop's sermon, with further references to the subject.
[5] Another curious preaching site is afforded by the case of Thos. Richmond, Franciscan, who discoursed "in quadam capella de novo constructa super pontem stagni fossae civitatis (York)...coram clero et populo in multitudine copiosa" (1426; see Wilkins, *Conc.* vol. iii, p. 487). This is a bridge-chapel, of course (cf. at Wakefield and Huntingdon). But where did "the copious multitude" stand? There is also record in MS. Lansd. 393, fol. 56, of a sermon by Archbp. Fitzralph "apud pontem" (1348).

finest sense, out of an "evil liver."[1] As regards the respective advantages of the two situations, it would seem that the amazing irreverences of which men were capable in church, the added splendour and attraction of the scene in the open must have tended to equalize them from the point of view of the pulpit. At the best of times, however, its work was never easy, or too eagerly applauded. Of one Carmelite orator of the later fourteenth century it is written that the people flocked to hear him "as to a show," so great was the universal admiration he commanded[2]. The same could be said of the great clergyman from Gloucester who, four centuries later, was to number a Chesterfield, a Garrick, and a Hume among his fascinated listeners in their thousands on the greensward[3]. But mere numbers without quality, as Bromyard rightly pointed out, do not necessarily constitute a preacher's greatest compliment, from the spiritual quarter. Otherwise we might all have to bow the knee to Messrs Moody and Sankey, to the many short-lived heroes of Exeter Hall, or the Tabernacle in Brooklyn. Where the audience is concerned, however, the pulpit giants of modern time may surely humble themselves at thought of these by-gone preaching scenes. How gentle the manners, how comfortable the surroundings of the tamed listeners of to-day!

[1] Our preachers do not fail to emphasize this point themselves: cf. Bromyard's story (*S.P.—Pred.*) of the woman, who, when she had listened to a certain preacher, whom she had known in his youth, would say to her neighbours—"Don't believe him, nor fear his words, for in his youth he was a terrible liar" (maximus mentitor)! "Tales heraldis assimilantur armorum, qui facta clamant armorum quae non faciunt. Et sunt sicut 'cymbalum tiniens, aut aes sonans,' quod extra ecclesiam sonat, et homines ad ecclesiam vocat, et nec ecclesiam intrat, sed seipsum sonando consumit." See also Rypon, MS. Harl. 4894, fols. 84, 215, etc.; and anon. on p. 7, above. Also Walleys, below, p. 352.
[2] Wm. Badby (fl. 1380), Oxf. Doctor; in MS. Harl. 3838, fol. 79 b.
[3] Of George Whitefield, Garrick is reported to have said: "I would give a 100 guineas if I could say 'Oh!' like Mr Whitefield." Chesterfield and Hume were equally impressed. No *ordinary* judges surely!

PART THREE

THE SERMONS

CHAPTER VI

THE SERMON LITERATURE AND ITS TYPES

Aᶠᵀᴱᴿ the activities of the mediaeval preachers and their audiences have been considered, the next task is to sort out and arrange the heterogeneous mass of special literature created to help them. That this is not so easy as might appear, the often arbitrary classifications of Mr J. E. Wells in his useful manual of Middle-English works, or some editors' extravagances in their prefaces to texts, can testify. Too often the cry of originality has been raised over a phrase or a preacher which would have been checked by any careful survey of this much-despised class of writings. Even for so short a period as that chosen out for our particular study of the subject, there will have to be considered under the heading of sermon material much that might justly seem irrelevant at first sight. Beside the obvious variety in language and in the object of address already suggested in previous chapters, we shall have sermons reported at the time of delivery, sermons systematically collected and re-edited afterwards, sermons in skeleton for later amplification, expanded sermons, both in prose and verse, arranged to be read aloud in their entirety. But apart from all this there are numerous treatises and manuals to be dealt with, now a veritable encyclopaedia of the art, now the simplest outline of the lay-folk's faith roughly cast into didactic form, now a mere collection of moralized stories, or an index of themes. In external appearance alone, contrasts are not wanting. On the one hand, a dignified and embellished folio, with flourished title-page, former treasure, very likely, of the great library at Durham, contains the collected orations of a learned sub-prior in church and synod[1]. On the other, vernacular treatises of the

---

[1] MS. Harl. 4894. Gasquet supplies a reading (*O.E.B.* 2nd ed. 1908, p. 24) of the half obliterated title, which after treatment of the MS. he says, showed

same age, often providing after all the most vivid and attractive reading to-day, may be drab and unadorned little octavo manuscripts on paper, "robed in russett," as M. Jusserand would say.

The problems of language, which raised a small controversy during last century among the French archivists concerned, have in our case been shorn of most of their difficulties already. M. Lecoy de la Marche's original view of the vernacular as the invariable medium for preaching to lay-folk, and of Latin for sermons to the clergy, monks, and scholars is clearly vindicated in the similar literature of this country, which affords repeated examples of both types from Anglo-Saxon times. True it is that we shall have to make one slight alteration in adjusting to our later centuries the summary conclusion of the Abbé Bourgain[1] who supports him, that is to say, in the case of the nuns, who must now be transferred to the vernacular side[2]. But otherwise the verdict for twelfth-century France remains equally good for our fourteenth-century England. The real difficulty which the learned author of *Notices et Extraits de quelques Manuscrits Latins* felt in the argument of one whom he treats somewhat caustically as "ce jeune érudit," was occasioned by the great Latin sermon collections and manuals issued often explicitly for the benefit of those preaching "ad populum."[3] Is it reasonable to suppose, argues M. Hauréau, that, after having been delivered originally in the vernacular, these sermons were translated by their authors into Latin, thus rendering them less intelligible and less handy for the average priest who was to rely on their help for his own vernacular addresses to precisely the same kind of audience? In reply, La Marche and Bourgain point us to actual cases where such translation is admitted by the compilers themselves. They go further and adduce some important reasons for the practice. Universality of appeal, for example, throughout clerical Christendom, might thus be commanded by means of the power of

agreement with an entry in the Durham Catalogues (See *Catalogi Veteres*, Surtees Soc. p. 76) of the "Sermones Mag. Roberti Rypon," thus: "Librarie Monachorum Dunelm., cum tabula." Traces of this full title are still discernible, but Gasquet has misread "Librarie" for "de communi Libraria."

[1] See *La chaire franç. au xiie siècle*, p. 186.
[2] See below, p. 258.
[3] See *Hist. Litt. de la France*, vol. xxvi, pp. 388–9, etc.

"Latinity" in the middle ages, as Bourgain puts it[1]. Again the suggestion is made that, in using this language for their manuscripts, the preachers confined them almost exclusively to clerical readers, and thus kept them away safely from the inquisitive eyes of the laity. Antony Méray, indeed, when speaking of the latest pre-Reformation sermon-writers, has here made valuable contribution to the debate. For in the Introduction to his *Libres Prêcheurs* he points out how many Latin editions of sermons full of the typical attacks on current ecclesiastical abuses and the general state of the Church have escaped the expurgation which has fallen on their vernacular neighbours[2]. In other words, our preacher, warned so repeatedly against encouraging an anti-clerical temper among the lay-folk by indiscreet revelations in the pulpit, could thus shield from the vulgar gaze what he had written down, when out of it, for the use of his clerical brethren before special audiences "in synodo" or "in capitulo." How thoroughly pertinent to the situation in England this whole question remains, even with the full tide of the vernacular movement set in, will only become clear as we proceed. What in fact is incomparably the greatest homiletic production of Chaucer's era by an Englishman, was written not in English but in Latin, and apparently never presented in the vernacular at all. For actual proof of the width of appeal in the case of this volume, we have only to point, in the days of the printing press alone, to the significance of at least nine successive editions, none of which are English, but issued abroad in places so scattered as Basle, Lübeck, Nuremberg, Paris, Lyons, Venice and Antwerp[3].

Gasquet, rejoicing with a new enthusiasm over the rediscovered treasure of pre-Reformation preaching, would have us believe that his erudite fourteenth-century parson went so far as to *prepare* his popular sermon in Latin[4]. But this is surely as wide of the truth as Hauréau's assertion that he sometimes

[1] For illustration, in the case of English authors here, we might point to the *Summa Pred.*, to Wycliffe's sermons (see here, on p. 239, n. 1), and to such foreign MSS. as the fifteenth century German MS. (Add. 21429) of Holcot's *Moralitates*, now in the Brit. Mus.

[2] *La vie au temps des Libres Prêcheurs*, vol. i, pp. 18–19. Geiler von Kaiserberg is given as an illustration.

[3] I.e. Bromyard's *Summa Predic.* cf. below p. 306, n. 7 (*Destr. Vic.*)

[4] *O.E.B.* p. 204.

preached in it to the laity. At all events we can find no facts to support the theory. Is it not possible rather to recognize the typical order of events in such cases as the following, where the friar Thomas Richmond of York[1] exhibits at his trial the sermon he had preached *and afterwards written out* with his own hand "in quodam papyro"; or where another friar, John Russell[2], two years earlier, confesses, in a like situation, that he had "upon Corpus Christi day, in this town of Stamford taught and openly preached (*in vulgari*) 'evel et wekkedly' this errour...*and afterwards wrot this conclusion in Latyn*, and so hit was sette up on this churche dore"? First the sermon is prepared for delivery in English. Then if it is to be perpetuated in writing, it is carefully set out afresh in Latin, like the challenge to an ecclesiastical debate or the conclusions of any thesis in the schools[3].

But, beyond surmise, there is positive evidence in our centuries for the making up of the "clerical" versions in this very fashion. The imposing series of over eighty Latin sermons by Archbishop Richard Fitzralph[4] declares explicitly that in every case these were delivered "in vulgari," with the exception of a paltry half-dozen or so. When, again, at the request of the Tynemouth monks, John Waldeby throws into book-form the discourses on the Creed, "which I had preached not long ago to

[1] 1426. See Wilkins, *Conc.* vol. iii, p. 487.
[2] At St Paul's, London, 1424. See ibid. vol. iii, p. 425. An interesting parallel case seems to be recorded of sermons preached by John Bredon, S.T.P., a Franciscan, in the parish church of Coventry, in 1445, involving "offensive" opinions, which the preacher had subsequently to recant (MS. Linc. Cath. Libr. A. 4. 16; printed in Leland, *Collectanea*, vol. v, p. 303): "Also that I in my billes that I made to be sette upon the chirche dores in the seide cite...," etc. See above, pp. 77–79. Rev. H. S. Cronin's recent discussion of the fastening of the twelve Conclusions of the Lollards on the doors of Westminster Hall and St Paul's Cathedral, in 1395 (see *Rogeri Dymmok Liber*, Wyclif Soc. 1922, pp. xxvi–xlii) should be read in the light of these other English examples.
[3] So, too, Cruel (*Geschichte der Deut. Pred.*): "The Latin language therefore belongs here, as in all similar cases, only to the written report, not to the public delivery." For the *writing out of sermons after* delivery, cf. in Bp. Pecock's *Folewer to the Donet*, recently printed in E.E.T.S., O.S. No. 164 (1924), p. 104, and the Prologues to various sermon collections, I mention, besides that of friar Waldeby above, e.g. John Felton, Robert of Ware, etc. For the use of Latin for this purpose (in the case of sermons preached specifically in the vernacular) cf. again the sermons of St Bernardino (e.g. Ferrers-Howell's *Life*, Chap. III).
[4] MS. Lansd. 393. See above, pp. 10–15.

O   15

the people in York,"[1] very naturally it is in Latin that they now make their appearance, although English must necessarily have been the language of original delivery. In the history of this particular work we can go actually a step further, and behold it turned back into English again, though now in a very free and divergent metrical edition:

> Ye that have herde, I you pray
> That ye wald pray specialy
> ffor freer John['s] soule of Waldby,
> That fast studyd day and nyght,   [nyght and day
> And preched it wt. full good cheer
> To lered and lewed that hymn wold here.
> Ther Jhu Crist graunt hym mede
> In hewyn for his good dede.
> Prays also wt. devocion
> ffor William['s] soule of Nassyngton,
> That gaf hym als full besyly
> Night and day to grete study,
> And made this tale in Ynglys tonge,
> Prays for hym old and yonge[2].

William, the Yorkshire notary, from the above would seem to imagine that Waldeby actually preached his "tale" in Latin to the unlettered in the first instance. But this would be palpably absurd, even had we not the friar's own account of the Tyne-mouth origin, which the other must have lacked. With the full evidence of both versions before us, however, it is easy to see that here is a worthy illustration of two important and distinctive classes of homiletic composition. The one, in Latin, is restricted to the mediation of the educated "clericus," and always characteristic of the friar. The other is issued in the vernacular, and characteristic of the great Yorkshire school of didactic writers which included hermit and secular, monk and canon in its ranks, *but not the Mendicant* as a rule[3]. From this conclusion there arises a fresh point which the researches of the

---

[1] MS. Caius Coll. Camb. 334, fol. 150; MS. Roy. 7. E. ii (B.M.), fol. 50, etc.

[2] MS. Roy. 17. C. viii (dated 1418), fol. 335.

[3] An exception must be made for John Lacy, who though *a recluse*, was also Dominican friar (see above, Chap. III, p. 119, n. 4); also, as translators, for one Richard Misyn (see ibid., p. 119), who translated works of Rolle (cf. MS. Add. 37790, fol. 95: "Liber de incendio amoris Ricardi Hampole, translatus in Anglicum, *instanciis domine Margarete Heslyngton recluse*, per fratrem Ricardum Misyn, S.T.B., tunc priorem Lyncoln., ordinis Carmeli-

present writer have induced him to add to the discussion, perhaps for the first time. This writing-out of sermons and manuals in Latin may well be an important mark of the friar's exclusiveness, as it certainly is of his vastly superior educational attainments. It reflects the desire to keep the fruits of his own labours to his equals if not entirely to his own orders, away from the half-literate priest or the layman, of whose progress in theological mysteries he became so jealous[1]. It may be one more quiet thrust at his old enemies the parish clergy, for whom others were now writing in the vernacular. Think, for example, of the best-known authors of these innumerable little treatises now issued in English, primarily for their use, as we shall see—Michel, Mannyng, Gaytrige, Rolle, Nassyngton, Hilton, Myrc, and the rest[2]. The Mendicants seem to be conspicuous for their absence. Then turn to such Mendicant works as have little of the more specialized character of Conciliar or University disputations about them. The sermons, tracts, story-books of Gorham, Holcot, Bromyard, Ringstead, Waldeby, Walleys[3], Hugh of Newcastle[4], Robert of Ware[5], Philip, Brackley, Spicer[6], and the throng of anonymous Dominican or Franciscan authors, are in the official language of the Church. If translated eventu-

tarum, A.D. 1435"), and Jo. Morton, Austin friar, probable translator of Bonaventura's *Spec. Vitae Christi*. As these works belong to the fifteenth century, they suggest that here and there a friar ventured at length to follow the popular movement.

[1] Cf. Wycliffe's remarkable testimony to the friars' desire to preach in a manner superior to that of the "sacerdos ruralis exiliter literatus" (*Sermones*, vol. i, pref. p. xvii), and see further above, p. 229.

[2] Of these, Michel, translator of the *Ayenbite*, was a monk of Canterbury (1340); Robert Mannyng (*Handlyng Synne*, etc.), a Gilbertine canon (1303); Gaytrige (see above, p. 53; below, p. 282), monk of St Mary's Abbey, York (1357); Rolle, a hermit (d. 1349); Nassyngton (*Spec. Vitae*, etc.), an advocate of York (1384); Hilton, Austin canon of Thurgarton (d. 1396?); Myrc(*Festiall*, etc.), an Austin canon of Lilleshall (c. 1420?). To these we may add the translators Nich. Love, Carthusian prior of Mount Grace, and another Yorkshire monk (of Sawley), translator of the *Chasteau d'Amour* (see below, p. 288, n. 5), and perhaps Jo. Walton, Austin Canon of Osney (see below, p. 291).

[3] *John*, a Franciscan (fl. 1280), author of the *Tractatus de Viciis*, etc. (cf. MS. Roy. 4. D. iv), here referred to, must not be confounded with the Dominican, *Thomas*, mentioned elsewhere.

[4] Franciscan author of a *Liber de victoria Christi contra Antichristum* (fl. 1320) (MS. Add. 36984).

[5] Franciscan author of a *Rosarium* of sermons on the B.V.M. (fl. c. 1280) (MS. Grays Inn 7).

[6] Spicer (or Selke?), author (Franc.) of the *Fasciculus Morum*, fl. c. 1320. For full description, see A. G. Little, *Studies in Engl. Franc. Hist.* pp. 139–57.

ally, it is by other pens, like those of the former group, or of Trevisa, and Chaucer[1]. Even friar Staunton, whoever he is, in a world of similar treatises in the vernacular, chooses to write thus on the Ten Commandments[2], though in the most simple and anecdotal way, in the language of his Order. Bozon, with his moralized tales in French, seems to be almost a lonely exception; and French after all is no tongue for the common herd, though the more educated townsmen might perhaps read as well as speak it[3].

But on the other hand, it will be retorted that Latin remains the language of secular parsons like Pagula or Burgo, manual-writers, even of John Felton with his ever popular "Sermones Dominicales." The answer is that the *Oculus Sacerdotis* and the *Pupilla Oculi* of the former are in truth much more akin to cut-and-dried legal compendia for priests—like the "Summae de Divinis Officiis" or the Canon-Law Books—than readers of Cutts or Gasquet might imagine; while the perpetual Vicar of St Mary Magdalene, Oxford, states expressly in his prologue that his work is for the student. Further exceptions on this side, too, we might expect. For the mere ability to write in the language of the learned could win the esteem of men, and be hailed as a mark of distinct superiority over the ordinary run of parochial clergy. If our theory be correct, however, its significance does not end here. The deadening effects of a high-and-dry isolation upon the monastic pulpit have been noticed already. Here there is an indication that the same danger was threatening the friars, however much their present proud position was due to faithful and hard-won achievements along the highways of the past. For all their continuous preaching at street-corners, they were now losing touch with the deeper religious life and needs of the masses. The mysterious mantle of prophecy

---

[1] Cf. the poet's own confession (explic. of the *Cant. Tales*) "of the translacion of....bokes of Legendes of Seintes, and *Omelies*, and moralitee, and devocioun" he had made. [2] MS. Gray's Inn Libr. 15.

[3] Cf. below, p. 265 (Nassyngton's *Spec. Vitae*, and the *N. Engl. Homily Collection*). MS. Bodl. 90 is said to contain sermons in French, in an English MS. of the late 13th century, (i.e. a little earlier than Bozon's day.) Mr Chaytor's assumption (*Troubadours & Engl.*, p. 12, quoting P. Studer) that the merchant's oath must necessarily have been administered to all in the language of the written document seems to me doubtful. What about our *Latin* sermon MSS. here?

received by their humble and heroic predecessors was gradually slipping, slipping from them on to other shoulders—those of the mystical hermit and his kind, of the Lollard, and soon of others "smelling somewhat of the pan,"—as the most illustrious preacher of the English Reformation was once described by a prelate in his audience[1].

One further reason suggests itself in the second half of our period for the continued preference for Latin—a fear of the taint of heresy. No one indeed expressed more vividly a sense of this haughty exclusiveness of the friar and his orthodox preaching than did the Lollard. It became one of the principal targets of his own homiletic assault—"sith prelates as scribes, and religious as Pharisees sayen it falleth not to hem [i.e. the laity and simple priests] to know God's Law; for they sayen it is so high, so subtle, so holy, that all only scribes and Pharisees should speak of this law....And these religious ben Pharisees, for they be divided fro common men of living."[2] "They hyden trewht," complains another, "as seith Isaie the profite—'this peple is of high sermone,' so that we may not undirstonde the sleghtnes of her tong in whiche is no wisdome."[3] Accordingly in days when the little vernacular books won an evil repute, and were cause of so much suspicion on the part of the authorities[4], small wonder that the champions of orthodoxy and status shunned anything that savoured of the opposite camp. The very closeness of the relations between much writing of the Northern vernacular school and that of the Wycliffites, which often constitutes our difficulty to-day in distinguishing what is really orthodox from what is not[5], would appear to justify such an attitude up to the hilt.

An interesting sidelight on this situation is afforded us by one of the rare cases in which both Latin and English versions still survive of the same sermon. Cambridge libraries possess at

[1] I.e. Latimer (by Bp. West of Ely). My theory *re* Mendicant sermon literature helps to explain Little, *Studies in Engl. Franc. Hist.* p. 135.

[2] MS. Trin. Coll. Camb. 60, fol. 2 b.

[3] MS. Laing 140, Univ. Libr. Edinburgh, fol. 3 b [the glosers]. Cf. further, Loserth's references to Wycliffe himself in *Sermones J. W.* (Wyclif Soc.), vol. i, p. ix, etc.

[4] Cf. Amundesham, *Annales* (Rolls S.), vol. i, p. 222 et seq. and Wilkins, *Conc.* vol. iii passim.

[5] See above, p. 131, Chap. III, and pp. 292–4, in Chap. VII. below.

least three copies in manuscript of Thomas Wimbledon's popular tirade at Paul's Cross in 1388. Of these, the two in Latin are to be found in collections of apparently unquestioned orthodoxy, one containing Waldeby's well-known Treatises[1]. The version in English, however (that is, the original language of delivery), appears at the end of a volume of Lollard treatises[2]. Although elsewhere[3] vernacular copies can be seen in quite unexceptionable company, the fact remains that the Latin versions are at the least symptomatic, in this respect, of a desire to keep inflammable material away from the people.

It might seem only natural to follow up what has been suggested in explanation of this survival of Latin, with some account of the renewed activity towards an English sermon literature, from Rolle to Wycliffe. So much depends in this case, however, upon the details of the texts concerned, that the subject will be postponed. Until the vernacular religious renaissance has begun in the North, about the middle of the fourteenth century, we shall expect to find few fresh sermon collections in Old English, after the age of Aelfric. But when once the movement has started, in spite of this policy of the friars, it needs little explanation. It springs naturally from ordinances for the instruction of the more ill-equipped preachers, like that of Archbishop Peckham, himself a friar, and spreads to the reading layman, as, in an age of growing enlightenment, it was at length bound to do. Before, however, the question of language is finally put aside, one or two special features call for remark. The kind of Latin itself used in the sermons has been well described by other writers[4], and the centuries

---

[1] MSS. Caius Coll. Camb. 334, and Camb. Univ. Libr. Ii. iii. 8.

[2] MS. Sidney Sussex Coll. Camb. 74, fols. 168–79. The vernacular copy in MS. Roy. 18. A. xvii, again, is in once-suspect Lollard company. Curiously enough, a parallel case is afforded by a sermon of Richard Alkerton, which appears in *English* along with the above, and sermons attributed to Wycliffe himself, in MS. Add. 37677, fols. 57–61 (fragmentary); but in *Latin* apparently in MS. Trin. Coll. Oxf. 42 (cf. Cat. Add. MSS. in B.M., 1906–10, p. 102, and see above, p. 24).

[3] Notably at the Brit. Mus. (MS. Roy. 18. B. xxiii, fol. 39; 18. A. xvii, fol. 184 b; MS. Harl. 2398, fol. 140, etc.); also Univ. Coll. Oxf. 97 (in company with Michel's *Ayenbite*, an Austin friar's sermon, etc., noted in Horstmann, vol. ii, p. 455, n.). See below, Appdx. v. Since writing the above, the author has noticed another English version of Wimbledon at Cambridge, viz. in MS. Corpus Christi Coll. 357. ii.

[4] Cf. Bourgain (*La Chaire franç. au xiie siècle*), p. 193 et seq.; Lecoy de la Marche; *Hist. Litt. de la France*, etc. passim.

here show little change. The non-classical constructions, the literal transference of popular idioms of speech into the Latin, the numbers of words of a Romance form, which seem to find no place even in the glossary of Ducange, are all aptly illustrated in the single case of the *Summa Predicantium*. As in earlier macaronic homilies abroad, vernacular phrases and quotations occur frequently, untranslated, in the body of the Latin text. The sermon-compiler is recording some favourite *bon-mot* or proverb of the day, some carefully chosen word, that it may spring again to the preacher's lips at the critical moment. Bromyard provides us with a vast number of these sayings in French as well as English, and in respect of the latter he follows the rule rather than the exception of his time[1].

Now and then a quotation from contemporary English verse finds its way to the end or the middle of a Latin discourse[2], thereby calling to mind, perhaps, Archbishop Stephen Langton's still more novel use of the refrain of a popular ditty for his theme, in an earlier century[3], or St Francis' text borrowed from the couplet of a love-song. But the quaint mixture of tongues appears occasionally from the opposite side. An artless preacher in the vernacular will introduce a few Latin words into the structure of his narrative, for no apparent reason other than to impress his audience with some high-sounding dignified syllables in the speech of the learned[4]: "Hereto have we story acordynge the wiche telleth a grett clerke: Et est Anselme in ecclesiastica Historia, and also the maister of stories...."[5] The titles of

---

[1] Cf. Rypon, MS. Harl. 4894, fols. 84 b, 92, etc.; Bp. Brunton, MS. Harl. 3760, fol. 62 b ("et sic precipue hiis diebus"—"flatrie flowrith, treuthe plourith"); MS. Add. 38819, fols. 228, 229 ("of gode ȝer and of plenteȝ"), 231, etc.; anon., MS. Camb. Univ. Libr. Ii. iii. 8, fol. 146 b ("now nys no God but gold alone"), etc.; Philip. MS. Bodl. Lat. Th. d. i, passim; Waldeby, MS. Caius Coll. Camb. 334, fols. 173, 176 ("feynt and feeble," etc.), 179 b; etc., etc.; many with the much-loved alliteration.

[2] Cf. below, p. 272, etc. (MS. Worcester Cath. Libr. F. 19, etc., etc.)

[3] "Bele Aliz matin leva." Cf. Lecoy de la Marche, *La Chaire franç.* pp. 91–3.

[4] Cf. here Chaucer's Pardoner (*Cant. Tales*, Pardoner's Tale, Prologue, l. 344):

"And in Latyn I speke a wordes fewe,
To saffron with my predicacioun."

[5] MS. Roy. 18. B. xxiii, fol. 82 (again, fol. 119), etc.; cf. also MS. Camb. Univ. Libr. Gg. vi. 16, fol. 40: "Quia secundum canones—there should no creature hear this name...," etc.; another given below, p. 270, etc. Similarly, regularly in the vernacular sermons of MS. Linc. Cath. Libr. A. 6. 2

books comprised about all the Latin he knew outside the Offices, no doubt! Finally, we may have even an echo of the popular love for macaronic poetry so well exhibited in Christmas carols, or in that scandalous little fifteenth-century satire against the Cambridge Carmelites, beginning, "Flen, flyys, and freris, populum Domini male caedunt!"[1] For such is suggested by the quaint jumble of Latin and old English verse which occurs in some versions of Watton's *Speculum Christiani*[2], and in even greater quantity in friar Grimston's *Sermon Commonplace Book*[3].

What sermons, it will be asked, if any, could fairly claim to have been set down precisely as they were delivered in the first case? The answer is not so simple. English utterances "ad populum" recast in Latin form are obviously out of the running; so too are others left untranslated but reduced to skeleton outline, even when directions for future amplification by the preachers using them, like those given in Wycliffe's[4] homilies, may be few and far between. Another Latin collection[5] with a uniform length of discourse agreeing with the likely requirements of monastic audiences for which it appears to have been composed, might suggest itself at first sight. But when we come suddenly upon cross-references in the text, in the manner of Fitzralph or of the *Summa Predicantium*—"De hoc quere in sermone 'Redde rationem villicationis tuae,'"[6]—we know that this is the sign of a later editorial pen. Sermons again in the popular idiom, having none of these indications, and retaining a peculiar directness of style, may yet be no nearer the mark, so far as we know, than any one of the several later variations of the celebrated *Festiall*. Textual criticism may disclose the earliest and purest manuscript in our possession; but how many

---

(cf. fol. 21: "Et est Petrus Blesensis in a sermon that he made," etc.). Cf. also the rude copying of scholastic forms of disputation in these sermons mentioned in Chap. VIII.

[1] In *Reliquiae Ant.* vol. i, p. 91. Mr H. B. Collins (Director of Music at the Birmingham Oratory) tells me there are numerous Old English Christmas Carols of this character. See also E. Rickert, *Ancient English Christmas Carols* (Chatto and Windus).

[2] Cf. MSS. Harl. 206, 2250; Roy. 8. E. v; Add. 15237, 21202, etc.

[3] MS. Advoc. Libr. Edinburgh 18. 7. 21 passim.

[4] See above, Chap. III, p. 135. Cf. also Felton ("Note about the man in Bristol," etc. with Gasquet's comment in *O.E.B.* p. 209), and Bozon's "Ici on peut conter de…" (cf. P. Meyer's ed., Introd. p. x, etc.).

[5] MS. Add. 21253.   [6] Ibid. fol. 166 b (cf. also fol. 171, etc.).

more, nearer to the original, may have been lost altogether, leaving behind them problems of construction or of authorship as acute perhaps as those of the *Gesta Romanorum*? Do they not all belong to a day when copyists and translators dealt much as they liked with their sources?

For practical purposes, however, the appearance of some little remark which could only apply to one particular audience or occasion, some special plea in an Invocation—"for the good and virtuose prosperite and encrese of owre soveraygne *here presente*,"[1] for example—must be taken as adequate testimony. Here at last survives the undoubted work of a reporter or else of some very conscientious sermon-diarist. The same may be said, too, of the quaint and fulsome repetitions of an anonymous preacher in a certain Cambridge manuscript, with his "moste worchifull ffrendys," and his homely directions in the style of Myrc[2]. But these primitive collections are comparative rarities. In one such, Thomas Looke, a self-assertive scribe, whose frequent name in its pages we could well spare for that of the unknown preacher himself, appears on more than one occasion to have finished off, later, the incomplete report of the day, by copying in the preacher's "exemplum," direct and in full, from some Latin source book, without even troubling about a translation to fit the rest[3]. A new kind of *sermon macaronic*, to be sure!

The comments which give to the Fitzralph collection the character of a personal sermon-diary put together apparently by the preacher, were noticed in a previous chapter. Evidences, on the other hand, of the systematic "reportatio" of sermons, by scholars and clerics in earlier periods, on the continent, may be taken as reasonably applicable to our own case. After all, other University students, like those to whom the famous English Dominican, John of St Giles, cried in his day from a Parisian pulpit—"I say to you scholars, put these sermons in your hearts, if not in your note-books! (in quaternis)"—must have

---

[1] MS. Roy. 18. B. xxiii, fol. 129 b; and many others here (cf. quotation given on p. 169, above). Cf. the repeated *3e, sirs* (fols. 57, 142, etc.).

[2] MS. Camb. Univ. Libr. Gg. vi. 16.

[3] MS. Roy. 18. B. xxiii, fols. 71 b–72, 117, 122 b, etc. Here an extra "exemplum" is frequently given in Latin, towards the sermon's end, while the conclusion returns to the vernacular again.

maintained the practice of note-books in Oxford and in Cambridge. So the taking down of sermons in outline would soon grow to be a popular habit elsewhere, first learnt, like so much else in our mediaeval preaching, in the lecture-room of the schools. However, the custom at Paris, described by Lecoy de la Marche[1], of employing special writers to report the University sermons of its members seems to have had no place here. For, according to an Oxford Statute of 1432[2], doctors and bachelors concerned were to furnish their own copies ("veras et integras copias"), within eight days of their delivery in the Church of St Mary the Virgin—"ad utilitatem studentium in sacra theologia, necnon quorumlibet aliorum predicare volentium saltem graduatorum." Nevertheless, while these are busy writing out their Latin effusions, and the occasional re-copying of older homilies goes on from time to time in the cloister, we may yet picture some faithful monk or clerk in a prelate's following, busily engaged at sermon-time in monastery, church, or churchyard, jotting down the words of his bishop or prior, with the regularity of a private secretary. From the results of these labours will come some at least of our more ambitious sermon manuscripts. Others will be copies supplied by the author to personal friends[3]. If they seem dry and unenlivening to us now, may it not be sometimes because we miss many of the more subtle touches in narrative and colour, the pointed "asides," the delicate amplifications, which our scribe lacked either time or ability to preserve?

On turning to examine in detail the chief manuscript types and classes, it will be natural to begin with what are usually termed "Sermones de tempore" ("sive in dies Dominicos et festivales per anni cursum")[4]. These may be taken to represent a model equipment for the priest of Sunday and feast-day

---

[1] See *La chaire franç. au moyen âge*, p. 326.

[2] See *Munimenta Acad. Oxon.* (Rolls S.), vol. i, p. 307. The Doctors were preachers for special Sundays, the Bachelors were delivering *Sermones Examinatorii*. See below, p. 259.

[3] Cf. friar Robert of Ware, for his brother (*Rosarium*, MS. Grays Inn Libr. 7, fol. 62), like the author of the *Fasciculus Morum*; friar John Waldeby for the monks of Tynemouth (see above, Chap. II, p. 64); the author of *Spec. Laic.* in Prol. (MS. Add. 17723, fol. 1); etc. And see Prologue to *Spec. Sacerd.* here following, p. 244 (MS. Add. 36791). There are many others.

[4] MS. Arundel 206.

addresses[1]—generally an admixture of both—prepared for the Church's preaching year, with themes drawn as a rule from the Gospel or Epistle at Mass, or else made appropriate for the occasion in some other way. More often than not the series as we find it is incomplete. The compiler may well have grown weary with such a task before the end. But it is easier to recognize that in most cases, as preacher, he has had some special preference or duty for certain seasons rather than for others. When his collection is finally put together, he does not trouble to fill up the gaps. It is another silent witness, perhaps, to the fact that continuous Sunday preaching was still quite the exception, never the rule. The sub-prior, Master Rypon, thus displays a quite disproportionate activity, for Lent[2]; while his incomplete "de tempore" series, closing with a sermon for Trinity Sunday, is followed up by a curious little isolated set of six Saint's-Day homilies—three for St Mary Magdalene, and three, as befits a monk of Durham, for the Festival of St Cuthbert.

No better illustration could be chosen of this particular class as a whole than the Latin *Sermones Dominicales* of John Felton[3]. These are fifty-eight in number, provided with short Prologue, and comprehensive alphabetical index. For all their overloading with quotations and authorities, "figures" and divisions, and their abbreviated style, they formed a remarkably popular production in their day. Another and more diminutive contemporary series[4], covering the same ground, brings us one stage further in the process of dry-compression, until practically all the sixty or seventy "Narrationes" which helped to enliven the former have now disappeared. The discourses, like those of other little duodecimo volumes, are clearly meant to be expanded by the preacher, as he stands, book in hand, to deliver his address. The bare skeleton character of the work is enhanced

---

[1] Cf. above, Chap. IV. Sometimes as many as five for a Sunday.

[2] MS. Harl. 4894. Sometimes as many as eight sermons supplied for a single occasion.

[3] Some MSS. are: Harl. 861, 868, 238, 5396; Add. 20727, 22572; Corpus Christi Coll. Camb. 360; Bodl., etc. However, Gasquet's inclusion of MS. Harl. 5396, fols. 143–209, must now give way to Herbert's correction in his *Cat. of Romances in the Brit. Mus.* vol. iii, p. 117 et seq., where authorship is attributed to Holcot.

[4] MS. Add. 21253.

still further by diagrammatic "schemata" of the sermon divisions sketched out over the lower margins of the pages, such as attain to really baffling proportions in taller manuscripts[1]. It was by glancing at these marginal diagrams from time to time, that the speaker prompted his memory as he discoursed[2].

As soon as the text is given out, the preacher proceeds at once to develope his exposition along the lines of a formal symbolism suggested therein. This leads up to almost invariable discussion of typical vices and virtues, and closes generally on a note of rewards for the righteous, and penalties for the wicked. No truckling to the pretty fancies and tastes of the audience shows itself here in this little pulpit volume. A short marginal "scheme" occurring in a sermon on the well-known text: "Hi, qui in stadio currunt"[3] will illustrate "diagrams," "divisions" and "figures," without need of further comment for the present:

$$5 \text{ impediunt cursum hominum} \begin{cases} \text{Lutum luxurie.} \\ \text{Pulvis inanis glorie.} \\ \text{Spine avaritie cupiditatis} \\ \text{Lapides obstinationis et duritie} \\ \text{Zabulum accidie}[4] \end{cases}$$

Struggling along the heavy, lifeless course of so "painful" a preacher with his tedious maze of tropes and allegories, we are reminded of the prudery of a Franciscan sermon-writer of the thirteenth century, whose dull *Sermones Dominicales in Evangelia* were destined to exercise as strong an influence on the English pulpit as on the French. Nicholas de Aquavilla[5], or "Waterton," as English moralists often prefer to call him[6], attacked "trufas et fabulas" in his sermons, warning his listeners that the preacher's duty was to instruct, not to amuse or even terrify. But what is far more remarkable and unusual, Fran-

---

[1] Cf. Harl. 1483, etc.

[2] Cf. in Cruel (*Geschichte der Deut. Pred.* § 633), referring to the *Manuale Curatorum* of Ulrich Sargant.   [3] 1 Cor. ix, 24.

[4] MS. Add. 21253, fol. 36 b (cf. also MS. Roy. 8. A. v, fol. 110 et seq.).

[5] Some MSS. in English Collections are: Gray's Inn Libr. 20 (xiii c.); Brit. Mus. Roy. MSS. 8. F. iv and 5. F. xvii (xv c.) etc.; C.C.C. Oxon.; Lincoln Coll. Oxon., etc.

[6] Cf. *Jacob's Well*, E.E.T.S., O.S. No. 115, p. 168, etc. ("Secundum Watertoun") and MS. Gray's Inn 20. This throws valuable light on Lampen's recent discussion of the identity of "R. Middleton" (*de Mediavilla*), in *Archivum Franc. Hist.*, xviii (ii), pp. 298–300.

ciscan as he was, he did not hesitate for once to adhere rigidly to his own principle, and exclude the stories altogether. M. Victor le Clerc's comment, after remarking on his dulness, is quite the best that can be said of him and his kind: "Le nombre des MSS. atteste combien les sermons dominicaux de Nicholas d'Hacqueville furent goûtés au xiiie et au xive siècle: on ne peut donc s'étonner de voir un copiste les honorer de cette qualification, 'valde boni.'"[1]

The interest evinced by the last-named work but one in matters relating to the life of Religious[2], and further the subsequent ownership of the manuscript in question, might go to prove that it was both used and intended for monastic audiences. But the same cannot be said of famous collections "de tempore" and "de sanctis," which under the somewhat droll names of *Dormi Secure* and *Abjiciamus et Suspendium* became at length by-words for mediocrity and uninspired traditionalism in preaching. An English authorship has actually been claimed for the former, that of the Carmelite Richard Maidstone, who flourished as a prolific homilist about the year 1396. But it is now more than probable that this and similar works had their origin on the continent. *Dormi Secure* was to be a handbook of outline sermons for the parish parsons, who thereby might sleep out their Saturday nights in peace, in sure and certain knowledge that a message needing no prolonged preparation lay ready for them on the morrow[3]. So dreary, however, is this once so welcome compilation, with its thirty printed editions and more—at least fourteen of which may be found in the British Museum alone[4]—that there has been manifested, since the days of its usefulness, the keenest anxiety on the part of Franciscans

---

[1] *Hist. Litt. de la France*, vol. xxxi, p. 95 et seq. For further details see Wadding, p. 262; Tanner, p. 46; Fabricius, vol. v, p. 103.

[2] Cf. MS. Add. 21253, fols. 19, 22, 22 b, 39, 72: "obedire superioribus nostris, ut quilibet religiosus...," etc.; 79 b, 135: "et maxime viri religiosi..."; 146: "Castellum religionis," in full.

[3] "Sermones dominicales cum expositionibus evangeliorum per annum, satis nobiles, et utiles omnibus sacerdotibus, pastoribus, et capellanis, qui alio nomine *Dormi secure*, vel *Dormi sine cura*, sunt nuncupati, eo quod absque magno studio faciliter possint incorporari et populo predicari incipiunt feliciter."

[4] Cf. A. G. Little in *D.N.B.* (under "Maidston, R."), 1475 (?)–1530; and M. le Clerc, in *Hist. Litt. de la France*, vol. xxv, p. 74 et seq.; Sbaraglia; Hartsheim, J.: "comme dispensant de tout travail ceux qui prêchent."

and others to disclaim any responsibility for it. But if the name of a friar Minor, John of Werden (or Verdena)[1], has been mentioned most freely in this connection, he can at least have been only the first of a subsequent line of writers to employ the seductive title. For not a few different collections have been observed to make use of it, with little in common but the name and the purpose[2]. The equally commonplace *Abjiciamus* and *Suspendium* courses[3] have here at least one small service to do. Their very titles, representing the opening word of the "de tempore" and the "de sanctis" themes respectively[4], remind us that even the choice of texts for regular seasons became stereotyped in due time.

Amid days of conventionalism and stagnation of mind in the pulpits, little wonder that audiences turned to their gossip and other diversions again, as the preacher mounted the stairs. Where newspapers and periodicals did not exist, and the practised memories of laymen were not infrequently exercised in storing up sermons and other pious instruction[5], they must often have known what was coming, almost as well as the speaker himself. It is the first Sunday in Advent. Then "'Behold thy King cometh' (Ecce Rex tuus venit)[6], is your theme for the day," echo the *Formae Predicandi*, as with one voice, and innumerable sermon collections after them. From the text itself the same fatal influence of the past seems to creep onward through the discourse: the same allegorical turns of exposition, the same "figurae" from animals or things, the same old sayings of "the great clerks," the same anecdotes, where anecdotes are to be found. The landscape is barren and monotonous to a degree. He who boldly sets out to follow the dust-laden tracks

---

[1] B. at Cologne, apparently, fl. c. 1300 (?). Or was the author another J. de W., fl. c. 1440?

[2] As witness the present author's own 15th cent. MS. *Dormi Secure*, which would appear to be by Ludolph of Saxony (d. c. 1370). Le Clerc mentions (p. 77) 1481 as the earliest *dated* MS. known.

[3] Attributed to William of Mailli, Dominican (1294). Numerous MSS. in England. Cf. MS. Roy. 3. A. xiii (c. 1300), etc.; MS. Bodl. 29 (fol. 168 et seq.).

[4] "Let us cast away the works of darkness" (Rom. xiii, 12), First Sunday in Advent.

[5] Cf. the interesting thirteenth century example cited in Coulton's *From St Francis to Dante*, p. 302: "Learned by heart within that year 40 Sunday gospels...and *other extracts from sermons* and prayers."

[6] Matth. xxi, 5.

of the ancient preachers, will pass by these dry bones, that whiten the road still further with their testimony to a decaying art, not without some sign of relief. Fortunately, there are better sights in store for him. Yet we fail to do justice even to the authors of such tedious stuff, unless we see in their efforts a genuine desire, like that expressed in Felton's *Prologue*, to serve their poorer brethren, who especially in penurious student days "are deprived of a sufficiency of books." Who knows but that the writer may have found his work wearisome, too. Often he is little more than a mere compiler himself, and, in an age of plagiarism wholesale, sometimes open enough to admit the fact. His own sermons or treatises are only "ex variis diversorum doctorum sermonibus collecti, et in unum compilati."

In the face of such degenerate tendencies in the pulpit of the day, the idea of fresh "de tempore" collections, adhering more faithfully to the plain text of Scripture, and now written in the vernacular, might well be expected to have commended itself to the reforming genius of Wycliffe and his party. This idea may be said to have been fully embodied in the Reformer's own English sermons; although his more imposing Latin series was compiled, as befits a great schoolman, appealing to the mind of clerical Christendom rather than to the common people, in the language of the *De civili Dominio*[1]. John Purvey and others eventually added further popular English contributions to the same literature[2]. Our present interest lies, however, not with these, but with some less-known vernacular sets of the period which, while they bear no distinctive mark of heterodoxy about them, yet show clearly the influence of the Lollard enthusiasm for "Goddis lawe," and of the new demand for English. In

[1] These *Latin* sermons provide a most interesting illustration of our remarks, above, on "universality of appeal." Prof. Loserth of Cernowitz describing their influence in Bohemia (Wyclif Soc. *Sermones*, vol. ii, p. xx), says: "There (among the Hussites) they were passed from hand to hand by the learned.... From the pulpits, the public mind was excited by these sermons of Wyclif, and inflamed with hatred for many decades against the prelates and monks. The effect of these sermons must have been the greater, that they were taken by many for sermons of Hus, as is evident from the marginal notes of our MS. D." (i.e. Codex pal. Vindobonensis 3928). See further the parallels given in Loserth's preface to Wycliffe's *Sermones*, vol. i.

[2] Cf. MS. Trin. Coll. Camb. B. 14. 50 (James' *Cat.* No. 333). For similar Lollard development of the vernacular religious treatises, see in Chap. VII, pp. 283, 291, below.

view of what has been said in modern times about the treatment of scripture narrative in mediaeval preaching, they receive an additional interest and importance. One of them, still "of the dominical gospels and of other certeyn grete feastis th^t ben comynli rad thorou3 out the 3eer in holi chirche,"[1] has already furnished us with a lengthy and vivid picture of the contemporary heretic that is anything but flattering[2]. Yet at the same time its author declares unreservedly that "the vertu of doctours techyng shuld be in the bokis of the foure evangelies," and declaims the Gospel text as loyally as ever Wycliffe himself in the pulpit. The elements of miracle and legend, of story-telling from the *example-books*, and learned arguments from the great clerks are here reduced to a minimum, or else disappear out of sight altogether. Symbolic interpretation, and analogues from nature, the latter often of a most charming and delicate kind, survive, as with the Reformer. But, in addition, we have each discourse opened with a brief outline of the literal Gospel narrative for the day, reinforced later on by careful translations of all separate texts as they occur, and generally rounded off with some appeal for more faithful instruction along these same lines. Other vernacular sets disclose the identical feature, where, indeed, "These wordes of this pistell buth thus muche to dey on Englische to 3our understondyng,"[3] or "This is the litterall sence off the gospell off thys deye," and "undurstond qwhat scripture seythe,"[4] are no mere empty phrases, but represent genuine attempts at their fulfilment. "Cristene men, as I have ydo her byfore, I wole do 3it thurgh the grace of God, I wole first telle 3ow the gospel as it was red byfore 3ow. After, I wole expoune it to 3ow and opene it to 3ow...."[5]

A "mirour" among the Parker MSS.[6] at first sight looks like

[1] MS. Harl. 2276, fol. 146 b. Another copy is MS. Roy. 18. A. xvii, fols. 1–184.

[2] See above, Chap. III, pp. 139–140.

[3] MS. Bodl. 95, fol. 104. Cf. also MS. Roy. 18. B. xxiii, fol. 105 b, etc., etc.

[4] MS. Camb. Univ. Libr. Gg. vi. 16, fols. 44 b and 47, etc. Cf. again MSS. Linc. Cath. Libr. A. 6. 2 and A. 7. 1: "So gostly to our purpose, the understondyng of this gospel *aftyr the litterall sence* [and *the sayng of docturs*...]," fols. 9 b–10, etc.

[5] MS. Harl. 2398, fol. 175 b (an Easter sermon in Myrc's style).

[6] MS. Corpus Christi Coll. Camb. 282. Other copies are MSS. Harl. 5085, Magd. Coll. Camb. 2498 and Holkham Hall. See Miss Deanesley's *Lollard Bible* (Camb. Univ. Press), pp. 315–16, where she points out that the

one of the several larger English treatises which frequently bear that name. It turns out on inspection, however, to be none other than an interesting "de tempore" sermon-series of this very class, concluding with simple material—"de sanctis," in the shape of homilies "in makyng mynde of apostoles," and "in the comune of on martir," "mani martir," and "one confessour." The unknown author's attitude to Scripture is expressed in the Prologue, where his elaborate insistence on the efficacy and authority of the divine message, however evil the life of the priest who delivers it[1], sounds like a rejoinder to the Lollard attacks, and an echo of Myrc himself on the Sacrament:

All ne hav nou3t al holi writ, ne alle ne understonde nou3t lettrure: swiche hereth the gospelles and redeth hit, that ne understondeth nou3t what he saith. And for to don alle understanden hit, in God ich dar wel taken this werk underhond, that alle may heren opinliche what the gospel techeth hem and al he mai sen in this writ that the Latin spekith and seithe suffisantliche[2].

Apart, however, from vernacular sermon collections which show something of the Lollard devotion to 'naked scripture' and contempt for the 'chronicle,' the 'comedy,' and the 'fable,' there are others in the same tongue, of a more picturesque character, which provided the unlettered parson with everything needed to instruct and satisfy a popular audience along the old lines: "Wherfore, sires myne, taketh here youre werke, occupacion, and besynes, that ye mowe have ther by a more profitable forme and better matere; that is to say, of the pronunsyng of solempnitees and festyvall tymes, right as ye have hadde and saide sermones in the same tymes here afore endytid to your honde in latyn or romayne tonge."[3] Whether for Saints' Days

work is based on Robert of Greatham's *Mirror*. When to these we have added such *further* collections of vernacular (non-Lollard) sermons as I have just indicated, however, Miss Deanesley's original "few" are found to be steadily mounting up, and her remarks (pp. 344–5) to the effect that the English lay-folk had no sermons in which the Sunday gospel was closely translated are found to be untenable. The Wycliffite agitation *did* bear fruit in this direction. See too the quotation from Walleys below on p. 311, espec. n. 3.

[1] The statement is clearly derived from Augustine, *De Doctr. Christiana*, lib. iv.

[2] MS. Corpus Christi Coll. Camb. 282, fol. 7. Another MS. series "de tempore" and "de sanctis" originally belonging to Wyggeston Hosp., Leicester, should be noticed in *The Old Service Books of the English Church*, p. 140. Cf. also MS. Bodl. 806.

[3] MS. Add. 36791, fols. 2–2 b. (*Speculum Sacerdotale* of sermons.)

A SERMON FOR NEW YEAR'S DAY
(from the *Festiall*, MS. Harl. 2403, lf. 30 b)

or for the ordinary Sunday, these English homilies have all of them one marked feature in common. They set out to give the common people that simple instruction in points of ritual and religious duties—the coming to Easter Communion or Lenten shrift well prepared in mind and conscience, the proper observance of the Sunday, the meaning of the Mass, the tasks of parents and servants, the avoidance of witchcraft and superstition—in short everything[1] that the Church deemed needful for the ordinary man and woman to know. When their worst crudities and most extravagant "examples" have been duly noted, the general verdict upon them must be one of generous approval. In an age of wild manners, untamed passions, open vice, it is the glory of the Catholic Church that she did clearly set herself to redeem the peasant and the labourer from the primitive error of their ways with direct, practical warnings and advice, wherever such homely sermons were preached. They must be judged in the light of what subsequent generations have been able to accomplish towards gentler modes of life and conduct, greater education and spiritual achievement, among the masses. Without their quaint thunder, their homely thrusts, their melodramatic narrations to hold the rustics' attention to higher things, our social progress might have been even slower.

To the modern reader, however, their greatest attraction will lie, probably, in the naïve explanations given of the various feasts and observances of the Sacred Calendar as they occur. Thus when "Newe-ȝer" day comes round, one simple homilist tells his flock that he has found "iiii causes in special," in the *Legenda Sanctorum*, why they should hold in great reverence and worship this feast of Our Lord's Circumcision[2]. On Ash Wednesday he is busy again with the quaintest information, teeming

---

[1] The body of instruction as outlined from previous Constitutions in such manuals as the *Cil. Oc. Sac.* (MS. Harl. 4968, fol. 43 b) should be compared with the sermons themselves.

[2] MS. Camb. Univ. Libr. Gg. vi. 16, fol. 40. See also sermon for "Neweris Day" in MS. Harl. 2276, fol. 22 et seq.; though the only reference to the day itself seems to be in the opening sentence: "ȝit we owen to hau this maidens sone freisshe in mynd, bi cause of newnesse of this feest" (i.e. Circumcision). Cf. also ibid. fol. 29 b ("Candelmasse Day"). Another "Newȝeres day" sermon in Myrc, *Festiall*, p. 44 (E.E.T.S., Ext. S. No. 96), and in MS. Linc. Cath. Libr. A. 6. 2, fol. 30 b.

with repetitions, much as John Myrc will explain in his *Festiall*[1]
the mysteries of "Teneblus," or of "Astyr-day":

> Worchypull ffrendys, ʒe shall ffast on Wedunsdaye as the com-
> mendabyll constitucion off holy ffaders off holy chyrche hathe
> ordenyd. It is called *caput jejunii*, the principall and the begynynge
> off that holy ffaste that our soffereyne saveour Criste Jhu halwed in
> hys manhode, quhan he fastyd....This faste is called also *Dies
> cinericius*, Pulver Wedunsdeye, or ellys Asche Wedunsdeye; ffor
> that deye every man off goode condicions shulde dispose hym to
> cum to God and holy chyrche mekely to take the halwed asches in
> syne to token of grete mekeness: ffor that the mynystres of holy
> cherche exorte and styrr men to mekeness, qwhen thei leyd the
> halowed asches up on theyr hedys, seynge thus—*Memento homo
> quod cinis es, et in cinerem reverteris*—"Remembyr thou man that
> thou art bot erthe, and to the erthe thou shalte turne aʒen."[2]

So another explains, with regard to "The Commemoracioun of
Alle Sowles," that "the memorye of the departynge of all
Cristen Sowles yˢ establyssched to be solempnysed in the
cherche of Cryste on thys daye to the ende thᵗ they maye hafe
generall ayde and comforte...."[3] Examples could be multiplied with ease[4].

It is time to turn, however, to the "de sanctis" sets, in particular. Here, in a hitherto unnoticed and unprinted *Speculum
Sacerdotale* of English homilies, for Festivals of Apostles and
Martyrs, the author sets forth in a Prologue the reasons for his
work:

> ...In alle the chirches of the worlde, the prestes of hem, whiche
> are sette to the governaunce of the parishenes,...schulden comende
> and prayse the solempnitees of god and of his seyntes excellentely
> with all here myghtes, and the cause wherfore they ben ordeyned
> openly to schewe and for to declare schortly some myracles that
> perteyneth un to the festes, that the peple of God may be lyghtenyd
> with, unto the knowlige of sothfastnes, and to the love therof be
> inflamyd and styred. Therfore the serteyn prestes which ben dere
> and famyliare un to me be fore alle other, unto you I redresse my
> speche, and seeth [i.e. since] that for the instance and prayers whiche

---

[1] E.E.T.S., Ext. S. xcvi, pp. 117 and 129. Many examples elsewhere in
this work.
[2] MS. Camb. Univ. Libr. Gg. vi. 16, fol. 51.
[3] MS. Lansd. 379, fol. 21 b. Others in MS. Roy. 18. B. xxv, fols. 134 b
and 137.
[4] Cf. e.g. MS. Roy. 18. B. xxiii, fols. 49, 111 (the "crisome," etc.); MS.
Harl. 2247, fol. 49 b; MS. Linc. Cath. Libr. A. 6. 2, fols. 84 b, 90 b; etc., etc.

that ye have makyd un to me for this present werke, I have here dis-
posyd and writen aftur my sympilnes of the solempnytees of alle
seyntes, the whiche schulden worshipfully eche Sonneday be schewid
un to youre peple....[1]

The *Festiall* of John Myrc[2], from its printed editions, both in
earlier and modern times, has almost come to be looked upon by
some as comprising everything characteristic of mediaeval
preaching as a whole. In reality, of course, it is but the outstanding example of the popular festival sermon-book. To
compare it to the English sermon collections recently mentioned, is but to compare the Blickling homilies of the tenth
century to the homilies of Aelfric over again. One need not
turn many pages of the Austin Canon to discover the secret of
his vast popularity five centuries later. A description once
given of the Blickling homilies themselves fits equally well in
respect of his work:—"The festival group with its fantastic incidents indicates the vogue of narrative sermons based on the
lives of holy men: it also shows lack of restraint on the part of
the preachers, and the marvellous credulity of contemporary
audiences."[3] With Myrc the text of canonical scriptures would
seem almost out of favour. He revels in the most fanciful and
impossible anecdotes about sacred characters; he is fascinated
irresistibly by the lurid and the painful; he seems to offer his
listeners little short of a new superstition and wizardry blessed
by the Church, in place of the old forbidden paganisms to
which they still cling so lovingly. In a word we feel transported
back again, at times, with all the suddenness of one of his
favourite "steyngs up" (like the Arabian traveller on the magic
carpet who actually figures in the *Gesta Romanorum*[4]), to the
ages when Egyptian Isis first became a Christian Virgin Mary,
or the Pantheon at Rome, rehallowed "in the honoure of oure
lady, Saynt Marye and all the Martyrs" became christened as
Sancta Maria Rotunda.[5] Are we not given in the *Festiall* a

---

[1] MS. Add. 36791, fols. 1 b–2.
[2] E.E.T.S., Ext. S. No. 96. To Dr Erbe's six MSS. there must be added,
amongst others, at Oxford, Bodl. MS. Rawl. A. 381 (wrongly catalogued as
Disciplina Simplicium) and MS. Hatton 96; at the Brit. Mus.: MSS. Roy.
18. B. xxv, and 17. C. xvii.
[3] J. A. Mosher, *The Exemplum in England*, p. 28.
[4] E.E.T.S., Ext. S. No. 33, p. 181 et seq.: "a rialle clothe...."
[5] I have deliberately selected these two pagan creations, because they

whole sermon on the death of Nero, full of the most unsavoury matter, in between the Feast of the Blessed Apostles Peter and Paul, and the Translation of St Thomas[1]! Yet the extravagances of pardoner and "jesting" friar, along with the subsequent complaints of the Reformers, ought to have prepared us for such an apparition, no worse than some of the original monstrosities of the *Exemplaria* themselves, behind their more sombre veil of Latin. A "de sanctis" collection of this kind is valuable just because it reveals how, in this particular instance, the sober author of the *Manuale*, set free, as it were, from the constraint of quasi-legal programmes of instruction for preachers, and stimulated by the popular passion, could indulge in the marvels and even some of the indecencies of the travelling entertainer. It is the stern Cromwell of the "de modo inquirendi de vii peccatis mortalibus,"[2] if you will, unbending at his ease, astride a pulpit instead of a table, to "jest" in homely fashion with his fellows. From the side of the mediaeval audiences, it is eloquent of the ineradicable popular love of saints and saint-lore. For the *Sermo de Sancto* is here one with the rejoicing of the patronal festival, the gay procession of the relics, the brilliant shrines, the pilgrimages, the guardian spirits of the air, or the great miracle-collections of a Gautier de Coinci.

Nevertheless, if it were not for a certain genuine though morbid zeal that peeps out here and there between the legs of devils, or the flames of an unending hell, we might find it hard to forgive the Shropshire canon, for all his entertainment. In fairness to him, and in spite of our knowledge of the "risus et cachinnationes" which greeted even the very solemn thunder of the preachers on occasion, the possibility of a complete though credulous faith in his own legends and absurdities on

happen to find curious mention in our sermon literature—of the style and period of Myrc. For the first, see MS. Roy. 18. B. xxiii, fol. 172: "Austinus, libro 19⁰, cap. 4, seth that men of Egipte worshipped a woman for a godesse whos name was Ysys...." For the second, MS. Lansd. 379, fol. 18 (Myrc? as in the *Festiall*), in a sermon "in die Omnium Sanctorum" ("when the Romayns reseyvyd Crystyn feythe...". Also in Bromyard, *S.P.*—*Dedicatio*. (The vernacular preacher carefully translates the new title for his folk, thus: "that ys, 'Maria, holy, the rounde!'")

[1] E.E.T.S., Ext. S. No. 96, p. 191: "De narratio de Morte Neronis Sermo."

[2] *Instructions for Parish Priests* (E.E.T.S., O.S. No. 31, p. 33, etc.), by the same author; see below, p. 297.

the part of the author must always be admitted. His mind was obviously steeped in the crude realism of mural paintings and carved grotesques that everywhere adorned the sacred places; although, on the other hand, something a little superior to such primitive *naïveté* might well be expected of an Austin canon, who became prior in his day, with the ability both to read and to write treatises in Latin[1]. Yet in spite of an orthodox Chaucer, a Lollard Oldcastle, the massive University Brom-yards of the same generation warn us now and then in their own simplicities not to expect too much from those who perforce lacked the more independent and matter-of-fact mentality of the educated laymen. So much, then, for the element in sermon books of what the English Reformer meant perhaps by the "drowsye dreams and idle imaginacions of Antichriste."[2] It should be clear that in this literature, as prepared for the Sunday and Saint's-Day preaching to popular audiences, there are already present a good many of the leading features that will attract our attention in the rest.

We are following what is actually a contemporary course, when passing next, in our survey, from the previous group, to the "Sermones ad Status," and the special occasions of preaching which found a place in the last chapter. In an *Ars Predicandi* attributed to Ranulf Higden[3], monastic author of the famous *Polychronicon*, a discussion on the proper choice of sermon themes leads up to the following three-fold division: "Sermo dominicalis, sermo festivalis, et sermo ad diversos status homi-num, sive ad diversa negocia rerum."[4] Immediately after, there follows the programme of the "negocia rerum" in question —visitations, elections, synods, processions and funerals—a queer medley perhaps, but one that corresponds most admirably with our sketches of the preaching scene. Sermons which bear specific evidence that they were intended for such times and audiences, will require a little more searching after than the previous. But, on the other hand, the strong family likeness,

---

[1] In addition to the fact of his own Latin *Manuale Sacerdotum*, he shows acquaintance with the usual fathers, Augustine, Gregory, Bede, etc., though he quotes them, no doubt, merely from other hand-books, and excerpts, at second-hand.

[2] Becon's *Supplicacyon* (Parker Soc.).

[3] MS. Bodl. 5.

[4] Ibid. fol. 5 b.

that generally pervades each group, makes any exhaustive search superfluous for such a purpose as the present. It tells us that when once we are acquainted with two or three, we may consider that we are acquainted with all. A certain conventionality indeed of topic and treatment has almost a right to be expected at visitation, for example, where the address is the prelude to business of a regularly recurrent sort. The thoughts of all present in the church or chapter-house flow in one particular direction. The speaker himself is drawn into the same stream. It is his task to prepare minds and stir hearts again to combat the old evils, to revive the old courage and open vision towards duly authorized reforms. If he deals only with side-issues, or delivers a pretty gospel exposition that is beside the point, he will be little better than a rock of offence or an eddy in the current. Mediaeval preachers at synods and visitations would seem to be singularly free from such faults. Their very texts still sound quaintly apposite. The freedom and violence of their denunciations and exposures startle us, and as a rule not a single anecdote relieves the sternness and the directness of the appeal. When Bishop Brunton holds a visitation of clergy in his cathedral church at Rochester, his chosen theme is "Appropinquaverunt visitationes urbis."[1] At another time it is the formidable "Visitabo in virga."[2] The regularity with which the same topic came to be used here, as at the special festivals, must have tended to introduce the same kind of monotony into the proceedings, even when it was all "very elegantly delivered in the Latin tongue." "Vide et visita vineam istam," an ever-popular example, will reappear now in a sermon manuscript of the thirteenth century[3], now in the visitation records of an Episcopal Register for the year 1438[4]. As for the violence, it is sufficient to say that no less a subject of discourse than the famous "Devil's Letter" itself—according to one version of the story—was thrust by the Prince of Darkness into a preacher's hand, as he made his way to the synod of clergy where he was due to deliver the opening

---

[1] Part of Ezech. ix, 1. Harl. 3760, fol. 51 : "Sermo 23us ad clerum in visitatione apud Roff."
[2] Ps. lxxxix, 32. Ibid. fol. 205 : "Sermo 75 in visitatione."
[3] MS. Roy. 8. F. ix.
[4] *Linc. Dioc. Reg.* vol. xxiv, p. 10.

sermon: "The Princes of Darkness to the Prelates of the Church send greeting!"[1]

Two further distinctions require to be made in this category of addresses before we proceed, namely, between utterances directed to the lower clergy, and those intended chiefly for the ears of prelates and superiors. A favourite burden of the first group indicated is the plea for greater purity in life and example, and an end to the appalling current immoralities of the priest-hood, couched usually in the blazing, indignant words of St Bernard. Higden suggests characteristically in his guide-book, "Mundamini qui fertis vasa Domini"[2] for a model text for the occasion. He knows, doubtless, how swiftly the storm can break then in all its fury on the tonsured heads. "Sicut populus, sic sacerdos." To speak of the rating of schoolboys in such a case would be almost to make a frivolous comparison. The lives of the clergy are declared to be the scandal of Christendom, and a leading cause of the people's ruin: divine punishment hangs over the nation for the vices of both![3] Then the long and oft-repeated procession of clerical sins is made to repass, the vanities and irregularities in dress, the absenteeism, the pro-fanity, the lust, the worldly covetousness and occupations, the illegitimate offspring, the horses, hawks, hounds, huntings, drinkings, gamblings, buyings and sellings, and what not. "The layman would not dare to spend his goods and his time as do the ecclesiastics on the lusts of the flesh and the vanities of the world!"[4] Another passage from the synodal sermon in the Oxford Manuscript of the Franciscan Nicholas Philip will illustrate the kind of language that could be em-ployed, although by no means the worst in this particular tirade, be it noted. The preacher has chosen a typical theme[5]—"Sacer-

---

[1] MS. Harl. 268, fol. 10 b: "...Demon obviavit ei, cui dixit, 'Quo vadis?' Dixit sacerdos, 'Ad sinodum, ut ibi predicem.' Dixit Demon, 'Dabo tibi sermonem bonum quem dices in sinodo,' et tradidit in cedula...." See also Hauréau, *Quelques MSS...* vol. iii, p. 120, *Contes Mor. de N. Bozon* (ed. Meyer), p. 269, and Coulton, *From St Francis to Dante*, 2nd ed. p. 398, n. 8. [2] Isaiah lii, 11. MS. Bodl. 5. fol. 6.
[3] See above, p. 35; also Philip, MS. Bodl. Lat. Th. d. i, fol. 87 et seq.; MS. C.C.C. Camb. 282, fol. 4; Bromyard; Rypon, MS. Harl. 4894, fol. 194, etc. (pena imminens propter peccata sacerdotum et populi).
[4] Philip, ibid.; cf. Rypon:—"Non est genus peccati in populo quin tale vel pejus exercetur in clero." [5] Exod. xix, 22.

dotes sanctificentur." After quoting from the book of Joel (ii, 17): "Let the priests weep between the porch and the altar, saying 'Spare, spare thy people, O Lord!'" he goes on:

But where, I ask, will you find many of the priests of to-day? Think you, mourning between the porch and the altar? Assuredly, I fear, in no wise [minime], but rather playing lasciviously around the prostitute and the brothel-house: nor by any means praying in the choir, but in truth wandering about the market-place; nor in the sanctuary, the temple of God, but rather in the tavern and the ale-house, where sometimes they imbibe so much that they can say neither vespers, nor matins properly[1].

Are we really to believe that English clergy listened regularly to such indictments from the lips of friar and monk? There seems to be no avoiding such a conclusion; and the fact that they were prepared to do so may well be in itself an argument for the ultimate truth of the charges. Master Rypon's eight synodal sermons at Durham, quite the most striking of the period so far disclosed, have already supplied us in an earlier chapter with much light on the *curatus* as a preacher. Each text in the series here is drawn from our Lord's Commission to the Seventy, according to the account in the third Gospel[2], and the whole is made to serve as the basis of a tremendous appeal for faithful parish preaching, and a judgement on the current apathy and ignorance. But what is still more to the point, the Benedictine sub-prior actually anticipates, in one of them[3], the hostility of many in his clerical audiences, much as we have seen him do with regard to the indignant layman:

If a religious possessioner preaches that word of truth, many will at once reply: "It is a shameful mockery [turpis est derisio] that this monk or canon should rebuke us thus! A single one of us has a better right to expend money than half his house. He thinks more of his goods than of his Order; and if he happened to know how to reckon correctly, or by what title he keeps his possessions, he would discover, perchance, that he owned scarcely three-pence on a just claim." Another will say: "Lo! that monk reproves us! There are none who live worse lives than monks and canons, because they do nothing that they are held to do!"[4]

---

[1] "With lips that have just kissed their mistresses, they kiss the Son of Mary. With hands that have embraced them they turn to embrace Jesus on the altar..."   [2] Luke x, 1–7.   [3] MS. Harl. 4894, fol. 161 et seq.

[4] Cf. also ibid. later: "Ista predicari murmurant moderni curati quamplures!"

In spite of this interesting and forcible comment, however, one alternative explanation of the state of affairs in these synods might be offered. Evidence there is in plenty that the knowledge of Latin possessed by even the average priest would hardly enable him to follow the intricacies of a Latin oration with any ease. Are we to believe, then, that, after all, little attention was paid to such indictments? The more ignorant among the parsons, who, as likely as not, would be the more worldly, too, and therefore the most guilty, sat heedless and unmoved while the storm lasted. The rest took it all much as an ordinary matter of course, in keeping with the general formalism and routine in organized religion, especially in the preaching "ad cleros" of the age. The very preacher himself was only fulfilling the duty which was there and then expected of him, and he might know the futility of his efforts, as well as a Brunton or a Bromyard. Familiarity, alas! still breeds inattention if not contempt as much around the pulpit as elsewhere. Had not these heard the same old denunciations of Bernard and the others, times without number, of which no manuscript record greets us to-day? The very fact of this continual haranguing in borrowed words, however authoritative they might be, would of itself tend to reduce the sting of the reprimand, even if once calculated to reinforce it. "Habent...aures ad audiendum, et non audiunt; quia domus exasperans est!"[1] As for that earnest monk, master Rypon, he at least was not incapable of pleading, at synod, in a more winsome and attractive tone[2]:

You priests, therefore, "tarrying in the same house"[3] of this church, beseech more devoutly, I beg of you, the Lord of the harvest, that is, Christ,...to send preachers into his harvest[4], that is, to send forth among the people of this church such preachers, I say, or labourers, as, in the words of Gorham, shall seek principally labour not leisure, burdens not honours, souls not tithes [opus non otium, onus non honores, animas non decimas];—for such men, I say, make your prayer....

---

[1] Ezech. xii, 2. Bede's *Epistle to Egbert* (cf. Browne, p. 279, etc.) gives a similar impression, I think, that this episcopal and clerical denunciation is mainly a tradition to be maintained.

[2] MS. Harl. 4894, fol. 199.

[3] He refers to Luke x, 7; his text.

[4] Thus used also by Odo of Cheriton, in the Prologue to his *Fabulae.* See Hervieux, *Fabul. Lat.* vol. iv, p. 174.

"All prelates of the Church, greater as well as lesser, are guardians,"[1] begins a conciliar preacher. The task of illustrating the exhortations to prelates is a comparatively easy one. Two favourite "figures," borrowed from Scripture, frequently set forth for their benefit the contemporary ideal of this guardianship. At least as far back as a papal legate's sermon before a council in St Paul's, at London, in 1237, we find the faithful prelates compared to the Beasts of the Apocalypse, "full of eyes before and behind," ever watchful alike in things temporal and things spiritual[2]. In an anonymous manuscript sermon of the early fourteenth century, now in the library of Gray's Inn, which the present writer has traced through the pages of Hauréau to Jacques de Lausanne, preaching "in capitulo," at Reims in 1307, they are identified with the Christmas shepherds "keeping watch over their flocks by night."[3] Both are the favourite analogues for such occasions. Archbishop Fitzralph combines these images, and adds a third, in a curious little sermon outline of only fourteen lines which stands at the head of his collected homilies:

Prelates, or whoever have the spiritual care of others, in holy scripture are called sometimes "eyes," sometimes "shepherds," sometimes "mediators." The reason is that they are the eyes of the mystical Body of Christ.... Because you are eyes, behold your flocks, visiting them with the greater solicitude.... Because you are shepherds, keep watch over your sheep, the more prudently guarding them.... Because you are mediators, pray, making peace the more devoutly with God and man....[4]

Before a Provincial Council held at Drogheda in 1350[5], he developes the second figure of the shepherds at greater length, according to a narrative in the book of Genesis[6]. Bishop Brunton, in his turn, shows what excellent pungent use can be made

[1] MS. Gray's Inn Libr. 12. iii., fols. 12 a–13 b. Text, "Super Muros tuos ...constitui custodes," Isa. lxii, 6.
[2] Ottobon in M. Paris, *Chron. Majora* (Rolls S.) Text from Rev. iv, 6; cf. also MS. Harl. 4894, fol. 206. MS. Roy. 7. E. ii, fol. 70 (Waldeby).
[3] MS. Gray's Inn. Libr. 12, fol. 13. See Hauréau, *Quelques MSS....* vol. iii, pp. 118–21. It is worth noting that the Gray's Inn MS. in question once belonged to the Franciscan Convent Library at Chester. MSS. abroad are Bibl. Nat. Paris, Nos. 18181 and 14799; Imper. Libr. Vienna, 631.
[4] MS. Lansd. 393, fol. 11 b. Text: "Videte, vigilate, et orate," Mark xiii, 33.
[5] Ibid. fol. 62 b et seq.   [6] Gen. xlvii, 3. (His text.)

of each detail in the Gospel Nativity scene[1]. "There were shepherds in that same region, keeping watch over their flocks," he quotes (Luke ii, 8).

"*Shepherds* they were, not hirelings," he continues, "to whom the sheep do not belong[2]; nor were they thieves and robbers, entering not by the door but by some other way—some by deceitfulness, like the crafty, some by influence, like the unfit of noble birth, some by worldly wisdom, like the ambitious. But they were shepherds feeding their flocks with the word of instruction [on fol. 60, 'preaching'], by example of life, and temporal support. '*In that same region.*'[3] He [i.e. the evangelist] does not say 'in a distant place,' where they could not exercise their pastoral office effectually. He does not say 'in the courts of princes and noblemen,' for prelates at court do not usually visit their flocks, except in the person of the sheep-shearers."

"Keeping watch," the Evangelist continues. Yes, indeed!—

Not as the voluptuous keep watch over their delicacies, not as the lecherous keep watch over their filthy lusts, not as the ambitious keep watch over the gathering together of their riches, not as the hypocrites keep watch to cultivate the praises of men, not as the vain keep watch, in huntings, dances, wrestlings and other excesses.

A relentless sermon this, for a prelate to make to his fellow-prelates! Bitter, no doubt, for the conscience-smitten were the stinging blows of that episcopal lash as wielded in Bishop Brunton's pulpit. M. Hauréau has a comment on the sermon of friar Jacques de Lausanne aforementioned, to the effect that these tirades against episcopal vice were characteristic of hostile Mendicant preaching in the chapter-houses, "behind closed doors." Such may well apply in this country to the case of Philip, the Franciscan, or of Bromyard, the Dominican. But however true here, or at Reims in 1307, it has certainly no place where, as at Rochester, it is a bishop who so fiercely denounces his own kind.

From the heat and condemnations of clerical assemblies, we think to turn now to the comparative placidity of the cloister.

---

[1] MS. Harl. 3760, fol. 191 et seq. This exposition is repeated again with only the slightest verbal alteration in another sermon, fol. 60.

[2] Cf. here the "fol. 60" version: "Pastores erant, non mercenarii qui serviunt ecclesiis pro propriis mercedibus et emolumentis, et non curant de animabus, et ideo tanquam fures sunt et latrones...."

[3] Fol. 60: "in hac auctoritate tangitur curatorum habitacio."

Do not the preachers themselves love to speak of its inmates as dwellers in a peaceful vineyard? "Operarii et cultores istius vineae sunt domus Israel, i.e. viri claustrales, contemplativi et videntes Deum per veram fidem et per veram contemplationem."[1] This may be true enough; but at the same time we must not forget that for the monk too there was the stern message of the visitation sermon. An interesting specimen in a fifteenth-century manuscript, apparently once connected with the priory of Ely[2], sets out in its opening lines a threefold conception of the task in hand: "Ponam visitationem tuam pacem"[3] (Isaiah lx, 17). "My beloved brethren, a visitation is ordained for a threefold purpose—that delinquents may be recovered from their sin, that the proficient may be encouraged in their good work, and that those who dwell together may be kept in rightful order." These points then furnish the speaker with the three "divisiones" of his discourse. Bishop Brunton's "Sermo ad religiosos,"[4] however, for once forgets the delinquents altogether, and, in its rejoicing over an act of virtue, employs a congratulatory tone together with a theme in the major key, which would appear to have been much in favour with monastic audiences[5]. The special cause of this outburst is explained in the sermon itself:

"The regular profession of true obedience," says the preacher, "is of such efficacy and power that it renders the man of religion as free as a little child at baptism from the stain of punishment and guilt. That unity of obedience and a pure conscience abounded in special degree among you, my brethren and friends, when your church was lately left destitute of the solace of a shepherd, and you did not decline to the right hand of favour, to elect him who if he had been

[1] MS. Add. 21253, fol. 39. Cf. the frequent texts: "Visita vineam istam" (Ps. lxxx, 14) as above, p. 248.

[2] MS. Corpus Christi Coll. Camb. 357, fol. 125 et seq.: "Amantissimi fratres mei, ratione triplici visitacio ordinatur, ut delinquentes a suo scelere retrahantur, ut proficientes in bono opere foveantur, et ut conviventes in debito ordine custodiantur." Others in MS. Roy. 7. A. viii, fols. 310 b–335.

[3] I find this same text recorded of a visitation sermon at Lincoln, preached by Mag. Thos. Duffeld, 1439; see above, p. 149, n. 5.

[4] MS. Harl. 3760, fol. 31 et seq.

[5] "Ecce quam bonum et quam jucundum est habitare fratres in unitate" (Ps. cxxxiii, 1); cf. also in MSS. Roy. 3. A. x, fol. 91, and 5. E. vii, fol. 100 (two thirteenth-century English Monastic sermon series); 4. B. x, fol. 48 b ("Sermo ad claustrales," early 13th cent.); MS. Harl. 52, fol. 37 b (a *Sermo Brevis*, in an English Monastic MS.).

elected, would not have looked upon you personally. Nor did you decline to the left hand of fear, by reason of the King's Letters sent to you, to the end that you should elect him whom you knew to be a man of not unstained reputation[1]. But rightly 'walking in the way,' you elected as your prior a learned man and one circumspect in things temporal; on account of which happy deed I shall love you the more eagerly, and deal with you the more gently, for the rest of my life. And there is good reason: for by this election you have kept your good name unspotted as much with regard to the world and your own conscience, as to God Himself. So that I may justly compare you to those kine [illis vaccis!] that went direct along the highway, bearing the ark, 'and turned not aside to the right hand or to the left.'"[2]

All this and much else in the same quaint strain is pleasant reading enough. But unfortunately such happy little incidents in the literature are as rare as the genius of Brunton himself. The dullness as well as the scarceness of the monastic sermon of the period has already been noted elsewhere; and, so far as we can judge from what remains, it is a pulpit that suggests something of cloister stagnation, as well as cloister calm. The word "exemplum" is probably still associated in most minds to-day with the literary activity of monks. Yet only fifteen *exempla* are tabulated for all the four hundred pages in modern reckoning, of Rypon's substantial Folio; and other monastic sermon compilations appear to tell the same tale, in spite of the early example set by our English Odo of Cheriton. It is the friar, indeed, who had actually bought up that market. On the other hand, the very convent library which presented the preacher with so much patristic and illustrative material ready to hand, may also explain, of course, why it became unnecessary to commit to parchment again the old narrations along with the new sermon. "Exemplaria," "Bestiaria," "Lapidaria," and the rest were to be found in the cloister book-presses, not a stone's throw from the place of declamation. Perhaps, after all, there is a still better reason in support of the theory that in convent preachings "exempla" were practically never used at all. The brethren had quite enough of them out of the pulpit, as it was, in the evening glow of the "calefactorium," that

---

[1] "et disparis religionis" is added in the margin.
[2] See I Sam. vi, 12.

ancient manufactory of "gestes" and fables, and friendly gossip. Their secrets were out; and the little points and conclusions of the stories that were wont to arrest men's attention in church were here common property already. However, if anecdotes are scarce, "similitudines" abound[1]. Whether it be actually the work of Dominican friar or monk, a Cambridge manuscript sermon-book[2], containing at least two addresses or postills labelled definitely "ad claustrales,"[3] presents a whole series of these expanded "figures," apart from the ordinary themes, and apparently complete in themselves. They compare the monk or his vocation, amongst other things, to fire, money, a tree, a gardener, and a draught of medicine! Besides "figures" and a typical "Consolatio religiosorum,"[4] the reader is supplied further with useful illustrations in outline of the kind of topic which would make special appeal to the monastic mind, "on the spiritual sacrifice of the monk," on his tonsure as a crown, on the familiar vices and virtues of cloister life. Here is "Accidia in genere," and that "Presumptio" which so often marks the reaction of some straitened and aggravated spirit in the cell. Among ideals of the straitened, "the curbing of desire," "the abnegation of one's own will," "fasting and abstinence," and others tell a similar tale, well summed up in a further heading of this same collection, "Admonitio ad fugam mundi."[5] Other homilies elsewhere of similar appearance and character remind us further, with a detailed list of no less than "ten mortal sins which often beset men of religion" ("peccata mortalia, quae saepe occupant homines religiosos"),[6] that monk as well as curate requires sometimes the note of solemn warning from his preachers.

---

[1] With this should be compared an interesting "Similitudinarium" by Wm. de Montibus [du Mont, of Leicester], in MS. Gray's Inn Libr. 13. ii (14th cent.): "ad declarandum in sermone quocunque propositorum similitudines," probably from a Franciscan Convent Library.

[2] MS. Caius Coll. Camb. 233.

[3] Another *Sermo ad claustrales* in MS. Gray's Inn Libr. 14, fols. 106 a–107 b (and Roy. 4. B. x, fol. 48); and a *Sermo ad religiosos* appears in the early fourteenth century MS. Arundel 206, fol. 65. Also *Sermones ad contemplativos* in a fourteenth-century (Engl.) MS. in the Univ. Libr. Edinburgh (MS. Db. iv. 17, fols. 111–115 b).

[4] Ibid. (Caius Coll. Camb. 233), fol. 131 b.

[5] Ibid. fols. 108 b–109.

[6] Cf. MS. Add. 21253, fol. 146 et seq.

In happier strain, and no less suggestive of the peculiar psychology of the convent, is the extraordinary warmth and delight manifested in frequent sermons on Our Lady, and indeed on the female saints generally. We never needed a monastic preacher, it is true, to tell us how fierce and relentless could be the battle there in the heart of the faithful to preserve unharmed their original vow of a perpetual chastity. Yet the annals of the cloister, too, confirming the view of commonsense, are full of such testimonies. So, for that same privileged spokesman there lay an unparalleled opportunity of bringing with his customary praise of the state of virginity, and its "hundred-fold," some gentler and less formal word of consolation into the pulpit. If, like that tempted clerk of Rome in the sermon-story[1], his audience might behold the radiant Queen of Heaven, as in a vision, coming to claim them in that very church, surely, as with him, their trials would be at an end, and their compensation full. "Nunc autem, fratres karissimi, semper tali serviamus reginae, quae nunquam dereliquit sperantes in se!"[2] In like fashion the penitent Mary Magdalene becomes an ever welcome subject of discourse. A homilist of our period, for example, who introduces her into an Easter sermon on "the three Maries,"[3] applies her discovery of Christ in the house of Symon to the case of men of religion, "bewailing their own sins in the cloister."[4]

That dwellers in the friaries as well as in the houses of older Orders looked for similar discourses from their distinguished visitors, there can be little doubt. Brunton[5], who like Archbishop Fitzralph[6] again, is a special preacher at the Carmelites on the Feast of the Annunciation, takes for his theme the "Nomen

---

[1] This actually occurs in a monastic sermon, for a feast of the B.V.M. in an early 15th cent. English MS., Add. 37787, fol. 27 b; cf. MSS. Harl. 2851, fol. 87 b and Add. 11579, fol. 11 (both fourteenth century).

[2] Ibid. (MS. Add. 37787). This early 15th cent. MS. promises us great things: "Hic incipiunt sermones anni festivitatum," but only one appears (for Advent)!

[3] MS. Add. 21253, fol. 79 b. Another sermon on the three Marys, for Easter Day, this time in the vernacular, may be found in MS. Roy. 18. B. xxiii, fol. 97 b et seq.

[4] Ibid. fol. 22 b. Cf. also Rypon's three sermons on the Magdalene in MS. Harl. 4894; and several in Brunton.

[5] MS. Harl. 3760, fol. 93 et seq.

[6] Drogheda, 1349. MS. Lansd. 393, fol. 58. (Text: "Ave Maria.")

Virginis Maria" of St Luke[1], which a Franciscan, brother
Robert of Ware, had once used for the opening text of his
Rosarium of twenty-five sermons on the Blessed Virgin[2], penned
in an earlier age of enthusiastic devotion to her memory and her
miracles. This was a cult well suited to blossom continually in
all such "gardens of holy religious orders."[3] Would that St
Catherine of Siena, Italian contemporary of our good Bishop of
Rochester, who uses the phrase[4], had not been compelled to tell
so sorry a tale of some of them! Sermons at the election of
abbot or prior gave the preacher his opportunity to hold up
afresh before his brethren a picture of the true ideal of monastic
manhood. "Eligite ex vobis virum!"[5] An unknown Abbot of
Dore in Herefordshire, probably of the early fourteenth century, singles out, for his topic, the virtue of humility, as that
which is the most desirable of all in one about to be chosen for
such an office. "Ideo licet in viro ecclesiae Dei proficiendo
vigere debeant omnia virtutum genera, in eo tamen maxime
humilitas est querenda."[6] Nor is there lacking a real significance
in his emphasis; for it was an age by no means innocent of the
sumptuous prelate riding to hounds or to court from his own
convent-gate, with the air and circumstance of a Wolsey.

A word must be added to this section with regard to preachings in the nunnery. Judging from the language in which
official correspondence was usually carried on with the sister-
hood, we may believe that religious instruction was often given
to them in French[7], save when some special occasion which
brought laity from the outside world into the nunnery chapel
demanded a use of the vernacular. The latter was the case, no

[1] Luke i, 27.
[2] MS. Gray's Inn Libr. 7, fols. 62–138. See *Dublin Review* (Apr. 1925),
as before.
[3] The anon. Religious, author of MS. Caius Coll. Camb. 233, shows a
similar fondness for St Katherine.
[4] *Dialogo*, cap. cxxv (1370).
[5] Brunton, in MS. Harl. 3760, fol. 267 et seq.: "Sermo...apud Roff., in
electione prioris Roff." This same text is reported of a sermon at the election
of Abbot Wm. Albon, at St Albans Abbey, 1465 (see Reg. Whethampst.
vol. ii, p. 30). For other similar sermons and themes, cf. MS. Bodl. 5, fol. 6,
and MS. Caius Coll. Camb. 233: "in electione prelati."
[6] MSS. Roy.8.A.v, fol. 129 b and 7. A. viii, fol.335: "in electione Abbatis."
[7] Cf. here the French *Sermun del secle* in verse, with other religious instruction, in the thirteenth century MS. Egerton 2710 (fol. 145, etc.), which
belonged to the nuns of the priory of Derby in the fifteenth century.

doubt, when Archbishop Fitzralph preached "in vulgari" on the Feast of Corpus Christi in 1355—"in ecclesia Monialium Londini."[1] Apart, however, from this quite characterless example, the present writer has found but two sermons definitely addressed to Nuns in English manuscripts even approximating in date to the chosen period of his study. One is a "Sermo in velatione monialis," on the text—"Vadet ad requiem suam."[2] The other is a short homily in Latin on the Lily, written down in a bare outline of thirty lines ("Florete flores quasi lilium, date odorem")[3]. If they are to be taken as representative of the species, we may gather that the nun was treated to the same high-and-dry formality of "figures" and expositions as her brother of the cloister. There is the usual plea for the appropriate religious virtues—purity of heart, holiness of conversation, white radiance of humility and innocence, and the rest—"ad modum lilii," in the latter case.

University sermons of the age would seem nowadays to be almost as hard to discover as those delivered in the nunneries. But a careful examination of forms of address might well reveal further examples scattered here and there in various Latin collections, which lack the more definite labels of "Oxon." or "Cantebrygge,"[4] at the head of the page. An interesting little volume in the Harleian collection[5], which so far appears to have escaped attention altogether, deserves to be singled out for its short series, all six of which were apparently delivered in Oxford about the year 1432, three being further detailed as "Sermones examinatorii." This date, it may be remembered, is none other than that of the introduction of the University Statute which required henceforth of each Oxford preacher a written copy of his oration, to be registered by the proctors, and preserved

---

[1] MS. Lansd. 393, fol. 96 b et seq. (Text: John vi, 54.)

[2] MS. Roy. 7. A. viii, fol. 307 b.

[3] (Ecclesiasticus xxxix, 14.) MS. Harl. 52, fol. 128. Both are in MSS. of early 14th century date; but they may be copied from earlier models. Along with *Sermones ad contemplativos* in MS. Univ. Libr. Edinburgh, Db. iv. 17 (Engl. 14th cent.), there is a *Sermo ad virgines* (fols. 116–18, incpl.), which is unnoticed in the Cat. of MSS. Further themes for nunnery visitation sermons may be found in the Alnwick Episc. Reg. (Dioc. Linc.), vol. xxiv, pp. 46, 89, etc.

[4] As in MS. Corpus Christi Coll. Camb. 392; cf. fol. 217 (Cambridge, in Lent), etc.

[5] MS. Harl. 5398, fol. 20 b et seq.

in the Common Library[1]. From the fact that the second of these sermons is further identified with "the First Sunday in Advent" (which is also the first occasion in the year to be mentioned in this particular decree), there is good reason for believing that we have actually before us in this manuscript the earliest fruits of the new regulation.

All that can be learnt from the opening number of the series is the name of its author, "Master John Shyrborne."[2] His use of such phrases of address as "peritissimi domini, patres, et magistri," "prestantissimi domini," and the like, however, agrees with the others. Turning to the second[3], we find from a more elaborate heading that the preacher in question is a Regent-Master, of the Carmelite convent in the city: "Sermo formalis et ordinaria magistri Johannis Haynton regentis claustralis Ordinis Carmelitarum Oxon.; dominica prima adventus, A.D. 1432." His ante-theme takes the form of a quaint Invocation in verse addressed to the Almighty as "Jupiter Omnipotens," "dux exercitum," and so forth. Though characteristically affected, it yet agrees with the topic of his discourse, the Holy Warfare and its weapons[4], thus beseeching Him to grant victory to His warriors, and peace to clergy, king and people[5]. The exhortation itself closes with a "Recapitulacio," first "in prosa," then "in metro."[6] The next sermon on the list is a Benedictine effusion "of the monk Rainold of Gloucester," beginning "Optulit immaculatum," ad Hebr. 9° [verse 14], "et pro hujus examinatorii sermonis themate designato, Reverendi magistri, patres, et domini...."[7] He sets out his two main

---

[1] See above, p. 234. Cf. further *Munim. Acad. Oxon.* (Rolls S.), vol. ii, p. 751 (1458). Moneys authorized from the University chest: "pro novo registro fiendo, in quo debent inscribi omnes sermones examinatorii."

[2] MS. ibid. fol. 21, etc. (See *Explicit*, fol. 26.)

[3] Ibid. fol. 40. For Haynton himself, see in MS. Harl. 3838, as before.

[4] Text: "Induamur arma lucis," etc. (Rom. xiii, 12).

[5] Cf. ll. 7 et seq.:
"Assis nunc bellis mentis, carnisque duellis,
Desque trophea tuis militibus meritis.
Vince tuos hostes, ut sors tua sit tibi sospes,
Lucis et exsortes sint modo participes.
Des pacem famulis, clero, regi, quoque regnis,
Praemia defunctis, cum sanctis luce perunctis
Pelle tenebras mentis, et ornes dote superna...," etc.

[6] fols. 44 b–45.

[7] Ibid. fol. 45 b.

divisions, the "legal act" involved in the "Obtulit," the moral purity of the "Immaculatum," then proceeds to apply them in regular formal style, first to the Son of God, and secondly to the case of each sanctified Christian. Authorities freely quoted include the works of Augustine, Peter of Blois[1], Gregory, and Gervase of Tilbury (*De ordinis sacerdotalis Instructione*). The theme developes finally into a plea for the religious life, supported by "contempt of the world," not unsuitable indeed for an incepting monk: "And what shall it profit a man, if he have the riches of Croesus, the glory of Solomon, whatever Julius Caesar, or Alexander the Great, and other mighty men possessed of lands, of treasures, and delights, if he suffer loss to his own soul?"[2] The discourse following[3], another "incultus sermo examinatorius," as the speaker himself terms it in addressing the "most distinguished lords, fathers, and masters" before him in the opening of his "processus," unfortunately lacks any descriptive rubric. With its discussion of the principles of "good stewardship," of the kind of wisdom required in the preacher, and especially of the "modus eligendi," it looks at first sight absurdly like a wordy and gratuitous charge delivered by the candidate to his own examiners. But the conclusion of the harangue suggests that nothing more unusual is implied by the "dispensatio" in question than that "of God's holy word and sacraments" by priests in the ordinary course[4]. The fifth is the examinatory sermon of the same brother John Haynton aforesaid, now appropriately described as "Bachelor of the faculty of Theology," without the title of Master[5]. Once again he employs verse for his ante-theme. In three plaintive little lines preceding his text, the anxious candidate, in typical mediaeval fashion, commends himself devoutly to his God, his "alma mater," and the saint of his own name, at the outset of

[1] Quoted no less than nine times.
[2] "Et quid prodest homini, si habeat divitias Cresi, gloriam Salamonis, quicquid Julius Caesar, aut Magnus Alexander, ceterique potentes in terris, in thesauris, in deliciis possiderunt, si suae animae detrimentum patiatur?"
[3] Ibid. fol. 51. (Text: "Estote boni dispensatores..." (1 Pet. iv, 10).)
[4] Ibid. fol. 53: "Vobis, qui dispensatores estis instituti, hoc ministerium specialius convenit de custodia et preparatione, ut et vos preparetis in adventu Judicis, quia pauci sunt qui commissam fideliter administrant dispensationem. Ille autem qui repertus fuerit annonam verbi administrans, et circa greges vigilans, eterna beatitudine glorificabitur."
[5] Ibid. fol. 54. (For the Fourth Sunday after Easter, 1432.)

the ordeal[1]. After the text there are another dozen lines of Latin, concluding, this time, with an offering of "the humble calves of his lips"[2] to the Deity. Fulsome self-depreciation, fatuous metaphors, lavish titles of honour for his auditors, stilted Latin verses, and a plentiful use of superlatives in the body of the discourse, reproduce the current affectations of the schools. The auditors are now "veritatis spiritus dulcedine delibuti doctissimi theodocti magistri, patres, atque domini," etc. or "perhonorandi magistri, ac sacrae milites disciplinae!"[3] His own effort is "this most unpolished examinatory collation," or "this exceedingly poor collation." Let us hope, at all events, that he met with the success for which he was obviously labouring so hard. Neither this sermon, nor the one which follows, need detain us any longer[4]. They suffice to illustrate the extravagances of scholastic preaching as satirized by Erasmus in the *Encomium Moriae*.

A little manuscript of the fifteenth century in the Library of Caius College, Cambridge, with matter relative to St Alban's Abbey, contains one Latin sermon for the Feast of the English proto-Martyr which must have been delivered before the University by some Bishop of Ely of the day[5]. From it we stop merely to take an unpublished example of the University Bidding Prayer, which preceded these orations, best left in its original Latin:

[1]   " Me doceant hii tres Jhesus, alma mater, Johannes;
            Spiritus omnidocens assit, modo nubila pellens,
            Hayntoun dictantem..."
(Another triplet on fol. 40.) Cf. a similar Invocation at the head, apparently, of another University sermon exercise in MS. Corpus Christi Coll. Camb. 392, fol. 253: "Maria, Jhs, Johannes, Thomas, Dunstanus assint principio meo."
[2] See Hosea xiv, 2.
[3] MS. Harl. 5398; ibid. fol. 56 b: (fol. 51 "serenissimi doctores").
[4] It may be worth remarking, however, that Haynton makes use of University imagery here; cf. God as the "doctor omnisciens et eternus"; "Universitas angelica," or "cherubica"; "Magister Veritatis," etc. For an Oxford sermon exercise for the D.D. degree, cf. John Lawerne's notes in MS. Bodl. 692, fols. 122–23 (1438).
[5] MS. Caius Coll. Camb. 230, fol. 130 et seq. (Begin: "Cani sunt sensus hominis"—Sap. iv—"et in epistola quam hodie in memoriam Passionis Sancti Protomartyris Anglorum, Albani, sua et suorum monachorum legit ecclesia....") By a Bishop of Ely, apparently because of the "jurisdictionis nostrae" following mention of the University (see Fuller's *History*, p. 55, etc.). Or was it an Archbishop of Canterbury, visiting the University, as in 1401?

In huius igitur collationis nostrae exordio, recommendo orationibus vestris sensus[1] brachii clericalis, dominum nostrum Papam, cardinales, et omnes prelatos ac ministros ecclesie, dominum nostrum cancellarium, caput hujus Universitatis venerabilis jurisdictionis nostre, cum omnibus scolaribus qui ad frugem meliorem scientiae laborant in ipsa. Ex alia parte commendo orationibus vestris predictis sensus brachii secularis, dominum nostrum regem, atque reginam, dominam matrem, dominum ducem, et omnes proceres hujus regni, cum omni populo Christiano. Et tertio commendo vobis omnes animas in purgatorio divinam misericordiam exspectantes....

The preacher ends with the usual request for Paternoster and Ave. "Sermones ad scholares"[1] may be detected in the catalogues, but they belong to other centuries than ours. There is, however, one of the kind—"to the Preachers (i.e. Dominicans) in Oxford,"[2]—in an anonymous collection presumably of the fourteenth century, to which repeated reference has been made in these pages. But beyond well-marked divisions and quotations from "Tullius," Seneca, and Isidore, in addition to the regular Fathers, no special feature appears. After so much wearisome prolixity at the seats of learning, we may be forgiven if, in passing from the scene, we refresh ourselves— according to the best models of homiletic art—with somewhat of a light and merry contrast. It comes from a vernacular homily of the period, which requires, for all its quaint eccentricity, as will be noticed, a University audience of some kind or other for its setting[3]. In expanding the story, from the "Legenda Aurea," of St Clement's conversion, among the philosophical students of Rome, the speaker has progressed as far as the unfriendly reception given to the preaching of St Barnabas, "for oure fey3the may not be preved by reson, and philosofres granteth no thinge but that resone enformeth hem." (Was all this the little scheme of a modest preacher, we are tempted to ask, tactfully introduced to smooth the way for his own simplicity[4] before another critical audience of students?)

Than oon of these philosofres come to Seynt Barnabe and asshed hym what was the cause that a flee that is so lityll a beeste hathe sixe

[1] Cf. the sermon text opps., p. 262, note 5.
[2] Cf. MS. Corpus Christi Coll. Camb. 217 (13th cent.).
[3] MS. Caius Coll. Camb. 233, fol. 229.
[4] MS. Roy. 18. B. xxiii, fol. 52 b. Cf. here, for his "uncunning," etc. Chap. I, pp. 21–22, above.

fete, and a camell that is so grete a beeste hathe but fowre. Than Barnabas answerd and seid, "I wolde answere 3ou to youre sotell question, 3iff 3e had ashed me for cause of knolache of the trowthe. But for all so muche that 3e knowe not that God that made 3ou, therfore it is well worthye that 3e erre in knolage of is creatures." Than Seynt Clement herde this wise answere of seynte Barnabe, and become oon of his disciples....The questioun that the philosofres ashed of Seynt Barnabe, I can not asoill it; but I preye the phylosofres of this worthy universite to asoyll itt, whan tham semeth good.

The *Sermones ad Status* thus passed rapidly in review, deal only with the cleric. Nor can we find to correspond to them a similar literature of the pulpit in this country as distinct in its application to the various ranks and professions of the laity[1]. At the same time we are by no means far from it, when we find ourselves listening to some mediaeval preacher in the open-air, at a public Intercessory procession, or at the regular sermon-time beneath the shadow of St Paul's. Here and in other places, as likely as not, description of one of the several familiar "figures" of the mediaeval realm will lead up to special counsel addressed in turn to the three principal estates that compose it, to clergy, nobility, and common people[2]. The speaker may possibly go further to differentiate the classes more minutely[3], to remind knighthood with Rypon[4], for example, of its particular duties and its present shortcomings; or with Brunton[5] to take the English "magnates," or the merchants to task, for their palpable lapses from the Christian ideal. "Sed ut veniamus ad exempla

---

[1] An interesting exception may have to be made in the case of MS. Add. 15095, a fifteenth-century series of "Sermones varii *ad mercatores*," in Latin, at all events written out here by an *English* scribe (Fleknowe). I have yet to discover whether from internal evidence they may be classed as an English production of the period.

[2] Cf. Wimbledon at Paul's Cross, 1388; Bromyard, *S.P.* s.v. "Compassio," "Miles," etc.; Rypon in MS. Harl. 4894, fol. 187; Brunton, as below; Myrc in the *Festiall* (E.E.T.S. ed. p. 65); MS. Roy. 18. B. xxiii; MS. Linc. Cath. Libr. A. 6. 2, fol. 68; etc., etc. Cf. also in the frequent *Moralization of Chess* (references below, on p. 326, n. 3).

[3] Cf. Bp. Brunton, in MS. Harl. 3760, fol. 61, where, in the favourite simile of the Body and the Members, he differentiates the king, princes and prelates, the judges, counsellors, doctors, knights, merchants and faithful mechanics, citizens and burgesses, peasants and labouring men. (Abroad, the *Prologue* to Jacques de Vitry's *Sermones Vulgares*, and Lecoy de la Marche, *La chaire fr.* pp. 133 et seq.)

[4] MS. Harl. 4894, fol. 188 b et seq. followed by a similar discussion of the "officium agricultorum" (and Brunton, MS. Harl. 3760, fols. 96, 152, etc.).

[5] MS. Harl. 3760, fols. 117, 124, 190 b, etc.

magis domestica," cries the latter, proceeding to discuss the "milicia Anglicana," now weak and degenerate in these days[1]. Much in the same way, the village preacher, whose detailed warnings in the *Great Sentence* have covered practically every activity and every walk of life, may put into his discourse a word for the young and for the old[2], or join with the friar in denouncing the characteristic enormities of the shop-keepers or the Law. The keen class-consciousness of feudalism is never very far from his mind, or his arguments.

Higden, whose programme of themes has been our guide thus far, passes finally from sermons at processions to sermons at funerals[3]. Again the list of examples is a small one, although, to judge from the researches of Bourgain for an earlier century[4], time was when these latter were numerous enough. Such remains as we possess, even for the fourteenth and fifteenth centuries, are yet sufficient to indicate how suitable themes— like the "Mortuus est in senectute bona, plenus dierum, divitiis et gloria," pronounced by Bishop Grandisson over the body of the Earl of Devon in 1341—were treated, "by applying them to the virtues and merits of the deceased."[5] In the case of this burial of Sir Hugh de Courtenay we are told that the funeral oration was given first in Latin, and then in French. The latter tongue was evidently a respectful concession to the nobility, who would share with the clergy present the places of honour and of chief mourning for the occasion. But one might have expected so enlightened a bishop to have suited himself to the condition of everyone in that "copious multitude" at once, by using English:

> ffor why that is your kyndly langage,
> that ʒe hafe here mast of usage,
> that cane ilk man undirstand,
> that is born in ynglande:
> ffor that langage is mast shewyd
> As wele amange lerede as lewede;

---

[1] Ibid. fol. 152.
[2] MS. Roy. 18. B. xxiii. Cf. also the special warnings for "domesmen" in MS. Harl. 45, fol. 86, or for servants (ibid. fol. 65), etc.
[3] Theme suggested, "Amicus noster dormit."
[4] Cf. *La chaire franç. au xii[e] s.* p. 202 et seq.
[5] Burial of Sir Hugh de Courtenay, Earl of Devon, at "Cowyke," near Exeter (Reg. Grandisson, Exeter, pt. ii, p. 939).

ffor Latyn as I trowe cane nane
Bot thai that hafe it of scole tane.
Some cane franche, and na latyn,
that used has court, and dwelled therin.
And some cane of latyn a party
that cane franch but feberly.
And some undirstandye ynglych,
that nouther cane latyn ne franche.
Bot lerede and lewed, alde & yonge,
All undirstandys ynglych tonge[1].

The explanation is evident, however, that in such pomps and ceremonies the vulgar tongue was looked upon as too outrageously vulgar. Latin and French alone would befit the dignified exequies of noble persons. Sir Thomas More's delightfully sarcastic picture, in a later day, of the "high solemne ceremonies about our funeralles, whereof the glory standeth us here, God wot, in very little stede, but hath on the tother side done us greate displeasure," comes forcibly to mind[2]. As a matter of fact his own complaint is heard already in the sermons of the period before us:

"Much superfluous charge used for boast and ostentacion," declared the great man, "namely, devised by the dede before his death, is of God greatly misliked;...as how we might be solemnly borne out to burying, have gay and goodly funerales, with herawdes at our hearses, and offering up our helmets, setting up our skouchin and cote armours on the wall, though ther never came harnesse on our backes, nor never ancester of oures ever bare armes before. Then devised we some doctor to make a sermon at our masse in our monthes mind, and there preache to our prayse, with some fond fantasy devised of our name; and after masse, muche feasting, ryotous and costly, and finally like mad men make men meri at our deth, and take our burying for a brideale."

Foxe makes some mention of Archbishop Arundel's eulogy at the burial of good Queen Anne of Bohemia in 1394, when that prelate, of doubtful virtue himself, actually "blamed in that sermon sharply the negligence of the prelates and other men," after the manner of our conciliar preachers, so stirred was he by the evidences of piety in the life of that lady[3]. But the

---

[1] MS. Roy. 17. C. viii, fol. 3 (Nassyngton's *Speculum Vitae*): cf. the unidentified quotation in Chaytor's *Troubadors and England*, p. 19, from MS. Camb. Univ. Libr. Ff. iv. 9.)   [2] *Supplication of Souls*, p. 335 (Engl. ed. 1557).
[3] *Acts and Mons.* vol. iii, p. 202, ed. (1855) Seeley (*Ch. Hists. of Engl.*), and compare Dean Hook, *Lives of the Archbishops*, vol. iv, p. 430.

Ꞓ Ꞇhis sermon folowynge was compyled & sayd in the Cathedrall chyrche of saynt Ꝓoule within þ cyte of Lon don by the ryght reucrende fader in god Ꝺohn byſſhop of Rocheſter, the body beynge preſent of the mooſt famouſe pꝛynce kynge Ꝺenry the.vij.the.ix.day of ꝳaye/the yere of our loꝛde god . ꝳ . CCCCC.ix. whiche sermon was enpꝛynted at the ſpecyall requeſt of þ ryght excellent pꝛyn ceſſe ꝳargarete moder vnto the sayd noble pꝛynce and Counteſſe of Rychemonde and Ꝺerby.

A ROYAL FUNERAL SERMON IN 1509
(ed. Wynkyn de Worde)

"locus classicus" for the period, will be Bishop Brunton's great funeral oration for the Black Prince, in his manuscript of sermons[1], with its echo of Poictiers, its rich praise for the uprightness, generosity, and loyalty of the great soldier "who loved the Holy Trinity above all things." It presents an interesting parallel to Bossuet's more famous utterance over the body of the Prince de Condé, with the victory of Rocroi extolled in the place of Poictiers. Thus were the mighty laid to rest. Yet the simple man, with no famous deeds to praise, might have a sermon, too. Myrc's *Festiall* offers one in which the grim fact of death itself, "the whiche iugylithe and sleithe us alle,"[2] irrespective of rank, together with the meaning of the last rites on earth, furnishes an equally potent object-lesson for the bystanders, where noble birth and rich pageantry are not. Who indeed was ever more eloquent in urging the efficacy of "the syght of corses and wepyng, that makyth a man to thenke on his deth, that ys the chefe helpe to put away synne[3]," than our mediaeval preacher himself? And his words are a vivid commentary on the more famous morality *Everyman*. The opening lines of Myrc's "In die sepulturae,"[4] then, strike the same familiar chord: "Gode men, as ȝe alle se, here is a myrroure to us alle; a corse browth to the chyrch. God have mercy on hym for hys mercy, and bryng hym into hys blysse that eure schal laston." It remains also the burden of his plaintive ending: "Wherefore uche man and womman that us wyse, make hym redy therto; for alle we schul dyon, and we wyte note how sone."

As the burial of the dead, with its grim spectacular appeal, was thus pressed into the service of preaching, in typical mediaeval fashion, so also was the marriage of the living. A "Sermo de Nupciis" in the *Festiall*[5] makes a precisely similar use of the situation, with details of the homely wedding cere-

---

[1] MS. Harl. 3760, fol. 212 et seq. (1376). Cf. fol. 213: "'Laudemus viros potentes et gloriosos"; et precipue in victoria apud Peyteris, ubi licet cum rege Francie tantus esset cuneus armatorum quod semper [the MS. here is corrupt, but the meaning is clear, 'there were 10 Frenchmen on their own soil opposed to one Englishman'], tamen, favente Deo justitie exercitui Anglicano, exercitus Francorum fuit dissipatus mirabiliter, et rex captus...."

[2] *Gesta Rom.*, 15th cent. Engl. vers. (E.E.T.S. ed. Ext. No. 33), p. 135.

[3] *Festiall* (E.E.T.S. ed.), p. 64. Cf. further in MS. Roy. 18. B. xxv, fol. 138, etc.   [4] Ibid. p. 294 et seq.   [5] Ibid. p. 289 et seq.

mony in place of the last rites of the dead. "But for ther ben many that takuth this sacrement and wyttuth lytal whatte charge is therwyth, therfore I wil schortely at this tyme schew ȝou what this sacrament is, that ȝe schullon in tyme comyng drede God the more and kepon ȝoure ordur the bettur." For the sake of variety and the unpublished page, a contemporary manuscript homily, "in solemnizatione matrimonii," will here best serve our purpose, as an illustration[1] of the discourse to be given:

"Most worchifull ffrendys," says this quaintly verbose homilist, "we be cume hedyr at this time in the name of the fader, son, & holy gost, in the honerabyll presens of our moder gostly, holy chyrche, to conjoynyn, knytt, and combyne thyse 2 persawnes by the holy sacrament of matrimonye, grauntyd to the holy dignite & ordyr of presthode. Qwyche sacrament of matrimonye is of this vertu and strengthe that thise 2 persawnes of whyche be nowe too bodyes and too sawles, durynge theyr lyves togeder schall be...one fflesche and too sawles."[2]

After what might be called a short historical preface, sketching the Genesis account of the creation of the sexes[3], he proceeds to elaborate three bonds or yokes of God which should unite the wedded—"honeste and worchep in werkynge," "true luff and ffeythefull in lyvynge,...obediens and continuall abydynge." The reader must rest satisfied with two excerpts, introducing typical features relative to the service itself. First of the ring:

And ffor this cawse is the ryng putt and sett by the husbonde upon the iiii[te] finger off the woman, ffor to showe that a true luff and precordiall affection must be betwyne hem. Cawse qwhy, as doctors sey, ther is a veyne cummynge frome the herte off a woman to the iiii[te] ffinger; and therfore the ringe is putt on the same finger, that sche shulde kepe unite and luff with hym, and he with hyr.

·   ·   ·   ·   ·   ·   ·   ·

[1] MS. Camb. Univ. Libr. Gg. vi. 16, fol. 32 et seq. With this, and the specimen in the *Festiall*, should be compared the relevant passages in MS. (Brit. Mus.) Add. 30506, leaf 25 (printed in E.E.T.S. 90, p. 5), a manual written for St Aldate's Church, Gloucester, in the fifteenth century.

[2] Cf. with Myrc's opening: "As ȝe here all seyne, a man and a woman ben weddut togydur, os the lawe of holy chyrch techuth...." Notice a sermon, "de matrimonio et ejus operibus," in MS. Salisb. Cath. Libr. 103, fols. 167–170 (e.g. (fol. 168): "aforn the sollemnyzacyon of weddyng, the banys owyn to ben askyd thre solenne dayes in holy cherche aforn the peple.")

[3] Begin: "This is wele figuryd—Gen. 4to—qwhan allmyȝty God had fformyd our forme-fadyr."

More on, ffor iiii cawses we do grettly to have thys sacrament of matromony in reverens and worschep. One cawse is ffor God hymselff was ffyrst fownder and maker of the sacrament of matrimonye. The secunde, for it was made and ordeyned off God in the most precious place that he wroghyt upon erthe, ffor it was "in paradiso terestre." The iiide cawse, for it was the ffirst sacrament that God ordeynde; and the iiiite, ffor holy chyrche hathe admytted it to be one of the vii sacraments off holy chyrche. And for thys cawse is the palle holden on theyr hedys in the messe tyme; ffor the palle representethe the dignite of matrimony. Also it is to wyte that this holy sacrament off matrimony muste be reseyvyd with a devoute herte and clene sawle, and a pure entente. Therffore holy chyrche exorteth, cownselythe, and ordenythe that bothe man and the woman be reconcylyd to clennes of lyffe by confessyon beforne the matrimony is solemnisyd ffor the encresynge and augmentynge off grace.

The learned Martène, who is not usually so generous in this respect, favours us, in his account of the dedication of a church, with a hint of the matter dealt with in the bishop's charge to the parishioners, which should form part of such proceedings[1]. When the procession, with relics, around the sacred edifice, has returned to the church-door, and the people are silent, let the prelate "have a word" to them "de honore ecclesiastico," concerning church tithes and oblations, and the anniversary of that dedication service to be observed. Let him announce to clergy and laity together in whose honour the fane has been built and consecrated, and the names of the saints whose bones are to repose there[2]. The fact that a good many of these dedicatory sermons actually remain in our manuscripts, suggests that in this country the practice was faithfully and continuously carried out[3]. Myrc's ever-ready *Festiall* again comes to the rescue, not of the bishops, of course, but rather of the parish priest, faced with the duty of supplying fresh explanatory addresses, "in memoriam," as the "chyrche-holyday" anniversary comes round[4]. That credulous ecclesiastic, yielding perhaps, even

---

[1] *Ant. Eccl. Rit.* vol. iii.

[2] For "Relike Sonday" sermons, see below in Chap. VIII, p. 351.

[3] At Cambridge alone, examples include: MSS. Jesus Coll. 65 (fol. 38 b); Corpus Christi Coll. 439 (fol. 141 b), 509 (fol. 244 b) and 524 (fol. 132); Caius Coll. 140, iii, 803 and 356; Camb. Univ. Libr. Dd. ix. 70.

[4] E.E.T.S. p. 277. Beginning: "Goode men and woymen, such a day N. ꝛe schull have your chyrche-holyday. The whech day ꝛe schull come to chyrch to worschyp God, hauyng yn mynde thre causes why the chyrche ys halowed...."

more than usual, to the festive mood of the hour, increases his racy anecdotes to the unprecedented number of five, until the expository section of his address is of the scantiest[1]. The fiends are wont to play such pranks on these occasions, and the old canon obviously enjoys the fun, as they run "among the pepullys fete hedyr and thedyr," and away out by the church door, sit on their shoulders at Mass-time, like gargoyles on the church-tower, or play the solemn bogey o' nights. So short is the little outline "in dedicatione ecclesie," of a more serious nature, in one of our Latin collections, that it seems justifiable to reproduce it here *in toto*[2]. For, apart from the interest of its references to contemporary custom, which, by the way, appear again in the *Summa Predicantium*, it serves to show how terse and vivid our Latin sermon-note can be:

"Sapientia edificavit sibi domum, excidit columpnas septem."[3] Cum aliquis princeps venturus est ad aliquem civitatem, ut teneat ibi curiam suam, cives illius civitatis preparant hospitia sua, et scutum sive aliud signum ante ostium ipsius constituunt, ad designandum ad cujus opus sit hospitium captum. Ita preparemus hospitia nostra ad recipiendum Dei sapientiam, qui hodie in nobis templum suum dedicare dignatus est. Egregium autem scutum ostio domus sue affigit, qui pallium vel tunicam utcunque vetustam collo pauperis suspendit. Premittendi sunt et precones qui moneant ut fiat panis et potus ad habundantiam. Precones sunt predicatores, de quorum numero, licet peccatorum summus, ego sum, qui moneo ut ista fiant—scil. bona opera et lacrime habundantes—quibus satiari et inebriari anima debet. Que ut nobis concedat dominus, dicat quilibet—"Pater Noster."

Our last group of sermons proper is to be determined not by subject-matter, but by style. These are the sermons in verse; therefore, presumably, in further contrast to the preceding, intended for reading or recitation in their entirety, without any expansions or amendment. The pulpit, as indeed we have seen already, was quite unable to escape a general contagion which involved alike the song of the minstrel, the cries of the street, and even such prosaic necessities as medical receipts. Stray

---

[1] These tales include a ghost-story from the neighbourhood ("Lulsull," or Lilleshall), and others from *Leg. Aurea, Gestes of Fraunce*, etc.

[2] MS. Caius Coll. Camb. 233, fols. 108 b–109. (It is likely, I think, that the ending proves this to be only an ante-theme, jotted down by the writer.)

[3] Prov. ix, 1.

verse in a Latin prose homily may denote one of two purposes. As in the recapitulation of a University sermon, recently mentioned[1], the lines, in this case themselves in Latin, may be there to assist the preacher, by recalling to his mind the chief divisions of his theme, as he progresses. On the other hand, and far more often, when appearing in English, they may serve to do a kindred work for the listeners, especially if the quotation takes the form of a popular rhyming summary of the day. Such, for example, are the quaint verses which repeatedly epitomize the Sacraments[2], or the Ten Commandments[3]. A homily collection in the Worcester Cathedral Library, containing an example of the latter, introduces similarly a warning quatrain for parents, calculated no doubt to arrest attention at the time of delivery, and afterwards to remain, "running in their heads," as the vulgar expression goes, until practice has become second nature:

> Chaste well (?) ʒoure childeryn, wyll thay ben ʒong,
> Of werke, of dede, of speche, of tong:
> For yf ʒe leten hym be to bold
> Hyt wol ʒow greve wen they ben olde[4].

Of all such collections of popular rhyming verse probably none can compare with that of friar John of Grimston's pulpit Commonplace Book, now in the Advocates' Library, in Edinburgh[5]. Its pages teem with crude English rhymes of anything from two to six lines, as well as longer and more tasteful compositions akin to the poetry of the better known Vernon MS.

---

[1] See above, p. 260.

[2] Cf. MS. Add. 24660, fol. 39 (a *Sermo de vii Sacramentis*).

[3] Cf. MS. Gray's Inn Libr. 15 (fol. ult. of Staunton's tract); MS. Bodl. 410, fol. 21 (*Fascic. Morum*); MSS. Add. 25031, fol. 5 b; 37049, fol. 20 b; Harl. 6580, 7578; Lansd. 344; Roy. 8. E. v; etc.; MS. Advoc. Libr. Edinburgh, 18. 7. 21, fol. 128 b (Grimston); *Reliq. Antiq.* vol. i, p. 49 (MS. Jesus Coll. Camb.).

[4] MS. Worc. Cath. Libr. F. 19, fol. 166. (This and a previous quotation have been kindly supplied to me by Canon J. M. Wilson.) Among transcripts kindly sent me by Canon R. M. Woolley, of Lincoln, I find the verse again in a *Sermo de Primo Mandato 2ᵉ Tabule*, MS. Linc. Cath. Libr. A. 6. 19, fol. 164:

> "Chasteyz ʒow children wyl thei be ʒownge
> Of werk, of dede, of speche, of townge.
> ffor ʒif ʒe lete them be to bolde,
> Thei wole ʒow greveyn wan ʒe be hold."

Again in MS. Bodl. 410, fol. 9 b (*Fasc. Mor.*).

[5] MS. 18. 7. 21. (Some French verse on fol. 46.)

at Oxford. Indeed, the compiler of a recently issued volume of *English Religious Lyrics of the Fourteenth Century* has actually gone to the former and to other homiletical works in Latin for no less than thirty of his pieces[1]. Furthermore, he is of the opinion[2] that friar Herebert's English translations of Latin hymns in Phillipps MS. 8336, "were designed primarily for pulpit use," and represent an early Franciscan attempt to introduce them thus to popular sermon audiences[3].

Such versifying, then, is but part of the orator's regular mode of strengthening the failing memories, or driving home particular points in a popular way. But now we are to be concerned with something on a much larger scale, where the entire homily becomes metrical. "Sermones Rimati," Latin sermons in rhymed prose, that is to say, and "Versus Colorati," had been the objects of special attacks on the part of the pulpit purists of the thirteenth century[4]. Considered by them as theatrical and unspiritual, grotesque enough to us nowadays, they were yet very much to the liking of audiences then. As Peter of Limoges pointed out, they had become a deadly snare for the fashionable preachers who sought to seduce the ear, rather than to convert the soul. But those early critics would have found little of the sort to distress them, had they been able to look into our own Latin compilations of the fourteenth and fifteenth centuries[5].

---

[1] Carleton Brown (Oxf. Univ. Press, 1924).
[2] Ibid. Introd., p. xiv.
[3] Herebert died in 1333. Among further examples of stray verse in *Latin* sermon collections, I note such, for example, as:
>"Godes grete godnysse and hys longe abydynge,
>Crystes open exemple, & hys holy techynge
>Hard dom ordayned for oure punyschement
>And grete mede y-schape for oure amendement"

(MS. Caius Coll. Camb. 334, fol. 179 b), or in a *Sermo de Primo Mandato*:
>"Alas, alas, that ever I was born
>ffor body and soule I am forlorn."

(MS. Linc. Cath. Libr. A. 6. 19, fol. 163). Cf. also further in the Franciscan *Fasciculus Morum*.
[4] Cf. Lecoy de la Marche (*La chaire fr.*), pp. 279–85: "Quod est contra illos qui faciunt sermones rimatos," etc.; Hauréau, *Quelques MSS.* vol. iv, p. 139; etc., etc.
[5] There is still, however, an interesting reference to be found to them in Thomas Walley's tractate on preaching (MS. Harl. 635, etc.; first half of the fourteenth century). He says: "...et tunc confunditur predicator; quia se verbis plus quam sententia alligavit, *quem defectum specialiter inducunt sermones multum rithmici*, vel nimis politi; et est culpa predicatoris, qui in curiositate conatur excedere." Cf. further, below, pp. 328–9.

In the vernacular literature of religious instruction, on the other hand, we are faced with a persistent and well-marked English metrical tradition; and the first task is to decide how much of this literature can be definitely ascribed to the actual work of the pulpit. Very few of these so-called didactic poems, to begin with, bear the titles of "sermon" or "homily." Nevertheless, many of them can be shown to possess important features which they share in common with those that are thus labelled. A good illustration occurs in the case of the Prologue to the so-called *North-English Homily Collection*, edited by John Small from a manuscript in the Library of the Royal College of Physicians in Edinburgh, which is repeated again and again, in some form or other, elsewhere. Clerks, it declares, in effect, can look into the mirror of their Latin and French books, and understand what they read, or else what is read to them in lessons at the Mass-time. "Bot all men can nought, i-wisse, undirstand latyne ne frankisse," especially the "lewid men" who long in vain to know the message of the gospels. Therefore for these is the work undertaken, while the "lered" may profit as well[1]. But although we may be well aware that of the many who could understand English, only a comparatively few could read it, such comments as these need not imply more than domestic reading aloud by the sufficiently literate "householder," who, as brother Whitford has depicted[2], religiously gathers his folk around the board at daily prayers, or on a Sunday afternoon. Yet for once it is possible to go farther. This same collection offers us a fragment of clearer evidence as to its use in church, in the shape of a direction to the preacher—for little else can it be—to omit certain Latin passages before lay-folk, which, by

---

[1] *Engl. Met. Homs.* ed. Small, Edinburgh, 1862, p. 3. By the kindness of the Librarian of the Royal College of Physicians, Edinburgh, I was recently able to examine this most interesting early 14th cent. MS. for myself. Since Small's day it has been handsomely remounted, page by page, in a quarto volume. Cf. with the above a French example:

> "A la simple gent
> Ai fait simplement
> Un simple sermon.
> Ne l'fiz as letrez
> Car il mit assez
> Escriz et raisum."
>
> (Lecoy de la Marche, p. 283.)

[2] *Werke for Housholders.*

implication, he very naturally means would only be suitable for the clerical audiences: "Isti versus omittantur a lectore *quando legit Anglicum coram laycis.*"[1] When, therefore, further parallels of treatment in the earlier prose homily collections of this country have been duly noted, and parallels of form, as offered by the "Li sermons" of Geoffrey of Waterford, and other sermons in rhymed verse on the continent[2], we may rest convinced that these English metrical lives of saints and gospel expositions were undoubtedly read or recited "ad populum" on feast-days and Sundays, in our own churches[3]. The same practice is reflected again in the closing lines of that highly apocryphal poem known as *The Develis Parlament*. Its extravagances and popular superstition are certainly no worse than much in the *Festiall*:

> This song that y have sunge ʒou heere,
> Is clepid the develis perlament:
> Thereof is red in tyme of ʒeere
> On the first Sunday of clene lent[4].

Finally, if a suspicion still lingers that the use of such rhyming verse as medium for serious and formal doctrine would be beneath the dignity of the priesthood, it is only necessary to point to Myrc's *Instructions for Parish Priests*, or Gaytrige's

---

[1] MS. Roy. Coll. of Phys. fol. 22 b, a rubric written between the lines of verse (*Engl. Met. Homs.* p. 26). Cf. also Miss Deanesly's remarks in her "Gospel-Harm. of Jo. de Caulibus," in *Collect. Franc.* vol. ii, p. 19.

[2] Lecoy de la Marche, p. 282, etc.

[3] Compare, for example, the Prologue to Nassyngton's *Spec. Vitae*, MS. Roy. 17. C. viii, fol. 2:

> "Good men and women, I yow pray,
> Takys goode keep to that I say,
> And takys no reward to my dedys,
> All if I be synfull that redys:
>
> . . . .
>
> Bot to my wordes anely takes kepe,
> And whiles I speke, kepe you fro slepp.". . .

or *The Spore of Love* (St Edmund's *Spec.*) in E.E.T.S., O.S. 89, p. 268:

> "God that art of miʒtes most,
> Ffadir, and sone, and holi gost,
> Thow graunte hem alle thi blessynge,
> That herken wel to this talkynge."

(cf. Myrc's regular phrase for preaching ("honest *talkyng*") *Festiall*, E.E.T.S. p. 191; and elsewhere, in a sermon in MS. Harl. 2398, fol. 175 b— "goede & lovelych *talkyng*").

[4] E.E.T.S., O.S. No. 24.

Sermon, two works of this character definitely "propter presbiterum parochialem instruendum,"[1] and not intended for direct consumption by the lay-folk at all. The rhyming sermons of the friars, indeed, had been one of Wycliffe's complaints[2].

When once the theory has been accepted, much in the structure of the poems and treatises themselves goes to confirm belief. Sometimes the opening lines have all the marks of the formal sermon ante-theme. This is clearly shown in Robert of Brunne's free translation of what is known as St Bonaventura's *Meditations on the Supper of Our Lord*[3]:

> Alle my3ty God yn trynyte,
> Now and ever wyth us be;
> For thy sones passyun,
> Save alle thys congregacyun;
> And graunte us grace of gode lyvyng
> To wynne us blysse wythouten endyng.
> Now every man, yn hys degre,
> Sey amen, amen, pur charyte....

Sometimes the typical Latin theme from Scripture stands at the head; and even so lengthy a work as the *Hali Maidenhed*[4] is rightly described, in the words of Ten Brink[5], as an alliterative homily on a text. Everywhere a use of "exempla" and the sermon-conclusion proclaims the same kinship. In our period the several versions of the metrical *Sermo de festo Corporis Christi*[6] incorporate every one of these traits, for an occasion, too, not out of keeping with the more festive spirit of song and poem. Fortunately there is little need to add anything here in illustration of a literature so well represented in modern reprint, apart from what has just been said of its relations with preaching[7].

---

[1] E.E.T.S., O.S. No. 31, p. 1; cf. again in the Preface to MS. Add. 36983 (c. 1442):

> "Bothe for clerkys and for lewed men
> This Englysch tale ys yfounde."

[2] I take it his remarks apply to metrical sermons in English, not Latin "sermones rythmici" (cf. his phrase "apocryphal poems"). See the references collected in Miss Deanesly's *Lollard Bible*, from Loserth, etc., pp. 148 and 244.

[3] E.E.T.S., O.S. No. 60. But see for authorship here, p. 288, n. 2.

[4] E.E.T.S., O.S. No. 60.

[5] See also his own discussion of the verse homily, p. 211 et seq. and p. 280 et seq. (*Hist. of Engl. Lit.* vol. i).

[6] E.E.T.S., O.S. No. 98, p. 168 ff.

[7] See especially the numerous references given in Carleton Brown's *Register of Middle English verse*.

The *Ormulum* of the thirteenth century, for example, whose somewhat long-winded author is at pains to explain himself in his preface, is again clearly homiletical in its intention:

> Icc hafe sammnedd of thiss boc   [gathered]
> Tha goddspelless neh alle,
> That sinndenn o the messe boc,   [that are within]
> Inn all the ʒer att messe:
> Annd azz affterr the goddspell staunt
> That tatt te Goddspell menethth,
> *Thatt mann birrth spellenn to the follc*   [ought to preach]
> Off theʒʒre sawle nede.

At the beginning of the next century the *Cursor Mundi* sets out for a similar mission, with the whole Scripture, both of Old Testament and New, as its message[1]. By the time that the age of Rolle and the Yorkshiremen is reached, the little one has become a thousand, overflowing the land, and blotting out all valid distinctions between treatise and poem and sermon proper[2]. Dan John Gaytrige's *Sermon*, which Skeat was apparently the first to recognize as imperfect alliterative verse, in spite of its being written in prose form in the manuscripts, belongs equally to all three categories[3]. So, too, Robert of Brunne's metrical translation of Waddington's *Manuel des Pechiez*[4], the *Ayenbite of Inwyt*, or the *Pricke of Conscience*, various English versions of Lorens' *Somme des vices et des vertus*, or Nassyngton's *Speculum Vitae*, and many treatises more with names now familiar in English literature[5]. All might well have been read from the pulpit in sections of suitable length, by priests more or less incapable of independent speech. Some works, like Lydgate's *Merita Missae* for example[6], have

[1] An incomplete text of this work is to be found alongside the *Engl. Met. Homs.* in the MS. Roy. Coll. of Phys., Edinburgh, recently alluded to, i.e. with definite pulpit matter.

[2] Thus, too, Ten Brink, *Hist. of Engl. Lit.* vol. i, p. 211.

[3] Cf. also the Didactic verse with "Tabula super Omelias" which accompanies it in MS. Add. 25006 (fol. 11 b).

[4] I.e. the *Handlynge Synne* (E.E.T.S., O.S. Nos. 119 and 123).

[5] Cf. the *Speculum* of St Edmund, two metrical versions of which may be found in the Vernon MS. (E.E.T.S., O.S. No. 89, pp. 221 et seq. and 268 et seq.); also the *Speculum* of Guy of Warwick (MS. Arund. 140, fol. 147 et seq.; also publ. in Horstmann, vol. ii, p. 24 et seq.); *Spiritus Guydonis* (Horstmann, vol. ii, p. 292 et seq.); a metrical Engl. vers. of Grossetête's *Castel of Love* in the Vernon MS. (E.E.T.S., O.S. No. 98, p. 355); etc., etc.

[6] Printed in E.E.T.S., O.S. No. 71, p. 148 et seq. (from MS. Cotton, Tit. A. xxvi, fol. 154).

actual length as well as style ready in their favour. Nor are there wanting here and there, in what are obviously preachers' manuscripts, rude and little-known metrical homilies, like one in a fifteenth-century Bodleian codex whose doggerel lines begin thus:

> My dere frendis I ȝou pray
> ffoure thingis in ȝour hertes bere away....[1]

Of the vernacular treatises in verse, something more will be said in the chapter that follows. Together with others in prose they constitute the important link between literature for the pulpit, and literature for the pew or the domestic hearth.

---

[1] MS. Douce, 107, fols. 62–65. Mem. also Bozon's seven little metrical sermons in French; see P. Meyer's ed. of the *Contes*, p. xlv, etc.

CHAPTER VII

MANUALS AND TREATISES

THE place of honour next to the sermon in any survey of
mediaeval pulpit literature should go by right to the great
Latin sermon "encyclopedias," which, though comparatively
few in this country, can yet boast of the *Summa Predicantium*
among their number, as an English *chef d'œuvre*. In the present
case, however, it is proposed to deal first with the more com-
plicated question of the ordinary religious treatises, leaving the
Summa and its kind to be viewed as the final culmination of all
types and tendencies in contemporary homiletic composition.
The student who gets to work in the later mediaeval library
finds before long that he has exhausted all the more concentrated
and independent sermon collections of his period. He has then
to fall back upon odd specimens and little isolated groups
scattered about among the pages of various volumes of devotional tracts and commentaries. Sooner or later the question
arises—should he include in his examination these tracts too?
The prospect is sufficiently unattractive to compel some preliminary taking of thought: "Ther beth so manye bokes and
tretees of vyces and vertues and of dyvers doctrynes, that this
schort lyfe schalle rathere have an end e of anye manne, thanne he
maye owthere studye hem or rede hem."[1] That, indeed, was a
contemporary opinion; but it seems almost as true to-day among
the Harleian Manuscripts at the British Museum, or the several
mediaeval Bodleian collections at Oxford. Many of these works
are in English, and would seem intended for devotional reading
by the lay-folk. Yet a sentence or two in a Prologue, the setting
of a text or a rubric, the turn of phrases, much as we have seen
in the sermons in verse, will show that their affinity with the
actual discoursing of the preachers cannot really be questioned[2].

---

[1] *Orologium Sapientie*, MS. Douce 114, fol. 90, printed in *Anglia*, vol. x,
p. 328.
[2] Cf. MS. Harl. 45, fol. 167 b: "he that wole ofte and devoutliche *hyre*
and understonde this writyng," etc. Even the *Ayenbite of Inwyt* is concluded
by a sermon from the author (MS. Arundel 57). Furthermore, compare the
frequent pulpit modes of address in such treatises as *Jacob's Well* in MS.
Salisb. Cath. Libr. 103, or the St Alban's MS. treatise on the Commandments: "A, dere frendis!"; "The other day I tolde ȝou...," etc.

Nor, moreover, do they raise merely the question of supplies *for* the pulpit. As often they are an important supply *from* it as well. They reveal to us how, as lay-reading increased, the simpler message declaimed in church passed eventually into the religious handbook of the home, there indeed to play no small part in creating in turn that peculiarly English type of staid and independent domestic piety which blossomed out into the Puritanism of subsequent centuries. When the present survey is complete, it will be seen that, in this work of evangelization by means of the vernacular page, *Piers Plowman's Vision* is as much the direct offspring of English mediaeval preaching as the most commonplace tracts on the Commandments, or the *Pricke of Conscience*. To be able thus to throw so remarkable a bridge across the chasm of the Reformation is no small achievement for our little sermon-books and treatises, and will be recognized, it is hoped, as one more justification of their study. This after all is where our stubborn Puritan temper comes from—not from Protestant Geneva or Wittenberg, but mediaeval Yorkshire. It is the vigorous unsacerdotalism of Rolle, coupled with the strict religious discipline for the household which he handed on from St Edmund Rich and others, that re-emerges, by means of this homely literature, in the sturdy sixteenth and seventeenth-century yeomen of England. His mystical fire may burn low for a while; but it will leap again in Bunyan and in Penn. Sometimes the subsequent careful notes and scoring, the rare erasures, the names entered by later hands in these very sermons and handbooks, seem to give almost tangible evidence of the continuity of use[1]. Their influence stalks on silent, but wonderfully real and alive from generation to generation, troubling little about the noisy clash of theologians and parties without. For round the family board, and in the hearts of the peasantry, the Reformation meant no such break with the past as many would have us believe.

---

[1] Cf. a marginal note in the Brunton sermons, MS. Harl. 3760, fol. 96: "Moderni papistae haec attribuunt papae...." An amusing case which has come to my notice is in MS. Linc. Cath. Libr. A. 6. 2, fol. 38. Against the passage in the sermon text—"To this we have a glorius exsampyll of our blessid lady..."—is a neat marginal comment, in a sixteenth century (?) hand—"Here begyndes a notabell lye...!" Evidently the same hand has cancelled the words "Pope of Rome," on fol. 133 b, etc. See also below in Appdx. v, and compare the Tudor editions of *Piers Plowman*, etc.

To speak thus early in generalities, while the task of investigating the tracts themselves remains still unattempted, might seem strangely out of place. Yet, as a prelude to what must follow, it is not so fanciful or irrelevant after all, since there is a smaller, though not dissimilar, gap bridged by them within the limits of our own two mediaeval centuries. The vernacular treatise itself, indeed, is often at first sight a strangely composite structure of mingled Wycliffite and Orthodox elements. More than twenty-five years ago, in an article published in the *Dublin Review*, Dr Gasquet attacked the "unwarranted assumption" with which many tracts and booklets of the period, as he said, which dealt openly with abuses needing correction, were ascribed to the Lollards[1]. Although some amends have been made since then, in the case of English tracts wrongly attributed to the Reformer himself, it would seem that there is more yet to be done in vindication of Dr Gasquet's words. The amazing charges and self-criticism that come from within the Church itself, from the lips of friars and prelates, have been pointed out already in some of our Latin sermons. But so far little has been heard from the sermon-books of the inferior clergy. We have now to learn that in these very "tracts and booklets" we have a pulpit literature, prepared for them by equally zealous writers, an activity in fact, already referred to in the opening sketch of the last chapter as an important parallel development which must not be overlooked.

Just because it is deliberately designed for the use of the simpler village parson who speaks only to his lay parishioners, it is natural enough that there should be comparatively very little actual criticism of fellow "clerici" in his preaching-guide. Yet, although its work lay elsewhere with elementary religious instruction, and its revelations come rather in the nature of casual "asides," the fact remains that the hypercritical Lollard himself on occasion found their spirit sufficiently to his liking to make use of them for his purposes. The history of a single composition of this kind exhibits, in most illuminating fashion, every distinctive stage in the process we are about to trace. The thirteenth-century Constitutions framed in Latin by Archbishop Peckham[2], himself a friar, for the non-preaching clergy,

---

[1] *Dublin Review*, 1897, art. i, p. 258.
[2] For similar earlier Constitutions, see in Wilkins, *Conc.* etc.

and re-stated by Archbishop Thoresby of York half a century later, were translated into English in expanded form, at the latter's request, for the benefit of those priests unable to understand them in their original tongue. Thus fashioned ready for the pulpit, and multiplied, "Dan Gaytrige's sermon" as the translation was sometimes called, survived long enough to undergo a further expansion at Lollard hands[1].

In the first place, then, Peckham's original outline of 1281 may be held to represent for us the several Latin tracts of his day, written by friar and bishop, which Rolle and his Yorkshire contemporaries were to offer at length to clergy and laity in a homely English[2]. The actual clauses of the Decree remind us that, whereas the polished argumentative utterances of men trained in the schools were not for such as these, even the most ill-equipped priest of all was expected to give his outline instruction to the parish, four times annually, on Paternoster, Ave, Creed, Commandments, vices and virtues, and the rest. But his knowledge of Latin was execrable, if not in many cases quite useless. Therefore the monk of St Mary's, the hermits, canons and other kindly folk, subsequently taking pity on him and his flock, give him outlines in English, and even better things, vernacular expositions enriched with charming "exempla" and similitudes, vying with the "beutis" of the Latin preachers, sometimes indistinguishable from the regular sermon courses themselves. So Myrc can cry in his rhyming manual:

> Wharefore, thou preste curatoure,
> ȝef thou plese thy sauyoure,
> Loke thou moste on thys werk;
> For here thou myȝte fynde and rede
> That the behoveth to conne nede,
> How thou schalt thy paresche preche,
> And what the nedeth hem to teche,
> And whyche thou moste thy self be[3].

---

[1] All the versions appear in E.E.T.S., O.S. No. 118. In one form or another this programme remains the backbone of every subsequent treatise. For another English translation made of the Peckham Decrees, see a letter from Bp. Stafford (Bath and Wells) to his archdeacon, 1435 (Reg. Stafford, Bath and Wells, Somerset Rec. Soc. p. 173).

[2] For a fifteenth century French example, cf. MS. Add. 29279 (fol. 49 b): "L'abc des simples gens...qui contient la patenostre...et l'ave Maria...et le credo...et les x commandemens, et plusieurs autres poins de nostre religion cretienne."

[3] E.E.T.S., O.S. No. 31, p. 1.

The introduction of these vernacular instruction-books, blessed by episcopal authority as we said, at length gave the Lollard his chance to adapt them for widespread propaganda among the reading lay-folk. With "enlightened" criticisms and doctrines added to the original texts, with fresh treatises of his own compiled on the old familiar lines, with a Bible in the vernacular, Wycliffe's dream of a reformed Christian people might well seem capable of realization by means of the written word alone, without waiting for a reformed hierarchy.

In accord with the more literary purposes of the present review, it is advisable merely to establish what relationship we can between these religious treatises and the pulpit proper, leaving their actual contents for some later study. First, then, of the relations of external form and style—a problem no harder than that presented by the metrical pieces. The method of explaining the Creed, clause by clause, in a sermon, is at least as old as the *Sermo de Symbolo ad catechumenos*, attributed to Augustine: commonsense suggests that it is a great deal older. Here, in later mediaeval England, a set of the briefest Latin sermons of the fourteenth century[1] will deal exclusively with each leading point of doctrine prescribed by the Peckham Decrees, in turn; while a later vernacular preacher of Myrc's style builds a continuous course of instruction on the Ten Commandments into the fabric of some consecutive Sunday discourses[2]. On the other hand, what are already familiar to us as John Waldeby's Latin treatises on the Lord's Prayer, Angelic Salutation (Ave), and the *Symbolum* (Creed), apart from their obvious structure and their source as popular sermons in York, may be seen still coupled with the word "Homilia" in the margins[3].

Furthermore, the metrical *Sermo de Festo Corporis Christi*, for example, in its various manuscript editions, ostensibly illustrates the very process of transformation from sermon to

---

[1] MS. Add. 24660, fols. 35–42. Cf. the late fifteenth-century vernacular preacher's presentation of the same in outline *in a sermon*, "Dom. v^a post oct. Epiphanie" (MS. Linc. Cath. Libr. A. 6. 2, fols. 64, 64 b).

[2] MS. Roy. 18. B. xxiii, fol. 86 et seq.; cf. also Rypon, in Latin (MS. Harl. 4894, fols. 67 and 187).

[3] Cf. MS. Roy. 8. C. i, fol. 46.

treatise, in the making[1]. In the oldest version of the text, apparently that of MS. Harl. 4196, the title "Sermo" stands clearly as above, and is followed by a Latin text from Psalm lxxvii, 25[2]. By the time MS. Camb. Univ. Libr. Dd. i. i is reached, the word "Sermo" has disappeared, although the text is retained, and the homily opens with a short Latin "exordium" —"In nomine summi salvatoris...." Finally, the Vernon Manuscript version (f. cxcv b), the latest of all, dispenses alike with "Sermo" and text. Our homily has now become a tract— *de festo Corporis Christi.* The composition which happens to follow this one in the Vernon MS. would seem to afford us a glimpse of the reverse process. For here an account of the seven miracles of the body of Christ is extracted from Robert of Brunne's *Handlynge Synne,* and given a formal sermon ante-theme and ending of its own by the new writer. In a similar way, it would be easy to show, in the case of compositions by Rolle, how frequently, with the omission of a name or the re-setting of a title, the adaptation of tract to sermon or sermon to tract is repeated according to the immediate intent of the compilation in hand[3].

Sometimes the treatise gives more special indication of the body of readers—clergy or laity—it was intended to serve. Wherever the familiar rubric occurs—"Sacerdos parochialis tenetur per canones docere et predicare in lingua materna quater in anno," etc.[4]—at the head of a typical instructional programme, the purport has been inscribed in the first word. Equally clearly for the priest alone are the treatises in Latin, such, for example, as a "Compilatio brevis et utilis," on the usual lines, by no less interesting a personage than the energetic friar,

---

[1] I follow, as to dates of the various MSS. concerned, the editor's judgement here: for the theory he is *not* responsible (E.E.T.S., O.S. No. 98).

[2] "Panem angelorum manducavit homo." ("Man etith (!) aungelis brede.")

[3] Cf. the *Judica me, Deus* in MS. Add. 21202 (fol. 87), identified by me with Rolle's *Libellus,* and other parallel MS. versions illustrated in Horstmann, again called "Sermo ejusdem Ric. Hampol," in MS. Douce 107, fol. 14 b. Cf., too, such *Adaptaciones* as supplied in MS. Salisb. Cath. Libr. 166, fol. 133, and below, p. 306, n. 2.

[4] Cf. MS. Bodl. 110, fol. 155; MS. Lansd. 379, fol. 23 (beginning "Constit. provinc. Johan. Peccham, de officio archipresbyteri, capitulo—Ignoranc. sac...."); MS. Burney 356, p. 80, and tracts by Burgo, Watton, etc.

"Thomas Brakkele," of the Paston Letters[1]. Its language confirms the statement of the Prologue—"ad instructionem juniorum, quibus non vacat opusculorum variorum prolixitatem perscrutari de dictis Catholicorum magistrorum, haec sequentia compilata sunt"—as expressed likewise in the Prologue to Felton's Latin *Sermones*. A vernacular *Memoriale Credentium*, on the other hand, followed in the manuscript volume[2] by a tract on the Commandments, and some odd sermons, gives significant advice direct to the layman, and throws further light on the dual use of these writings, which we have been trying to emphasize:

> Al that is y-wryte may be expounyd and y-seyde. Yf ʒe conneth nouʒt understonde what is y-wryte, thenne hyre ʒe blythely the goednesse that men seyth, when thou hyrest eny thynge of holy wryt in commune sermones, other in pryvy collatiouns[3].

Passing to relations in matter and authorship, we propose to deal only with some leading examples of the literature before us. If these can be connected together, and shown to spring from a general desire to supply the wants of the English pulpit in our period and the century preceding it, there is little need to worry about the rest. They are mere insignificant imitations that continue to increase through the remaining years. For the centuries thus selected we cannot do better than start with Rolle himself, and his ringing challenge: "Saltem vobis ostendam in scribendo, qui necessitatem habetis predicare!" The very fact that, like another Wycliffe, he has been loaded with too many anonymous works in the past, is only one more tribute to his lasting genius. Manuscript after manuscript of the fifteenth century will be found to contain some treatise or homily which at one time or another has been attributed to his authorship, especially those most likely to have constituted, within the one pair of covers, the "Preacher's Library" of some more fortunate

---

[1] MS. Camb. Univ. Libr. Ff. 1. 18, fol. 7 et seq. (Readers will recall the report of his sermon in MS. Add. 34888, fol. 171.) See also Bennett, *The Pastons and their England* (1922), *passim*.

[2] MS. Harl. 2398. This, I find, is, after all, only a free rendering of a passage of Rolle's (?) translation of the *Speculum of St Edmund* (see E.E.T.S. O.S. No. 26, p. 22). It provides therefore one more interesting link with the Yorkshire writers.

[3] Ibid. fol. 61 b. See further, above, Chap. VI, p. 274, etc.

parish priest[1]. Horstmann has called him a link between Bonaventura and the Reformers. But his significance, and that of his
Yorkshire fellow-writers for the mediaeval pulpit in England,
is something far wider. The treasured piety and mysticism
from the last great preaching revival of the thirteenth century,
as stored in the smaller French or Latin tracts, was now to be
opened up, as we have seen, to a much larger public, by the
medium of a virile English dialect[2]. The very words of earlier
friars and their friends were to be made available for the use
of their rivals, the "seculars," though no subsequent friar might
be found willing to do the work of such translation and
"vulgarization."

Early English tracts on vices and virtues[3] there had been,
indeed, even before Mannyng undertook his translation of
William of Waddington's *Le Manuel des Pechiez* in 1303; but
nothing in any way comparable to the really generous output
of these later popularisers, so well represented in Horstmann's
two capacious volumes. Leaving on one side the more slender
mystical pieces which may best stand for the hermit of Hampole's own unique personality, there is really little else than a
mass of translations, adaptations, expansions of the literature
of earlier moralists. Through these and successive vernacular
manuals of all kinds, there recur now and again certain marked
features betraying the common ancestry and kinship. Vivid

---

[1] Cf., for example, the MS. Add. 21202 (15th cent.) aforementioned, containing Watton's *Spec. Christ.* (fols. 1–70), a *Forma Sermonum* (fols. 71–73),
and the odd sermons (fols. 73–99), which include the *Libellus* of Rolle. This
MS. bears the name (15th cent.) of dom. Wm. Woddrest, doubtless a priest
of very modest learning, and certainly no graduate. Cf., further, MS. Linc.
Cath. Libr. C. 4. 6, containing much the same as in the *Flos Florum*, mentioned below on p. 298 (works of Rolle, *Medit.* of St Bernard, Anselm's
Elucid.); MS. Laing 140, Univ. Libr. Edinburgh; etc., etc. The examples of
this type of MS. in the Bodleian collections are exceedingly numerous. See,
for example, the revised edition of the *Catalogue of the Western MSS.* here
(Madan and Craster), vols. i and ii, etc.

[2] Even the mystical treatises of great fourteenth-century preachers of the
continent like Suso and Ruysbroek were made available for the English
pulpit, in English translations (cf. MS. Add. 37790, containing Ruysbroek's
Trettesse of perfeccion off the sonnys of God (fol. 115), Suso, *Horolog. Sapientiae* (fol. 135 b; part only as in MS. Add. 37049; but all in MS. Douce 114),
etc.; two of these translations here bear the dates 1434–5).

[3] Cf. *Vices and Virtues*, a middle Engl. Dialogue, c. 1200 (E.E.T.S., O.S.
Nos. 89 and 159); or *Sawle warde* (early 13th cent.) (E.E.T.S., O.S. No. 34);
MS. Stowe 34.

THE MASTER HOMILIST AND HIS PUPILS
(From a XV century edition of the *Meditationes* of
St Bonaventura (Pseud.))

sketches of the suffering Jesus in the Courtyard or on the Cross, plaintive appeals from the Virgin's woes[1], re-echo to us the original eloquence of St Bernard, or the so-called *Meditations of St Bonaventura*[2] in the naïve language of the translators. The somewhat ascetic piety of St Edmund Rich breathes likewise afresh through the many English versions of his *Speculum* in prose and verse—for at least one of which Rolle himself has been considered responsible[3]—or again, in the typical directions for private prayer incorporated elsewhere. A conclusion to the English version of the *Speculum Vitae Christi* acknowledges, in illuminating fashion, that free-and-easy treatment of the older sources by mediaeval translators, which has so often perplexed the modern investigator. Says the writer: "for als moche as hit ys here thus wreten in englysshe tonge, *lengere in many parties, and in othere maner than ys the latyn of Bonaventure,* therefore hit semeth not convenient to folowe the processe there of by the dayes of the wyke, aftir the entente of the forsayde Bonaventure, for hit were to tediose, as me thenketh...."[4] The formal treatment of virtues and vices will probably hark back most often to the famous model of Lorens; or the writer may prefer, with Lydgate, the method of personification that was used in Bishop Grossetête's *Castel of Love* (Chasteau d'amour)[5]. The tradition of the *Speculum* or *Mirrour* goes on and expands, as indeed every

---

[1] Cf. MS. Roy. 18. B. xxiii, fols. 83, 84 b (here the reference is to St Bernard by name), 88 b et seq.; MS. Harl. 2398, fol. 186 et seq., etc.; MS. St Albans Cath. fol. 20 (MS. Laud Misc. 23), etc., etc.

[2] These were apparently first translated by Mannyng, c. 1320 (E.E.T.S., O.S. No. 60). For a scholarly account of the English versions of this work and its original author, see Miss Deanesly's "Gospel-Harmony of John de Caulibus," in *Collect. Francisc.* (B.S.F.S.), II, ii, pp. 10–19.

[3] See Horstmann, vol. i, p. 219. Note also, in addition to metrical versions mentioned above, a prose version, in E.E.T.S., O.S. No. 26, p. 15 et seq. (from Thornton MS. Linc. Cath. Libr.). The meditations for the hours in *Memoriale Credentium* (MS. Harl. 2398, fol. 64 et seq.) seem to show the direct influence of this work.

[4] MS. Arundel 364, fol. 204.

[5] It is worth noting here, for our general argument, that a prose version of this work was made by another Yorkshire monk (of Sawley) with additions (MS. Egerton 927; see E.E.T.S., O.S. 98, Appdx. p. 407): "of al that a lewed man has nede for to knawe for hele of soule." Cf. also the survival of the same method of treatment in another work once attributed to Rolle, *The Abbey of the Holy Ghost* (in E.E.T.S., O.S. No. 26, p. 48 et seq.); see especially the Prologue of MS. Lamb. 432, fol. 37 b.

mediaeval student knows to his cost, who has ever had to do with them[1].

Exchanging these older influences for John Gaytrige's very free translation of Thoresby's Latin text in the middle of the century, here in his treatment of the Decalogue, we come actually upon a work which figures independently in the "Yorkshire" Collections[2], while his regular scheme of vices suggests once more the pattern of the *Somme le Roi*. Associated, it is believed[3], with Gaytrige, was William of Nassyngton, lawyer, of the same city, whom the researches of Miss Allen[4] would now make responsible for the *Prick of Conscience*, once ascribed to Rolle, but of a style too practical and commonplace, she well argues, for so individual and mystical a character. Her conclusion was based upon the remarkable likeness which that work bears to Nassyngton's own *Speculum Vitae*. The latter, in its turn, is found to be derived, not from any surviving treatise of Waldeby, as its author would suggest, but from the *Somme* of the Dominican Lorens, itself inspired by the *Summae* of William Perrault[5]. So we are back again to the original of Dan Michel's Kentish *Ayenbite of Inwyt*, of William of Waddington's *Manuel des Péchés* translated as the *Handlyng Synne* by Robert Mannyng of Brunne, and the prime model of many tractates more[6]. "The first three hundred lines of the

[1] On mediaeval "Specula," see P. Perdrizet, *Étude sur le Spec. Human. Salv.* Paris, 1908. MS. Add. 20771, *Notes on Specula*, by an English antiquary of the nineteenth century, J. Holmes, though incomplete, will be found useful.

[2] See Horstmann, vol. i, pp. 104 and 108; also pp. 132, 157.

[3] See Canon Raine (*Fasti Ebor.* vol. i, p. 470); Horstmann, vol. i, p. 104 and vol. ii, p. 274, n.

[4] *Radcliffe Coll. Monographs*, No. 15, p. 115 et seq. (Allen, H. E.); cf. (p. 144): "nearly 1000 lines on most elementary questions of the 'active life,' ...such as might be the concern of the commonest parish priest"; also p. 162, etc. ("a 'commonplace book'"). *Cat. of Roy. MSS. in B.M.* (1921), vol. ii, p. 140, suggests that Nassyngton is the same as the chaplain of Jo. Grandisson, Bp. of Exeter, who died in 1359. But this would seem to give him far too early a date (cf. footnote following, also Waldeby's date).

[5] Cf. ibid. p. 169. A colophon in MS. Bodl. 446, a copy of Nassyngton's *Speculum*, is quoted in the *Thornton Romances* (Camd. Soc. p. xx), to the effect that in 1384, this work was examined at Cambridge for heresy ("ne minus literati populum per eam negligenter fallant, et in varios errores fallaciter inducant") for four days, but declared sound and orthodox by all. Copies are numerous: cf. MSS. Add. 22283, 22558; Ryl. 17. C. viii.

[6] It is quite impossible here to give any adequate indication of the influence of the *Somme* of Lorens through its English translations, among

Speculum Vitae," we are told, "and pages 98 to 105 of the *Ayenbite of Inwyt* may be said to be close enough to each other to make them appear translations from the same work."[1] William of Nassyngton himself is an all too elusive figure[2]. Yet some further metrical works of his seem to provide a connection with the so-called *Northern Homily Collection*, edited by Messrs Small and Gerould[3]; while the *Mirror* of MS. Harl. 45 has been found, by the present writer, to be a most striking link midway between Michel's *Ayenbite* and the interesting homily series *Fons Jacob* in the Salisbury Cathedral Library[4]. Moreover, it is by no means impossible to justify Horstmann's inclusion of John Myrc's name amongst those who reflect the influence of Rolle and his associates, even if the emphasis has to be laid on the *Instructions*[5], at the expense of the *Festiall*. The mixed

further varieties and adaptations of which should be noticed those of MSS. Harl. 435 (metrical), Add. 17013 (and Bodl. 283) (early 15th cent.), Add. 37677 (along with Wimbledon's famous sermon, etc.), and Harl. 45 (see here below). Even the fifteenth-century tract "de v Sensibus" of so individual an orator as Dr Lichfield, already mentioned (see Chap. 1) in MS. Roy. 8. C. i, shows the same debt to it. As far as I understand, the development of the chief treatises may be represented thus:

Summae de Viciis et Virtutibus
(Guil. Perrault [Peraldus])
written before 1261

Le Manuel des Péchés (*Pechiez*) (Wm. of Waddington) not before 1272 (?)	*Somme des Vices et des Vertues* or *Somme le Roi* (Fr. Lorens, dominican) 1279
Handlyng Synne (Robert of Brunne, translator of above) 1303	*Ayenbite of Inwyt* (Dan Michel of Northgate) 1340

(See especially, Herbert, *Cat. of Romances*, vol. iii, pp. 273–4, etc.)

[1] "That is," she continues, "practically everything in the *Spec. Vitae* can be found in the *Ayenbite*, though the reverse is not true."

[2] See Miss Allen again, pp. 166–8.

[3] See Horstmann, vol. ii, p. 274 et seq. (poems from MS. Tib. E. vii), and Perry's *Rel. Pieces*, E.E.T.S. 1867, p. 60 for the *De Trinitate et Unitate* or *Bande of Lovynge* (from MS. Thornton, fol. 189). The latter poem also appears in MS. Add. 33995, with the *Mirror of Life* and the *Prick of Conscience*.

[4] Dr Brandeis, the editor of pt. i of this MS. for the E.E.T.S. has not realized that its "perfect little pictures" too are derived from the *Mirrour* of MS. Harl. 45.

[5] E.g. the layman's prayer at consecration here cited (see E.E.T.S., O.S. No. 31, p. 9) is Rolle's ("Welcome, Lord, in form of bread"). The vivid

sermon collection of MS. Roy. 18. B. xxiii, which Horstmann may never have seen, with its few unquestionable homilies from the *Festiall* series, among a host of others, brings us, indeed, very close to their spirit again. Here may be discerned the same detailed agonies of the Passion, the same touch of delight in the Nativity scene, or in the charms of childhood[1], the same picturesque treatment of "God's privities," or of the Lord's Prayer. Nor, finally, need we leave outside the charmed circle John Watton's popular *Speculum Christiani*[2], another manual drawn up explicitly for preachers, with its crude rhymes and its medley of Latin and English, which, as Miss Deanesly reminds us, "did for the south of England and the fifteenth century what Gaytrik's treatise had done for the north and the fourteenth." For Horstmann himself has discovered for us that passages of Rolle's *Form of Living* occur in it. How true the same kind of facts may be of many other smaller treatises and sermons, only a more protracted research is probably needed to show. Ten Brink, another student in the same field, does not exaggerate when he declares, "during the first half of the fifteenth century, the orthodox homily...still felt the prevailing influence of Hampole."[3] As we have said, there are Lollard affinities with this literature, too. But time permits only a passing reference to Wycliffe's own vernacular sermons, or to the Lambeth MS. version of Gaytrige's tract[4], done, so the editor of the *Lay Folks' Catechism* believed, by Wycliffe himself, at least with the archbishop's consent (!)[5]; or again to the record

passion scene of the *Festiall* (E.E.T.S., Ext. S. No. 96, pp. 121–2) should also be compared with the Rolle equivalent, etc. See also above, p. 47.

[1] Cf. the *Festiall* description of the Holy Innocents, and of the "Nativity" scene ("the oxe and the asse," etc.; see pp. 22–3).

[2] Numerous copies in the Brit. Mus. in Latin and English versions (cf. MS. Add. 22121, written by a Carthusian monk of Shene, as a penance, etc. For other MSS. and the above remark, see Miss Deanesly's *Lollard Bible* (Camb. Univ. Press), p. 346). *Warner and Gilson* suggest Jo. Morys of Wales as a more likely author (and *Wallensis* for "Watton"); but I notice that the 15th cent. MS. Linc. Cath. Libr. C. 4. 2, contains the sermons of Doctor Watton (in Latin). Further, a note in Sir Frederick Madden's hand (I am told) in MS. Add. 14408, suggests Jo. Watton as author of this English version of Vegetius, *de re Militari*. I suspect myself that he is really the "John Walton, Canon of Osney," reported translator of the *Consol. Boethii*, 1410. (Cf. *Cat. of Roy. MSS.* ii, p. 267.)

[3] *Hist. of Eng. Lit.* vol. ii, p. 329.   [4] MS. Lamb. 408.

[5] See E.E.T.S., O.S. No. 118, p. xxiv (Canon Nolloth).

of Lollard tamperings with the text of Rolle which dismayed the good nuns of Hampole[1].

In closing the present section it is proposed to illustrate the significance of some remarks already passed on the subject of pseudo-Wycliffite ascriptions, by the case of a little manuscript which came accidentally to the present writer's notice in the course of his researches. It belongs to the category of doubtful works which cannot be identified at all confidently either with the party of strict orthodoxy or its opponents. There is in the Bodleian Library an insignificant *Tractatus* in English on the Ten Commandments[2], many passages of which may be found in generally similar works in the British Museum[3]. These anonymous treatises have been attributed in the catalogues, hitherto apparently without much hesitation, to Wycliffe himself, and one of them was actually shown and described as such by Sir E. Maunde Thompson in the Wycliffe Exhibition of 1884[4]. Less than a year ago, however, another copy, which turned out to be identical, within limits, with the version in the Bodleian (when compared by the present author), was placed under glass in St Alban's Cathedral[5]. This time, incorporated in the text itself, at the end of the exposition, and in the same fifteenth-century hand, there appeared the following curious addition: "Thes beutis of this book, the whiche maister Wiliam Trebilvile, doctoure of decrees, Official of Seynt Albons, hath decreed necessarili and bi hovely cristis people to kunne in her modir tunge."[6] Now it is hardly to be believed that an Official of the Archdeaconry, connected with an institution whose action against Lollards and suspected literature was so notably

---

[1] See Horstmann, vol. ii, p. xxxiv. It is worth noticing also that works by Rolle and Wycliffe sometimes appear together in the same MS. (cf. MSS. Bodl. 52 and 938, etc.). Dr Craster reminds us, too, in a recent catalogue of Western MSS. in the Bodleian, that up to and including that of 1697 Rolle's *Commentary on the Psalms and Canticles* was definitely attributed to Wycliffe himself, in the Bodleian catalogues, so complete was the later confusion.

[2] MS. (Bodl.) Laud. Misc. 23.

[3] MS. Roy. 17. A. xxvi and MS. Harl. 211 (fols. 47–65). These and the foregoing are obviously related to the treatise of MS. Harl. 2398, also.

[4] See *Guide* (Thompson), p. 52; and reference to No. 40, Shirley's *Cat. of Wycl. Works.*

[5] Here regularly referred to as MS. St Albans Cath. See my article on this MS. in the *Trans. of the St Alban's and Herts. Archaeol. Soc.* for 1924.

[6] Ibid. fol. 44 b.

vigorous in the same century[1], would be found recommending a tract by the arch-heretic himself, or one of his followers. Nor can it be said, in spite of some frank remarks, that its contents in any way resemble those of the little Lollard books "in the vulgar idiom" which were actually condemned by the Abbot of St Albans at the Synod of 1427[2]. Unless the Official's name has been introduced without proper authority[3], we may consider, therefore, in the absence of any information respecting the said 'Trebilvile,'[4] that we have here a vernacular treatise which was deemed not merely respectable, but highly salutary in its day. Since, furthermore, it seems clear on inspection that the work was somewhat loosely constructed out of pulpit matter, we may well stop to ask what may be the worst that this author, once mistaken for Wycliffe, has to say to his readers. Its agreement with the tone of Bromyard and the Latin homilists is certainly most suggestive for the present study. While no definitely Lollard tenet is expressed throughout, there is the same fearless attitude of mind towards clerical shortcomings, with the hated friar now often bracketed with the much criticized parish "curate." "Loke what companye thu comest inne," says the irate moralist, this time sparing none, "be thei lordis, bischopis, personnys, vicaries, prestis, or freris, (which wolen be holde holi men in lyvynge), and thou schalt se for the moost part that al her daliaunce schal be of triflis, and of iapis, of nycyte, and othere syche vanytees, and not oo word of God, ne of his commaundementis."[5]

Besides worldliness, the writer is not afraid to accuse the prelates of a disastrous laxity in the performance of their duties; and prelates, we may remind ourselves, would assuredly be no more to the taste of monks of the great abbey[6], than to Bromyard, or to the hermit of Hampole. No attempt is made to conceal

---

[1] Cf. 1426–7, trial of suspects at St Peter's, St Alban's, by the abbot; 1429, similar enquiry at St Peter's again, Bp. of Lincoln presiding; 1431, similar enquiry at Hertford, for measures against Lollards, the abbot present; 1464, a Commission to three abbey officials for a like purpose, etc., etc. See Amundesham, *Annales* (Rolls S.), vol. i; Whethamstede, ibid. vol. ii (p. 22); Walsingham, etc.

[2] Amundesham, vol. i, pp. 222–4, etc.

[3] See my article aforementioned, p. 48.   [4] Turberville.

[5] Ibid. fol. 8 b. Cf. with this the Latin passage given above, p. 38.

[6] The officers of this archdeaconry were selected from their number.

the existence of immorality among priests and friars; while there is much of St Francis' charming spirit in the love and respect described as due to their ghostly father from parishioners, in the sorrow, and in the gentle reproof to be given in private, when he shows evil example. But even he is to be obeyed only *in as myche as he techith thee goddis lawe*[1]. Alms should be given to the helpless and crippled poor, but not to sturdy beggars well arrayed—"whether thei ben lewid prestis or freris."[2] There is scant respect for the pardoner and his penny[3]. As for "dede ymages" they seem to fare little better at first sight; but it is only the false rendering to them of "that worschipe and praier that is oonli dew to god and to his seyntis," and foolish miraculous honours, that are really condemned. Images, as elsewhere in orthodox literature, are to be rightly maintained as "lewid mennes bokes."[4] Antichrist's laws are further said to be rampant in the land. But that is a vague phrase, for all its taint of Lollardy almost as often used by their opponents, as by the Lollards themselves. As against it, we have to notice a surer test-case in favour of orthodoxy, namely, that the command "to rede goddis lawe" is carefully qualified by the previous condition—"if thou be a prest."[5] Such criticisms of lay vices as follow in its pages, with picturesque reference to current fashions in dress, in witchcrafts, in oaths, in domestic life, in buying and selling, the daily activities "in halle and in chambre, in chirche and in chepinge"[6] will be found scattered under the appropriate Prohibitions in almost every tractate of this kind. The student of social custom who turns to the great Latin *Summae* of the preachers will therefore do well to include these more modest little works on the Decalogue in his survey, also[7].

---

[1] Ibid. fol. 25. Cf. here, MS. Harl. 2276, fol. 34: "No man shuld have the offis of prechyng, neither cure in holi chirche, that wolde presume to teche or do besides that Crist hath tau3t hym bi his word," etc.

[2] Ibid. fol. 22.   [3] fol. 41. See Chap. III.

[4] fol. 10: "for suche dede ymagis ben lewid mennes bokes to lerne bi hem hou thei schulden worschipe the seyntis in hevene, aftir whom these dede ymagis ben mad, and also that men, whenne thei biholden these dede ymagis, schulden have...the more mynde of the seintis lyvynge that ben in hevene, and make these holi seintis her meenys bitwix God and hem, and not these dede ymagis, for neither thei mowe not helpe hem silfe, ne other men."

[5] fol. 21.   [6] fol. 24.

[7] Besides MSS. already indicated in Chap. III, cf. MS. Camb. Univ. Libr.

The English pulpit which thus gave birth to a didactic literature both in prose and verse, in Latin and in the vernacular, is as much the true parent of the contemporary satirical poem or the allegoric vision. To glance at that section of Mr Wells' manual of Middle-English writings which is entitled "Satire and Complaint," is merely to read a subject-index of typical sermon matter[1]. Here are the preacher's diatribes "against the pride of the Ladies, their luxury in dress," "the retinues of the great," the Church courts, "the evil times," the mendicant friars; his regular moralizings alike in the "Song of Nego," or the "Narration of Sir Penny," upon "The Devyl of Hell," or "The Earthquake of 1382." Whether the poems themselves were his own composition or that of others in his audience is a question to be left for some future discussion. A word can only be added in passing concerning the *Vision of Piers Plowman*, which as the greatest product of all has here rightly a final place in Mr Wells' series. Half a century and more of learned criticism has been expended on Langland's famous Vision. But, through modern contempt for a pulpit now shorn of its ancient glory, the one complete clue to the poem is still persistently ignored. In reality, it represents nothing more nor less than the quintessence of English mediaeval preaching gathered up into a single metrical piece of unusual charm and vivacity. Hardly a concept of the poet's mind, an authority quoted, a trick of symbolism, or a satirical portrait but is to be found characteristic of the literature of our present study. The fact applies equally, and indeed adequately, to the loosely-quoted references from "great clerks,"[2] or from Scripture, the quaint "saffron" of French[3] and Latin phrases, the knowledge of legal[4] or commercial

---

Ii. iii. 8 (two tracts); MS. Laing 140, Univ. Libr. Edinburgh; etc., and several more in the Bodleian.

[1] pp. 227–70.

[2] Which *do not* mean, as M. Jusserand imagined, that Langland has read them, "but quotes from memory." He is simply using the preachers' ordinary *Sententiae Patrum* and the popular treatises, with all their inaccuracies. (Ten Brink is equally misleading here. Cf. *E. E. Lit.*, ed. 1887, p. 354.)

[3] Which *does not* mean that he "knew French"; but that he used the popular *bons-mots* like other preachers.

[4] Which *does not* mean that he had special knowledge of lawyers or the law, as both Skeat and Jusserand suggested. That very acquaintance with "what renders a Latin charter *challengeable*," which impresses Jusserand, could have been derived *direct from the pages of the "Summa Predicantium"*!

practices, the mildly conservative attitude towards Authority as divinely constituted in Church and State, the passion for reforms[1], the biting satire of the classes[2], the criticisms of the churchmen, the whole apparatus of imagery[3], the stress on Love and good works, the unqualified praise of the virtuous labouring poor. To crown all, the very recensions, expansions, alterations of the original text which have raised mountains of difficulty in the critic's path, have been but the common fate, as we have seen, of every popular religious treatise of the age, copied and re-copied again. But to illustrate and develope this parallel would require the space of an independent volume. The task must wait[4].

In explaining how the needs of the ordinary parish priest were met by the Peckham-Thoresby outlines of Faith, allusion might have been made to clerical manuals which include in addition rules and directions for the whole round of parish duties. These handy little directories are best treated, perhaps, in a small class by themselves. Their common characteristics are that, with one exception, they are in Latin, and that amid a wealth of pithy information, the regular Peckham outline of instruction always finds a place to itself, normally accompanied by the articles of the Great Sentence[5]. In brief, they must be considered, for the most part, as still smaller and handier abridgements of the *Summae Juris Canonici* on the one hand, and compilations like John Beleth's *Rationale Divinorum Officiorum* on the other, a writer repeatedly quoted by Myrc in the course of his *Festiall* sermons. The *Oculus Sacerdotis* of William de

[1] Which, linked with the foregoing, is *not in the least* unique, as Prof. Ker stated. On the contrary, it is typical of every sermon collection we possess.

[2] Which *does not* make his poem a satire distinct from "the devotional treatise," as Mr Chambers suggests, and Mr Wells' classification also.

[3] *None* of which requires any acquaintance with "French allegory," to explain it, apart from the stock-in-trade of English homilists of the day.

[4] I have essayed a beginning in my article in the *Mod. Lang. Rev.* for July, 1925 (vol. xx, No. 3), pp. 270–279.

[5] The author is here inclined to disagree somewhat with Mr Littlehales (see *The Old Service Books*, p. 270), who says: "It would be expected that the text of the Great Sentence would be supplied in MS. Manuals, but this is not so...." He goes on to admit that it is to be found "at times," however. See below, Appdx. iv. However, there *is* evidence in the Registers that the custom of reading out the Great Sentence publicly in the churches had fallen into neglect, and lapsed in the fifteenth century (cf. Reg. Spofford, Hereford, p. 199 [1435]; and Wilkins, *Conc.* passim).

Pagula (or Page) would seem to be our oldest example of these English manuals, and the parent of not a few later varieties[1]. If the *Regimen Animarum* is dated correctly in the Harleian manuscript of that work, then Pagula's book could hardly be later than the middle of the first half of the fourteenth century[2]. For the former claims to have made use of it. It is perhaps the most comprehensive of the series, furnishing the parson with a wonderfully complete "vade-mecum" based upon the appropriate provincial and synodal decrees. In spite of Mr Peacock's difficulties in the matter[3], Myrc's vernacular *Instructions for Parish Priests*, after all, merely embodies a verse "translation," in the regular loose fashion of the day, of Part II of the former, preceded by the Latin rubric: "Quid et quomodo debet predicare parochianos suos." The essential knowledge here arranged for transmission to the laity embraces the proper method of baptism and the bringing up of children, marriage and confession, reverence and ritual in the church, cemetery behaviour, payment of tithes and even the conduct of secular business, from the ethical point of view[4]. The *Regimen Animarum* which, as its unknown author informs us in his Prologue, owes much to this same part of the *Oculus Sacerdotis* in its compilation, was written apparently in the year 1343, and based mainly upon the *Summa* of Raymund of Pennaforte[5]. Its second principal section[6] is concerned with "exhortations and

---

[1] MSS. are numerous (cf. MS. Roy. 6. E. i (B.M.); MS. Adv. Libr. Edinb. 18. 3. 6; MS. Guildhall Libr. London, 249; etc.).

[2] The date hitherto usually ascribed to it—c. 1350 (cf. Cutts, ed. 1914, p. 224)—will therefore be too late.

[3] See E.E.T.S., O.S. No. 31, pref. The editor says here (p. vi): "Mirk tells us that he translated this poem from a Latin book called 'Pars Oculi.' Some people have therefore thought that it is a versified translation of John de Burgo's 'Pupilla Oculi.'" (But why?) Peacock himself does not realize that Myrc refers to "Pars ii" of Pagula's work. Concerning further confusion over Myrc's Latin *Manuale Sac.*, see above, p. 47. (MS. Camb. Univ. Libr. Ff. i. 14, and MS. York Cath. Libr. xvi, L. 8 contain copies of this latter.)

[4] Cf. here, e.g., MS. Roy. 6. E. i, fol. 25 b et seq. (Pagula), with Myrc's *Instructions*, p. 3 (E.E.T.S.) et seq.

[5] Cf. the typical Prologue of MS. Harl. 2272, fol. 2: "O vos omnes sacerdotes qui laboratis et onerati et curati animarum estis, attendite et videte libellum istum.... Nam in isto opusculo perhibentur pericula et medicine que ad animas pertinent, et ideo Regimen vocatur Animarum. Compilavi enim hoc opusculum ex quibusdam libris, viz. Summa Summarum Raymundi, Summa confessoris et veritatis theologie, Pars Oculi sacerdotis, et de libro venerabilis Anselmi...," etc.

[6] Ibid. fol. 88 et seq.

good teaching" for the parishioners, and, after mention of the preacher's task, the usual Latin programme follows, with a particularly liberal treatment of the Deadly Sins and the subject of Temptation. Some quasi-legal advice on preaching and its privileges, which falls early in the first half of the book[1], introduces to the reader the curt method of question and answer typical of the Canon Law manuals, to which this class of treatises has already been compared[2]. The *Pupilla Oculi* of John de Burgo, Chancellor of Cambridge University (c. 1384), the popularity of which is clearly attested by printed editions in the sixteenth century[3] as well as by numerous earlier manuscripts, also claims kinship with Pagula's earlier work. It is, however, much less of a preaching manual, and much more of the compendium of legal information[4]. The early fifteenth-century *Flos Florum*[5], on the other hand, save for its introduction of the " Layfolk's Faith " (here partly in Latin, partly in English), and of other compositions directly intended for the preacher, seems to have but little right to be included in the group at all. For its character is simply that of an ample collection of earlier "libelli" and sermons put together in twenty-three books, without any attempt at literary unification

[1] Ibid. fol. 9 et seq.

[2] Cf. for a foreign example, the popular *Summa Angelica*, by Angelus of Clavasio (d. 1495).

[3] Cf. 1510 (Wolffgang), 1518 (Paris). The work occurs in Wills of the period; cf. a rector's will of 1410 (Great Heylingbury, Essex), with a " Legenda Sanctorum " (Sharpe's *Calendar of Wills*, London, vol. ii, p. 385). Cf. also an interesting note in MS. Gray's Inn Libr. 18, fol. 229 b, a volume of *Sermones Domin. per totum annum* by Januensis (i.e. Voragine): "A.D. millesimo cccc^mo lxxv^o, M. Jacobus Base emebat istum librum [i.e. the sermons, as above] de M. Thoma Boteler, in hospitio Sancti Nicolai de Civ. Cantabrigge, et alium librum vocatum *Pupilla Oculi*, et alium librum vocatum *Casus Bernardi* [i.e. Casus super Decret., by Bernard of Parma], et unum Decretum [i.e. ex Corp. Jur. Canon.], cum uno doctore vocato Brexiensis." [Gloss. on *Decret.* by Bartholomew of Brescia.] In short, a modest preacher's library!

[4] (Pars x here gives the "Peckham" programme.) Cf. MS. Roy. II. B. x; MS. Camb. Univ. Libr. Kk. i. 14; MS. Durham Cath. Libr. B. iv. 32, MSS. Salis. Cath. Libr. 126 and 147; etc. To the list of these works must be added the *Cilium Oculi Sacerdotis*, MS. Harl. 4968, MS. Guildhall Libr. London, 249, fols. 391–484 (here described as "quoddam additamentum *Oculo Sacerdotis*").

[5] MS. Burney 356 (over 400 pp.). The "Peckham" programme is No. 5, on p. 80 et seq. Cf. again the Prologue of the *Reg. Anim.* (MS. Harl. 2272, fol. 2): " ...Omnia precipua que per canones et constituciones provinciales precipiuntur scire, et parochianis exponere, et inter ipsos in ecclesia predicare, in hac modica summa per ordinem conscribuntur."

whatever. None the less it shows the same intention of grouping together under one heading all that the average priest requires for his guidance in the sacred office of instruction.

We take our final leave of the treatises, then, with the *Flos Florum*, a choice garland of homiletic flowers culled from Rolle, Grossetête, Anselm, and others, but one most loosely and promiscuously strung together. In the literature that closes the present survey, it will be the elaborate and finished systems of tabulating, alphabetical indexing, cross-referencing, as well as summarizing, linking up every detail of the whole in a truly wonderful order, that will impress us. "Exemplaria" or books of moralized stories and analogues for sermon illustration comprize the only branch of that literature that may be said to have attracted adequate attention in modern times. In the ordinary course of our survey the use and development of the "exemplum" would require more than a chapter to itself. But the published researches of Prof. Crane in America[1], and the learned volume in the Catalogue of Romances in the British Museum, by Mr Herbert[2], apart from single monographs, happily will enable us to dismiss the leading English collections here, in a sentence or two:

> Mira parabolica, que sunt racionis amica,
> Colligo per multos libros reddencia cultos,
> Et quasi mellitos sermones luce pollitos,
> Que faciunt mentes populi recreamen habentes....[3]

Although in a direct line with the *Dialogues* of Gregory or the primitive Greek "Physiologus,"[4] these were, in England as on the continent, the special fruit of Dominican and Franciscan

---

[1] The *Exempla of Jacques de Vitry* (Folklore Soc. 1890) and several later pamphlets, especially *Mediaeval Sermon Books and Stories, and their study, since* 1883. (Reprinted from *Proceedings of the American Philosophical Soc.* vol. lvi, No. 5, 1917.)

[2] *Cat. of Romances in the Dept. of MSS. of the B.M.* vol. iii. (An analysis of 109 "exempla" MSS., with reference to over 8000 stories!) See also J. H. Mosher, *The Exemplum in England* (Columbia Univ. Press, 1911), a short study from printed sources only. The author has missed at least one *printed* series of English sermons, containing "exempla," viz. those of Bp. Herbert de Losinga of Norwich (in *Life, Letters, and Sermons of Bp. Herbert de Losinga*, vol. ii, ed. Goulburn and Symonds; J. Parker, Oxf. 1878), c. 1050–1119.

[3] MS. Arundel 506, fol. 40.

[4] See art. "Physiologus" in *Encycl. Brit.* 11th ed.

labours. Even before the Mendicant appeared, however, in the opening years of the thirteenth century, Alexander Neckam of St Albans, in his *De Naturis Rerum*[1], and the Cistercian fabulist Odo of Cheriton[2], had produced between them, besides many examples of the weird symbolic animals of the bestiary, and the fable proper, a handful of entertaining "narrations," biblical, historical, monkish or purely legendary. When Bartholomew's vast treasure-house of natural wonders[3], in the shape of the *De Proprietatibus Rerum*, has been added, somewhere about the year 1230, already English authorship can boast of all the great Latin "exempla" types which eventually go to enrich the *Summa Predicantium* of our noteworthy Dominican chancellor. Two anonymous collections, most probably the work of a Franciscan in each case, mark a further stage, especially in their use of subject-headings, alphabetically arranged. These are the *Liber Exemplorum* (c. 1270–79)[4], and the *Speculum Laicorum* (c. 1279–92)[5]. The origins of the more famous *Gesta Romanorum* are still wrapped in mystery, in spite of the fact that a whole group of scholars has been busy upon them during the last fifty years or so[6]. But the latest and best opinion, at all events, is in favour of original compilation in this country. Amid the truly brilliant assemblage of tales, in its pages, from many nations and many periods, each followed by its own moralization, East meets West, and classical names parade in feudal habit. The whole provides a most entertaining and ever popular spectacle, of which subsequent English preachers were not slow to avail themselves.

All the collections so far named were written in the ecclesiastical tongue, and lay therefore at the disposal of the clerical reader alone[7]. By the time, however, that the age of Mannyng and Rolle is reached, and the "exempla" naturally appear in

[1] Ed. Wright (Rolls S.).

[2] See Hervieux, *Les Fabulistes Latins*, vol. iv. (Odo bids the preacher supply "auctoritates et exempla scripturarum," in his Prologue; see ibid. p. 174.)

[3] For treatises on "Moralized Properties of Things" consult M. L. Delisle in *Hist. Litt. de la Fr.* vol. xxx, Introd. p. xxxvi, etc.

[4] Ed. Little, A. G., *Br. Soc. of Franc. Studies*, 1908. See also his sketch of the "Fasciculus Morum" in his *Studies in Engl. Franc. Hist.* There are several MSS. of this work in the Bodleian, some explicitly called "Sermons."

[5] Ed. J. Th. Welter, Paris, 1914.

[6] One need only stop to mention here such names as Oesterley, Herrtage, Swan, Douce, Warton, Tyrrwhitt, and Madden (from 1879 back to 1838).

[7] Cf. here such headings as "Liber Exemplorum *ad usum predicantium*."

English among their treatises, another collection of "fabliaux" arrives on the scene, this time in French—language of the court and perhaps of the traders. But this is apparently as far as the Mendicant ever got in the direction of popularizing the example-books themselves[1]. Nicole Bozon's *Contes Moralizés*[2] are the last as they are the first known collection by an English friar to be issued, apparently, by the author himself, in anything but Latin. Unless, therefore, the explanation already offered—of the friar's unwillingness thus to give away his pulpit specialities —be accepted, we are at a loss to account for the situation[3]. Two Latin books of moralizations by the Dominican Robert Holcot[4], about this time, further typify admirably the kind of stiff and formal pedantry beloved of the contemporary university friar, even in so trivial a sphere. This writer takes particular delight in historical "exempla" from classical or pseudo-classical sources. His moralizations and metaphors must be full of the absurd extravagances and wearisome multi-plicity of scholastic divisions and scholastic symbolism[5]. The same thing is largely true of Bromyard. But to look back again at Bozon, for a moment. Besides the Natural History, the animal fables, the anecdotes, the "canonization of hard work" and the rest, he is interesting for the violence of his attack on abuses in Church and State. The bailiff, the bishop, and lawyer, the usurer, all come in for their share. So, while we may not agree with M. Meyer over the originality of all this criticism in what he claims unhesitatingly to be nothing less than a book of sermons actually preached[6], we gladly recognize the importance of its anticipation of another distinct element in the make-up of the *Summa Predicantium*. For Bozon's work is no mere

---

[1] It is worth noting, however, that French proverbs are sometimes quoted in the text of Latin sermon collections; cf. Bromyard, *S.P.*, and MS. Add. 24660, fol. 40, etc.

[2] Ed. P. Meyer and L. T. Smith (Soc. des Anciens Textes fr.), 1889. An important manuscript of this work is MS. Gray's Inn Libr. 12. iv. An English translation of this text has been published as *The Metaphors of Brother Bozon, a Friar Minor*, by J. R. MS. Harl. 1288 contains a *Latin* version.

[3] See above, Chap. VI, pp. 226–8.

[4] *Liber de Moralizationibus* and *Opus super Sapientiam Salomonis* (d. 1349).

[5] Cf. here Crane (*Exempla of J. de Vitry*), pp. xcviii–xcix, etc. See also the printed editions (Venice, 1505; Paris, 1510) of the *Moralitates pulchrae Historiarum in usum Predicatorum*.

[6] "Et, sans doute, plus d'une fois, avant d'être écrit," adds M. Meyer (p. xxviii). (For his claim of originality, see pp. xxvi (and xxii).)

sermon-series, but shares the character of the more or less systematic guide-book. No less worthy of the comparison are his strong popular sympathies; although his simple practical teaching may be more in a line with Myrc and the vernacularists. Even apart altogether from features noticed in the learned editor's preface, the *Contes Moralizés* are significant for their union at this stage of the fables, the moralized "narrations" and "properties of things" along with this strong topical interest.

As a last word in connection with the history of the greater example-books in our period, we call attention to the remarkable activity displayed in making English translations, and in multiplying generally the number of available copies. More often than not the thirteenth-century *Speculum Laicorum* will turn up in a fifteenth-century manuscript[1]; or we may find that the copy of the sixty fables in Latin elegiacs that we may be reading—known as *Aesopus in Fabulis* and compiled probably by one Walter the Englishman between the years 1169 and 1190—is in the hand of an Austin canon of the priory at Kenilworth, some two and a half centuries later[2]. Among notable translations are the two earlier vernacular manuscripts of the *Gesta Romanorum*, of about the year 1440[3], and contemporary English versions of Voragine's *Legenda Aurea*[4] and the *Alphabetum Narrationum*[5]. This last-named work, with a title that commands our notice, is now believed, in its Latin form, to have been put together originally by a Frenchman at the end of the fourteenth century[6]. Its two hundred "exempla" neatly arranged, "secundum ordinem alphabeti," from "Accidia" to "Xps" (Christ), are a not unworthy prelude to the volume which now claims our notice.

[1] Cf. MS. Salisb. Cath. Libr. 141; MS. Roy. 7. C. xv, and others in the Brit. Mus. (see *Cat. of Rom.* vol. iii, p. 408, etc.); MS. Bodl. 474, etc.

[2] MS. Add. 38665, fols. 41–56 b, by John Strecch (cf. MS. Add. 35295, c. 1422). Strecch[e] is known as a chronicler: see Kingsford, *Eng. Hist. Lit. in XV cent.*, p. 39.

[3] MSS. Harl. 7333 and Add. 9066. (See E.E.T.S. reprint, Ext. S. No. 33.)

[4] MSS. are Add. 11565 and 35298, Harl. 630 and 4775, Egerton 876, Douce 372, and Lamb. 72. See Pierce Butler, *Leg. Aur.*, Baltimore, 1899, pp. 50–75.

[5] MS. Add. 25719 (see E.E.T.S. ed. Banks, O.S. Nos. 126, 127). MS. Harl. 268 is said to be the Latin original of this particular version.

[6] See J. A. Herbert in *The Library*, New S. vol. vi (1905), p. 94 et seq. Mr Herbert, who here suggests Arnold of Liège as author, adds: "English preachers held it in even greater esteem than the *Speculum Laicorum*."

"Examples move men more than precepts" is a favourite quotation of the preachers from St Gregory onward; and the statement would seem equally true of the modern *littérateurs* who profess to have looked into the books of Jacques de Vitry, or John de Bromyard to-day. In fact, it might come as a surprise to some of them to hear that the *Summa Predicantium* of the latter contained anything but what one has termed the "histories." None the less, this colossal undertaking, with its hundred and eighty-nine topics disposed alphabetically, and its "exempla" now swollen to over a thousand, gathers up into itself practically every feature of importance in the literature with which we have been concerned. Hence, while defying any adequate analysis, it will yet serve us here as both final illustration and summary. In the first place, its Dominican authorship asserts once more the unrivalled supremacy of the Mendicants, not merely in the preservation of tales and wonders, but in everything that pertains to the formal preaching art. Secondly, its wholesale plagiarism, and with it the decay in originality of treatment, which resulted from a profusion of hand-books and helps for the pulpit, though not always clear to the casual reader, becomes more and more evident, as careful investigation proceeds. Acknowledged quotations from other sources are, to begin with, numerous enough. But, not content with these, the author must borrow in addition the most homely and natural little comparisons and sketches of every-day life from other minds. We fix with an innocent enthusiasm upon some vivid portraiture of the well-bred hounds of the chase, with the domestic dog lying asleep, in the foreground, by way of contrast, upon his cottage dung-heap. At another time it is a passage on the increased activities of bear-baiting on Sundays that arrests us. In each the lines of our British "primitive" of the middle ages are as few and as skilful as those of the contemporary wall-painting, or monumental brass, with a sympathy as keen as Landseer's. Yet to our surprise, and no little disappointment, the very phrases of Bromyard's Latin will turn up in French sermon manuscripts of at least a century earlier. Everywhere an unrestricted use of anterior forms seems to be the order of the day. The art of the pulpit has passed its zenith.

If we turn next to principles of style and construction, each topical section of the work, however uneven in length, is found to reproduce the invariable pattern of the elaborately "divided" sermon, with the chief heads of divisions set forth in the opening paragraph. The allegoric interpretations, noticed repeatedly elsewhere, reach the most tedious and absurd proportions imaginable in such "figures" as those of the well-known chess-men and their moves, reminiscent of de Cessolis; the Devil's Castle; or the separate hands, fingers, even finger-joints of God and the Evil One, subjected in turn to the same highly grotesque treatment as symbols of the truths to be imparted. The quintessence of the treatises we may consider incorporated and expanded under the headings of vices and virtues, which in all alphabetical "encyclopedias" of this kind occupy the chief place in the contents-tables. Bromyard has an eye not merely for their branches and characteristic penalties or prizes, but even for the regular excuses men make for them in the one case, or the widespread social advantages in the other. Furthermore the *Sermones ad Status* are not missing. For, scattered amongst the former, appear "capitula" with such titles as "Ordo Clericalis," "Judices," "Advocati," "Mercatio," "Nobilitas," "Militia," containing an ordered mass of detailed criticism, advice, warning, applied to the particular class concerned. That they are often intended to equip the preacher for the special occasions and audiences we have mentioned, there can be little doubt. The second "Divisio" of the subject "Ordo Clericalis," for example, is thus outlined: "Secundo prosequenda sunt quaedam themata *per modum collationum ad ordinandos et ordinatos* specialiter pertinentium." Emphasis of the way in which every conceivable history-book, example-book, legendary, bestiary and the rest seem to have been ransacked to provide adequate illustration for this huge enterprize, on an unprecedented scale, will be unnecessary. The writer repeats an old phrase in his own Prologue to the effect that "it is no sin to be taught by the enemy, and to enrich the Hebrews with the spoils of the Egyptian." Little wonder, therefore, that the sayings of pagan philosophers and men of letters[1], as well as fabulists, jostle quotations in his pages from Scripture, from the Fathers, or

---

[1] Cf. the Prologue: "Est aliud etiam advertendum quod frequenter in hoc tractatu adducuntur gentiles et eorum opera...," etc.

from Canon Law to all appearance, sometimes, with an equal authority and importance.

The thirteenth-century *Speculum Laicorum*[1] aforementioned, of all the antecedent compositions by Englishmen which adopted an alphabetical system, is perhaps most worthy to be singled out as the genuine prototype of our *Summa*. Here not only are the "exempla" but the typical opening definitions and divisions, the fondness for the citation of authorities, and the special warnings to social groups as well. With Bromyard, however, in the matter of arrangement, we go further, to mark how by means of a method of index-letters and numbers he heightens the possible efficiency of his book for the preacher with continuous cross-referencing in the body of the text[2]. Moreover, he informs us in his Prologue that his references to Canon Law are so ordered "that those who possess a sufficiency of the said books [lawyers' hand-books to the Digest, etc.] but have little skill or experience in turning them up, to find what is referred to, may not spend too much time in hunting about."

While so many libraries still remain unsearched, it is impossible to say how many attempts were made in this country to emulate the great achievement of the Dominican. Bromyard himself has been mentioned as author of a set of *Distinctiones Theologicae*, name common enough in recent Bodleian Catalogues of manuscripts for an encyclopaedic work of similar description. Three English Franciscans of the period, at the least, produced *Summae* of sermon-material alphabetically arranged—John of Lathbury[3], John de Grimston, whose small volume rich in vernacular verse, now in the Advocates' Library in Edinburgh[4], was compiled in the year 1376, and the Minorite

[1] Cf. the writer's preface (ed. Welter): "...et ut facilius inveniantur a querentibus optata, per modum alphabeti compegi tractaculum, materiarum capitula preponens ibi contentarum"; and that of MS. Roy. 6. E. vi. Sim. the mid. 14th cent. *Tabula Exemplorum* of MS. Add. 37670 (fol. 125): "ad omnem materiam in sermonibus secundum ordinem alphabeti ordinata," and MS. Add. 18351. See also *Cat. of B. M. Romances*, vol. iii, pp. 414, 422.

[2] Cf. his Prologue: "...compilationem a me prius collectam in isto libello ad meam et aliorum utilitatem emendavi et augmentavi, ponendo certas materias sub determinatis literis secundum ordinem alphabeti, per propria capitula distinguendo. Et quia frequenter contingit mittere de una litera et de uno capitulo ad aliud, propter similitudinem materie de qua agitur in loco de quo agitur et mittitur, quotantur litera et capitulum ad quod mittitur, et numerus in margine signatus sub quo queritur invenietur...."

[3] C. 1350, MS. Roy. 11. A. xiii.   [4] MS. 18. 7. 21, with 143 topics.

Gilbert[1], author of a more substantial "*Summa Sermonum* which is called the *Summa Abstinentiae*." Of the latter work the Bodleian Library contains more than one copy[2]. In addition to these, a bulky though sadly fragmentary Folio, not unlike the old Rochester Priory manuscript[3] of the *Summa Predicantium*, has come under the notice of the present writer, in the Cambridge University Library[4]. Though figuring under the dull name of "Sermon Commonplaces" (Loci Communes) in Mr Luard's catalogue, in reality it has nothing of the untidy notes and abominable jottings at volume-ends that one is wont to associate with that title. Unhappily stripped alike of opening and closing pages, it is yet recognizable as a finely executed copy of the *Florarium Bartholomei* of John of Mirfield, an Austin Canon of St Bartholomew's, Smithfield (c. 1370?). If its chapters are more skeleton in character than those of Bromyard, the variety of subjects in its alphabetical scheme far outshines his own[5]. Very similar but larger still is the dictionary of Canon Law and Theology by one James, a disciple of Fitzralph, bitterly hostile to the friars[6]. Further, there is the *Destructorium Viciorum* by an Englishman known variously as Alexander Anglus, Fabricius, or Carpenter, compiled in the year 1429[7], a vast unoriginal compendium of the vices, boasting an almost unrivalled succession of printed editions down to the year 1521[8]. Finally, a work in the Bodleian drawn from the *Pera Peregrini*

[1] "...edita a quodam fratre de Ordine Minorum, nomine Gilberto." (The earlier Franciscan *Fasciculus Morum*, c. 1320 (?), I have omitted in my sketch, as it is fully described by Mr Little in his *Studies in Franc. History* (Oxford), pp. 139–157.)
[2] MSS. Bodl. 45 and 542 (130 chapters, intended to be followed by "Adaptaciones omnium sermonum in hoc libello contentorum prout competunt sabbatis dominicis et feriis tocius anni." Cf. MS. Bodl. 45, fol. 117).
[3] MS. Roy. 7. E. 4.   [4] MS. Camb. Univ. Libr. Mm. ii. 10.
[5] I have identified it from the later and inferior copy, MS. Roy. 7. F. xi, in the B.M. (Cambridge cataloguers please note!) Cf. here such fresh topical headings as: De conviviis, decimis et oblationibus, indulgenciis, labore manuum, matrimonio et sponsalibus, medicis et medicinis, monachis et regularibus, mortificatione carnis, negociis secularibus, penis inferni, pollutione nocturna, purgatorio, sera conversatione ad Deum, sompniis. Another MS. is Gray's Inn Libr. 4.
[6] MS. Roy. 6. E. vi and vii (with numerous miniatures): by an Engl. Cistercian of the mid. 14th cent.? 23 Bks. corresponding to 23 letters of the Alphabet; with valuable lists in the *Prol.* of the sources used.
[7] Explic.: "...a cuiusdam fabri lignarii filio,...A.D. MCCCCXXIX collecta."
[8] Cologne, 1480, 1485; Nuremberg, 1491, 1500; Paris, 1497, 1500, 1505, 1509, 1516, 1521.

of John Felton recalls the abridgements made of these great pulpit compendia[1].

Prompted, no doubt, by the example of the *Summae*, and the current activity in reducing to handy proportions the vast stores of accumulated pulpit learning, sermon-writers and copyists now proceeded to furnish their homily sets with goodly alphabetical Tabulae or Indices[2]. This improvement naturally heightened the variety and suggestibility of their contents for the homilist, until the ordinary *De Tempore* volume in its turn could itself be used as a veritable encyclopaedia, by working from the table at its end, if the student so preferred[3]. Master Rypon's imposing Tabula to be found at the end of his volumes of sermons is actually furnished with a descriptive Prologue of its own[4]. The greatest achievement in systematic tabulation, of the period, however, stands apparently to the credit of a Carmelite Doctor of Theology, Alan of Lynn[5]. It was he who compiled the contents-table[6] for the immense *Reductorium Morale* of the monk Berchorius (Peter Bercheur)[7], French counterpart of the *Summa Predicantium*, whose fourteenth-century writer indeed has actually been put forward, like Brom-yard himself, as the likely author of the original *Gesta Roman-orum*. With his labours successfully accomplished, brother Alan could well boast in his preface: "per juvamen tabule supradicte, singulus predicator poterit processum super-effluentem ad omnem quasi materiam reperire...." To the same era belongs the list of monastic libraries, made in con-nection with a catalogue of theological literature, probably by a Franciscan, showing by reference numbers in what place each work was to be found[8]. Such might be thought to serve the

[1] MS. Laud. Misc. 389 ("ex procuratione fratris T., Rome S.T.P."). (Cf., in the realm of mediaeval medicine, the *Rosula Medicine* (MS. Add. 33996, fols. 168 b–210 b), abridgement of John of Gaddesden's *Rosa Anglica*, etc.)
[2] Cf. the MSS. of Armagh, Brunton, Waldeby, Felton, etc., etc.
[3] Cf. here the footnote added to the sermon, MS. Arundel 384, fol. 28: "Require tabulam horum ser[monum]...ad tale signum."
[4] MS. Harl. 4894, fol. 217. Even the little sermon-book, MS. Add. 21253, has an alphabetical index (incomplete), giving an outline idea of each subject item, generally the form of imagery used in the text. The method of actual reference is to the particular sermon-number and the particular *principale*.
[5] fl. 1420 (N.B. another *friar*.) [6] MS. Roy. 3. D. iii.
[7] There are several printed editions of this immense work (cf. Cologne, 1477).
[8] MS. Roy. 3. D. i, with an erased subscription (fol. 234 b): "Finitum (?)

needs of the man of letters rather than of eloquence. But we have no right to forget the sermon-*writer*, while remembering the preacher only, especially where Mendicants are concerned; and, as Gasquet points out, it is only another valuable witness to the painstaking efforts made for his equipment[1]. This very volume, as a matter of fact, in the early years of the next century, came into the hands of at least one "famous preacher."[2] To similar ends the multiplication of Biblical Concordances and Glosses were contributing; likewise the first English-Latin Dictionary that we possess, compiled by another friar of Lynn, this time a Dominican, somewhere about the year 1440[3]. Of Treatises on the Art of Preaching itself nothing need be added for the present. They will appear in due course in the final chapter that follows.

Looking back over our long survey with all its varieties we must admit that, whatever has to be said about the decline of notable preaching as the Reformation approaches, the pulpit reference-books have a career which only flourishes the more as later years increase the power and efficiency of the printing-press. Nevertheless, it is not hard to understand why, as an independent art, preaching wellnigh perished, overwhelmed with such a surfeit of written material. Over-refinement and development of the homiletic armour now hampered or even suffocated its wearer, instead of equipping him the better for the battle. To the eye of Richard de Bury, as early as the year 1334, his contemporaries were already spoilt children, degenerate sons of the great "Fishers of Men" in the past:

O idle fishermen, using only the nets of others, which when torn it is all ye can do to repair clumsily, but can net no new ones of your own! Ye enter on the labours of others, ye repeat the lessons of others, ye mouth with theatrical effort the superficially-repeated wisdom of other men![4]

per Ricardum Bottisham...A.D. 1452...[in] collegio Annunciationis Beatae Mariae, [Canta]brigie, nuncupato Gonnvillhalle." See further, Dr M. R. James' article, "List of Libraries prefixed to the Cat. of Jo. of Boston," in *Collect. Franc.* (B.S.F.S.), vol. ii, pp. 39–60.

[1] See *O.E.B.* (2nd ed.), pp. 188–98.

[2] As entered on fly-leaf here—Ralph Collingwood (Dean of Lichfield, 1512–21)—"famosus predicator et S.T.D."

[3] See ed. E.E.T.S. (*Prompt. Parvulorum*), Ext. S cii, 1908.

[4] *Philobiblon*, cap. vi.

CHAPTER VIII

SERMON-MAKING, OR THE THEORY AND PRACTICE OF SACRED ELOQUENCE

OF the several impressions left upon the mind, after a first survey of mediaeval sermon literature, that which is most likely to attract the reader further will be concerned with the sacred eloquence of the special occasions, or the words directed to some particular class of the community with their reference to current habit and idea. If he holds to the pursuit at all, he will henceforth be impatient to follow up suggestive tracks observed to lead whither a more familiar literature was leading him already; or to be away down the wind after fresh quarry like the ecclesiastical revelations we have sighted. True it is that the hunting over these much despised literary preserves may not prove as bad as some imagine. For what game there is has really been little disturbed as yet, and here fortunately the less painstaking huntsmen of letters do not venture as a rule. Conscientious research, on the other hand, requires that, before the pleasures of the chase, there shall be some preliminary groundwork. However dull the task, we must proceed to examine the various modes of actual sermon construction.

Three great influences in the matter of style can be detected at work among the sermon-types which found their place in the previous chapters. Ever since the thirteenth century, at least, they had stood offering their services, as it were, to the would-be preacher, waiting upon him not like the three friendly graces with linked arms, that Master Rypon describes[1], but rather as jealous rivals, each claiming from him an exclusive choice. The first was the genius of exposition "secundum ordinem textus," based, like the postill in its original sense[2],

---

[1] Cf. MS. Harl. 4894, fol. 59: "Ad modum ymaginum de quibus loquitur Seneca, in libro 1º, de beneficiis. Erant tres ymagines que vocabantur beneficiorum, depicte ad similitudinem trium virginum quarum quelibet habuit manus insertas in manibus alterius, ad modum tripudiencium in rotundo, sive in circulo. Habuerunt hillares vultus, et fuerunt iuvencule, et depingebantur tres virgines, et non plures...."

[2] I.e. "post illa—verba (textus)," etc.

on the text and narrative of Scripture, treated more or less in straightforward and simple fashion. To it preachers of our period, struggling in a wilderness of "divisions," allegories, and other subtleties, looked back sometimes as to a golden memory of the past. Dr Gascoigne, who can be as loquacious as ever on these points[1], bewails the hopelessness of the present style, the lost advantages of the old, as though there had never been any serious attempts made to revive the latter. Yet we must agree perhaps that even the reforming Wycliffe, his enemy, had been as careful as any other schoolman to maintain the scholastic divisions as well as the tropology intact in his preaching, in spite of all his zeal for the naked Biblical text. It was the complete freedom from logical thematic development and the regular constraints of "form,"—such as the Abbé Bourgain actually deplores in his twelfth-century preacher[2],—that the Oxford Chancellor would have men strive after in the fifteenth. Now among the Rivers of Babylon[3] he sighs after the ancient music they cannot sing:

> Which method the saints of old did not use, as is seen in the sermons and homilies of St Augustine and St Bernard, who preached to clergy and people by the method of "postillating" and expounding the text of some apostle, according to the order of the text. And sometimes they used to preach, neither postillating nor expounding the text of any chapter, but making straightforward assertion—when they used to declare the points pertaining to those matters which they set forth, without any text, before clergy and people, to be asserted according to reason and Scripture[4].

In another place[5] he speaks of the free, unconventional methods of Christ. His comments might equally well be those of the Reformer himself:

> For Christ, in the gospel preached by him, preserved such order in his speaking that within a short space of time he would discourse

[1] See *Loci e Libro Veritatum* (ed. Rogers, as before).
[2] Cf. *La chaire franç.* p. 261.
[3] I venture to use the phrase because it is the theme of a remarkable sermon by him, incorporated in his *Dict. Theol.* ("Super flumina Babylonis," Ps. 137). The Seven Rivers here stand for the seven great contemporary ills of the Church.
[4] Ibid. (Rogers), p. 42. (Begin.: "Predicare modo usitato, scil. accipiendo thema et uti inductione thematis per narrationem materiae quae concludit verba thematis repeti et recitari, et tunc divisiones facere....")
[5] Ibid. p. 179.

of matters, diverse, dissimilar, and unlike, as is clear in different parts of the Gospel. For a fanciful method of speaking hinders perception of the matter to be grasped, and does not manifest the truth, as it is manifested in plain words and good modes of speech when instruction is given and the hearers understand[1].

Strangely enough, on the outskirts of the period we have chosen, there seems to be an echo of the same judgement. A private letter, dated 1329, appears among the correspondence of good Bishop Grandisson[2], which hitherto probably unnoticed, assumes in the light of our enquiry a new interest. He is writing to thank Master Richard de Ratforde for securing for him a *Liber Sermonum* "of the blessed Augustine," which he now proposes to buy. To his directions, however, he adds a further request, which shows where his preference lies: "Libros etiam theologicos originales, veteres saltem et raros, *ac sermones antiquos etiam, sine divisionibus thematum, pro nostris usibus,* exploretis." Furthermore, the Dominican Thomas Walleys refers in his *Ars Predicandi* to this "method of the Saints in their Homilies," with strong approval of those who are still "wont to expound the whole Gospel or Epistle in regular order" after their pattern[3]. The influence of this traditional mode, then, in our centuries is genuine enough. As for the talk of a golden age of oratory in the past, apart from the triumphs of leading individuals, we do well to be a little suspicious about it. For the gold here as in other cases has ever a habit, like Maeterlinck's Blue Bird, of disappearing on our approach. The phantom will draw us further and further into the dim recesses of religious history, until we find ourselves, with a shock, at the gate of that first mythical garden with its golden fruit. We may believe that the art of homiletics has had always a majority of the rambling unpolished speakers among its disciples of the

[1] Derived from Augustine, *De Doctr. Christiana.*
[2] Letter 169, Reg. Grandiss. (Exeter), pt. i, p. 240.
[3] Cf. MS. Harl. 635, fol. 8 b: "Aliqui solent totum evangelium vel epistolam ordinatim exponere, et bene proficiunt, et forte saepe vulgo utilior...." This is further orthodox evidence, from the first half of the fourteenth century, of that close exposition of the scriptural text by the preachers which Miss Deanesly is inclined to deny (see above, Chap. vi, p. 240, n. 6). I should understand the above method to be one with Colet's, as described by Erasmus (expounding the Scriptures, not by retail, but by wholesale), or indeed with that of Wycliffe himself, as described by Miss Deanesly (p. 317).

rank and file. The rambling catechetical address was possibly as common and as dull in Augustine's day as were the later "divisiones"; and Bernards or Bernardinos have been the rarest exceptions in any era of faith.

The second great style is that to be associated intimately with the method of the University schools. Gascoigne does not hesitate to identify its influence with the work of the earlier friars: "This modern mode of preaching came into fashion after the coming of the Orders of friars into the Church."[1] Nor is it likely that the innovation, when it came, was looked upon other than as a welcome improvement on the disjointed, ill-planned efforts that preceded. Indeed, there is positive evidence that the new way, with its logical distinctions, and its pretty formality—with what Wycliffe scorns in his preaching as "the argumentis that sophistis maken"—proved so much to the taste of learned and fashionable audiences, that many were in the habit of overlooking the sermon-matter, in their rapt appreciation of the form. Says one, preaching before the canons of St Victor in Paris, at the close of the thirteenth century:

> There are many, who, when they come to sermon, . . . do not care what the preacher says; but only how he says it. And if the sermon be well "rhymed," if the theme be well "divided," if the brother discourses well, if he pursues his argument well, if he "harmonizes" well, they say: "How well that brother preached!" "What a fine sermon he made!" That is all they look for in the sermon, nor do they attend to what he says[2].

Such worldly preoccupation could be still charged against English sermon-critics a century and a half later[3]. Side by side, too, with this dry pedantry of form, must be put the famous extravagances of scriptural interpretation, "historial," "allegorik," "tropologik," and "anagogik"—"foure reulis of holi scripture, tht ben clepid foure maner undirstondyngs; and these

---

[1] Rogers, p. 44, etc.: and again,—"Modus enim predicandi per divisiones et per theme incepit circa annum Domini 1000 et fere 200, ut patet per auctores talium sermonum."

[2] Hauréau, *Quelques MSS.* . . . , vol. iv, p. 139.

[3] "Moderni enim inimici veritatis, audientes sermonem veritatis, dicunt, 'Iste sermo non habet formam, sed locutus est, et nescivit quae dixit, nec intellexit quae dixit, nec habet formatum ingenium': (quia predicavit ea quae sunt contra eorum appetitum)." Gascoigne (ed. Rogers, p. 179).

as it were foure feet, beren up the bord of Goddes lawe."[1] Like
the amazing accumulations of imagery and quotation[2], which
grew from cultivation of the same habit of mind in other depart-
ments of knowledge, they reflect directly the vast commentaries
and encyclopaedias which now brought the current learning to
the preacher's study desk. For "glosing was a glorious thing,
for certain" in days when the "naked text" might shame the
none-too-exemplary clerk. From being the fashion of the hour
among "literati," we shall see how the "modus predicandi per
divisiones" and the rest creep into what appears to be the
simplest kind of homily series in the vernacular, with even an
occasional caricature of the lordly theological argument itself:

> Thise cokes, how they stampe, and streyne, and grinde,
> And turnen substaunce into accident[3].

The anecdote, the fable, the entertaining legend and marvel
provide us with our third great element from the sermon-
making of the past, in a word everything that sprang from
contact with the people and the popular taste. Those who had
made good one deficiency in the art by introducing the method
of the schools into the pulpits, were destined to satisfy another.
For the sermon of the early thirteenth century, besides lacking
style, lacked also that bright familiarity and raciness which
when once developed would be capable of holding the attention
of the masses. This the friar had been able to provide, fresh
from his further contact with the mean and vulgar in country
lanes and crowded areas. Regret it as the mere stylists may, even
his written homily collections in Latin retain yet their little
popular idioms of speech, saws and couplets, preserved in the
vernacular along with the old wives' fables so dear to the
common heart. His moralized story and miracle books became
at length models for sermon-writers in English, as was indicated
above. Here, then, was a substantial, not to say formidable
threefold heritage for every future preacher. We now proceed

---

[1] MS. Harl. 2276, fol. 32 b. (Yet a sermon collection notably *simple* in its
expositions!)
[2] Cf. here Luther: "When I was young,...I dealt largely in allegories,
and tropes, and a quantity of idle craft; but now I have let all that slip, and
my best craft is to give the Scripture with its plain meaning, for the plain
meaning is learning and life."
[3] The Pardoner's Tale (*Cant. Tales*), ll. 538–9.

to enquire what use they could make of it in the two centuries that concern us, and in what particular framework it was to appear.

A prominent English Dominican has declared in a recent book[1] that in mediaeval England strictly formal preaching had little or no place. But, even if he had disdained the evidence of Gascoigne and Grandisson, and had never looked into a manuscript of Latin homilies in his life, one would have imagined it impossible for any Catholic to have made such a statement. Tracts by Englishmen on the formal art of preaching, on dilating and dividing the sermon are so numerous from the second half of the thirteenth century onwards, that the practice might almost be looked upon as a speciality of our pulpits. Langlois[2] has even noticed in France a *Tractatus de dilatione sermonum* of about the year 1288 or so, by brother Richard the Englishman. To the same epoch belong *Formae Predicandi* by Richard de Tefford or Thetford[3], and by Robert of Basevorn (?)[4], who appears to have dedicated his composition to an Irish Cistercian abbot. There is also another work on the subject variously ascribed to the same Richard, and with less authority to the Franciscan Richard Middleton, and to one Thomas Lemman, of whom nothing appears to be known[5]. A discourse "de artificioso modo predicandi" by a

[1] Bede Jarrett, *The Engl. Domin.* (Burns and Oates), 1921.
[2] Article in *Revue des deux mondes*, Jan. 1, 1893, pp. 170–201.
[3] MS. Bodl. 631, fol. 4. *Inc.* "Primo per qualemcunque termini notificationem...."
[4] Cf. MS. Roy. 7. C. i, fol. 215 b, etc. (belonged to Romsey Abbey); and MS. Add. 38818, fol. 191, etc.
[5] *Inc.*: "Quoniam emulatores estis spirituum ad edificationem ecclesie...." Starting with MS. Roy. 4. B. viii (fol. 263 b), an anon. copy, we find that the editors of the new *Cat. of Royal MSS. in the B. M.* (Warner and Gilson), basing their reference on Mr Little's *Initia Op. Lat.* (ed. 1904, p. 200), refer solely to Richard Middleton, or Thomas Lemman, apparently ignoring the fact that in MS. Harl. 3244 (fol. 186) they have a copy of the work *with a contemporary rubric heading* ascribing it to Richard of Thetford (secundum Ricardum de Theford). Furthermore, Mr Little's ascription to Rich. Middleton is apparently based on nothing else than the heading to MS. Merton Coll. Oxf. 249 (fol. 175), which reads "Sermo fratris Ricardi de dilatatione sermonum" (see *Oxf. Greyfriars*, p. 215), properly referring, I take it, to R. de Thetford, as above. MS. Bodl. 848 is anon. again. As for Thos. Lemman, this ascription must be based on MS. Linc. Cath. Libr. A. 6. 10 (fol. 227 b), from which Tanner got his one reference to Lemman, of whom he admits further nothing is known. Now I have seen this MS. at Lincoln, and I find the ascription is in the hand of Dean Honeywood (late in the

"Prior de Essebi"[1] is a further example. Coming to our period we find besides the works, already familiar in these pages, of Ranulf Higden[2], monk of Chester, and Thomas Walleys, Dominican[3], more than one copy is extant of Simon Alcock's "Tractatus de modo dividendi thema, pro materia sermonis dilatanda."[4] Bale's lists again provide us with some further authors—"de Arte Predicandi," a Dominican Doctor, Hugo de Sueth, or Suexth[5], and a Carmelite, John Folsham[6], of Norfolk (d. 1348). How many anonymous tractates on the subject[7], apart from mere summaries of Alain de Lille's best-known directory of all, are to be discovered in our mediaeval libraries to-day, it would be hard to estimate. A work like the *Summa Predicantium* itself is a monument of the formal style in its most lengthy and "divided" state. But finally, who shall assess, when all is examined, the number of the lost and destroyed, of which John Bale's list of Carmelites is so mournful a reminder? Dull and dreary enough in their treatment, these little guides for the sacred orator, spread over a folio or two, are none the less witness that there must have been more genuine declamation

seventeenth century), who cannot be trusted in these matters (cf. other ascriptions by him in the same MS. here). Clearly, then, for the present, evidence favours Rich. of Thetford as author.

[1] Mr Little (ibid. p. 126) repeats Tanner's suggestion of the Franciscan William of Esseby as author of this tract preserved in MS. Camb. Univ. Libr. Ii. i. 24, p. 332 (14th cent.). But he adds, "'Prior' was a title unknown in the Franciscan Order. The author was probably a prior of Canons Ashby." Reference to Bale, I think, proves this latter supposition to be correct. I identify him with one Alexander of Ashby (fl. 1220), called "Essebiensis," and also "prior de Essebi," precisely as above, and reported author of a treatise on the art of preaching. (See Bale, Oxf. ed. 1902, p. 22).

[2] MSS. Bodl. 5 and 316. The latter (with the *Policronicon*) begins: "Circa sermones artificialiter faciendos," and ends: "Expl. ars comp. serm..." (fol. 176). I have used the Bodl. MS. 5. See also MS. Harl. 3634 (c. 1388).

[3] Cf. MS. Harl. 635, fol. 6, etc. ("De theoria, sive arte predicandi.")

[4] MS. Harl. 635, fols. 1 b–5 b ("editus a magistro Simone Alcok, sacre pagine professore"); and MS. Bodl. 52, fol. 102 b, etc.

[5] Of whom nothing further is known (Quétif et Echard, vol. i, 471 A).

[6] In MS. Harl. 3838, only. Notice also Jo. Goldstone (fl. 1320), author of *Divisiones Sermonum*.

[7] Cf. MSS. Caius Coll. Camb. 240, fol. 525, etc. and 407; MSS. Add. 21202, fol. 71 and 24361, fol. 52 (a *Tractatus de sermonibus faciendis*, in a fifteenth-century MS. once belonging to St Mary's Abbey, York); MSS. Roy. 5. C. iii; Cotton, Vitell., C. xiv, fols. 72 b–78 (unfinished); MS. Gray's Inn Libr. 12. ii; (an *Ars dividendi themata*, by Cardinal Bertrand de la Tour, Franciscan, may be noticed in MS. Balliol Coll. Oxf. 179; his *Collations* (de temp. et de sanct.) appear in MS. Gray's Inn Libr. 7. ix, a MS. from an Engl. Franciscan convent).

and less reading of "homiliaria" than many would have us believe. They tell us that, apart altogether from the village "curate" with his manual of outlines, childish in their simplicity, friar and bishop and graduate priest still demanded their set of instructions, to deal correctly with themes of their own. The speaker himself needed preparation as well as his address, sometimes for that most awful duty of dilating "when one has really nothing to say."

Our mediaeval preacher, then, is sitting down to his lesson in sermon construction. His *Tractatus de forma Sermonum* lies open before him: "Preaching involves the taking up of a Theme, the division of the same theme, the sub-division of the theme, the appropriate citing of concordant points, and the clear and devout explanation of the Authorities brought forward."[1] It is obviously no light task that he is to undertake. Preaching, his instructor goes on, must have proper form and order. The first step is to put forward a *theme*, or text from Scripture, "in which the message is virtually contained."[2] Walleys says on this point: "And this *theme* may be taken from the lesson, the epistle, or the gospel of that day, with the exception of the very solemn days, such as Easter, Whitsunday, or the like. For then, because many are wont to preach, they may take their *theme* as they wish."[3] Such, at all events, is the "approved modern style." Of the actual choice of suitable subject-matter for these special occasions, nothing further need be added. The care with which it was expected to be done has been amply illustrated in a previous chapter from the pages of Higden[4].

Next follows the *ante-theme*. Here there is general agreement among the authorities that prayer and invocation are to be the keynote, so that at the very outset "divine help may be im-

[1] MS. Add. 21202, fol. 71: "Predicatio est thematis assumpcio, ejusdemque thematis divisio, thematis subdivisio, concordantiarum congrua citacio, et auctoritatum adductarum clara et devota explanatio."

[2] Cf. Walleys, cap. ii, MS. Harl. 635, fol. 8: "Consuetudo est apud modernos approbata primo thema proponere...."

[3] Ibid. fol. 8 b: "Quod thema accipiatur de lectione, epistola, vel evangelio illius diei, exceptis diebus multum solemnibus, ut paschae, pentecostes, vel similibus. Tunc enim, quia plures solent predicare, accipiant thema ut volunt."

[4] See above, Chap. VI; and MS. Bodl. 5, fol. 5 b, etc.: "De congruitate thematis."

plored," and "the word of the Lord have free course and be fruitful."[1] Actual examples, abounding in both Latin and English collections, show us, as a rule, ante-themes of the briefest pattern, in which the preacher's call to intercession is directly followed by the repetition of "Pater" and "Ave" by all present: "Devoto corde simul omnes offeramus Christo orationem quam docuit, et matri ejus ac virgini salutationem angelicam, qua illum ipsa concepit, dicentes pr. nr., et ave...."[2] This habit often led to two very natural elaborations of the ante-theme prayer, one for special help for the speaker himself, the other calling to remembrance before the Mercy-Seat all the people of God, that mighty audience of the living and the dead, seen and unseen. A charming invocation of the first type, not unworthy of our Prayer-Book Collects, stands at the head of an English homily on the Assumption of the Blessed Virgin:

All myȝhty God, to whos powere and goodenes ynfinite all creatures bethe suget, at the besechynge of thi glorious modur, gracious lady, and of all thi seyntes, helpe oure febulnes with thi powre, oure ignoraunce with thi wisdom, oure freelte with thin sufficiaunt goodnes, that we may resceyve here thin helpe and grace continuall, and finally everlastynge blisse. To the wiche bliss thou toke this blissed lady this day as to hur eternall felicite. Amen[3].

From the same manuscript we venture to borrow an equally pleasing illustration of the second type:

...But forasmuche as grace in this acte is to us ryght nedefull, pray we to God specially for grace, havynge recommended to oure devoute prayours all the parties of cristis church, the clergy from the hiest astate unto the lowest degre, seynge thus, "Sacerdotes tui in-

---

[1] Cf. MS. Add. 21202: "quaedam via ad divinum auxilium implorandum"; Walleys: "ad invitandum ad orationes"; Higden: "Posuerunt nonulli post thema propositum statim promittere orationem, et hoc quidem bene"; Felton, beginning a sermon (MS. Harl. 5396, fol. 55): "quod predicator debet ante sermonem orare, ut sermo Dei currat et fructiferat in auditoribus." Ibid. MS. Roy. 8. B. xii, fol. 73.

[2] MS. Lansd. 393, fol. 27 (Fitzralph). Cf. again MS. Harl. 5398, fol. 21: "ei offerentes illud sacrificium orationis consuetum," and, for vernacular example, MS. Roy. 18. B. xxiii, fol. 121: "...and therefore, that we better love God and oure sowles, iche man, per charite, sey a 'pr. nr.' and 'ave.'"

[3] MS. Roy. 18. B. xxiii, fol. 135 b. For a Latin example, cf. MS. Add. 21202, fol. 74: "Nunc in principio sermonis invocabimus ut impetret [Xtus.] nobis gratiam, mihi ad dicendum, et vobis ad audiendum, et intendere quod sit Deo et sibi ad laudem et gloriam, et nobis omnibus ad salutem."

duantur justitiam," etc.—"Lord, late thi prestes be of such lyvynge in right wisnes that every good man may have ioye thereof" (Ps. 13[2]). The second, pray we tendirly for oure sovereyn lorde the kynge and all is lege peple, saying thus, "Domine salvum fac regem...,"—"Lord God, save oure most cristen kynge, and here us cristen peple, what day that ever we call upon the" (Ps. 19); and for all is lordes; and in especiall pray we for the sowles that ben passed hens. ffor tho we pray for the sowles that ben in heven, other in hell, our prayoure is not lost. Loo a full fayre figure here of!... [The preacher breaks off most quaintly here with his figure of "Noe's culver," or dove.]...Praye we than for all thise, and for grace to us necessare, with "pr. nr." and "ave."[1]

No happier hunting-ground for those interested in quaint and picturesque forms of the Bidding Prayer could be found than amongst these Old English sermon ante-themes. Metrical homilies naturally employ a metrical ante-theme to fit, if such appears[2]. The University preacher in prose, however, may fancy some pious Latin couplet in rhyme to suit the affected taste of his hearers:

> Per consueta suffragia pulsentur mente pia,
> Pater, proles deifica, spiramen cum Maria[3].

Robert Rypon's manuscript possesses many homilies where the ante-theme, which is here regularly marked "Ante-thema" or "Prologus" in the margins[4], has often some message of its own in keeping with the chosen *theme*. In one of his eight sermons on the preaching task, for instance, where the text is a single word—"Ite," interpreted according to the gloss—"ad predicandum," he has something to add both of the subject-matter to be preached, and the supply of the preachers, thereby opening up the way to his threefold "divisio" of the theme. In place of the more sober prayer for speaker and listeners, the "Prologus" ends here with an arresting appeal to his audience

---

[1] For a Latin example of contrasted brevity, cf. MS. Camb. Univ. Libr. Ii. iii. 8, fol. 126: "In principio hujus collationis, recommendatis omnibus quae debent hic recommendari, dicat quisque mente pia—'pater nr.' et 'ave maria.'"

[2] Cf. MS. Camb. Univ. Libr. Dd. i. 1, version of the *Sermo festo Corp. Christi*, printed in E.E.T.S., O.S. No. 89, p. 168.

[3] MS. Harl. 5398, fol. 51 (cf. again fol. 54).

[4] The word "Prologus" is here preferred where the preacher is long-winded; "ante-thema" for the shorter openings, sometimes only of a line or two.

to pray that the Almighty may send true "preachers of his Word among Christian people."[1] From the vernacular side, this might be matched with another good illustration of the shrewdness and force of which the contemporary pulpit was capable. Rather than waste even the breath of an Introduction upon hackneyed phrases, the homilist seizes his opportunity to recall men to the real meaning of the "Pater Noster." It is a prayer these wandering, unlettered minds have repeated so often and so carelessly in their crude Latin, and have forgotten so soon. They are now about to repeat it again, as the sermon opens. With spiritual discernment he would make it not the mere idle passing repetition of phrases, but a common act of worship:

> Good men and good women, oure Lord Jhu Crist techyng his disciplus, and by hem alle cristyne, that in every good werk ferst godus worschep and afturwarde hele of soule principalyche is to be desyred, seyet hem in this wyse, "pater n. qui es in celes (sic!), sanct. nomen t." etc., that is to seyngge, "ffader oure, that hert in hevene, y halwed by thi name, thy kyngdom be ous to commyng"; werfore, suth no werk is of more vertu tha[n] the word of God, skylfullyche in the bygynnyngge of godus word, we schulde desyre to worschepe god and helpe oure soules. Werfore, suth oure purpos at this tyme is to speke sumwhat to the worschep of God and help of oure soules, it is ful skylful that we sey and *wt. oure herte desyre* as Crist us hath y-tawyth, that is to wyte—*pat. nr....*etc.; havyng in ʒoure prayre y-recommendyd alle lyves and dethus, the wyche Go(o)d wole at this tyme that we have in mynde....[2]

An almost infallible indication that the ante-theme has ended and the *processus* of the theme has begun is afforded by a clear repetition of the text: "After the prayer, the principal *theme* ought to be repeated again. Then let some brief, fitting introduction be made, so that the theme may seem to have been

---

[1] MS. Harl. 4894, fol. 195 b. A *Forma Predicandi* thus describes how the more stylish ante-theme should be constructed (MS. Add. 21202, fol. 71 et seq.): "Ut haec clarius videantur, ponamus exemplum; et proponatur hoc thema—'Beatus vir qui timet dominum' in proposito. Et accipiatur pro themate haec auctoritas—'Beati qui audiunt verbum Dei,' Luc. vi. Sic in hoc verbo potestis videre quod devota auditio verbi Dei inducit nos ad eternam beatitudinem. Ideo, si voluistis eternae beatitudinis esse participes, oportet vos libenter et devote audire verbum Dei. Ideo in principio nostrae sermonis rogemus Deum ut mihi det gratiam proponendi, et vobis audiendi..." etc.

[2] MS. Bodl. 110, fol. 168.

opened in a reasonable fashion."[1] Preliminaries are now over, and the real preacher will begin to disclose himself. So much hangs for our human nature upon the starting-point, the first impression made, the first stride which will proclaim the master or the tyro. Our orator is upon his trial. The real battle in actual preparation, no doubt, which wages around the division of the theme, has been fought and won before ever the time comes to mount the rostrum. But equally vital must be that psychological moment in the pulpit which may win or lose a sympathetic hearing for the rest of sermon-time. Thomas Walleys is perfectly candid in his guide-book about the fact that "many have difficulty in introducing their themes in a pertinent manner."[2] He therefore offers his reader a choice of three pleasing ways— "by an authority" (that is a quotation, of course)[3], "by an 'exemplum,'" or "by natural reason." These are illustrated in turn. If, for example, it please you to select the last named, what could be better than some appropriate little message for the particular occasion or audience of the day? There lie the sick or infirm. Let the preacher then win his way to their hearts with a word of the divine consolation, "something useful for them to know," such as the future joys of heaven that await the patient and the faithful. Argument for the mind, kindling emotion, the attraction of the illustrative story might well be expected to play their part together. In view of what has been said by way of modern comment[4] upon the wiles and eccentricities of the mediaeval "preambulum," the "Quo nunc se proripit ille?" and so forth, it is worth noting that something akin to this appears to be suggested by our English Higden: "At the beginning it is expedient that the preacher, so far as he can without giving offence to God, should win the good-will of his hearers, rendering them apt to hear, and eager to pursue his words to the end."[5] This can be accomplished by de-

---

[1] MS. Add. 21202, as before. "Post orationem debet repeti thema principale etiam. Tunc fiat aliqua brevis decens introductio, ut videatur quod thema fuit rationabiliter sumptum."

[2] MS. Harl. 635, fol. 9.

[3] MS. Add. 21202 is more explicit: "per auctoritates Bibliae vel alicujus doctoris."

[4] See e.g. J. Ker, *Hist. of Preaching* (1888), p. 143.

[5] MS. Bodl. 5, fol. 12: "Expedit in principio predicatori ut, quantum poterit, Deo inoffenso, auditores reddat benevolos et aptos ad audiendum, et sollicitos ad exequendum."

scribing "something strange, subtle, and curious," or else by startling them into attention with some terrible anecdote as example. For the latter there were plenty to hand of ghoulish devil-stories, terrifying death-bed scenes, the graves of "wormes mete and rotye,"[1] the tortures of an enduring hell, all calculated to freeze the blood and raise the hair of the simple. Long before black-gowned Calvinists started to gnash teeth in the pulpit, or Protestant parents and nursemaids held up an awful fiendish finger at their charges, like the archdeacons and others in our miniatures[2], the same threatening of sinners was almost a commonplace of religious instruction. For openings subtle and curious on the other hand we might turn back to Thomas Walleys. He advises that after the preacher has laid out in his own mind the groundwork of a suitable Introduction, he should proceed to cover it, as it were, with a purely ornamental super-structure, in such a way that when presented in the pulpit to his audience, only the sharpest intellects among them will detect at once what lies beneath[3]. As illustration of the method in actual practice, we have only to listen to some Introductions of Bishop Brunton, with their weird galaxy of the most diverse metaphors imaginable. Thus does he seek on occasion to dazzle and arouse the half-awakened congregation before him[4]: "Whither is he hurrying now?"

But Introductions, as Walleys reminds us, should never be long[5]. "Causa brevitatis," indeed they may sometimes be omitted, when the preacher is pressed for time[6]. From the making of *divisions* for the "processus thematis" following there can be no escape. When the sermon is based upon an ordinary text of Scripture, the task of extracting three convenient ideas, upon which to hang the rest of the discourse

[1] MS. Harl. 2398, fol. 91. (And see below, pp. 336–344.)
[2] Cf. MSS. Roy. 6. E. vi, fol. 132 and 6. E. vii, fol. 197. Reproduced in Cutts' *Parish Priests* (ed. 1914), p. 167; etc.
[3] MS. Harl. 635, fol. 11: "...quod non apparebit statim audientibus nisi bene intelligentibus."
[4] Cf. e.g. his strange opening for the striking sermon on "Simul in unum dives et pauper" (MS. Harl. 3760, fol. 111 b): "Sicut ab uno mari manant diversi rivuli, ab una luce diversi radii, ab uno puncto diverse linee, multa opera ab uno artifice, ab uno Deo procedunt omnia...," etc.
[5] MS. Harl. 635, fol. 14.
[6] Cf. Waldeby, MS. Caius Coll. Camb. 334, fol. 195 b: "Omissa thematis introductione causa brevitatis, pro processu...," etc.

does not appear very difficult. For three, with that characteristic mediaeval love of symbolic numbers[1] perhaps, is a regular
choice for the main "divisio." If "Dies mali sunt" be your
theme[2], for example, you may observe a threefold evil, which
flourishes in these days, to wit "excessus voluptatis," "defectus
sanitatis," and "contemptus humilitatis." They may sound a
little vague and dreary, it is true. To those, doomed like ourselves to look back over five centuries more since friar John
Waldeby preached upon them, the whole world still lying, as
he saw it then, "in wickedness, with these three vices," they
may be even a little futile and annoying. But sermon-headings
after all are not expected to be as provoking as the head-lines
of the news-sheets. Once let the mediaeval homilist get astride
the vices, and then the virtues which ever accompany them,
and he may be safely trusted to gallop triumphantly to his conclusion[3]. What a vista of separate crimes, follies, excuses, pains
and penalties, they open up to Dr Bromyard, with his searching
eye ever upon the contemporary scene! By thus "dividing the
branches of the vices" with him, as with Gower[4], you may
obtain a dozen sub-headings, figures, and examples more, with
the minimum of reflection. The relentless Dominican doctor,
indeed, urges his pupils to make pointed attacks on specific
evils: "As the mummer when describing or mocking anyone

---

[1] Cf. for a curious example of "Holy Numbers" in a sermon, Myrc's
Festiall (E.E.T.S. ed. p. 215, l. 28). (Three children and no more, in worship
of the Trinity.)

[2] Cf. MS. Caius Coll. Camb. 334, fol. 195 b (as treated above).

[3] This and the Decalogue (together with Heaven and Hell) in a word are
considered the *marrow of all preaching* by contemporaries; cf. Rypon, MS.
Harl. 4894, fol. 130 b: "ad mores instruere, vicia reprehendere, et ad peni-
tentiam excitare"; MS. Add. 21253, fol. 140: "vocem predicatoris Xti de
poenis inferni, et gloria paradisi, et de virtutibus, et viciis, et judicio";
similarly *Cil. Oc. Sac.*, MS. Harl. 4968, fol. 43 (answering—"Quid sit predicandum?"); and similarly Walleys in MS. Harl. 635, fol. 17 b; Spicer (?) in
Fascic. Morum, Prologue: "in regula beati fratris Francisci, et...alibi,
tenemur primo denunciare, et predicare vicia et virtutes, penam et gloriam..."; Myrc's *Festiall*, E.E.T.S. p. 161: "tell the people their vices";
Dives et Pauper, prec. x, cap. x: "For it longeth to the prechoure of goddis
worde to commende vertuis, and despise vices," etc.; MS. Harl. 45, fol. 77:
"...how thei schulde flee synne, and use vertu, and so schone the pyne of
helle, and come to the blisse of hevene"; MS. Linc. Cath. Libr. A. 6. 2, fol.
64 b: "the seedys and cornys of the doctrine of God"; etc., etc.

[4] *Conf. Amant.* bk. v, etc. Cf. any of our moral treatises, e.g. MS. Harl.
2398, fol. 21 b (five types of covetousness, etc.); MS. Harl. 45 and the
works mentioned here in Chap. VII.

recites intimate details about him, as the doctor gives his specific prescriptions, so let the preacher deliver a detailed account of the sinner's state and its dangers, with special reproofs."[1] Thus do the greatest homiletical works of the age resolve themselves very naturally into vast repositories of current criticism and rebuke—for the mediaeval cleric his chief weapons, "smooth stones out of the brook"—not five, but five hundred for the holy warfare of the pulpit, for the modern social historian a mine of fresh and illuminating facts[2].

Not every text, on the other hand, may yield so easy a solution. Like the blessed Edmund of old, worn out with the burden of his Oxford lectures and other duties, faced with the task of preparing a sermon for the morrow, our preacher too, "burdened with drowsiness" as he sits at his desk in the nightwatches, may drop off to sleep. He can hardly expect a visit from that heaven-sent dove, however, which brought inspiration to the saint of old, at his prayer[3]. Nevertheless, for the clerk who struggles helplessly, with the nightmare of the "divisio" and the "subdivisio" before him, an empty head, and time fast running out with his ideas, there is a further expedient at hand. Kindly "Professors of Sacred Theology" and other learned persons have evolved for his use cunning Latin verses, usually of eight lines or so, which are to be found in most treatises on sermon division and dilation[4]. A compiler shall explain the scheme in his own pious way:

[1] S.P.—Predic. (Cf. also, preaching should be—"contra vicia,...in speciali.")

[2] For further illustration, I submit the following *numbers of references to the chief vices* extracted from the contemporary Tabula to MS. Roy. 8. C. i, a copy of Waldeby's well-known sermon-treatises. They refer to passages occurring in the text:

Avaritia	...	...	56	Invidia	23
Luxuria	...	...	33	Gula	19
Superbia	...	...	32		

(The leading two are here characteristically the most common English vices to be denounced by our pulpit. For "Luxuria" we are even told England has the worst reputation of any country in the world! (cf. frequent references to St Boniface's prophecy). "Homicidia" might have figured as the third to be representative, perhaps.)

[3] MS. Roy. 7. D. i, fol. 92. A sermon story of St Edmund of Canterbury in an English Dominican collection, told to the writer by the Saint's confessor.

[4] Cf. Simon Alcock, S.T.P. in MS. Harl. 635, fol. 1 b: "Ad quare, per, propter notat...," etc. I give Thos. Walleys' verse as it is shorter (MS. Harl. 635, fol. 15 b):

In the aforesaid verses hints are contained, by means of which a *division* in the sermon matter can be fashioned from the *theme*; and in addition, by means of the same hints the preacher can multiply his matter, and dilate the same. And although not every *theme* can be easily "divided" by any one of the aforesaid hints, nevertheless rarely is a *theme* assigned which cannot be "divided" by many ways indicated in the verses aforesaid, if the preacher's effort is directed by the noblest Master of all, who is the Spirit of Truth[1].

Now take, for example, the second word "quare" as supplied in such verses as are referred to. This should prompt you "to seek for 'questiones' in the theme, and to give reasons in the reply." When the ordinary meanings of Scripture have been exhausted, further points of discussion can be raised by developing the various symbolic meanings[2]. To these can be added in due time imagery from nature and social life, duly expanded in its turn, authoritative statements or examples from the Fathers[3], the Histories, the "Exemplaria," until the whole becomes as intricate, though hardly as beautiful as the tracery of a Gothic "rose-window." Leaving aside the latter, perhaps, as something too choice and unspoilt for the comparison, it is possible for us to see in the riot of shallow, trivial ornamentation, the petty groupings and lack of dignified proportion in the last great decorative styles, the fondness for diagrams, "Catherine-wheels," emblems and devices[4], and further in these same fantastic niceties of later preaching and Scholasticism in general, some common expressions of the Age-Spirit.

"Regule dilatande materie in sermonibus patent in hiis versibus:
　　　　Hic dilatandi modus est sermonibus aptus,
　　　　Divide, diffini, tribus argue per methaphoras,
　　　　Bis binos sensus expone, triformiter adduc,
　　　　Conjuga, multiplica, dic facta rei quoque causas."

[1] MS. Roy. 8. E. xii, fol. 53 et seq.

[2] To indicate the importance of this sermon dilation and division in the eyes of English preachers, one has merely to point to the headings of sections in so diminutive a work as Higden's *Forma Pred.* (cf. MS. Bodl. 5, fols. 16–26 b: "De thematis divisione; de clavibus divisionis; de sermonis dilatatione; de membrorum subdivisione; de dilatacione per auctoritates; de regulis dilatationum," etc.). Cf. also Walleys, in his final summary (MS. Harl. 635, fol. 17 b) on the *Causa Formalis* of the sermon art.

[3] Such simple collections of sayings as the *Sententie ex patribus* in MS. Linc. Cath. Libr. C. 4. 6, fols. 47–62 b (here adorned with little marginal portraits, occasionally!), or *The Vertewes of the Mass*, ed. from MS. Camb. Univ. Libr. Kk. i. 5, in E.E.T.S., Old S. No. 43, p. 113, etc. illustrate perfectly where the "great clerks'" sayings come from in the vernacular sermons.

[4] Cf. the favourite devices of the Trinity, emblems of the Passion, Vices and Virtues, etc. in ecclesiastical art, with the typical sermon *schemata* described.

The final method of dilating suggested by Walleys is that of developing the several features of some natural object chosen as symbol, a scriptural method easy to apply, as he points out[1]. The formal preachers seem to have seized upon it with avidity. Prominent among the homiletical conceits of the twelfth and thirteenth centuries had been the curious Heavenly Chariot, with its four wheels, their spokes and axles, the body of the conveyance, its occupants, its team of oxen and much else, all discussed allegorically in turn[2]. There is an echo of "the verb and its tenses," from the same period, in a comparison of the six noun-cases of the school grammar-books with the "Six Cases of Pride" which is to be found in the *Gesta Romanorum*[3]. Similarly, in English homilies of our period, familiar objects, whether from Scripture or from every-day life, provide the preacher with a whole series of pegs upon which to hang the chief points of his theme. From Scripture comes Jacob's Ladder, or that Galilean boat of the Gospel story in which Christ sat to preach, as figured by Rypon. From current life come the "Castellum Diaboli," or "Castellum Religionis," and the social parable set forth by the chessmen and their moves. As Dr Brandeis says, the symbol "is set in motion, as it were, by expanding it into a sort of allegorical action." Mention of the "fortress" leads on naturally to a description of its formidable walls, the hardened sinners, built of stone of the hardest vices, joined together with the cement of impiety. Then there is the "dych," or moat, with its symbolic water, the "drawbryge," the inner and outer keep, the lofty tower, and within "capten," and constable, officials and garrison troops[4]. Forced though many of the analogues may be, all this is certainly an improvement over "the beeste" that "hath not but oon fote," with five

---

[1] MS. Harl. 635, fol. 17 b, cap. ix: " ...Restat ergo in talibus locutionibus considerare proprietates et conditiones rerum ex quibus accipitur similitudo, et conditiones illas aptare ad propositum..." (e.g. qualitas, operatio, finis, causa efficiens, etc.).

[2] Cf. Bourgain, p. 256, etc. Cf. here the weird drawing of "the Cart of the Fayth" in a fifteenth-century English MS.—Add. 37049, fol. 81.

[3] Cf. MS. Add. 9066, fol. 82 b (E.E.T.S. ed. O.S. No. 33, p. 416) from the *Donet*. (*Nominatif* = pride of name; *Genetif* = pride of birth; *Datif* = of gifts; *Accusatif* = in false accusations; *Vocatyf* = of being *called* to the king's counsel; *Ablatif* = in theft and confiscation!)

[4] Cf. Bromyard, *S.P.* s.v. *Anima*; MS. Camb. Univ. Libr. Ii. iii. 8, fol. 150; MS. Add. 21253, fol. 146 et seq.; Myrc's *Festiall* (E.E.T.S. ed. p. 228: the Castle of Our Lady): the latter derived from Grossetête's *Castle of Love*.

tediously moralized toes[1] on it, or the fingers and finger-joints of the Almighty[2]. But for its familiarity, one could imagine that the favourite Moralization of Chess[3] excited a considerable interest among the contemporary sermon audiences, when developed in the same fashion. It must surely have been otherwise with that rural congregation treated for "this hool tweyne monythys and more" to a sermon course which dilated upon the single figure of *Jacob's Well*[4] with talk of "skeet and skavel," "spade and laddere," "wyndas," "roop," "bokett" and all manner of soils and deposits, as well. We are left wondering at the first how intelligent persons could have survived the practice. But the mediaeval preacher generally knows well enough what is best suited to his age. Here was a scheme cleverly calculated to stimulate memories. Those two compass points[5] you despise, those three corners of the shield[6], those "dyvers drynkes" of the Devil[7], those "sixe leves" and "thre greynes,...faire endored" of the lily-flower[8], when the sermon was over, would be remembered yet. Behold the pious mediaeval household seated around the Sunday dinner-table recalling the speaker's points: "Lust consumes the body. It destroys the tongue of confession,...the eyes of the intelligence, the ears of obedience, the nose of discretion, the hairs of good thoughts, the beard of fortitude, the eyebrows of holy religion...."[9] It may seem trivial, but you cannot stop till the whole physiognomy has been accounted for. When books were rare, amusements childish, and the summer evenings long, how many ancestors of the race may have gained their religious instruction that way? Brick by brick the simple mind builds up its "Castellum Diaboli" or its "Castellum Religionis" again, with all the child's delight in his plaything upon the hearth-rug.

However, for those who discard clear logical thinking and

---

[1] MS. Roy. 18. B. xxiii, fol. 77. The 'Cyclops.'
[2] Cf. Bromyard, above, on p. 304; and MS. Harl. 2398, fol. 141 b, etc.
[3] Cf. Bromyard, *S.P.* s.v. *Mundus*; the *Communiloquium* of Jo. Walleys (see Little, *Studies*, Appdx. 5, p. 232); *Gesta Rom.* (E.E.T.S. ed. pp. 70–71); MSS. Harl. 2253, fol. 135 b, Bodl. 52, fol. 59 b, Bodl. 58, fol. 51 (*Engl. MS.* of de Cessolis, c. 1400). See also *Archaeol.* vol. xxiv, p. 203.
[4] See MS. Salisb. Cath. Libr. 103, fol. 214 b (and ed. of Pt. i, E.E.T.S.).
[5] Lichfield, in MS. Roy. 8. C. i; MS. Harl. 45, fol. 131.
[6] Bromyard, *S.P.* s.v. *Fides*.   [7] MS. Roy. 18. B. xxiii, fol. 131 b.
[8] MS. Harl. 45, fol. 124 b.   [9] MS. Add. 21253, fol. 27 b.

precise observation for such strings of analogies where more educated audiences are concerned, there can be little praise. Such is invariably the mark of puerile, undisciplined thought. Without doubt, the contemporary pulpit shows us its worst side in its "scholastic" preaching; and puerility of style becomes the more glaring, as the fashion increases. Where English survivals of this class occur, the passion for shaping everything "secundum formam syllogisticam,"[1] or according to the method of propounding questions and defending conclusions "in the schools of Theology at Oxford,"[2] is not concealed. Master Rypon actually borrows the whole syllogistic machinery, with talk of major and minor premise, qualities and essence of things, to demonstrate an initial point—that the priest should be what he calls "sacer dux, sacra dans, et sacra docens."[3] A more ridiculous admixture of the trivial and the pompous it would be hard to imagine. Hear him, again, as he discourses on what the mediaeval logician calls the "propria passio" of a subject. The sermon is proceeding:

...In qua quidem demonstratione, sicut satis moverunt logici, concluditur propria passio de subjecto per medium quod est diffinitio. Et voco propriam passionem proprietatem specificam, quae convenit uni soli specie, ut, verb. grat., risibilitas, vel esse risibile est propria passio seu proprietas speciei humanae, cujus speciei diffinitio est haec—homo est animal rationale mortale—per quam diffinitionem concluditur dicta passio seu proprietas de hoc subjecto "homo," ut verb. grat. haec est demonstratio sillogica: Omne animal rationale mortale est risibile. Omnis homo est animal mortale. Igitur, omnis homo est risibilis. Hinc concluditur propria passio de subjecto per medium quod est diffinitio....

So he goes on to the end of his "demonstratio sillogica." But further, in gross defiance of Father Bede Jarrett, and even of

[1] Cf. also *Hist. Litt. de la Fr.* vol. xxiv, p. 363 et seq.

[2] Cf. Walleys' reference to the Oxford style of preaching, or Gascoigne (in Rogers' ed. *Loci e Libro Ver.* p. 183, etc.). Similarly in Richard of Thetford's treatise.

[3] MS. Harl. 4894, fol. 205 et seq.: "Sic igitur, pro presenti subjectum nostrae demonstrationis similitudinarie 'Sacerdos,' cujus propria passio sive proprietas est ut sit sacer dux, sacra dans, et sacra docens. Et in hoc 'est operarius dignus mercede.'" (This is his text—another violent clash of ideas and tastes!) N.B. also, here, he starts off with the typical "scholastic" questions: "Quae est propria proprietas per quam res est?"; "Quid res est, scil. in sua essentia vel diffinitione?"; etc.

their own manual writers in the centuries concerned[1], the simpler preachers in the vulgar tongue, copying their "Masters," with little pretence of scholastic achievement themselves, will sometimes fall into the same habit of procedure. Now they will talk of "my anteteme" in the body of their address[2], or again, with carefully "divided" subject-matter, of "resonable certeyn questions" couched superbly in Latin, one by one, to impress their admiring hearers: "'Beatus est rex....' Uppon thise wordes may be moved resonable certeyn questions: 'Quis est rex iste?'; 'Qualis est?'; 'Quantus est?'; et 'Ubi?'.... The firste question is of personall dignite; the secounde is of is maner of lyvynge; the third is of is auctorite; the fourthe is of is dwellyng."[3] What would Bishop Croft of Hereford have said to them[4]?

The more practised orators of the pulpit were never slow to make whatever "play" they could out of carefully chosen words, forced etymologies[5], and the like. Reference has been made already to a theme of the Durham sub-prior which was fashioned of a single word of three letters. So Fitzralph and others had based their discourses upon "texts" of a like simplicity for listeners to recall, such as the name "Jhesus."[6] Clear enunciation of the headings of "divisiones" which, by right, followed immediately upon the opening of the theme itself, was sometimes made even more impressive by repeated use of end-syllables in rhyme. Such had been the method of the *Sermones*

[1] Cf. *Cil. Oc. Sac.* in MS. Harl. 4968, fol. 43: "...Nam laicis gramatica, fabule, nec alia subtilia, ut divisiones vel conclusiones scolastice, predicari non debent." Apart from the above, if a general scheme of construction for the simple vernacular sermons were to be made out from surviving examples, it would be roughly as follows: (1) a paraphrase of the Gospel (or Epistle, etc.) for the day; (2) an exposition of the same, with the usual practical instruction; (3) two or more "exempla" to end the sermon.
[2] MS. Roy. 18. B. xxiii, fol. 53. Cf. also what might be a quaint imitation of Rypon's style above (MS. Harl. 2398, fol. 86): "The name of God ys the wisdom of the fader; for as phylosophers seyth, the propre name of a thyng ys the forme that ys y-founded in that and non other...."
[3] MS. Roy. 18. B. xxiii, fol. 129 b, etc. Cf. also ibid. fol. 136: "In thise wordes ben moved iiii questions...," and fol. 59 b, etc.
[4] *The Naked Truth*, 1675, Chap. VII, "Concerning Preaching." (A plea for simple religious instruction, *versus* those who preach "in demonstration of their Learning." Curiously like mediaeval attacks on those who have "learnt a little to chop Logick," in the pulpits.) Ed. Hensley Henson, 1919.
[5] As satirized by Erasmus (*Enc. Moriae*). Cf. examples above, pp. 38, 327.
[6] Cf. another, simply "Videte!" (Mk. xiii), (MS. Lansd. 393, serm. xxvii); and Waldeby, in MS. Caius Coll. Camb. 334, fol. 177 (Jhesus).

Rimati. Punning upon words is a not infrequent device, and actually figures in at least one funeral oration of the times, where one would have thought the solemnity of the occasion might have forbidden it[1]. The versatile Rypon of Durham, preaching on the text, "Ecce ego mitto vos," reads his clerical congregation what sounds strangely like a lesson in grammar, on the triple uses of the adverb "Ecce," and the pronoun "Ego."[2] Finally we get an element of acrostic-making, when each letter of sacred names like "Maria" or "Jesus,"[3] ordinary nouns like "Cor,"[4] are made to introduce significant words of their own, thereby supplying the speaker with sermon divisions of a most facile sort. If used with a measure of reverence, we need not sneer at these little tricks of oratorical ingenuity, as nothing more than idle vanities on the part of the speaker, mere offences against good taste. They had their value, then, like the sermons in verse and the narrations, which aided the attention and the memory of all too human audiences. What may be written down as oppressive and scandalous, indeed, is the case of the sermon-compiler who inflicts upon us his serried ranks of divisions, threefold for almost every word of his text, plentifully besprinkled with superlatives, and grossly artificial in their relations[5].

So much then for what one preacher, in his discourse, calls

[1] MS. Harl. 3760, fol. 214. Bp. Brunton—for the death of the Black Prince: "Edwardus, dum vixit, nos wardavit." For another, cf. Rypon, above ("sacerdos"), etc.

[2] MS. Harl. 4894, fol. 214 b: "Pro fundamento processus, breviter est notandum quod hoc adverbium—'ecce' in scriptura sacra, sicut et pronomen —'ego,' tripliciter est acceptum. Sumitur enim admirative, demonstrative, et excitative....Conformiter, hoc pronomen 'ego,' congruenter ad hoc adverbium 'ecce,' secundum grammaticos, accipitur trino modo: est enim discretivum, demonstrativum, et super se alterius nominis susceptivum...." With this cf. the treatment of the *Donet* case-endings of nouns in the *Gesta Rom.* aforementioned. Anything and everything could be "moralized."

[3] Cf. Bromyard, *S.P.*—*Maria*; also in *Juramentum*: "Fatuum et Idonea," treated similarly. In Rypon (MS. Harl. 4894): "De significatis litterarum hujus nominis 'Jhesus.'" (See Tabula at end.)

[4] MS. Roy. 8. C. i: "This latyn worde 'Cor,' that betokyneth a hert in Engliche, hath iii letteris—C, O, R. C for camera, that is 'chaumbre'; O for Omnipotentis, that is 'Almyghty'; and R for regis, that is 'of a kyng.' So that 'Cor,' that is to mene 'manes herte,' scholde be the chaumbre of the kyng almyʒty...." (This is another vernacular address in *formal* style.) Cf. also the sermon-story of MS. Harl. 2316, fol. 3, and of MSS. Roy. 8. F. vi, fol. 13 b; Harl. 219, fol. 14 b; etc.

[5] Cf. the amazing *schema* of a sermon "on St Bernard," in MS. Roy. 8. A. v, fol. 128. (On the text: "Ecce vir unus vestitus lineis," Dan. x, 5.)

"the gronde and the substaunce of my sermon."[1] The theme is now ended, and there remains but to add the appropriate finishing touch to the homiletic masterpiece. The tactful preacher has probably taken care to leave as his parting impression the bold, stark outline of future penalties and future bliss. If this latter be mentioned last, then "Ad quem nos perducat, qui sine fine vivit et regnat. Amen." will be an effective yet simple conclusion, whether expressed in the language of the Church or of the common people[2]. Dignified and more polished speakers on the other hand may indulge in a more stylish peroration with some final reference to their original text, and the chief points of discourse. Thus Rypon concludes a synodal oration: "Redeundo igitur ad propositum principale, et finem faciendo, vos sacerdotes et curati—'Dicite'! [i.e. the text, 'Dicite—"pax huic domui"']—primo mentaliter, pacem internam in domo conscientiae mentem a contagione purgando contra insolenciam et superbiam. 'Dicite,' secundo, vocaliter, pacem externam in domo ecclesiae gentem predicatione informando..."[3] and so on, through the heads of divisions once more. There may even be a tactful politeness about the orator's mode of cessation, as when Archbishop Fitzralph commends his earnest appeal to the distinguished throng at Avignon[4], with a final gesture, thus: "But I have i-travailled ʒowre holynes inow, and the reverens of my lordes the cardenalis. Therefore I conclude, and pray meke liche and devout-liche as I prayde in the firste that I touchede, 'Demeth nouʒt by the face, but riʒtful doome ʒe deme.' Qui cum patre..., etc."[5] The English is the graceful English of John de Trevisa, translator, but behind it we discern the grace of a no less polished master of assemblies, who "lowed to speke in latyn" before the rulers of the Church.

[1] MS. Roy. 18. B. xxiii, fol. 59 b.
[2] Cf. our *Tractatus de Forma Serm.* as quoted here, MS. Add. 21202, fol. 73; or Waldeby, e.g. MS. Caius Coll. Camb. 334, fol. 198: "Ad quam Dei laetitiam nos perducant beata Trinitas, pater, et filius, et spiritus sanctus. Amen."
[3] MS. Harl. 4894, fol. 195.
[4] In the year 1357. This sermon is *wrongly dated* in the published *Brit. Mus. Cat. of Add. MSS.* It may easily be corrected by reference to the Latin version in MS. Lansd. 393 (8th Nov. 1357), or in the *D.N.B.* (Fitzralph of Armagh).
[5] MS. Add. 24194, fol. 21. For "rhymes coués" endings to vernacular

If there was no chapter in the mediaeval *Ars Predicandi* actually entitled "The Psychology of Preacher and Congregation,"[1] yet it is a fact that a remarkable amount of attention was paid by those practising as well as teaching the art, to the mentality of audiences, and the effects of varying modes of presentation. This has been well illustrated already in our pages in the case of the sermons in procession. The principle laid down by Walleys and others—"the conditions of the hearers are to be carefully pondered, and in accord with these the sermon is to be set forth" ("Auditorum etiam condiciones ponderande sunt, et juxta has proferendus est sermo")— usually referred to the more urgent matter of certain vices for certain audiences, but may here be taken to apply with equal force on a wider scale. In a previous account of the mediaeval preaching scene[2] we had occasion to notice the external behaviour of those present, more particularly as viewed from the speaker's standpoint. Wycliffe, then, is probably voicing the general opinion of preachers of his age, when, despairing of the manners of the unrepentant, he decides to concentrate upon the men of good will: "Where a gedrynge of peple is, summe comynly ben goode, and for hem principaly men prechen goddis word, and not for houndis that berken aȝenst God and his lawis, ne for swyn that bathen hem in synne, and wolle nevere leven hem for drede of peyne ne hope of blisse."[3] The learned doctor was apparently no more anxious to play the part of a Salvationist Booth than was friar Doctor Bromyard to become a foreign missionary. But those who might abstain when in Church from the grosser sins of laughing, chattering, sleeping, or fooling, were always liable to wandering thoughts, if not deliberate

homilies, cf. *Jacob's Well* (E.E.T.S. ed.), p. 76: "...Qui se humiliat, exaltabitur":

> "This lownes here in oure lyvyng
> That we mowe be heyghed in hevene in oure endynge,
> Graunte us he
> That for us deyed on rode tre."

For metrical endings to metrical homilies, cf. E.E.T.S., O.S. No. 98, p. 333.

[1] Cf. chapter in *The Minister in the Mod. World* (1923), by Rev. R. C. Gillie, a readable little modern book on the subject.

[2] Chaps. V and VI.

[3] See ed. Matthew (*English Works*), E.E.T.S., O.S. No. 74, pp. 110–11.

inattention[1]. The mediaeval pulpit delights to compare the guilty who will not heed its rebukes to the asp that stops her two ears, one with the "tail of vicious habit," the other against the "ground of sensuality," when the charmer mutters his incantation[2]. More particularly your "great rich and powerful noblemen" though sitting peacefully in their pews, as Bromyard sees them, may yet have no inclination to attend to the sermon. They indulge their fancy with dreams of avarice and carnal delights[3]. A rustic preacher knows too the fickle moods and day-dreams of his humble villagers, moods that will play like shifting sunlight and shadow among the trees: "for hevynes sumtyme, settyst no pryce be thi lyif; and sumtyme thou art to overdone mery, and sumtyme to ovyrdone sory, and to ovyrdone hevy." Even thus will they come to church, from their labours or their holiday sports; and "thof the tunge praye, the herte prayeth noȝt."[4] Perchance the air is heavy with summer heat, and the dreary voice is irksome to listen to. Then

the feendys skyppedyn aforne hem in lyknes of wommen, and thanne tho men in here herte were temptyd to leccherye. Afore summe the feendys drovyn beestys, and thanne thei thouȝtyn on here beestys. Aforn summe the feendys teldyn nobelys, and thanne tho men settyn here thouȝt on here tresoure. Afore summe feendys komyn as merchauntys; thanne the folk thouȝtyn all on byggyng and sellyng. Afore summe feendys komyn as tylmen wyth here hors and carte, and thanne tho folk settyn all herte on husbondrye, on here lond and tylthe, on here howsyng, and on here worldly good. So the feendys made hem ydell...in thouȝtys[5].

The preacher sums up the several types of these day-dreams with almost the care of a psychologist. Idle thoughts themselves lead on to drowsiness again:

> And men may call the fendes drink
> on vanitese thare for to think

[1] Cf. Bp. Brunton's quaint simile (MS. Harl. 3760, fol. 176): "Sed est hodie de multis auditoribus verbi Dei, sicut de fatuis scolaribus per parentes missis Parissiis, in expensis maximis, ad studendum, qui licet pro forma ad scolas vadant, nec tamen student in libris, nec attendunt verba doctorum, sed vage respiciunt fenestras, et indicant transeuntes...."
[2] Cf. MS. Harl. 4894, fol. 17 b. So, too, Fitzralph blames the simple, who fail to learn from preaching, through their own fault: MS. Lansd. 393, fol. 43 b.
[3] S.P.—Predicatio.   [4] Jacob's Well (E.E.T.S., O.S. No. 115, p. 107).
[5] Ibid. p. 237. From a tale of Macarius, the abbot. Sim. p. 231 ('thinking on thy muck'). Cf. Piers Plowman, C text, pass. vii, ll. 282–5.

and on thaire tresore in thaire hord
so that thai here noght Goddes worde.
And when that idell thoght es levid
a hevynes cumes in thaire hevid,⠀⠀⠀⠀[head]
that thai may noght thaire eghen lift
to here no wordes of goddes gift.
Thus drink thai of the devils gowrd
that unto him es nobill bowrd.
Thus dose the fende the folk to lett,
when thai er at the sarmon sett[1].

For rich and for poor alike, then, the old problem is continually facing the preacher, how to unstop the ears of the deaf, and outwit the diabolical plan. The use of the story and the subtleties to arrest attention have already been dealt with sufficiently: "Modo audite narrationem in cronicis!"[2] There remain, however, certain other appeals to the senses, and through them to the emotions, of which the mediaeval homilist is by no means slow to take advantage. These can be collected together for our present purpose under two heads—oratorical and visual.

An ardent champion of the formal theory of sermon construction like friar Walleys is yet in no way scornful of the emotional element in sacred oratory. "The preacher's task is not only to stir the intelligence towards what is true by means of the inevitable conclusions of arguments, but also, by means of narrative and likely persuasion, to stir the emotions to piety."[3] He is to keep to a middle course in this respect, declares the Dominican, employing both methods, as he sees fit, for the audience before him. Earlier in the same work Walleys' interpretation of the phrase, "ad cor principaliter loquitur" goes straight to the root of the matter. It is the goal to which he would lead his pupils by way of the primary elimination of faults in elocution, memory, and gesture. Then "in fervour of spirit," the speaker's heart will become one with the hearts of his hearers[4]. "Distinctions of tongue and listening ears dis-

[1] MS. Harl. 4196, fol. 88 b (*Eng. Met. Homs.*), and compare a little earlier, here:

> "On werldis welth thai think so mekill,
> That ever es fail and fals and fekyll,
> And thar on thai sett thaire thoght.
> That sarmon savers tham right noght."

[2] Waldeby, in MS. Caius Coll. Camb. 334.
[3] MS. Harl. 635, fol. 11.⠀⠀⠀⠀[4] Cf. here the language of mysticism.

appear, as it were, and to him it seems that the message wells up in his own soul, and flows direct into those of his audience," without any intermedium. Then come the "brennyng wordys," such as Myrc mentions[1], kindled with apostolic fire, making the cold, hard hearts "nesch," and fervent. Two great contrasted types of emotional appeal force themselves upon our attention in the pages of the sermon-books[2]. There is the threat of terror and reproof, and there are the gentle references to the love and mercy of the Crucified, both methods fundamentally as old and as primitive as the human race. Among the preachers themselves there seems to be no small difference of opinion on their respective merits. Dr Bromyard may be taken as a typical supporter of the opinion of the majority in favour of that "sad undirnymyng" which, in the words of another, "letteth freyll peple from synne, and in speciall from lechery, and therefore... shuld be had in every prechoure of the worde of God."[3] His motto for the pulpit is "Primo, argue frequenter; secundo obsecra importune; tertio increpa perseveranter."[4] It is to be pre-eminently a system of forcible feeding for the young. As the nurse fails not ever to put more nourishment to the wilful infant mouth that has stubbornly rejected the previous help-ings, so let the preacher persevere with the food of the Word, until successful. There is to be no pampering here with soothing sweetmeats. To spend the greater part of one's sermon in com-mendation of the saints, who need no such commendation from us mortals, he declares, is nothing less than sheer folly. The proper duty of preaching is the reproof of vice, and beyond reproof, the threat of divine fury and future punishments[5].

Victorian Evangelicalism has twitted the "modernist" for his wholesome contempt of the stimulus of hell-fire and eternal damnation as a pious means of frightening sinners into the

[1] The *Festiall*, E.E.T.S. ed. p. 161: "The Apostolys, and all othyr pre-chours aftyr hom schold speke brennyng wordys...."
[2] Cf. Prologue to MS. Add. 33956, fol. 2: "...auditores aliquos feriant timoris malleo, alios autem alliciant amoris incendio...." The interesting contemporary discussion of the elements of *Passion and Anger* in the work of preaching, and the praising and blaming of the preachers, as recently pub-lished in the new E.E.T.S. ed. of Pecock's *Folewer to the Donet* (O.S. No. 164, pp. 102–7) should be consulted in connection with my remarks here.
[3] MS. Roy. 18. B. xxiii, fol. 135 b.
[4] *S.P.—Predic.* Cf. 2 Timothy iv, 2.
[5] Cf. other statements given here in a recent footnote. (Vices and virtues.)

kingdom of Heaven. It is at least fitting for her to know that the whole weight of mediaeval Catholic tradition lies at her back. Our popular friar, Dr John Waldeby, voices the general opinion:

There is a fish in the sea[1], in whose mouth the bitterest water turns to sweetness. Therefore on account of the sweet water the little fishes are attracted to his mouth. But when they have got inside it, he swallows them up, rends them with his teeth, and slays them. So, spiritually speaking, the preacher who always talks of the piety and pity of God, and of the sweetness of the Lord Jesus to sinners, pleases them hugely and right gladly do they listen to him.... But assuredly when the preacher dwells too much on the divine mercy, and says nought of punishment, he makes the people presume too greatly on the mercy of God, and thus to lie and perish in their sins[2].

A curious agreement manifests itself among contemporary moralists of all classes with regard to the fact that this "presumpcion and over-hopynge in the mercy of God" is one if not actually the most potent and deadly of current popular heresies[3]. Bromyard recognizes it as a characteristic subtlety of the devil's predication, and of all heretics after him:

"*Howsoever great thy sins may be, greater is His mercy.*" And in this third point he deceives many, nay rather well-nigh the whole world. And therefore more preaching is to be made against this deception of the devil's, and little or nothing of the mercy of God. Because, as against a hundred who attend preaching, and sin in presuming overmuch upon the Divine mercy, there is not one who sins in desperation.

The mediaeval preacher then is prepared at all times to combat the fallacies of the ever-forgiving Redeemer, the "large lyf," and its many opportunities of repentance, with a terrifying

---

[1] Quoted here from Solinus, *de mirabilibus mundi*. The figure occurs also in MS. Arundel 231. ii, fol. 69, containing Odo of Cheriton's sermons, though not in Hervieux's ed. of them.

[2] MS. Caius Coll. Camb. 334, fol. 177 et seq.

[3] Cf. MS. Harl. 2398, fol. 46: "Some men weneth that God be so merciable that he wol nou3t punysche a mannes synnes"; Myrc's *Festiall*, E.E.T.S. ed. p. 55: "God will not lose that he hath bought with his heart-blood," they say; MS. Add. 37049, fol. 96: "Mykil folkes ther is that hopes that God wil dampne no men...."; MS. Harl. 211, fol. 50b: "God is merciful, they seyn, & iust, & therfore he wil not dampne no men for a ly3t ooth...."; Bromy. *S.P.—Damnatio*, etc.: "Deus nullum Christianum, quem ita care redemit, perdere vult vel damnare," they say; and see my article, "Some Franciscan Memorials," *Dublin Review* (April, 1925), p. 279.

message of death, burial, judgement and hell-pains. Students of the tenth-century Blickling homilies[1], and subsequent early English collections, which have been edited by Messrs Morris[2] and Belfour[3] will have noticed the sudden amazing warmth which the homilists bring to the subject of these tragedies. The rest of the series may have been dull and commonplace enough. In a moment one sees the eye flash, the body sway and tremble, as with a native eloquence, almost prophetic in its grandeur, the lurid tale is re-told. No sceptical mind is needed to realize how clumsy and artificial is the vast formal theological super-structure that weighs upon the mediaeval pulpit. Yet, here freed for an hour from pious platitudes and points of doctrine, the preacher shall escape, if he will, into a world of primitive human nature, ancient as the Sagas, and the curse of black death-dealing Alberic:

> Hearest thou this great voice that shakes the world
> And wastes the narrow realm whereon we move
> And beats upon the faces of the dead[4]?

Gazing into the unknown abyss, helpless upon his death-bed, the devils whirling above him, or lurking under the furniture, friends and acquaintances waiting at his side, the stoutest mediaeval sinner becomes a trembling savage again[5]. There in the awful air, in every nook and cranny we behold primeval monsters of the past, implacable spirits returned to haunt the enfeebled race.

First, not in order of the time, but in oratorical force and picturesqueness for the preacher's appeal, undoubtedly stood the horrors of Hell. If all else failed to carry the day, this would not:

And be oon wey I shall meve men to drawe thereto [contrition], and that is for the drede of the peynes of hell. I trow ther is no man that leveth, and he wold considre ynwardly what peyn is ordeynt for

---

[1] E.E.T.S., O.S. Nos. 58, 63, 73; cf. pp. 60, 92 et seq., 112, 194, etc.

[2] *Old English Homilies*, E.E.T.S., O.S. Nos. 29, 34, etc., p. 172 (The Fate of the Wicked), etc.

[3] 12-*century Homilies*, ibid. No. 137, p. 125 (The Voice from the Tomb; Doom and Hell, etc.).

[4] Tennyson, *The Passing of Arthur*.

[5] H. S. Bennett brings this point out well in his recently published *Pastons and their England*, cf. p. 196 (Camb. Univ. Press). See also my sermon evidence here following, and the vivid illustrations in the block-books of the *Ars Moriendi* treatises.

synnes in hell, I trowe a wold drede hym sore and full sone amende
hym. I shew this by ensampull. Iff ther were here a towne [tun]
so ordeyned that it were full of nayles longe and sharpe, the poyntes
beyng inward, and that all thise nayles were fure hote, I trow ther is
no man that wold be rolled a myle wey in this tonne for all the reame
of ynglonde. And 3itt were this peyn but in towchynge all-on,...and
bot a myle wey! A good lord! How gret peyn shall ther be eternally in
every parte of mans V wittes, not only a myle wey, but while god is god
in heven...3iff that a dampned man desire to se delectabull thinges,
ther shall oribull devels be seyn, whos faces ben brent and blake in
semblance; *ffacies eorum combuste*! ys. 13....Certeyn the si3th of
hem is so orybull that a man wold for all the world [not] ons loke on
hem: as it is rad of a religius man that saw on, and seid that he had
lever to renne in to the hote fuyre than ons see hym ageyn. What
trowe we than what si3the woll it be thousaundes of dewels that bethe
ther. 3iff a dampned man coveyt to here delectabull thinges, ther
is no songe but oribull rorynge of dewels, and wepynge, and gnas-
tynge of tethe, and weylyng of dampned men, crying: "Ve, ve, ve,
quante sunt tenebre!"—"Vo, Vo, Vo, how gret is this derkenes!"[1]
3iff a dampned man coveit to tast swete metes and drynkes ther is no
swetnes, ne delicacye, but fuyre and brymston is parte of ther drynke.
...3iff on of hem wold 3eve a thousaund li [i.e. pounds] for on drope
of water, he 3ettes non. The riche gloton ashed a drope of water, as
the gospell seyth, more than a thowsaund 3ere agoyn, and 3it had he
non. And 3iff anny dampned men desiren anny delicate clothinge
and riche, thei shall fynde non ther. Undir hem, I rede, shall be flies
that shall bite ther flessh, and ther clothynge shall be wormes....
And shortely to sey, ther is all maner of turmentes in all the V wittys;
and abowen all this, ther is *pena dampni*—"peyn of privacion of the
blis of heven," the wiche is a peyn of all peynes. For jesu cristes
love, remember inwardly on thise peynes; and I trust to God that
thei shall stere the to a vomyte of all thi dronkelew lyvyng[2]!

---

[1] Apparently derived from Chrysostom. It occurs again in *Jacob's Well*,
E.E.T.S. ed., pp. 228, 319: "Yelling, roaring, and weeping, thou shalt cryen
with fiends in hell, without end—'Ve, ve, ve! Quantae sunt tenebrae!'—
'Wo, wo, wo, great are my "therknessis" in pain!'"

[2] MS. Roy. 18. B. xxiii, fol. 134 b et seq. Again, fol. 113 et seq.: "Ryght
so thei that shall be dampned in hell shall have dyvers peynes and turmen-
tynge, som with smale devels and som with grett devels, so beynge in sorowe
and care with owten ende. And som shall brenne in the grett flameth of fyre,
the wiche is ix tymes hotter than is anny fyre in this worlde; 3e, and som
shall be hangged be the necke, and devels with owte nowmbre shall all to
drawe hure lymmes in sondre, and shall smyte here bodies thorowe with fury
bronndes. Tho be thise proude men that falsely robben other men in this
world to make hure wreched bodies gaye and hure eres ryche. And som shall
be hanged be the tonge, and devels inow to turment that membre...Som shall
also be drawen in to the fyre...and here bowels...drawen owte...," etc.

Much indeed could be reproduced to show how fascinated the preacher became by this "Inferno"-scene. Almost everything in the current decorative and histrionic arts tended to encourage him. Myrc indeed seems to be actually reading off to us from the walls of some ancient Shropshire church, where he is preaching[1], the fiend, pitch-black "as a man of Inde," with sharp nose, loathful face, and blazing eyes, blowing flames of fire from his mouth[2], the burning brands thrust into men's throats, the boiling cauldron[3], the worms and adders[4] that come out of it. Few laymen then but must have known the formal *Pains* by heart, as well as any "Paternoster" and "Ave": "Caligo, vinculum, flagellum, frigor, flamma, timor, vermis, confusio, fetor,"[5] etc.

Except for the fact that the state of the damned was that of "Ending and none end,"[6]—"per milia milium annorum cruciandi...nec unquam inde liberandi,"[7]—the General Doom which preceded, would seem to present almost as many terrors for the unregenerate. Fifteen days of as many terrifying portents in the world of nature were to usher it in, the sea standing up and falling again to turn to blood, the fishes crying upon the land, grinding rocks and falling castles, earthquakes, tempests, fires, waning constellations, opening graves, men going mad,

---

[1] Cf. St Alkmund (mentioned in this sermon; E.E.T.S. ed. p. 240, l. 29). Besides the numerous "Doom" paintings in churches showing Hell-Mouth, etc., cf. the typical drawings in such English MSS. as Add. 37049, fols. 17 and 74, and Linc. Cath. Libr. C. 4. 6, fols. 34 and 120.

[2] See *Festiall* (E.E.T.S. ed., p. 238).

[3] Ibid. (in a *Narratio*). Cf. again *Gesta Rom.* (Engl. vers.), E.E.T.S. ed. p. 384, etc.: "And sone aftyr come ii devyls yellyn, and broughtyn a cawderon full of hote wellyng brasse, and sette it downe besyde the stone.... Than the ii devyls tokyn bothe the man and the woman that they brought, and caste hem into a cawderone, and helden hem there, till the fleshe was sothyn fro the bone...," etc. See also *Jacob's Well* (E.E.T.S. ed.), "the wicked clerk Odo."

[4] Cf. MS. Linc. Cath. Libr. A. 6. 2, fol. 81: "an untollerabyll tormentis of devylls, and grete multitude of serpentis and dragons, wormys th[t] turment the sowlys that ben ther in." Cf. also R. Alkerton in MS. Add. 37677, fol. 60 b: "Venemous wormes and naddris shul gnawe alle here membris withouten seessyng; and the worm of conscience,...shal gnawe the soule...," etc.

[5] Cf. MS. Add. 21253, fol. 163, etc. Also MS. Camb. Univ. Libr. Gg. vi. 16, fol. 49, etc.

[6] Ibid. (Camb. Univ. Libr.), quoted from St Gregory; MS. Linc. Cath. Libr. A. 6. 2, fol. 81 b.

[7] MS. Add. 21253, fol. 172.

like the beasts, for fear[1]. "Alwey when I thenke on the last Day, for drede my bodie quaketh."[2] A favourite thrust in this connection was to remind men that all sin unconfessed at death would be made public then before the whole universe assembled at that awful bar of justice[3]. "And behold that terrible word which the Lord shall speak in the Day of Judgement to each Christian: 'Give account of thy stewardship!'"[4] No secret bribes, no private meddling with judge or jury there!

> The angell shall blowe afore God that all the world shall rise; when Criste shall sey thise wordes, "...Arise ȝe dede, and comyth to the dome!" Ther shall be no man askape with no meynprise, for no drede ne favour of lordeshyppe, ne for no mede. For ther shall noon be saved but thoo that be owte of dedely synne. For and thou be than foundon in anny dedely synne, thoo oure ladie, and all thouwȝ seyntes, that been in hevene, prey for the, thei shall not be herde[5].

The same naïve homilist is equally certain that there is really little to choose in sheer discomfort between the two situations in hell or in actual Judgement:

> Sirs, I counsell all maner of men fully to thenke on this dome.... I concell and I preye everich on of you to conceyve and knowe that oure lorde God at the day of dome shall shewe ryght withoute mercye, full rygorysly, full sturnely, and aske of us howe that we have spende the vii workes of mercy[6]....He shall seme so crucll, ȝe sir, he shall be to hem as styborne as a wode man....As a grete clerke Barnard seyth, the dampned had lever be in hell withowte ende than ons loke

---

[1] Cf. MS. Linc. Cath. Libr. A. 6. 2, fols. 11–13: "...as Seynt Jerom seythe, tht xv dayes by fore the dredfull dome, almyȝthi god wil schewe xv mervellus tokens...." Similarly, MS. Harl. 4196, fol. 4 (*Eng. Met. Homs.*); MS. Arund. 506, fol. 29 (ibid.), and MS. Harl. 3232, fol. 1 b. (All from St Jerome.)

[2] MS. Roy. 18. B. xxiii, fol. 169, quoted from "Seynte Barnarde." Again, in a sermon in MS. Linc. Cath. Libr. A. 6. 2, fol. 10 b: "of the whiche rehersithe Seint Barnarde in the personys of synfull pepyll, and seythe thus—Et est in sermone de adventu iudicis, ubi sic semper inquid (sic), 'diem illum extremum considerans, toto corpore contremesco....'"

[3] Cf. Bromyard, *S.P.*—*Contritio*; Myrc's *Festiall* (E.E.T.S.), pp. 89, 95; MS. Harl. 2398, fol. 45 b; etc.

[4] MS. Add. 21253, fol. 130. See also Wimbledon's sermon at Paul's Cross, and cf. above, p. 40.

[5] MS. Roy. 18. B. xxiii, fol. 89 b. Cf. again, fol. 113 b.

[6] Ibid. fol. 57. Cf. also MS. St Albans Cath. fol. 29 b: "Which of us thinkith on the dredfull day of doom?—and we witen not whethir it fallith to nyȝt or to morowe....But yit for al this, who takith heede of this dredful day of Doom, who dradith it, who purveieth eny thinge bifore it? As who seith but fewe or wel nyȝ noon...."

hym in the face.... For sothe that chastismente is full harde ther—
as shall be everelastynge peyne withowte anny reste, other ese[1].

A London preacher we have met, one Richard Alkerton,
appropriately likens his Doom-scene to a Parliament summoned by the sovereign. His congregation would recall the
familiar bustle and excitement, the splendid progress of the
mighty through the streets:

> ffor these defautes and other it behoveth that this king make his
> parlement in schorte tyme. Wherfore this king ordeineth with assent
> of his councel that a parlement be maad; and for this parlement the
> kings writtis ben sent out thoru3 out al the worlde bi the hooly gos-
> peleris, apostlis and prophetis, which hav writyn of the day of
> doom.... And al the worlde is somoned, but no day is sette to hem.
> ...The cause of delaying of this parlement is noon other, no, but
> the abidyng of kni3tis of the king, that fi3tin 3it in werris of the king
> in diveris cuntrees. And whan thei comen and been redi to go with
> the king to the parlement, outhere than to meete him there, than the
> parlement schal be maad.... And anone the king schal come fro
> heven to the doom, and schal be compacid with al the chevalrie of
> heven[2].

With blare of trumpets, and the rest, it was an impressive
spectacle; for none knew better than our mediaeval preacher
how to choose a telling simile. Guilty souls, listening in that
city church[3], might well shrink at thought of so formidable an
array at the bar of Heaven.

Amid the ever-growing scepticism, concerning which our
sermon-makers are by no means silent, the ideas of Doom and
Damnation might seem to many a trifle absurd and old-fashioned
in their way[4]. "Not to say a little humorous by now," some

---

[1] MS. Roy. 18. B. xxiii, fol. 60 b. David is also quoted here, concerning a
God that "shalte seme wode" in his fury. The preacher explains that the
Almighty permits such horrors—"for to shewe is lordshype, and that he ys
lorde of all the worlde," etc. An arbitrary mediaeval tyrant! Cf. MS. Linc.
Cath. Libr. A. 6. 2, fol. 82 b: "God as chefe justice, sittyng in his mageste,
all this worlde demyng." See also the Doom scene in MS. Camb. Univ.
Libr. Gg. vi. 16, fol. 50 b (including the fact that "all the world shall be
burning, all on fire"); and Myrc's *Festiall*, p. 155, etc. (E.E.T.S. ed.).

[2] MS. Add. 37677, fol. 59, etc.

[3] St Mary, Spital. See Chap. 1 above, p. 23.

[4] In an illuminating passage, Bromyard provides for precisely this situation (*S.P.—Ebrietas*): "Et ponatur quod aliqui ita sunt illo peccato excoecati
quod infamiam vel inferni poenas non timeant, quia forte eas non vident, vel
non credunt. Saltem timeant rerum et bonorum diminutionem.... Ideo istam
poenam post precedentes posui, quia plus apud mundiales timetur...," etc.

would add, thinking, perhaps, of the roaring demons and gaping canvas hell-mouths that ran about town from time to time, like Parisian revellers and their properties in "mi-carême." But who could deny the grim reality of the valley of the shadow of Death, the Tomb where none shall give praise? Here was the unfailing cure for the flippant, as well as for human pride and self-complacency in general. When the pulpit was not actually raised amid the tombs, as it must often have been, or over some freshly-dug grave, the mournful cry of its occupants was ever calling men back to the same scene:

Go to the buryeles of thy fader & moder; and suche schalt thou be, be he never so fayr, never so kunnynge, never so strong, never so gay, never so ly3t. Loke also what fruyt cometh of a man at alle yssues of his body, as at nose, atte mouthe, at ey3en, and atte alle the othe y33ues of the body, and of othe pryvey membres, and he schall have mater to lowe his herte[1]!

It is all the same sad story from cradle to grave:

Ri3t as a worme is but litel and a foul thinge and of no prise, and cometh crepynge naked bare out of the erthe where he was bred, ri3t so a man at his begynnynge is a foule thing, litel and pore.... Therfore seith the holy man Bernard thus: "Quid est homo nisi sperma fetidum, saccus stercorum, esca vermium?" What is man, he seith, but a stynkynge slyme, and after that a sake ful of donge, and at the laste mete to wormes[2].

"Wormes mete and rotye!" "Stinking frog's meat,"[3] says another, who in his sermon bids men "see folk die!" "Thise 3onge peple weneth that thei shall never die, and specially afore that thei be old! And treuly thei ben oft beguiled." They protest: "I am 3onge 3itt. When that I drawe to age I will amende me."[4] Ah! How soon that sense of longevity perishes!

---

[1] MS. Harl. 2398, fol. 11 (cf. Bromyard, *S.P.*—*Mors*, as quoted here later: "Nos vero debemus speculum nobis facere—et exemplum accipere de mortuis et pulverizatis..."). See, too, above, Chap. VI, p. 268.

[2] MS. Harl. 45, fol. 112 b; and again, fol. 106 b; and MS. Linc. Cath. Libr. A. 6. 2, fols. 31 and 121. The first part of the above (as "Seint Austen seythe"), on fol. 36 b. See also MS. Camb. Univ. Libr. Ee. vi. 29, as given in *Reliq. Ant.* vol. I, p. 138, and John Lydgate's (?) poem with the alluring title, "Remember man thow art but wormes mete" (MS. Add. 29729, fol. 7).

[3] *Jacob's Well* (E.E.T.S. ed.), pp. 217, 218. Again, Myrc's *Festiall*, p. 64; Bromyard, *S.P.*—*Mors, Exemplum*, etc.

[4] MS. Roy. 18. B. xxiii, fol. 145; also fol. 142 b.

"For who so had lyved an hondred yere, whan he cometh to the dethe, hym shall seme that he hath lyved but the space of an houre."[1] To modern ears this tragic sentiment of death and the grave will sound pagan indeed coming from such lips. But an uncritical use of the Old Testament, and the surviving influences of classical literature[2] are together quite sufficient to account for the strange liberties taken. Apart from such evil accompaniment of healthy life in the healthiest of mortals as has been mentioned, Bromyard[3], Wimbledon[4] and Myrc[5]—to take three random examples—all tell eloquently of the wrinkled face, the hoar head ("quae secundum libros medicorum est vexillum mortis"), the bent back, the failing sight, hearing, limbs, the livid nose and nails, the evil breath, the hollow eye, one of them, even the crazy mirth that seems to forget its approaching end. Behold now, "how that at the last death cometh and casteth him down, sick in his bed, groaning and sighing....And so at the last, with deep sobbing yieldeth up the ghost." If that were all indeed, the dying might almost count themselves happy as they pass. "Knowe all men, douȝtless, that men that dyen, in her last siknesse and ende have grettest and most grevouse temptacions, and such as thei never had befor in all her lyfe."[6] Alas, the "harde storme of the perilous assaut of the fende" is upon them! "And it is to suppose that thes fendes beth most aboute to tempte men and women in the houre

[1] *Gesta Rom.* (15th cent. Engl. vers.), E.E.T.S. ed. p. 439.

[2] Thus Bromyard, *S.P.—Exemplum*, quotes the famous saying: "Count no man happy before his death" though here probably from the Bk. of Wisdom.

[3] *S.P.—Mors.* (Cf., in verse, examples in *Rel. Antiq.* i, 64–65, ii, 211.)

[4] Paul's Cross sermon, 1388. (N.B. Here especially the famous "Three Messengers.") Cf. sermon for First Sunday in Lent in MS. Camb. Univ. Libr. Ii. iii. 8, fol. 127 b (Latin).

[5] *Festiall* (E.E.T.S. ed.), p. 84. Cf. similarly, MS. Linc. Cath. Libr. A. 6. 2, fols. 5, 46, etc. (sermon for Second Sunday—"post Oct. Epiphanie," fol. 46): "ffor then is chaungyng of chere; for he that was be fore full roddy & wel colowrde then becommythe he all pale. then the yeen wynkythe, the mowthe frowt, the tethe gryndythe, & the hed schakythe, & the armys spredithe abrode, the hondythe (sic!) pullythe & pluckythe, the feete rubbythe, the herte syȝhethe, the voyce gronythe, & gruntithe. & thus all the lymmys of the body schewt the grete sorowȝe of his departyng."

[6] From *The Boke of the Craft of dying* (MS. Rawl. C. 894, etc.), cap. ii (printed in Horstmann, *Yorkshire Writers*, vol. ii, p. 406 et seq.; see especially cap. ii). See also some useful notes in *The Bk. of the Craft of Dying, and other Early Engl. Tracts concerning Death, taken from MSS. and printed books in the Brit. Mus. and Bodleian Libraries* (*now first done into mod. spelling*), ed. F. M. M. Comper, Longmans, 1917.

of here deth; and never in here lyf so fast aboute to combre men as at the laste stounde to make hem to have an yvel ende and so be dampned."[1] Of the wretched victim himself, dramatically pourtrayed by Bromyard, we have spoken already:

so feeble that scarce can he think of anything but his own weakness, or utter a last confession to the priest, or even move a limb. Not merely does he see a crowd of grinning demons waiting to snatch away his soul with their infernal claws, but hard by his own friends and executors waiting too with "adhesive fingers" (manibus viscosis!) to burst open his coffer and his money-bags, and carry off his worldly possessions....How can such an one turn to God with all these conditions about him?[2]

How, indeed!

Last of all come bitter humiliations beneath the sod. "And the prophet seythe he schall have somewhat w^t hym, and that is but smalle. firste he schall have vii foote of erthe to ley his body in, and a wyndyng schete."[3] After a particularly long and sorrowful glance at the "good old days"—"when the earth possessed a more long-lived race which could attain to ninety years and more," and was not overcrowded, as he believes, our English author of the *Summa Predicantium* seems to take positively savage delight in mocking the material state of the dead. But he is no exception.

If we would but consider well how quickly we shall be placed beneath the feet not only of men, friend and foe alike, but of dogs, and the beasts of the field—where he who now rears and possesses mighty palaces shall have a hall whose roof touches his nose—he who now can hardly decide which robe he wishes to wear, shall have a garment of earth and worms—he who now, taking offence at a word, fights the offender, then if he have a sword in his hand, could not defend himself from the vilest beasts, even the worms,—we should find little reason for pride.....*Sic transit gloria mundi!*

[1] MS. Harl. 2398, fol. 181, etc. (The author proceeds to deal at length with the correct arguments with which the dying must meet the taunts of the demons.) Cf. also MS. Add. 21253, fol. 134; Myrc's *Festiall*, p. 84, etc. (The fiends sit at the dead man's head, raking after his soul, etc.)

[2] *S.P.*—*Mors, Desperatio*, etc. Cf. again: "Videbunt demones ipsos irridentes et in desperationem ponentes...." For the *false Executors* around the death-bed, see ibid.—*Executores*; MS. Roy. 18. B. xxiii, fol. 80; MS. Harl. 45, fol. 66, etc. With these compare the quaint English drawings of the death-bed scene in MSS. Cotton Faust. B. vi, pt. ii, fol. 2; Stowe 39, fol. 32 b, etc.

[3] MS. Linc. Cath. Libr. A. 6. 2, fol. 6.

little later he will point his audience to the skulls and bones of the departed, bidding them reflect how through the mouth once so delectable to kiss, so delicate in its eating and its drinking, through eyes but a short while before so fair to see, worms now crawl in and out. The body or the head, once so richly attired[1], so proudly displayed, now boasts no covering but the soil, no bed of softness, no proud retinue save worms for the flesh, and, if its life was evil, demons for the soul. Therefore let all going forth to God's eternal banquet prepare themselves beforehand—by looking into the mirror of the Dead[2]. Two centuries and more before the age of this learned friar, some English preacher had proclaimed a similar message from the Tomb: "Look on my bones here in this dust, and think of thyself. Before I was such a one as thou art now. Look on my bones and my dust, and leave thy evil desires!"[3] His warning is reiterated in Bromyard's own day by the Franciscan John of Grimston in his Sermon Commonplace Book:

> Wat so thu art th^t gost her be me
> W^{t}stand and be hold and wel be thenk the
> Th^t suich as thu art was i wone to be
> And suich as i am nou saltu sone be[4].

He, too, lay in his turn under the greensward where perchance the Dominican now paces, fashioning his message for the morrow: "Loca et specula sepulcrorum et cimiteriorum viridia, ubi illi qui nos precesserunt sunt sepulti."[5]

From the dignified but morbid language echoing St Bernard,

[1] Elsewhere, under *Mors*, he cries to the fine ladies, etc.: "Utinam haec saperent et intelligerent, qui nunc de pulchritudine inaniter gloriantur, et quae *se pingunt*, et superbe ornant, ut pulchriores appareant quam sint; cogitare deberent tales quomodo erit *pro crispanti crine* [the 'crespine' head-dress, perhaps] calvitium...," etc. (cf. Isaiah iii, 18–24).

[2] Under *Exemplum* he says quaintly: "Sicut ergo qui vult statum suum speculari, respicit speculum quod est in plumbo vel ligno positum, ita spiritualiter speculum nostrum debent esse mortui, qui in plumbo vel ligno, i.e. in cista plumbea vel lignea positi sub terra, conducuntur!" With these references cf. the weird "disputacion betwyx the body and wormes," with crude illustrations, in MS. Add. 37049, fol. 33, and the very numerous tales in sermon "exempla" collections of the toads and worms found upon the dead when tombs are opened, etc.

[3] *12th cent. E. E. Homilies*, in E.E.T.S., O.S. No. 137 (ed. Belfour), pp. 125, etc.

[4] MS. Advoc. Libr. Edinburgh, 18. 7. 21, fols. 87–87 b. There is a quantity of vernacular verse here on the subject (*Mors*).

[5] *S.P.—Gloria.*

if not those earlier churchmen, too, troubled witnesses of the fall of a great world-empire, it is still possible to descend to lower forms of the coercive "verba terribilia." We need go no further than the pages of the *Fons Jacob* to guess of the hectoring tone which the pulpit could adopt sometimes toward the pew[1]. Yet its author declares that the mere deterrent dread of hell is not in itself sufficient to bring a man to heaven, although valuable as what he calls "a beginning dread." When all is said, however, the radical failure of scolding and threats was sufficiently clear even to those who were loudest in their support. Dr Bromyard, always ready to give us the fashionable excuses and opinions of his day, tells how "glosing their consciences" his contemporaries were capable of doubting the divine threat of Damnation as expressed in the very Scriptures[2]. It was bad enough when they sniffed audibly at the men in the pulpit: "Those things which God teaches we believe. But there is no need to put faith in the *narrations* and *exempla* of other preachers because they only narrate such terrible things to terrify the sinner, or for some other purpose!"[3] Such at long last will always be the result of expedients used in sacred oratory, however swift and impressive their early promises of success, which yet do an inward violence to the moral sense. The far-reaching evils and aggravations of this particular resort need little comment from us. For, it would not be wholly unjust to say, in modern parlance, that the acerbity of Reformation Protestantism was only the acute neurosis of once-terrified children reared in the mediaeval nursery.

Though much less is said in the homiletic guide-books about what old brother Whitford of Syon would call "a solempne and mervaylous swete sermon, makyng speciall mencion of love,

---

[1] Cf. E.E.T.S. ed. p. 111 (in a sermon-ending, following the *Narrationes*): "Chese thou thanne whethir thou wylt be slaw3 and sluggy in goddys servyse, in gode werkys, and prayerys, and usyn iangelyng in cherche, and be dampned; or ellys to leve thi sleuthe,...and be savyd in blysse. Here thou may chese. 3if thou chese to be dampnyd, wyte it thi self, and no3t God!"

[2] They say: "...Exempla in libris posita et scripturis sunt ad timorem!"

[3] *S.P.—Damnatio*: "His quae Deus dicit credimus. Sed narrationibus et exemplis aliorum predicantium non oportet fidem adhibere, quia ipsi, vel ad terrorem peccatorum, vel propter alias causas talia terribilia narrant." ("Sed quae major stulticia quam cogitare quod aliquis mendacio suo se perdere velit, ut alios salvet..." is his retort!)

unite, peace, and concorde,"[1] it is worth noting that Thomas Walleys, Dominican as he is, does warn the preacher against being "too austere or harsh in his rebuking of vice." There is special danger, says he, that simple folk in the audience may think that all his remarks are levelled at them, and shrink accordingly from making their confessions to him later on. Every sermon, too, that omits to make mention of Our Lady of Grace and of Christ, the Redeemer, is to be censured[2]. The criticism of opponents, on the other hand, witnesses itself to the use of this gentler mode of appeal, as well as the familiar eloquence of the Yorkshire pietists, dwelling sweetly upon Our Lady's tears, the humility and frailness of the Christmas babe, or the anguish of the Crucified. A like sermon it must have been that touched the poor harlot of our "Preaching Scene," till she "was right sorye and wepte faste," a sermon "mych of the mercy of God,"[3] of how in His great love He would pardon the contrite. "And patientlyche he suffreth despyt from dey to dey, of alle maner false peple."[4] Who could help confessing, with her, to so gentle a parson, true "mirror of the Christian"?

> He was to sinful man not despitous,
> Ne of his speche daungerous, ne digne[5].

With a charming disregard of the risks of inconsistency, John Waldeby, the Austin friar, who warned us of "the fishes" that turn the bitter waters of their preaching to a fatal sweetness, has yet tender passages in his own Latin homily series in the best manner of his northern fellow-countrymen. He, too, appeals to the sufferings of Jesus—at birth, in His labours, at His Passion[6]. First, then, of His birth:

satis penalis quoad tria, locum, apparatum, tempus. Quia fuit in maximo frigore, utpote in medio yeme, et media nocte. Locus fuit stabulum et presepe. Apparatus in quo erat involutus pauper, coram

---

[1] A *Werke for Housholders*.   [2] MS. Harl. 635, fol. 11.
[3] *Gesta Rom.* (Engl. vers. E.E.T.S. ed.), p. 391. See above, pp. 167, 191.
[4] MS. Harl. 2398, fol. 20 b.
[5] Chaucer, *Cant. Tales, Prologue*, ll. 516–17.
[6] Cf. also, in the vernacular, MS. St Albans Cath. fol. 20 (printed in my article, q.v.); MS. Salisb. Cath. Libr. 103, fol. 103; MS. Linc. Cath. Libr. A. 6. 2, fol. 41 et seq., and the works of Rolle, etc.; also above, pp. 120–1. In friar Grimston's Sermon Note Book there is more vernacular verse on this subject than on any other (MS. Advoc. Libr. Edinburgh, 18. 7. 21, fols 116–26).

bove et asina. O quam dura initia tenerrimo puero, utpote virginis filio!

Of his progress:

nos docuit penitenciam in deserto, fatigationem etiam in discur-
rendo, pernoctationem in orando, que satis videntur multum
laboriosa.

Finally, of his ending:

Quanta sustinuit nullus sermo explicare potest. Cogitare tamen
aliqualiter possumus, scil. sputa, flagella, et dura crucis tormenta.
Sed, O bone Jhesu, quomodo potest humana mens sine lacrimis
cogitare quomodo pulchritudo talis conspuitur, mansuetudo flagel-
latur, et innocenti morti crudelissime condemnatur. Ecce bene-
dictum caput, summis splendoribus reverendum, spinis pungentibus
coronatum, manus et pedes confossi, et latus perforatum, totumque
corpus tenerrimum dire cruentatum....O bone Jhesu, durior est
finis tuus quam principium! Ecce, Maria mater, Jhesus quem pannis
involvisti pendet omnino nudatus; quem reclinasti in presepio,
plenus crucis supplicio; quem etiam suaviter fovebas in gremio,
dilaceratur et distenditur, latere ejus transfixo[1].

Now, for those to whom the Latin makes no appeal, we choose
another unpublished example—in English—from a "Sermon
on the Passion." Belonging to the very eve of the Reformation,
late in the fifteenth century, when preaching was supposed to
be at its lowest ebb, it reminds us that, even if all originality
has disappeared, the "solempne and mervaylous swete sermon"
yet persists:

What defawte fynde ʒow in me, seithe Crist, and why go ʒe a wey
fro me, and will not kepe my preceptis and my commawndementis?
If I have trespasyd to ʒow, tell it me. Se now the goodnes of almyʒthi
god, and beholde the pride of man, and se the mekenes of criste. And
ʒit he is in the ryʒte, and tretithe feyre w^t us, and proferythe us mercy,
or that we aske it. He mekythe hym to us, and we be obstynate and
rebell to hym. ffor the herd stonys brake in the tyme of cristis
passion; but oure herttys ben herddar in synne then the stonys, for
they wyll not breke w^t contriscion. Crist is oure moste special
frende, and we be to hym worse then the jewys were. he is passyng
lovyng to us, and we schewe to him grete unkyndnes. he schewythe
to us obediens, and we schewe to hym disobediens. he is ever to us
gracius and good, and we be to him wickyd and ungentill. Ever th^t
good lorde that is mercyfull callythe to us and seythe: "loo, I am

[1] MS. Caius Coll. Camb. 334, fol. 80 et seq.

lyfte up on hy3e up on the cros for the, synfull creature, that th^u scholde here my voyce, turne to me a 3ene, and I wyll 3iffe the remission and mercy. loo, myne armys ben sprede a brode for to clyppe the and to take the to grace, and myne hedde I bow doune for to gyfe the a kisse of luffe. And my syde is openyd for to schewe how kynde I have ben to the, and how lovyng, and myne hertt is clyfte a two for the love of the, my hondys and my feete bledythe for to schewe what I suffyrde for the. And 3it th^u turneste a wey, and wil not come to me at my callyng. 3it turne to me, and I wil gyfe the joye and reste perpetually.... ”[1]

Type of wellnigh all in the contemporary oratory—perhaps all in contemporary art—that avoids the harsh and the grotesque, this fragrant appeal has remained characteristic of the finest Catholic preaching in subsequent ages. Whatever the critics may say, its glory will never fade until the Cradle and the Cross alike have disappeared from human experience.

For sheer tenderness and delicacy of speech in a simple homilist, it would be hard to improve upon what, in its detailed account of the calling of Samuel, is in effect a "Children's Sermon" of the middle ages:

...But trowe we that God calleth this 3onge peple? 3e, sirs. Every gracious sterynge to God is the callyng of God. I rede that almy3thy God called Samuel, when that he was 3onge.... So dothe thise fresh 3onge peple, when God calleth hem in here soul, and meveth hem to vertewe.... It is prophetabull to a 3onge man to be vertewous in is 3onge age. I shall tell the cause why: for he that refuseth grace and goddes callyng in 3oug3, grace is not with hym in is old age...,"[2] etc.

Chaucer's parson must have talked in that tone to the folk he loved and served so well, easily but none the less earnestly. For simple and honest men and women of toil there is not a trick of oratory or argument to compete with the eloquence of true sympathy, be it that of scholar, or of clerk that "can nat geste—rum, ram, ruf—by lettre."

Thus trewe doctours in hooli chirche hav as it were firen tongis; for whil bi trewe love thei prechen God, thei enflawmen the hertis of her herers. For if ferventnesse of love be not in the doctour that prechith, thanne it falleth ful ofte that his word is ful idil to the puple[3].

[1] MS. Linc. Cath. Libr. A. 6. 2, fols. 130–31.
[2] MS. Roy. 18. B. xxiii, fol. 142 b, etc.   [3] MS. Harl. 2276, fol. 92.

Of appeals to the visual in English mediaeval preaching direct evidence may be scarce; but there are tales enough of graphic appearances in the clouds, spectacular sights in the audience at sermon-time to indicate their importance in the contemporary view[1]. What we know of the popular love of pictures and relics as aids to devotion leads to the same conclusion. In Italy of the early fifteenth century, St Bernardino's monogram painted on tablets, itself devised in part to replace the current fondness for badges and charms, became, for a time at least, the triumphant standard of his preaching tours. Exposed above the pulpit, it filled men with wondrous emotion as they listened. But this particular emblem was admittedly an innovation. None the less in Sano di Pietro's paintings at Siena we behold the saint again upon his rostrum in the market-place, pointing this time like any other preacher of the day to the wooden crucifix he holds. It is a regular companion of the preacher's art, greeting us alike upon the wall of Savonarola's Florentine cell in the monastery of San Marco, or carved in a bishop's hands as he leans from his miniature pulpit upon a stall-end in the Lady Chapel of Winchester Cathedral[2]:

For I sauh the feld ful of folk, that ich of bi-fore schewede,
And Conscience with a crois com for to preche[3].

The case of the Pardoner whose oratorical efforts depended so much for their ultimate success upon the relics and seals that he could exhibit, has been immortalized already in the *Canterbury Tales*. But it would seem that more dignified and reputable speakers made a good use of such objects "in the sermon-time," like the Archbishop in Creton's illumination, with his Papal Bull, forged but none the less imposing for that[4]. An entry in the *French Chronicle of London*[5] describes how somewhere about the year 1314 certain relics were found in the old Cross on the steeple of St Paul's Cathedral[6]. They were

---

[1] Cf. MS. Add. 26770, fol. 77; MS. Egert. 117, fol. 177 b; etc.
[2] When I visited the cathedral in 1924, this cross appeared to have been knocked off. See illustration over, p. 350.
[3] *Piers Plowman* (A text), pass. v, ll. 10–11.
[4] MS. Harl. 1319. See illus. in Chap. I, above, p. 9.
[5] Ed. H. T. Riley (Camden Soc.), p. 251.
[6] For relics in so seemingly unexpected a place (as protection against lightning!), cf. Prof. Jenkins, *The Monastic Chronicler* (S.P.C.K.), p. 75.

of the usual rarity and splendour. A piece of the true Cross, a stone of the Holy Sepulchre, other stones from the place of Ascension and the Mount of Calvary, bones of martyred Virgins were amongst them. "These relics Master Robert de Clothale

PREACHING WITH A CROSS
(Lady Chapel, Winchester Cathedral)

(Chancellor of the Cathedral) showed to the people during his preaching on the Sunday, before the Feast of St Botolph, and after the same the relics were replaced in the cross." Occasionally a sermon for the Feast of Relics makes its appearance in our manuscripts to remind us further of their connection with the pulpit:

Syrres, than on relike Sonday next commyng we shall reverens, honour, and worship the precius sacrament of the awter, verey Goddis body,...and in generall all the reverent relikes of patriackes, prophetes, apostelles, martirs, confessours, and virtuous virgins, and other holy and devoute men and women, whoos blessid bodyes, holy bones, and other relikes th^t be left in erth to cristen mannes socour, comfort, and recreacion, and their names be regestrede in the boke of life[1].

A century after the incident at St Paul's, we have the interesting information from a chronicler of St Albans that a certain book left defaced by Lollards and forwarded to the king by the abbot, was sent on to the Archbishop of Canterbury "to be displayed at the sermons to be delivered at St. Paul's Cross in London."[2] From events like that in which Bishop Pecock and his volumes figured at the same spot, it is reasonable to believe that their exhibition would be used directly by the spokesman of the occasion to enliven the point of his anti-Wycliffite arguments. Book in hand, he could give the crowds such an object-lesson in heresy as would not fail to impress many, to whom mere words meant little. More arresting still might be the object chosen for some humbler occasion. There is a story told by way of "exemplum" in a fifteenth-century manuscript entitled *Tractatus de Abundantia Exemplorum*, of "a certain preacher who to strike terror into his audience"—the holy terror of earthly vanities—"suddenly displayed the skull of a dead man which he had been carrying under his cloak."[3] If the Pardoner brought the contents of the reliquaries into the pulpit, this man could claim to have brought with him the gruesome content of the cemeteries, another dramatic warning in the midst of a sermon of the fate that no man can avoid. Finally, where litera-ture itself fails, the manuscript pictures prevent us from forget-ting further details of the scene which once helped to keep the attention in similar ways. Such was digital mnemotechny, for example. With a finger for each leading point in his discourse,

[1] MS. Harl. 2247, fol. 170 b; sim. in MS. Roy. 18. B. xxv, fol. 108 b. Cf. the notes of a sermon at Bury, in MS. Caius Coll. Camb. 356, mentioned above on p. 60. A sermon "de Reliquiis" (text: "Reliquias dedit eis," Luc. ult.) occurs in MS. Salisb. Cath. Libr. 174, fol. 286, a *Liber Sermonum* (early 14th cent.), which belonged to one of the canons, who flourished c. 1431.

[2] "...ut *in sermonibus* faciendis ad crucem Sancti Pauli, Londoniis, osten-deretur, *ut vel sic civibus innotesceret quanta furia Lollardi vehebantur...*" Walsingham (Rolls S.), vol. ii, p. 326 (c. 1417).

[3] MS. Sloane 3102, fol. 80: "...caput defuncti quod sub capa ferebat subito ostendebat...." This collection has been identified by Mr Herbert with the *Liber de Dono Timoris*.

the priest is rallying his hearers again; or some friar handles the beads of his long rosary in the pulpit, like the cowled preaching fox before his audience of fowls, on a Misericord carving at Beverley Minster. Nothing was too trivial for the art of these ancient sermon-makers.

Rules for elocution, and rules for deportment are not omitted from Thomas Walleys'[1] careful tractate for the pupil in homiletics. Some of them, indeed, have been translated and set forth already in the volume of essays by Dr Gasquet. Neither the mediaeval friar nor the modern cardinal, however, afford us the hint, given by Higden in his own *Ars componendi sermones*[2], that they are probably inspired by the *De Institutione Novitiorum* of Hugh of St Victor. Walleys begins with the usual remark about purity of life and example—"munditia quedam vite ultra homines quos habet informare."[3] His next is a warning against vainglory and ostentation in the pulpit. Thirdly, let the preacher seek the wisdom that comes from God through frequent prayer. Fourthly, let him seek moderation in dress, to avoid any charge of hypocrisy; fifthly, in the matter of gestures, a like classical mean between the immobility of a statue on the other hand, and the restless jerking of a fighter, on the other. His deportment in public is to be nothing less than that of an angel or messenger, sent from on high. As for elocution itself, sixthly, the greatest stress is laid on the necessity and value of a clear enunciation:

Therefore let him not speak too noisily, or too softly: not too noisily lest he confound the hearing of those near him, not too softly lest those standing far off cannot understand; neither let him suddenly raise his voice from low pitch to high, or *vice versa*. The method of speaking, therefore, although not entirely uniform, is to be at least not too varied as regards elevation and depression of the voice[4].

[1] Capit. i, "de qualitate predicatoris," is devoted to this subject (MS. Harl. 635, fols. 6–8). See also here, below, note on p. 362.

[2] MS. Bodl. 5, fol. 3.

[3] Cf. also Rypon's most forcible manner of pointing the same truth in a synodal sermon to clergy, on preaching (MS. Harl. 4894, fol. 215).

[4] "Igitur non nimis clamose, aut nimis submisse loquatur; non nimis clamose ne prope sibi assistencium auditum confundat, aut nimis submisse ne procul stantes non intelligant; nec subito vocem exaltet ab ymo in altum, aut econtra. Modus igitur loquendi, etsi non in toto uniformis, saltem non multum difformis quoad elevationem et depressionem est servandus." Cf. again on fol. 17 b.

Another most subtle mean for the beginner! Seventhly, equal care is to be expended upon questions of pace and emphasis. Let there be appropriate pauses at appropriate stages; no unintelligible gabbling, "like a school-boy reading his *Donet* and not knowing what he is uttering." Some preachers merely fill their listeners' ears with sound, and nothing else. Hearts remain empty because the message has no chance to sink gently and intelligently into them. Would that some of our modern missioners indeed, had given heed to the fourteenth-century missioner's advice, in this as in so many respects! "Si incertam vocem dat tuba," he would quote to them, "quis parabit se ad bellum?"[1] There is more than one good meaning to be got out of most texts.

Quality, not quantity, then, is to be the great aim:

Wherefore saith the Apostle—[1 Cor. xiv, 19]—"I would rather speak five words with my understanding, that I might instruct others, than ten thousand words in a tongue." Therefore let the preacher weigh his words, and utter them with due weight; because, if he himself ponder not, how shall the others ponder? And the more that things are to be pondered, the more must they be lingered over: if it should seem necessary, he should repeat them twice or thrice[2].

The theme, its divisions, and leading ideas should be emphasized with especial care, lest the audience fail to get the hang of what is to follow. It is either ignorance, indevotion, or the bad habit of indecent haste that is responsible, we are told, for this lack of due emphasis and reflection. The eighth section of the work is a lesson on the memory. Here the proud and affected who busy themselves over little tricks of speech, the pretty polished phrases, the "sermones rithmici," the too-lengthy quotation, are warned to beware. They may suffer a fate their self-ambition deserves. He, on the other hand, who attends chiefly to the meaning of what he has to say, putting choice of words in a second place, and not talking like a magpie—*ex solo usu*— need fear little. Once again to our mind the ancient preacher,

---

[1] 1 Cor. xiv, 8.
[2] "Unde apostolus, 'Malo 5 verba sensu meo loqui, ut alios instruant, quam decem milia verborum in lingua.' Ponderet ergo predicator verba sua, et cum debito pondere proferat; quia, si ipse non ponderet, quomodo alii ponderabunt? Et in magis ponderandis magis immoretur, ut, si necesse videatur, ea bis vel ter replicet."

from his close observation of human nature, and his sound common-sense, is a pattern for all the generations.

In view of what has been said elsewhere, we pass over his treatment of the "vanities and curiosities," of tact and restraint in giving rebuke, of the choice of special matter for special audiences, and the avoidance of too-learned argument. The eleventh section broadens out into a warning against undue length[1]; for this only wearies the congregation and spoils their future appetite. As Higden reminds us, he who clumsily stretches "the strings of the mind" too far may end in snapping them[2]. With his word of advice on the subject of private practice beforehand, we may leave the astute Dominican and his remarkable booklet. The tyro is here bidden to betake himself to some quiet spot, where there will be none to mock him, there to accustom his speech and gesture to their proper use. Thus do the knights who go through their paces before the contest. Then, if he throws to the wind his fears, as he mounts the rostrum—that faintheartedness which vexes the memory, brings on forgetfulness, impedes the work of tongue and members— all will be well. "PROCEDAT ERGO PREDICATOR!"[3]

---

[1] Cf. the tactful homilist of MS. Roy. 18. B. xxiii, fol. 134 b: "Sirs, the right order of prechyng wold aske too ordinate remedies..., but the tyme suffreth not now." See also above, p. 179, etc.

[2] MS. Bodl. 5, fols. 4–5. Bromyard also warns against a long theme (*S.P.—Predic.*). Cf. here the story in MS. Cotton Cleop. D. viii, fol. 113 b— of a sinful priest struck with remorse during the hearing of a sermon. He resolves to confess. *But the sermon is so long* that he puts confession off till next day, with disastrous results!

[3] MS. Harl. 635, fol. 8. The treatise ends (fol. 18) with a model sermon. (I have deliberately abstained from speaking of pulpit *satire* here, as the manuals themselves do not really prescribe it, and an adequate account of its use in the sermons would require almost a whole chapter to itself. I hope to discuss this subject, with further aspects of the preaching, in its relation to the general literature, art, and life of the times, in a later study.)

APPENDICES

APPENDIX I

CHAPTER IV

FOR the place of the sermon at Mass, I have collected the following:

(i) *Durandus, "Rationale"* (c. 1286):

Quoniam ut praemissum est Evangelium praedicatio est, et symbolum fidei professio, ideo *post illa* fit populo praedicatio, quasi evangelici verbi et simboli sive novi et veteri testamenti expositio.... Communiter tamen *post predicationem simbolum decantatur.*

(Canon Simmons in *The Lay Folks Mass Book*, E.E.T.S., O.S. No. 71, Notes, pp. 317, etc. seems to have overlooked this last alternative. Otherwise he would have been compelled to modify his remark on the existing Roman practice, in connection with this subject.)

(ii) *Officium S. Ricardi*, York Breviary, Surtees Soc. vol. ii, Appdx. 5, col. 791:

Cum autem in Missa Evangelium esset lectum, petita prius benedictione presbyteri, pulpitum predicantium adiit, et sermonem ...fecit ad populum.

(iii) *Acts of a Chapter of Canons*, 1446 (Salter, as in Chap. IV): "Sermo in Anglicis," in the parish church of All Saints, Northampton:

Missa vero ibidem de sancto spiritu solemniter inchoata, et *usque ad post offertorium* continuata, ven. pater Mag. J. Kyngestone, S.T.P.,...solemnem sermonem in Anglicis in pulpito ejusdem ecclesiae...proposuit.

(iv) Powell and Trevelyan, *Docs. on the Peasant Revolt*, p. 46 (c. 1390):

...which preacher did assend the pulpit to preache, when the viccar of the church *after the effertorie* in the masse parochiell retourned to the aulter....

(v) Prologue to the *Speculum Sacerdotale*, a fifteenth-century collection of English festival sermons (MS. Add. 36791, fol. 1 b):

...the prestes...*aftur the redyng of the gospel, and of the offertorie* at masse, turne hem unto the peple and schewe openliche unto hem alle the solempnitees and festes whiche shall falle and be hadde in the weke folowyng. And afturwarde...pray for pees,...the clergie,...the peple..., etc.

Then preach (fol. 2). (See above, Chap. VI, pp. 244–5.)

(vi) Sermon *after the offertory* in: Wm. Lyndwood's *Provinciale*, bk. v, § v; Sarum Pontifical (1315–29), Office at the Consecration; and similar Office (c. 1500) for St Mary's, Winchester[1]. Thomas Netter's *Doctrinale*, vol. i, § iv, chap. 33. The *Book of Precedence* (ed. Furnivall, E.E.T.S.) (after 1386), for funerals. Sir David Lyndesay's *Testament of Squyer Meldrum* (see E.E.T.S. ed.). [All these are given by Canon Simmons, as above, in reference i.]

(vii) J. D. Chambers, *Divine Worship in England in the Thirteenth and Fourteenth Centuries*, p. 337, declares that a sermon (if any) after the Creed, and before the offertory sentences was the usual custom in England and France.

APPENDIX II

CHAPTER IV

For the sermon on Sunday afternoons:

(i) References given above in Chap. IV, from *The Rites of Durham* (Surtees Soc.); and MS. Vernon, in E.E.T.S., O.S. No. 98, p. 351.

(ii) Rich. Whitforde's *Werke for Housholders* (early 16th cent.). From directions for the Sunday afternoon:

Appoynt them also the place (for their pastime, after luncheon), that you may call or sende for them whan case requyreth. For yf there be a sermon ony tyme of the daye, let them be there present....

(iii) The case of violent assault in St Dunstan's Church, London, 1417, in Wilkins, *Conc.* vol. iii, p. 385, and here in Chap. IV. This occurs "hora quasi vesperarum, *post solennem verbi Dei predicationem*, in ecclesia Sti. Dunstani...populo in ibi congregato factam," on Easter Day. This agrees with the 'MS. Vernon' Sunday, of vespers following the afternoon sermon.

(iv) Powell and Trevelyan (as in Appdx. I, ref. iv):

And the same daie, *after dynner*, the saide parson came...to preach in the said church.

[1] In Maskell's *Monum. Rit.*

(v) For Sunday sermons at Paul's Cross, cf. 1408 (Wilkins, *Conc.* vol. iii, p. 310); 1417 (ibid. p. 388: "cum major ibidem ad sermonem audiendum affluerit populi multitudo"); 1424 (ibid. p. 439); 1425 (ibid. p. 437); 1428 (ibid. p. 502), etc.

APPENDIX III

CHAPTER III, etc.

Types of sermon indulgences.

(In addition in Archbishop Fitzralph of Armagh's sermon indulgence, quoted from MS. Lansd. 393, fol. 112, above, p. 101, n. 2.)
N.B. The pardon is never given for mere *hearing* alone.

(i) *At the Sermon Close* (MS. Roy. 18. B. xxiii, fol. 69 b):

> ...And all that have herde my sermon, and waketh oute of synne, and preyth to God V tymes here "pr. nr." and here "Ave", with a good herte in the maner as I have seid before, and name Goddes hi3 name Jhs in the ende of the Ave Maria, divers popes have granted hem CCC daies to pardon, and Goddes blissynge and pees. And ther fore wake 3e and preye, and kepe you owt of synne, as I seid you afore, and than 3e shall com to the blisse that ever shall laste. Amen.
> Qui cum deo, patre, etc. In nomine patris.

Cf. also the indulgences at the end of the metrical sermon— "de festo Corporis Christi"—for hearing or reading "this servise," etc. (MS. Harl. 4196 vers. "De Indulgenciis inde concessis," also MS. Camb. vers.) printed in E.E.T.S., O.S. No. 98, pp. 95–97.
(The total here seems to mount up to 41 years 60 days!)

(ii) Among *The Indulgences of the Monasterie of Syon* (MS. Ashmol. 750, fol. 140 b):

Also to all verraie contrite and shryven that arne present with devocion whenne the worde of God is preched by the brethren of this ordre, so often pope Boniface the IX relesseth mercifullie an C daies of penaunce enioynded, wyche al other popes sithen have confermed. And the Archebysshop of Cauntirburye hath graunted with the same XL daies of pardon, and the Archebysshop of York also XL dayes, and the Bysshop of London XL dayes, and the bysshop of Duram XL dayes.

(iii) With these compare further the *Thoresby Indulgence* (1357. Cawode, York.) accompanying the English version of the *Lay Folk's Faith*, as printed in E.E.T.S., O.S. No. 118, p. 98.

Omnibus subditis nostris infra nostras civitatem, diocesim, et provinciam constitutis, et aliis quorum diocesani hanc nostram indulgentiam ratam habuerint, de peccatis suis vere confessis poenitentibus et contritis, qui praemissa in predicando, docendo, audiendo, et erudiendo devote servaverint et adimpleverint XL dies indulgentiae misericorditer duximus concedendos.... Nostrae tamen intentionis non existit aliquibus personis ad predicandum per praesentes in aliquo prejudicare.

(iv) Also the terms of such a preaching license, as that granted to John Borard, S.T.P., Canon of Twynham, by William of Wykeham, c. 1381; printed in Reg. Wykeham (Winchester Record Soc.), vol. ii, p. 326:

> ...Hiis quoque, qui predicacioni tuae interfuerint, volentes per hoc te favore prosequi gracioso, de peccatis suis vere contritis etiam et confessis indulgencias concedimus in talibus consuetas..., etc.

See also other preaching indulgences in *Cal. of Papal Registers*, (cf. vol. iv, p. 165 [1371]).

(v) Finally, compare this remarkable comment on indulgences in a *Sermon by Master Robert Rypon, Sub-prior of Durham* (fl. 1401), MS. Harl. 4894, fol. 102 b et seq.:

> ...Ideo illi qui in indulgenciis spem venie reponunt quandoque multipliciter sunt decepti. Praesertim illi qui optenta Domini pape indulgencia a poena, ut vulgariter dicitur, et a culpa, credentes quod virtute bullarum indulgentie una cum verbali confessione facta electo sacerdoti, omnis tam poena quam culpa eis totaliter remittetur. O spes frivola atque vana, cum in hujusmodi litteris indulgentie scribatur, "vere" nedum "confessis" sed et "contritis," quibus predictus dolor secundus est omnino necessarius ad hoc quod per confessionem seu pena remittetur vel culpa!
>
> Quod si vera precedat contricio, tunc cum confessione electo scienti sacerdoti jurisdictionem sui officii legitime exercenti, virtute papalis indulgentie, commutatur pena perpetua in temporalem; et insuper pena temporalis peccatis debita et condigna remitti potest, magna conticione preveniente in penam modicam ad discretum arbitrium sacerdotis, et hoc ex meritis totius ecclesiae militantis.

APPENDIX IV

CHAPTER VI

The "Great Sentence," or Curse, in preachers' manuals:—

Two examples (unpublished) of the Introduction:

(i) MS. Rawl. A. 381, fol. 1 b. (With a copy of Myrc's *Festiall*, wrongly catalogued as *Doctrina Simplicium*):

Gode men and women, I do you to understande we tha[t] have care of your soulles be commaundet of our ordinaries, ande by the constituciouns and lau of holy churche, to shew to you foure tymes in the ȝere, in eche quarter of the ȝere onys, whan the peple is moost plenerye in holy churche, the artycles of the sentence of cursynge; so that not for our defaut, no man nor woman fal there.

(ii) MS. Burney 356, fol. 50 b (*Flos Florum*):

Gowd men, thees poyntes and artycles that y shal to yow shewe of corsynge or mansynge beth y-ordeyned, and y-stabeled, and y-confermyd of popes, herchebysshopes, bysshopes, and pre-lates of holy cherche, hotynge and comawndynge alle thulke that haveth cure of mannys saule, as persones, vicares, and par[i]she prestes, that they shewe hare par[i]shones fowre tymes in the ȝere thes poyntes and artycles of corsynge, that they thorw onknowynge or defawte of techynge falle in to no corsynge....

A Conclusion (with special heading): MS. Advoc. Libr. Edin-burgh, 18. 3. 6, fols. 7 b–8. (With the *Oculus Sacerdotum*, here mistakenly entitled *Grosseti Oc. Sac.* from the last item— "Diversitates...Rob. Grossete" [*sic*!]):

Nota, dicitur ulterius in pronunciacione. Be the autorite of oure lord jhesu crist, and of his modur seynte marie, and of alle the holy companye of hevene, be angeles, archangeles, evangelistes, apostolis, and martyres, and confessoures, and virgines, thei ben acorsed fro the heyyst her of here hed to the sole of here fot, etyng, drynkyng, sitting, stonding, sleping, and wakyng. Ant rith as the lith of this candel sal ben for don by fore oure sith, rit so al here godnes and alle here soules ben departed fro godes face til thei hau mad s... [satisfacioun?], or comen to amende-ment. Fiat, fiat. Amen.

[For a further contemporary example of the "Great Sentence," with full details of the custom, see *Jacob's Well*, pt. i, E.E.T.S., O.S. No. 115, p. 13 et seq.]

APPENDIX V

A NOTE ON THOMAS (OR RICHARD) WIMBLEDON
AND HIS SERMON AT PAUL'S CROSS IN 1388

No direct reference to the preaching of any *Chaplain* has yet been made in the course of our survey. It may happen, however, that in a certain sermon of the year 1388–9, which seems to have enjoyed a popularity out of all proportion to its apparent value, we may have an example.

Among the preaching licenses of William of Wykeham for his diocese of Winchester, appears one granted, in the year 1385, to a certain Thomas Wymbledone, Chaplain to Sir John Sandes. The terms in which it is set out require, in usual fashion, that the preaching of rectors and vicars shall in no way be interfered with in the parishes he visits. There is also a clause "expressly inhibiting you from asserting or preaching any heretical conclusions or errors, which might subvert the state of our church of Winchester, and the tranquillity of our subjects."[1] Now there can be so single sermon by an Englishman of our two centuries of which so many copies in contemporary manuscript, and later printed book can be found than one on the favourite text: "Redde rationem villicationis tuae,"[2]— "prechyd atte Paulis crosse, at two tymes, of maister Thomas Wymbilton."[3] Preached at a time when Lollard influences were strong in the city, it seems innocent nevertheless of any taint of heresy. Its solemn warnings of Judgement, its attacks on ecclesiastical corruption, its call to all classes to give "reckoning of thy Bailiwicke," when compared with the utterances of Bishop Brunton and others we have considered, can hardly be called extreme. Yet it made considerable stir at the time, and according to Foxe[4] was afterwards exhibited to Archbishop Courtney. Otherwise there is no reason to suppose the faith of its author was ever called in question. Rather must we believe that the personality and status of the speaker may have had as much to do with its fame as the unbroken note of gloom and foreboding with which it seems to voice the religious

---

[1] See Reg. Wykeham (Winch. Rec. Soc.), vol. ii.　　　　[2] Luke xvi, 2.

[3] From vers. MS. Roy. 18. A. xvii (fol. 184 b et seq.); cf. "apud crucem in cimiterio," MS. Harl. 2398 (fol. 140). MS. Sidney Sussex Coll. Camb. 74 (fol. 168) adds, "Quinquagesima Sunday." "Explicit sermo factus et compilatus per maister Thomam Wymbeldon." (Engl. vers.) The "two tymes" correspond to the two parts into which the sermon is divided. The Christian name Richard has somehow replaced that of Thomas in the printed editions.

[4] Who reproduces it in his *Acts and Mons.* (Seeley's *Ch. Hist.* ser. 1885, vol. iii, pt. i, pp. 292–307).

mood of the times. Once again, like the preaching in public places which brought others to trial for definite heresy, it may have seemed daring and impertinent enough for a mere priest to utter from so prominent a pulpit. He was crying from the house-tops what others less exalted than Brunton whispered before nobility or clergy in inner chambers, things fit for select prelatical lips to utter, and select ears to hear.

Be this as it may, the Word in this case had free course, and was multiplied indeed. The sermon appears again and again in Latin dress in the most respectable homily collections[1]. The Lollards liked it apparently, and preserved it with the discourses of their great master[2], as they did the sayings of Rolle. Finally, "found out hid in a wall,"[3] in the reign of Queen Elizabeth, it was again brought into the open to stir the hearts of the Reformers. Edition after edition[4] was issued in print, and subsequent Puritans seem to have delighted to bind it up with their own volumes of sermons[5]. From a copy of the 12th edition, of the year 1617, by W. Jaggard, in the University Library at Cambridge, I take the following from a characteristic preface which now recommends it—"to the Christian Reader":

Lo, Christian reader, while the worlde not slumbred, but routed and snorted in the deepe and dead sleep of ignorance, some lively spirits were waking, and ceased not to call uppon the drowsie multitude of men, and to stirre them up from the long dreames of sinfull living, that once at the last they would creepe out of darknesse, and come forth to the hot shining Sunne of God's Word, that both the filthy mists of their harts might be driven away, and also their heavy and dying spirits recreated, refreshed, and quickened. So that no man can alleadge that in any age there wanted Preachers of God's word. For he that keepeth Israel sleepeth not, nor slumbreth....

Reade, therefore, diligently this little sermon, so long since written, and thou shalt perceive the same quicke spirit in the Author thereof that thou now marvailest at in others of our time. He sharply, earnestly, and wittily rebuketh the sinnes of all sorts of men, and speaketh as one

[1] See above, Chap. VI, pp. 229–30. Also found with Waldeby in MS. Caius Coll. Camb. 334; and in MS. Roy. 18. B. xxiii with Myrc (?).

[2] Cf. MS. Sidney Sussex Coll. Camb. 74; and possibly MS. Add. 37677.

[3] This is the normal way in which it is described in the printed editions.

[4] The first seems to be J. Kynge, c. 1550–60. Others in 1563, 1570, 1572, 1575, 1582, 1584, 1603, 1617, 1629, 1634, 1635, 1738, etc.

[5] An interesting case in which whole sections of the sermon have been incorporated practically verbatim by a pre-Reformation preacher in *his own* vernacular homilies, is afforded by MS. Linc. Cath. Libr. A. 6. 2. Here the simile of the Vine and the labourers (the three orders of Holy Church, and their tasks) appears on fols. 67 b–70 (Serm., Dom. Septuages.); and the "iii maner of baylis" summoned to "ȝelde rekenyng" at the Doom, on fols. 217 to end (Serm., Dom. ixª post fest. S. trinitatis).

362 APPENDICES

having authority, and not as the Scribes and Pharisees, which, with their leaden and blunt dart, could never touch the quicke, tho' they have occupied the Pulpets for many yeares....

Thus speak the sons of gospel liberty, the really superior preachers, as Presbyterian Mr Stalker[1] would insist, certain themselves, at any rate, of their own salvation and superiority. For our own part we will feel grateful to them for their contribution to the little romance of a mediaeval sermon, and there let the matter rest.

One point more. The present writer has found a Latin version of this work in the heart of a series of Latin sermons of the period, with the same vigorous style, amongst the manuscripts of the Cambridge University Library[2]. In this case no identification of preacher or of place of delivery is given. The anonymous collection in question was actually used to good purpose by Petit-Dutaillis for a study we have alluded to, concerning the influences of the pulpit upon the Peasants' Revolt. With a certain interest, therefore, a likely name for its author can now be put forward, that of Thomas Wimbledon, the pulpit-hero of 1388. Among the "gravamina" presented by the inferior clergy to the Bishops in Convocation in 1399, was a request that *unbeneficed chaplains* should not be licensed to preach for the future[3]. Was the relentless denunciation of Thomas and his kind too much for their nerves?

[1] Article on "Preaching" (Hist. of Christian) in Hastings' *Encycl. of Rel. and Ethics*, all too scanty of mediaeval preachers and preaching.
[2] MS. Camb. Univ. Libr. Ii. iii. 8 (also used in this study: see *passim*).
[3] See also the complaint in Reg. Brantingh. (Exeter), pt. ii, p. 692.

NOTE. As I go to press for the last time, my attention has been drawn to a recent article by M. Etienne Gilson, in *Revue d'histoire franciscaine* (Paris), for July, 1925, vol. ii, no. 3, which should be worth consulting, on:—"Michel Menot, et la technique du sermon médiéval."

INDEX

CAMBRIDGE: PRINTED BY
W. LEWIS, M.A.
AT THE UNIVERSITY PRESS